A
HARD
FOUGHT
SHIP

The story of HMS *Venomous*

Robert J Moore

John A Rodgaard

HOLYWELL HOUSE PUBLISHING

First published in Great Britain by Robert J Moore in 1990

This edition published in 2010 by

Holywell House Publishing
88 Holywell Hill
St Albans
Hertfordshire
AL1 1DH

http://www.holywellhousepublishing.co.uk/

British Library Cataloguing in Publication Data
A catalogue record for this book is available from The British Library

ISBN 978-0-9559382-0-7

The cover design is based on a painting by Peter Hsu showing
HMS *Venomous* under attack by Stuka dive bombers
at Boulogne on the 23 May 1940

Rear cover painting by Herbert McWilliams of torpedo striking
HMS *Marne* as HMS *Hecla* sinks
Image ART LD 002612. *The Imperial War Mueum*

Designed by John Robertshaw
Printed in Great Britain by Antony Rowe Co Ltd SN14 6LH

This book is dedicated to the memory of
all those who served on HMS *Venomous*
between 1919 and 1946

Hostibus nocens amicis innocens
"Deadly to foes, harmless to Friends"

Motto of HMS *Venomous*

"It is upon the Navy that under the good providence of God the wealth, prosperity and peace of these islands and of the Empire do mainly depend."

Original Articles of War

CONTENTS

List of illustrations   vi

Foreword   xi

Introduction   xiii

Acknowledgements   xvi

Chapter one   Pedigree   1

Chapter two   To the Baltic and back   13
                 1919 – 23

Chapter three   The Mediterranean years   41
                 1923 – 29

Chapter four   Off to war   62
                 September 1938 – June 1940

Chapter five   The North Sea and beyond   118
                 June 1940 – December 1941

Chapter six   Refit, re-commissioning and Russia   168
                 January – June 1942

Chapter seven   Back to the Mediterranean   193
                 June – November 1942

Chapter eight   A very, very long night   211
                 11 – 12 November 1942

Chapter nine   To the Med for the last time   245
                 November 1942 – October 1943

Chapter ten	On other duties assigned December 1943 – May 1945	276
Chapter eleven	A last Hurrah 12 – 17 May 1945	295
Chapter twelve	The end of the road May 1945 – November 1948	311
	Postscript	313
Appendices	1 Specification and battle honours	314
	2 Commanding officers	315
	3 List of officers	316
	4 List of ratings	320
	5 Shipboard organisation	324
	6 Life aboard *Venomous*	330
	7 TS *Venomous*	338
	8 The sixty-nine V & Ws	340
	9 Abbreviations	346
Bibliography	Primary sources	348
	Secondary sources	349
	Index	353

LIST OF ILLUSTRATIONS

Frontispiece – HMS *Venomous* in 1942   xxi

HMS *Hood* and HMS *Venomous* in the fitting-out basin on the Clyde, 1919   13

The bow and stern of HMS *Venomous* in John Brown's shipyard in 1919   14

HMS *Venomous* with crew members on fo'c'sle in 1919   15

The German High Sea Fleet in Scapa Flow after their internment   17

The Baltic Campaign memorial in Portsmouth cathedral   27

The officers and ship's company of HMS *Venomous* at Hull in April 1921   32

Programme for "Grand Naval Concert" by the 'Jolliboys" from HMS *Venomous*   34

HMS *Venomous* leaving Valetta harbour, Malta, in the 1920s   46

HMS *Venomous* in the 1920s   50

HMS *Venomous* with pendant D75 taken in the Mediterranean in the 1920s   56

Damage done in collision with the tug, *Swarthey*, 6 March 1940   73

Disembarking Royal Marines and their stores, Hook of Holland, 12 May 1940   76

Taking aboard Dutch refugees from the tug *Atjeh*, 15 May 1940   79

Embarking refugees, including nuns and school girls, at Calais, 21 May 1940   83

Mona's Queen landing troops at Boulogne on 22 May 1940   85

Venomous returning from Boulogne with refugees, 22 May 1940   86

HMS *Venetia* on fire leaving Boulogne harbour stern first, 23 May 1940   92

Regimental painting of the Welsh Guards at Boulogne, 23 May 1940   94

Burning truck as *Venomous* leaves Boulogne, 23 May 1940   96

Boulogne photographed from *Venomous* as it leaves harbour, 23 May 1940   97

Portrait page: **Desperate times aboard HMS *Venomous***   101

HMS *Malcolm* approaching the entrance to Dunkirk   102

HMS *Basilisk* alongside the Mole at Dunkirk, 31 May 1940   103

Troops boarding HMS *Vanquisher* at the Mole at Dunkirk   104

HMS Venomous off the beaches Dunkirk with small boat alongside   106

Evacuating French troops from the Mole at Dunkirk on the last night   113

Oil tanks burning at Dunkirk after demolition   113

Venomous and sister ships wait to berth at Dover with troops from Dunkirk 114

French troops landing at Dover from *Venomous*, 2 June 1940 115

HMS *Venomous* in the Thames Estuary on the 2 July 1940 122

Venomous escorting HMS *Formidable* on her trials, December 1940 131

HMS *Formidable* on its sea trials in the Clyde estuary 132

Capt P. Ruck-Keene, Captain (D) at Londonderry, inspecting *Venomous* 134

Venomous needing a tow after hitting a mine, 136

HMS Venomous *with* Atlantic camouflage 142

Atlantic convoys, 1941 145

AB "Freddo" Thomas, RDF operator 146

Portrait page: the officers and men escorting Atlantic convoys, 1941 147

Group portrait of Cdr Henderson with his officers 148

Gunner Thompson and Lt Walter Wells firing at mines 148

Maylands on signalling lamp 148

HMS *Hecla* at Iceland (Hvalfjord), 1941 149

Venomous refuelling alongside AMC*Springbank* 151

Gnr (T) Thompson, Mid. R.J. Knight, Cdr H.P. Henderson with USN Officer 152

Captain Lohmeyer of *U-651* watches his men come ashore at Londonderry 153

Two COs: Cdr H.P. Henderson RN and Cdr H. Falcon-Steward RN 154

Venomous being towed to Hvalfjord, 11 July 1941, and alongside HMS *Hecla* 155

Lockheed built Hudson with ASV radar on anti-submarine patrol 156

AB Sydney T. Charles, Bosun's Mate (on left), with his 'pipe' 158

Surgeon Lt Browning being taken in the ship's whaler to a sick seaman 159

USS *Kearny* alongside USS *Vulcan* at Hvalfjord after being torpedoed 160

HMS *Venomous* at Loch Ewe after the collision with *Keppel* 164

The bronze plaque presented to HMS *Venomous* by Loughborough 174

"Climbing to Victory" war fund target on Loughborough Town Hall 174

Lord Teynham and his officers during the refit at Troon in Spring 1942 176

Venomous alongside the depot ship HMS *Sandhurst*, Londonderry 178

HMS *London*, at Seidisfjord prior to joining Convoy PQ.15 179

HMS *Venomous* with zig-zag camouflage at Seidisfjord, Iceland 179

USS *Wichita* provided support for Convoy PQ.15 181

Portrait page: with Cdr H.W. Falcon-Steward to Arctic Russia 185

HMS *Trinidad* at the Russian naval base of Polyanyy 186

Polyarnyy, the Russian naval base where *Venomous* berthed, 1942   187

Venomous "Oiling alongside HMS *Nelson* at sea" in 1942   197

Flotilla in line ahead with ships offset   197

HMS Rodney framed by "B" Gun of another V & W in the Mediterranean   198

Aerial photograph of the aircraft carriers used in Operation *Pedestal*   199

HMS Eagle sinking, with merchant ship in foreground; Cyril Hely   200

Eagle survivors being transferred from HMS *Laforey*   202

Eagle survivors on HMS *Venomous*   203

Venomous escorted HMS *Furious* whilst taking Spitfires to Malta   204

A typical wartime painting by Robert Back of a Captain Class frigate   208

HMS *Hecla* with torpedo striking HMS *Marne* in background   220

HMS *Marne* torpedoed in the stern by U-515   221

HMS *Hecla* sinking whilst the survivors struggle in the water   225

Hecla survivors on Carley floats at dawn on the 12 November 1942   230

Exhausted survivors of HMS *Hecla*   233

HMS *Venomous* alongside USS *Augusta* at Casablanca   234

The *Hecla* dead sewn in hammocks on the deck of *Venomous* at Casablanca   234

Hecla survivors on *Venomous* as it come alongside USS *Chenango*   235

Venomous on her way to Gibraltar with *Hecla* survivors, 14-15 November   237

"Burial at sea of the unlucky ones" whilst en-route to Gibraltar   238

HMS *Marne* at Gibraltar, November 1942   239

Falcon-Steward with Max Horton at Western Approaches HQ,   246

The six CW candidates who spent five months on *Venomous*   250

Floating dock at "MEK" naval base just outside Oran   252

Portrait page: hot work in the Mediterranean   254

Announcement of awards for HMS *Hecla*, signed by Lt Durell   255

HMS *Venomous* crossing the stern of HMS *Formidable* at high speed   256

Passing the blockships at the entrance to Tripoli harbour, 23 May 1943   259

HMS *Venomous* and HMS *Liddersdale* refuelling in Tripoli harbour   260

Searchlights directing the fire on German aircraft attacking Bone   261

Lt Christopher R.V. Holt RNVR   262

A caricature of HMS *"Verminous"* presented to Lt H.D.Durell RN   262

Venomous escorting convoy for landing in Sicily, 1943   266

At Gibraltar in October 1943 before *Venomous* limped home for a refit   272

Venomous stripped of its armament after its refit at Falmouth in 1944	278
The officers for *Venomous'* last commission, August 1944	279
The Skipper, Lt Cdr Derek Lawson RNVR	280
Young Midshipman Wilfred Beckerman RNVR	280
HMS *Venomous* working as a target ship in the Irish Sea, August 1944	284
Portrait page: officers and crew in home waters but still with a job to do	286
Lt Cdr J.A.J. Dennis RN, the CO of HMS *Valorous*	296
HMS *Venomous* and HMS *Valorous* at Kristiansand harbour, 14 May 1945	299
Lord Teynham and Brigadier "Mad" Mike Calvert of the SAS going ashore	301
German naval officer boards HMS *Valorous* for the surrender ceremony	302
German officers waiting on the quarterdeck of HMS *Valorous*	302
SAS driving through Kristiansand in their jeeps in May 1940	307
Children wave the national flag on National Day, 17 May 1945	307
Sailors from HMS *Valorous* parade through Kristiansand, 17 May 1945	308
The commemorative scroll signed by King Olav	309

List of maps and plans

The Baltic theatre of operations, 1919-22	21
East Mediterranean theatre of operations, 1922-9	45
English Channel theatre of operations, 1939-41	69
Port of Boulogne	88
Plan of ship positions in Boulogne harbour on 23 May 1940	89
Dispositions of Channel and Harwich Forces, July 1940	121
Royal Navy Command Areas, 1939-42	133
Atlantic theatre of operations with convoy routes designators	140
Arctic Convoy routes (1941-4) with probable route of Convoy PQ.15	180
Mediterranean theatre of operations, 1941-3	201
The position of *Hecla, Marne* and *Venomous* during the attack by *U-515*	214
Mediterranean operations, 1943	249

FOREWORD

It is both a pleasure and an honour to contribute a foreword to this, significantly enhanced, edition of Bob Moore's book outlining the life of the destroyer HMS *Venomous*. I met Bob in 1985, when, after passing out of Dartmouth and having completed Fleet training, I was sent to Loughborough University to read history. During these three years I became the seamanship and navigation officer at the local Sea Cadets unit, named after the town's Second World War affiliation, HMS *Venomous*. I was fortunate, therefore, to become a friend of Bob, then a fellow instructor at the unit, and to learn a little about *Venomous*. Hence the invitation as a Sub Lieutenant to proof read the original book and some 22 years later to contribute to this.

I commend this book to you. It tells the story of one of the many Royal Navy destroyers that served in the inter war years and went on to play such a critical role during the Second World War. But perhaps more importantly this book tells the story of the officers and men that gave *Venomous*, and the ships like her, their character. It is clear that she served the nation well and, in the best traditions of the Royal Navy, did all that was asked of her thoroughly deserving the description as a hard fought ship. Indeed, having had the enormous privilege of commanding three ships I can think of no greater tribute to the men of *Venomous*, and her sister ships, than this book and its title.

J M L Kingwell
Captain Royal Navy
Commanding Officer
HMS *Albion*

FOREWORD TO THE FIRST EDITION

To read this book is to read the private diary of a member of a great family. The family is the V & W Class Destroyers, the member is HMS *Venomous* and the setting is 1919 to 1946.

I knew this family well, having sailed with three of them – *Vidette, Vivian, Warwick* – and started the Second World War in one of their Class Leaders, *Malcolm*. So the story of HMS *Venomous* freshens the nip of past experience; of days at sea when it was perilous to venture on deck even with the aid of a lifeline; of iron decks spotless and shining for Captain's rounds thanks to the application of the special mixture of beeswax, soot, boot polish and heaven knows what in a recipe known only to Chief Boatswain's Mates; of using the ship's only typewriter and the awful jelly needed for duplicating; of fiddles on the Mess table or sandwiches when even the fiddles were insufficient; of the ship's motor boat battling its way through wild winds and currents at Invergordon; of making a sternboard to the buoys in Sliema Creek. So many memories so many moons ago.

It is fitting that the deeds of this family should be recorded in a book of history and of personal detail, and it is good that the name *Venomous* should act as an inspiration by gracing a vigorous and active Sea Cadet Unit today.

Admiral Sir Frank R. Twiss KCB DSC

INTRODUCTION

The following pages tell the story of a ship and the hundreds of men who served on her. She was a V & W class destroyer of the Royal Navy, and her name was *Venomous*. HMS *Venomous* was commissioned just after the Great War of 1914 – 1918 and during the next decade, her commissions took her from the Baltic to the Red Sea. The major defence cuts the Royal Navy experienced during the latter part of the 1920s led to this new destroyer being placed into reserve but with the outbreak of the Second World War, *Venomous* was called back to service. She was a lucky ship and at the end of the war, *Venomous* found herself sitting on a mud bank, awaiting disposal. She had survived the savagery of war and the remorselessness of a "Cruel Sea." Today, *Venomous* lives on in the name of a Royal Navy Sea Cadet Unit.

Shortly after his appointment to Training Ship *Venomous* in April 1985, Lt Cdr (SCC) Robert J. Moore RNR became aware that the sea cadet unit was the namesake of no ordinary Royal Navy warship, and her achievements, and those of her men, merited closer scrutiny. At that time, Robert, who in civilian life was a surveyor in Loughborough, did not realise that he was embarking on four and a half years of increasingly detailed research. Like Topsy, the project grew and grew into a book, which was first published in 1990.

Robert's book received many favourable reviews, especially from former crew members and their families who were often able to provide additional information. Robert continued to research the history of HMS *Venomous* throughout the 1990s, and when I first met him in May 2001, he had acquired sufficient material to warrant a second edition.

In October 2005, when my wife Judy and I visited Robert and his wife Pat, he gave me one of the last copies of *A Hard Fought Ship*. I was immediately taken by the story, especially the richness and the sheer number of first-hand accounts by the men who served on

Venomous. One chapter especially caught my interest. I suggested that we collaborate in writing an article about the ship's operations in May and June 1940. To me this was a tremendous story and if published in America, might make Robert better known over there and boost the prospects for the new edition. The article was submitted to the United States Naval Institute's *Naval History Magazine*, and the editor, Mr. Richard Latture accepted it for publication.

By this time, Robert had retired from his firm and had begun work on the new edition. He and Pat would spend days at a time running down leads all over Britain, obtaining those last first-hand accounts from the few surviving members of *Venomous*' World War Two crew.

Tragically, Robert died suddenly when he was only 63. This came as a terrible shock to all who knew him, especially as he was an avid jogger and exceptionally fit.

Having some experience in naval matters, I asked the publisher if I could pick up Robert's "shield" and continue the book in his name. Mr. Forster agreed, and what you have before you is my attempt to fulfil Robert's dream.

However, this edition is very different from that written and published by Robert in 1990. At first I only wanted to expand the book to incorporate the additional research Robert had done since the publication of the first edition but I then decided to place *Venomous* and her men within their historical context. I wanted to explain "why" *Venomous* and her men were at a particular place at a certain time.

The reader will note that I include numerous quotations without reference to sources. These were taken directly from the first edition and from Robert's notes for his second edition. They are first-hand accounts obtained through correspondence or by interviewing former crew members of HMS *Venomous*, almost all of whom have since died. In my attempt to frame the story in its historical context I have added additional first and second-hand sources.

I have also searched the Internet for new material but whilst doing so I kept a sailor's watchful eye on the content of the sites that I visited. I took care to include only information that I could verify based on my own knowledge of British naval history, naval operations and naval intelligence and through the application of my own research methods.

Finally, I encourage the reader to follow *Venomous* and her men by their own use of the Internet. I analysed several of the photographs taken by former crew members using Google Earth. I also used this source to better understand what the ship and her men experienced: the starkness of a Baltic Winter; the bitter cold of the Kola Inlet; the sweltering heat of the Red Sea; the summer-parched shoreline of the Dardanelles peninsula and the historic battlements surrounding Malta's Grand Harbour.

I feel the result is a book that remains true to Robert's aim to honour the ship and the men who served on board *Venomous* during times of peace and war. I also feel that I have taken Robert's work further by placing the story of *Venomous* within the context of the tumultuous events of the first half of the twentieth century.

For Robert Moore, I hope you will enjoy the account that follows and recognise the paradox. *Venomous*, like every ship that served in the Royal Navy during the first half of the last century, had a crew of ordinary men but they, and the rest of the ships and men of the Royal Navy, were extraordinary in their performance. Is this not True Glory?

John A. Rodgaard
Captain USN
Burke, Virginia
2010

ACKNOWLEDGEMENTS

First and foremost, I wish to thank my friend Robert Moore, who had dedicated so much time to find the former crewmen of HMS *Venomous* and engage them to tell their stories of their naval service and life on board. I also wish to thank his wife, Pat, who so graciously gave me all of Robert's papers pertaining to the book.

I also wish to thank my wife Judy, who, in her own words, "played devil's advocate" with my manuscript. A beautiful writer in her own right, Dr. Judy Pearson's editing greatly improved my effort. To her, I am lovingly grateful.

I also wish to thank the Director of the Naval Historical Branch, Ministry of Defence, Capt Christopher Page, RN (Ret.), for his generous and very personal help with my research at the Naval Historical Centre, Portsmouth. Captain Page's professional seaman's eye on the manuscript was very important, as I worked through the events that embroiled HMS *Venomous* during a very long night in November 1942.

To Mr. W.J.R. "Jock" Gardner, also of the Naval Historical Branch, I am also appreciative for his efforts on my behalf. Between many hot cups of tea, he guided me through the archives. This Scottish gentleman cast his scholarly expertise on my work and it has benefited a great deal as a result. I am most appreciative.

I also wish to thank Mr. Peter C. Smith, the author of many books on military and naval history for his review of the new edition in manuscript. Peter is the author of HMS *Wild Swan, Venomous'* sister ship, and his insight into my work was especially appreciated.

I was most fortunate to be able to call on John Appleby, the Secretary of the V & W Association, for an insight into life aboard V & Ws and to Mr Edwin Walker, probably the foremost expert on destroyer ship movements alive today, for clarification of certain points.

I would also like to acknowledge the permission of Gordon Smith to use the maps on his website as the basis for the maps in this edition. I would recommend his website, www.naval-history.net to the reader for its wealth of information on the Royal Navy and the Commonwealth Navies during the twentieth century.

I also tip my hat to Ms. Kelly Erlinger of the United States Naval Institute. Kelly has illustrated several of my articles that have appeared in the Institute's *Naval History* magazine, and I am grateful for her artistry and technical proficiency.

To my dear friend and "Renaissance man," Mr. Peter Hsu, I am so grateful for his artistry that adorns the cover of this book. His depiction of *Venomous* conveys a realism that is rare indeed. It is no wonder that the US Navy commissions him to paint the official portraits of its newly commissioned ships.

Finally, I wish to thank Bill Forster whose imprint published this edition. For him this was a work of love, because his father served on board *Venomous* during the Second World War. Bill, I am most grateful for the opportunity to have been able to carry on in Bob Moore's stead. I also wish to acknowledge the attention to detail shown by Anthony R. Ford in proof checking the final manuscript.

The photographs and paintings reproduced in this edition are by courtesy of Richard Kershaw, the son of Lt Peter Kershaw RNVR; Leslie Eaton, son of Lt Leslie 'Slogger' Eaton; Professor Wilfred Beckerman, Mid. RNVR; Dorothy Hely, widow of Cyril Hely; F.N.G. 'Freddo' Thomas; Sydney Compston; George Male; Marie Cliffe, the widow of Harry Cliffe; David and Penny Durell, the son and daughter in law of Lt H.D. Durell RN; Nicholas Holt, the son of Lt C.R.V. Holt RNVR; Alison Travis, the daughter of Robert Back; Arthur Charles the son of Sidney T. Charles; Mervyn Mansell; William Leslie Collister; Alan Dennis, the son of Cdr J.A.J. Dennis RN, DSC; Knut Maesel, Christer Andvik; The Imperial War Museum and the Welsh Guards Regiment. It has not always been possible to trace the copyright owners but should they be identified after publication due acknowledgement will be made in future editions.

Further significant contributions came from the following:

HMS *Venomous*

Stephen Barney (Midshipman and Sub Lt RNVR, 1943); John Tucker (Sub Lt RNR, 1941); F.N.G. 'Freddo' Thomas, Radar Operator (RDF) 1940-3; Professor Wilfred Beckerman (Sub Lt RNVR, 1944-5); Thomas Arthur 'Yorkie' Russell, Stoker 1945; William Leslie Collister (CPO 1940-5); Cdr D.A.R. Duff (First Lt 1939); Arthur J. 'Mervyn' Mansell

MBE (Ordinary Seaman and Commission Warrant Officer candidate1942-3); Alexander M Campbell (Ordinary Seaman and Commission Warrant Officer candidate 1942-3); Arthur L Bowler (Gunner 1942-3); Harry Haddon (AB 1940-3) and Sydney Compston (AB 1940-1).

The families of those who served on HMS *Venomous*

Chris Eaton (son of Leslie 'Slogger' Eaton, Lt RNVR 1942-3); Jeremy Greenaway (son of Frank Greenaway, Lt RN 1944); Arthur Charles (son of Sidney Thomas Charles, Bosun's Mate 1939-42); Dr Malcolm Birkin (son of George Arnold Birkin, Gunner 1939-42); Leon Bennett (grandson of Arthur Malcolm Bennett, Chief ERA 1944-5); Annie Mercer (widow of Frederick Mercer, AB 1945); Richard Bishop Miller (great nephew of John C Robb, AB); Alison Travis (daughter of Robert Back, Gunner and marine artist); Dorothy Hely (widow of Cyril Hely, OS 1940-3) Walter McPhee (the son of Lt Arthur D. McPhee RN); Sheena Mckenzie (the daughter of Lt A.A. Mackenzie RNR).

HMS *Hecla*

George Male (medical orderly, 1940-2); Norman Johns (2nd Class Stoker); Marie Cliffe (widow of Harry Cliffe); Fred Lemberg (AB 1942); Greg Clark (Sub Lt, 'Schoolie', 1941-2).

British Expeditionary Force

Douglas King (Corporal, later Captain D. King, Green Howards) and Lou Warn (Sergeant, Green Howards)

John A. Rodgaard,
2010

ACKNOWLEDGMENTS TO THE FIRST EDITION

I wish to acknowledge the assistance of the following, without whose help this book could not have been written.

My thanks to Mr. Peter Smith for permission to quote from his book *Wild Swan*, which proved to me the catalyst for this work and to Mr. Walter Lord for the use of passages from *The Miracle of Dunkirk*.

Lt Cdr Arnold Hague RSR of the World Ship Society, Mr. Peter Melton of the Naval Historical Branch, Mr. Roderick Suddaby of the Imperial War Museum, the staff of the Public Record Office, Kew and Mr. E. Walker for the provision of essential documents.

Cdr Christopher Gotto RN, Mrs. Veronica Wells, Mrs. R. Esson, Mrs. C.G. Lapthorne, Mrs. W. Holgate, Mrs. S. Ommanney and Mrs. B. Vaughan-Lewis, for the loan of papers relevant to this account, Mrs. Cecile Holman for the receipt of photographs and reports, the property of the late Rear Admiral J.E.H. McBeath CB, DSO, DSC, DL.

I also wish to record my appreciation to Lt Cdr H.H. McGeeney DSM, RN (Ret) and Lt Cdr A. d'E. T. Sangster RN (Ret) and Sub Lt John Kingwell RN for their ongoing perusal of my work and for the helpful comments and advice they have given.

Finally I wish to thank Miss Tina Highton, for her preparation of the printed text.

Further significant contributions came from the following:

HMS *Venomous*

Rear Admiral Sir Peter Dawney KCV CB DSC DL, Capt J.F. Coleman RN RD BNR, Capt S.B. de Courcy-Ireland RN, Capt C.L. Robertson RN, Cdr R. Moore RN, Cdr R.H.S. Rodger OBE RN, Cdr D.A.R. Duff DSC RN, Cdr H.W. Falcon-Steward OBE RN, Cdr D.H. Maitland-Makgill-Crichton DSO DSC RN, Cdr F.S.H. Greenaway RNR, Lt Cdr A.G. Prideaux RNVR, Lt Cdr M. Cashman RN, Lt Cdr S.J. Barney RD RNR, Lt Cdr F.L.W. Hunter RN, Lt D.M. Caudle RNVR, Lt J.W. Martin RNVR, Lt J. Blair

RNVR, Lt A.E. Parkes DSC RN, Lt P. Kershaw RNVR, Lt J.C. Tucker RNR, Surg. Lt P.B. Woodyatt RNVR, Surg. Lt R. Browning, RNVR.

Messrs. J. Irlam, H. Worsnip, A.G. Upton, F.W.A. Notton, J. Compston DSM, H. Knapton DSM, L.W. Dagley DSM, R.A. Craddock, L.T. May, A. Willett, T. Davies, H.T. Willmott, W.J. Barnfield, J. Baton.

HMS *Marne*
Mr. F. Todd

HMS *Eagle*
Mr. W.H.E. Loades

HMS *Hecla*
Mr. S. Rowles

U-515
Herren R. Tahbert and H. Hahn

British Expeditionary Force
Messrs. D.J.W. Marr and R. Lockerby

Other Sources
Capt C. Bogh-Tobiassen Royal Norwegian Navy, Mssrs. J. Esslemont and C.E. Hurry

Robert J. Moore,
1990

HMS _Venomous_ in 1942.
View aft on port side from bridge.
Photographed by Lt Leslie "Slogger" Eaton.

CHAPTER ONE

PEDIGREE

The stripped hulls, slinking through the gloom,
At gaze and gone again –
The Brides of Death that wait the groom –
The Choosers of the Slain!

The Destroyers; by Rudyard Kipling, 1898[1]

At the close of the nineteenth century and twenty-one years before the commissioning of HMS *Venomous*, Rudyard Kipling wrote a nine-verse poem about a new type of warship that appeared on the scene with the Royal Navy. The poem, "The Destroyers" was Kipling's impression of this new type of warship. By today's standards, his poem seems overtly romanticised, especially when he turned the phrase, *"dash, flash and boom."*

As the experiences of the Great War of 1914-8 showed, there were those moments of dash, flash and boom for the destroyers of the Royal Navy. At the battles of the Dogger Bank, Jutland and several minor actions, Kipling's verse rang true. But, for the most part, the destroyers and their crews followed a routine existence of manoeuvring in packs with the battle fleet on fruitless sweeps across the North Sea in search of the German High Sea Fleet, when their greatest danger was from collision or an errant sea mine.

Yes, Kipling did accurately describe the destroyer's speed and deadliness but, for many a destroyer and her crew, patrol duty in the North Sea and escort duty protecting merchant ships were a long way from the dash, flash and boom of the battle fleet.

Destroyer operations during that war illustrated another of Kipling's poetic phrases – *"the white hot wake, the wildering speed…"* of the destroyer's main weapon, the torpedo. In his own way, Kipling accurately described ships such as *Venomous* – a fast ship, possessing a weapon of incredible underwater speed and deadliness.

The war also confirmed the capability of another new type of warship that possessed the same weapon, the submarine and its torpedo, and also demonstrated the devastating potential of the new flying machines in finding, then sinking, ships at sea.

Capt Wayne P. Hughes, USN (Ret.) wrote about the role reversal of the destroyer from its original concept prior to the Great War to that of the interwar years and those of the Second World War: "... light cruisers designed as destroyer leaders became anti-aircraft (A.A.) escorts for carriers; destroyers conceived for defending the van and rear of the battle line against torpedo attacks from other destroyers were adapted to function as anti-submarine (A.S.) and A.A. escorts ... "[2]

The German U-boat would become a determined and merciless foe to *Venomous* and her crews 41 years after Kipling penned *"The Destroyer."* The role this venerable ship would play would morph away from the dash, flash and boom of the battle fleet and toward the relentless and exhausting work of protecting Britain's merchant marine from the U-boat.

The *"wildering speed"* of aircraft such as the German Stuka dive-bomber plummeting down from the sky would often place *Venomous* and her crew in mortal danger. The early days of the Second World War would find *Venomous* and her sister ships nearly defenceless against this new *"Chooser of the Slain."*

What, then, was this "Bride of Death" that Kipling penned?

HMS *Venomous* was a member of the Admiralty Modified W Class, 1st Group of destroyers. This class of destroyer comes from a prolific pedigree of British destroyer classes, which saw service with the Royal Navy between 1906 and 1920.[3] In setting the stage for the story of *Venomous'* service and recounting the experiences of her crew members, it would be helpful to explore first the background of the destroyer as a type of warship that was adopted by the world's navies at the beginning of the twentieth century. This chapter will trace the lineage of British destroyer design from 1906 to the introduction of the Admiralty Modified W Class ships. A final step will take the design characteristics of *Venomous* and compare them with contemporary destroyer designs from other navies. With this final comparison, one will see that *Venomous* and the other sixty-six similar ships that comprised the overall V & W Class were the most capable class of destroyers built during the Great War period, and their attributes were carried forward in succeeding British destroyer designs from the inter-war years through the immediate post Second World War era.

The emergence of the destroyer as a specific type of warship can be traced directly to the English engineer Robert Whitehead, who invented the "locomotive torpedo." Although the torpedo as a weapon was in existence prior to Whitehead's invention, it was a submerged, anchored explosive charge (today's underwater mine) or it was carried by a small vessel that had at its bow a long pole or spar with the explosive charge fitted at its tip. Whitehead took the concept of the torpedo in another direction, and put an end to the extremely dangerous practice of "engaging the enemy more closely" by ramming another vessel with an explosive device extended from one's own vessel on a long pole (spar), or trying to fix the charge on the hull of the enemy ship from one's own vessel.[4] This technology and suicidal tactics were replaced by launching a self-propelled torpedo at much greater and potentially safer distances.

During the next thirty years, fast craft carrying Whitehead's invention became known as torpedo boats. By the 1880s, they had evolved into a larger and more effective weapon system, possessing greater lethality, range and speed but, as with all new weapon systems, a counter was developed – the "Catcher" or the Torpedo Boat Destroyer.

By the beginning of the twentieth century both types of warship had begun to merge into a larger vessel that could protect the capital ships of the fleet from torpedo boat attacks and conduct its own torpedo attacks against the enemy's manoeuvring battle fleet. Equipped with a range of lightweight and quick-firing guns, together with more advanced torpedoes (larger warheads, higher speeds and extended ranges), the destroyer became a major type of warship in its own right.[5]

The first ships to bear this official destroyer designator for the Royal Navy were two ships of the Havock Class launched in 1893. The lead ship, HMS *Havock*, supposedly had a remarkable speed of 27 knots, and the ability to keep up with the battle fleet but only under certain conditions:

> "*Havock* and *Hornet* might have been able to keep up with the battle fleet, but only in good weather, calm seas and with picked coal and stokers. All the Turtle Backs, listed as 27 and 30-knotters, could make around those speeds in those conditions but this was for short bursts only and soon fell off in anything of a seaway. It was not until the River class destroyers that realistic seagoing speeds were credited..."[6]

With her torpedoes and quick-firing guns, *Havock* and her sister HMS *Hornet* would lay the foundation for future destroyer design.

Additional developments in engineering and improvements in hull design enhanced the capabilities of this new type of destroyer. The invention of the steam turbine engine enabled them to approach and even exceed 30 knots. Within five years of the outbreak of the Great War, the steam turbine was standard for destroyer type ships of all the world's major navies.

Destroyers and their forerunners were originally powered by coal but the introduction of oil-fired boilers further improved the efficiency of the steam turbine engine, boosting the speed of destroyers to beyond 30 knots. Oil burners eliminated the time-consuming logistics required for loading, handling and stowing the coal within the hull but oil presents its own challenges that persist to this day.

Changes in the shape of the destroyer's hull also improved its capability. As originally conceived, the destroyer possessed a hull with extremely fine lines built for speed – long and narrow with a low freeboard and a shallow draft, and very little superstructure. This made the early destroyers extremely uncomfortable in anything but relatively calm seas. The British introduced the raised fo'c'sle, which placed an extra deck on the forward one third of the hull. This improved the sea-keeping capability of the design, and also provided an enlarged berthing arrangement for the ship's company. The after two thirds of the hull accommodated the large engine room, while the long weather deck served as the primary platform for the destroyer's main weapon – the torpedo. The raised fo'c'sle would become the hull characteristic of the dozens of British destroyer classes built in the twentieth century.

A widely-known reference book of the early twentieth century, Conway's *Warships of the World, 1906 – 1920*, listed twenty-three class names of British destroyers built during the fourteen years covered by this authoritative guide to the world's navies (Jane's *Fighting Ships* was more widely recognised as the standard work). Of these twenty-three, there were eighteen distinct classes (but the Swift Class destroyer had only one ship and was excluded from this analysis) and of these, four classes had successive modified batches – the M, R, and the V & W Classes. The sixteen destroyers of the M Class were followed by a second batch of ninety ships identified as the Repeat M Class. The same occurred with the fifty-one destroyers of the R Class, and this class had a second batch of sixteen ships identified as the Modified R Class. The V & W Classes would also have several batches, and *Venomous* would be part of the last batch of fourteen ships referred to as the Admiralty Modified W Class First Group.

With a fully-loaded displacement of 1,550 tons, a maximum trials speed of 34 knots, and armed principally with torpedoes and four 4.7-inch guns, *Venomous* and her sisters were, at the time, the last word in destroyer development. She and her sisters compared very favourably to contemporaries found in the other major navies of the world. Arguably, they were the most powerful destroyers in the world in 1919, the year when *Venomous* was commissioned. After the Great War only the navies of Britain, France, Italy, Japan and the United States continued to build destroyers of any consequence (Germany was limited in its ability to improve or advance its destroyer designs by the Treaty of Versailles).

The table below compares the main features of the Admiralty Modified W class First Group (or the V & W Class as a whole) with those of destroyers of the US Navy, the French Navy, the Italian Navy and the Imperial Japanese Navy. All these destroyers were commissioned around the same time as *Venomous* and her sisters, and all except the French Arabe Class served during the Second World War.

For the US Navy, the Wickes Class destroyer was selected. This class was part of the largest composite class of destroyers ever built. They were the famous 'flush deck' or 'four pipers' destroyers that served with the US Navy through the Second World War.[7] Fifty of these ships were transferred to the Royal Navy in 1940 as part of the Lend Lease Programme, and their appearance flying the White Ensign filled a critical hole created as a result of increased demand for destroyer type ships and the terrible losses suffered by Royal Navy destroyers during the first two years of the Second World War.

The fourteen ships of the Arabe Class were the largest class built during the Great War for the French Navy. They were built in Japan along the lines of their Kaba Class destroyers as the needs of the French Army for steel were given a higher priority than that of the French Navy. In fact, French shipyards had great difficulty building ships of any kind while the Japanese shipyards had both the steel and the building capacity.[8] Ironically, Japan sent five of the Kaba class to serve alongside the French Navy in the Mediterranean during the war.

The Italian Palestro Class destroyers were selected because they were chronological contemporaries to *Venomous* and her sisters, and they served during the Second World War with the Italian Navy and then with the German Navy after Italy surrendered and came over to the Allies' side.

As in the case of France the Italian Army's need for steel prevented the Italian shipyards from building the number of ships that were ordered for the Palestro Class.

The Palestro Class were enlarged improvements of the Italian Audace Class destroyer, and the Audace Class were improvements of the six ships of the Indomito Class destroyers that were commissioned just before the war.[9]

	RN **Modified W Class** 1919	USN **Wickes Class** 1917	FN **Arabe Class** 1917	IN **Palestro Class** 1919	IJN **Minekaze Class** 1920
Displacement	1,550 tons	1,247 tons	685 tons	1076 tons	1,215 tons
Dimensions (ft)					
Length	312 ft	314.5 ft	271.9 ft	268.75 ft	336.5 ft
Beam	30 ft	30.9 ft	23.9 ft	26.2 ft	29 ft
Draught	10 ft 11 in	11.6 ft	7.9 ft	9.1 ft	10 ft
Armament					
Main guns	4 - 4.7"	4 - 4"/50 cal	1 - 4.7"	4- 4"	4- 4.7"/45 cal S.P.
Secondary guns	2-2 pdr pom poms	1-3"/25 cal A.A.	3-76 mm 1-76 mm A.A.	2-3" 2- 6.5 mm A.A.	2-7.7 mm A.A.
Torpedoe tubes Number & type	2 mounts w/ 3 tubes 6-21" torpedoes	4 mounts w/ 3 tubes 12-21" torpedoes	2 mounts w/ 2 tubes 4-17.7" torpedoes	2 mounts w/2 tubes 4-17.7" torpedoes	3 mounts w/ 2 tubes 6-21" torpedoes
Propulsion					
Steam boilers	3 Yarrow	4 White-Foster	4 Kampon	4 Thornycroft	4 Kampon
Geared turbines	2 Brown-Curtis	2 Parson	3 VTE	2 Zoelly	2 Parsons
Shafts	2	2	3	2	2
Horse power	30,000	24,200	10,000	18,000	38,500
Speed	32 knots	35 knots	29 knots	32 knots	Up to 39 knots
Range					
Cruising speed	3,500 nm @15 kts	2,500 nm @ 20 kts	2,000 nm @12 kts	1,970 nm @ 15 kts	4,000 nm @15 kts
Full speed	900 nm @ 32 kts			370 nm @ 27 kts	
Complement	134	114	86	118	148

Comparative table of destroyer characteristics

The table provides a simple comparison of the displacement, dimensions and corresponding propulsion plants and operational ranges of these classes, the characteristics which reflect the operational role the navies saw for their destroyers.

The length and short cruising range of the French Arabe Class and Italian Palestro Class destroyers reflected the operational requirements of their battle fleets. Both France and Italy concentrated their battle fleets in the confines of the Mediterranean Sea and larger longer-range destroyers were not required. The smaller capacity propulsion plant of the French Arabe Class gave a cruising range of just 2,000 nautical miles at 12 knots, whilst the even smaller propulsion plant of the Palestro Class had a cruising range of less than 2,000 nautical miles at 15 knots.

Compare these characteristics with those of the British, Japanese and American destroyers whose dimensions, displacement, propulsion plants and corresponding cruising ranges reflected the global operating requirements of their navies.[10] From this perspective, *Venomous* and her sisters were on a par with the Japanese Minekaze Class and superior to all the others. It is interesting to note, however, that the maximum speed of *Venomous* was less than that of her American and Japanese counterparts. This reflects the requirement to 'keep up' with their respective battle fleets and a clear understanding of the over-riding importance of the destroyer's main armament – the torpedo.

By the end of the Great War, the top speeds of the battleships serving in the Royal Navy averaged 21 knots while US and Japanese battleships averaged 21 and 23 knots respectively. The dash speeds of all three classes of destroyers gave them the tactical ability to maintain station with their respective battle fleets but the reality of the Great War at sea for Britain's battle fleet was that "engineering speed used to achieve tactical advantage usually went for nought."[11] The speed of the fleet was a measure of the speed of its slowest battleship, and as such the need for very high-speed destroyers was not as great.[12]

The underlying reason why the American and Japanese destroyers were faster than *Venomous* and her sisters was the role of the torpedo. For the Americans and the Japanese, the emphasis was on the ability of their destroyers to dash toward the enemy's battle fleet to deliver a mass torpedo attack. It was an offensively oriented doctrine. For the British, the emphasis was on screening the battle fleet against torpedo attack, whilst providing a credible torpedo attack capability of its own. Thwart attack first, and then counter the attack with your own torpedoes.

A destroyer's torpedoes were considered the main armament during this period, and *Venomous* was on a par with most contemporaries with regard to the number of torpedo tubes and torpedoes carried. The Wickes Class was, however, far superior to all the others with twelve 21-inch torpedo tubes, but these tubes were arranged in four 3-tube mounts set two on either side of the main deck. This would allow a maximum of only six torpedoes to be launched in one salvo. To launch the remaining six torpedoes, this US destroyer class would have to rapidly turn away or toward the enemy to unmask the disengaged two torpedo tube mounts. This could expose the ship to countermeasures, including a deluge of well-directed gunfire.

Complementing the torpedo armament for these destroyers would be their main gun armament. Examining the main gun armament characteristics of these destroyers, as well as their placement on their hull, can tell us a great deal about their capabilities. *Venomous* and her sisters were heavily armed with the 4.7-inch gun. Only the Minekaze Class possessed the same size gun with an equal number of mounts. This shows that both the *Venomous* and the Minekaze were the fruits of a balanced approach in their respective designs. Each design recognised the torpedo as its main offensive weapon, but also recognised the need for a large-size gun to blunt the torpedo attack by enemy destroyers.[13] In the end, what it really boiled down to was how the Royal Navy and the Imperial Japanese Navy would employ their respective destroyers in combat with their battle fleets.

During the last years of the Great War, British Intelligence reported that the German Navy had developed a larger calibre gun for their destroyers. In fact, although a 5.9-inch gun had been installed on a few destroyers it never saw action on German destroyers until the Second World War.[14] In response to this perceived improvement in German destroyer armament, the new 4.7-inch 45-calibre gun was developed for the class, making them the most heavily armed destroyers of the period.[15] However, as we will see later, this 4.7-inch gun's performance was a mixed blessing – it was certainly an excellent weapon against surface targets but the gun lacked sufficient elevation capability against attacking aircraft.

Not only was *Venomous* heavily armed, but the main battery of guns and torpedoes were well positioned on her long quarterdeck, allowing most of these weapons to be engaged from any firing quarter. This had much to do with the arrangement of the guns and the hull design. For the guns, the two forward mounts ("A" and "B" mounts) were superimposed – "A" mount was placed on the raised fo'c'sle, whilst "B" mount was placed aft of "A" and above on the forward deck house of the ship. This was a rather novel concept at the time, and in future the design of destroyers of the major navies would all follow this concept. The two after gun mounts were similarly arranged with one superimposed above the other, with "X" mount situated on the after deck house and above "Y" mount.[16] As for her torpedo armament, the two triple torpedo tube mounts were located aft of amidships and on the main deck. These could be directed on both sides and well forward toward the bow of the ship.

The American approach in positioning the guns of the Wickes Class was a throwback to earlier designs and remained a unique characteristic of this class. The Wickes' arrangement of waist guns on a rise or "bandstand" above the main deck and just forward of amidships was an attempt to enable those two guns to be trained forward. This allowed the American to train three of her four main guns just shy of dead ahead or dead astern.

It is also important to compare the hull form of each class. The first two characteristics of the table – displacement and dimensions – will help us in this assessment. With a displacement of over 1,500 tons fully loaded (fl), *Venomous* and her sisters were heavier than the other destroyer classes in the table. Nevertheless, her hull dimensions were very similar to all but the Japanese Minekaze Class.

The Minekaze Class was nearly 25 feet longer, but it had the same beam. This gave the Minekaze Class an extraordinary length to beam ratio of 11.6 to 1. In other words, for every ten feet of length, there was one foot of beam, and for destroyers, a ratio approximating or exceeding 10 to 1 allows the hull to cut through the water more efficiently and at very high speeds. For the Minekaze Class, a top speed approaching 39 knots was attainable. *Venomous* and her sisters had a ratio of 10.4 to 1 and a top speed of 32 knots.[17] On the face of it, the Minekaze Class possessed a tremendous advantage but such an extreme ratio subjects the hull to considerable rolling in heavy seas and a fair comparison needs to take into account the shape of the hull.

Except for the Wickes Class, all of the destroyer classes identified in the table had a raised fo'c'sle. A raised fo'c'sle, together with a noticeable forward "V" shape to the hull, a traceable sheer line running from the bow on the raised foredeck, and a noticeably higher freeboard along the entire length of the hull, gave the *Venomous* and her Japanese contemporary better sea-keeping ability – the ability to remain fairly stable at high speeds and in rough seas. This was extremely important to enable a destroyer to effectively launch her torpedoes and lay her guns on target.

One can see that the Wickes Class destroyers' "flush decked" hull form lacked sufficient sheer forward and freeboard (height) along the entire hull to prevent water from washing over the hull in moderate seas. The most pronounced feature of the after portion of the hull is the lack of freeboard. With the ill-designed placement of the torpedo tube mounts with two mounts on either side on the main deck, this meant a very wet experience for the torpedo men. The 10.4 to 1 length to beam ratio, together with the fore mentioned hull form, would result in heavy rolls in moderate seas. These combined factors could affect the efficiency of the torpedo attack. With all things considered, the V & Ws and the Minekaze Class had the same potential to deliver a torpedo salvo of six torpedoes but the fact that the American destroyers had six extra torpedoes did give them a major advantage over their contemporaries when destroyers normally did not carry reloads.

The arrangement of the lightweight torpedo tubes of the V & W Class was a unique concept which was only copied by the US Navy fifty years later when it introduced its Mark 32 anti-submarine torpedo mount on its post Second World War destroyer classes. This arrangement had the tubes in a triangular configuration, with the third tube situated above the lower two. This saved considerable deck space on either side of the weather deck of these ships.

This comparison of *Venomous* to her contemporaries shows that she possessed well thought out design characteristics, which would become standard on future classes of destroyers. It also shows that *Venomous* was a capable and powerful ship for the period. As Anthony Preston wrote in his definitive account about the V & W Class destroyers,

> "The 'V & W' boats had something more: the detailed design work was good...the paradox answer is that the design was both progressive and conservative; it met an important criterion of any design in not

introducing too many innovations, but rather concentrating on new combinations of tried components. Thus their geared turbines...the superimposed gun...their method of construction used the well-tried transverse framing...with a larger hull, to accommodate greater armament and seaworthiness. In addition, the Director of Naval Construction...insisted on sturdy construction and a good margin of stability as prerequisites for destroyers."[18]

But, in the end, a warship's ability to perform in combat rested upon the quality of the crew and a little bit of luck. We will see that *Venomous* had both.

Notes

1   Rudyard Kipling's poem, *The Destroyers*, was published in 1898, and it can be found at http://www.poetryloverspage.com/poets/kipling/kipling_ind.html

2   CAPT Wayne P. Hughes, USN Ret., *Fleet Tactics: Theory and Practice*, Naval Institute Press, Annapolis, Maryland, 1986, p 89.

3   Officially, a member of the Admiralty Modified W Class, 1st Group HMS *Venomous* was a member of the greater V & W Class of British destroyers. This class comprised six similarly designed ships. *Venomous* was in the last batch of the V & W Class.

4   "Engage the Enemy More Closely" was Nelson's more favoured signal when directing the captains of his fleet in action.

5   The torpedo boat would continue to evolve as its own type of naval craft that would see wartime service in both great wars at sea during the twentieth century.

6   Peter C. Smith's email dated 8 February 2009 noted that both *Havock* and *Hornet* did not perform as advertised and referenced his own work on the subject: *Hard Lying – The Birth of the Destroyer, 1893-1913* (Kimber, 1971). ISBN 7183 01927

7   The Wickes Class consisted of 110 ships, whilst the very near sister class, the Clemson Class consisted of nearly 150 ships. This compares to the 67 ships of the V & W Class.

8   Moreover, the major shipyards for the French Navy had existed along the northern coast of France, and these fell into the hands of the German Army.

9   *Conway's All the World's Fighting Ships 1906-1921* (Conway Maritime Press, 1985) Reprinted by the United States Naval Institute Press, 2006, p 268 – 270.

10 The Palestro Class was based on the earlier Japanese Kaba Class which, compared to the new Minekaze Class, was a second rate destroyer.

11 Hughes, p. 87.

12 According to *Conway's All the World's Fighting Ships 1906-1921*, the slowest battleship class that fought for the Royal Navy at Jutland was the *Bellerophon* Class, which had a top speed of 20.75 knots.

13 Japanese torpedoes were superior to all other torpedoes of the world's navies. This proved tragically so for the US Navy during the early days of the Second World War in the Pacific.

14 According to *Conway's Warships* only a few of the German destroyers carried this size gun, but it would be standard for follow-on classes of German destroyers that would see action during the Second World War.

15 The 4.7-inch gun was the naval version of the British Army's 4.7-inch field gun.

16 The Royal Navy and the Commonwealth Navies adopted the lettering designator to indicate the position of each major gun on board, whilst the US Navy used a numerical designator that corresponded with the calibre of the gun. For example, the forward 5-inch gun on a destroyer was designated as Mount 51. For the Royal Navy it would be designated "A" gun.

17 *Venomous* reached 34 knots during her builder's trials and her sisters reached comparable speeds. In CPO Collister's account of his service on board *Venomous* during the Second World War he said the ship hit 34 knots, up until she was placed into reserve status and sent to the breakers.

18 Anthony Preston, *V & W Class Destroyers 1917-1945*, MacDonald & Co. Ltd., London, 1971, p. 19.

CHAPTER TWO

TO THE BALTIC AND BACK
1919 – 23

"Tell Raskolnikov that the British ships must be sunk come what may." Leon Trotsky[1]

Originally named HMS *Venom*, HMS *Venomous* began as Ship No. 482 in the upper Clyde shipyards of John Brown and Company Limited, Glasgow Scotland.[2] She formed part of a double order with her sister ship, HMS *Verity* (No. 483). The two ships were laid down on 31 May and 17 May 1918 respectively.[3] *Venomous* was launched on 17 April 1919, and together with another sister ship, HMS *Veteran,* the three destroyers shared the same fitting-out basin as the battle-cruiser, HMS *Hood*.

HMS *Hood* and HMS *Venomous* in the fitting-out basin at John Brown's shipyard on the Clyde
A photocopy which was found in the papers of Robert J. Moore after his death. The publishers would like to know the present whereabouts of this photograph.

Views of the bow and stern of HMS *Venomous* fitting out in John Brown's shipyard on the Clyde in 1919. *Courtesy of Warships on Clydesite, see http://www.clydesite.co.uk/warships/index.asp*

The ship's first commanding officer was Cdr Somerville P.B. Russell RN who took up his duties on 28 April 1919 and oversaw the completion of his ship. His contemporaries considered Russell to be "a nice little man, if rather dull," but respected him as a keen player of the game of bridge. Considering what lay ahead Russell's traits were probably those most required. His Executive Officer, Lt John A.B. Wilson RN, was recognised as "quite a character" and known as the "Big White Chief." Sub Lt Edward Hurry RN joined as the ship's

Torpedo Officer. He was delighted with the appointment but it's not known if young Hurry had read Kipling's poem.

Under her new commander and with a ship's company of 134 men, *Venomous* proceeded down the Clyde for acceptance trials on 4 June. The ship's log records *Venomous* weighing anchor at 0930 on 4 June and proceeding down the Clyde for Tail O' the Bank to calibrate her compass. This brand new destroyer must have made a fine sight cutting through the waters of the Clyde at a steady 12 knots. Who could have predicted the long and eventful career that this new addition to the fleet would experience in the years ahead?

Russell put *Venomous* through various engineering, gunnery, torpedo, and operational exercises, including the uploading of ammunition, to ensure the ship met fleet standards and to bring the ship's company up to operational proficiency. The various drills and exercises detailed in the ship's log were intermingled with such mundane entries as on "5 June… one boathook lost overboard" followed by another entry on 6 June for "A hand scrubber lost overboard."

With her acceptance trials completed, Russell received orders to take *Venomous* to her new homeport. During the long twilight hours of 17 June 1919, Russell ordered the special sea duty men to be closed up to their stations for getting underway and for the port watch to be

HMS *Venomous* with crew members on fo'c'sle taken shortly after its launch in 1919.
The G98 pendant number changed to D75 in 1920. *Courtesy of the Imperial War Museum.*

mustered on the fo'c'sle. Minutes later, the Royal Navy's newest destroyer weighed anchor and proceeded down the Clyde. Once in open waters, she headed north and up the west coast of Scotland, bound for Rosyth, the Royal Navy's principal dockyard and base in Scotland, on the Firth of Forth upstream from Edinburgh. Arriving at Rosyth on 19 June, *Venomous* officially joined the Third Flotilla of the Atlantic Fleet with the Scott class destroyer HMS *Campbell* as her flotilla leader.[4] Whilst moored with the Third Flotilla on 28 June, *Venomous'* crew received news that peace had come – The Great War had officially ended. The ship's log simply recorded the event… "Cleared lower deck and ship's company assembled on deck for the announcement that peace had been signed. Dressed ship. Fleet fired 101 gun salutes to Port Edgar."

Her first assignment was to participate in the Fleet Review off Southend in the Thames to celebrate the end of the Great War and the peace.[5] In company with sister ship, HMS *Valkyrie*, and the Caroline Class light cruiser, HMS *Carysfort*, *Venomous* steamed south on 14 July. All three ships arrived alongside the Royal Fleet Auxiliary oiler RFA *Scotch* off Southend Pier at 1800 the following day, an exceedingly swift passage! With the celebrations over, *Venomous* weighed anchor on 23 July and steamed back north to the wartime Fleet anchorage of Scapa Flow.

On arrival at Scapa Flow in the Orkney Islands on 25 July they saw the ghostly remains of the German Navy's scuttled High Sea Fleet. Five weeks earlier, on 21 June 1919, on learning of the conclusion of peace negotiations, the Fleet Commander, Admiral von Reuter, had activated previously issued orders for his warships to be scuttled. As this drama unfolded, and with the Grand Fleet at sea, the single guard ship, the destroyer *Westcott*, was powerless to prevent the wholesale destruction of the German vessels. In *Westcott* that day was Sub Lt S. Brian de Courcy Ireland RN, whose next appointment would be to *Venomous*.[6] This young officer described this incredible event in his journal:

> "On 21 June 1919 we were lying in Gutter Sound doing our turn, having a gin before lunch, when the senior Sub-Lt came running into the wardroom and said 'The Germans are abandoning ship.' We thought at first he was being funny. However, we rushed up on deck and indeed they were abandoning ship, every ship. In fact, they were scuttling

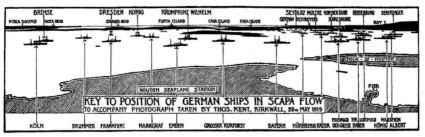

The German High Sea Fleet at anchor in Scapa Flow after its internment.
Photograph and drawing by Thomas Kent. *Courtesy of Orkney Library and Archive.*

them. They were flying various signals and laying boats, but there was nothing that we could do. There was no way we could prevent seventy ships from being scuttled. Our C-in-C had rather foolishly taken the rest of the Fleet out on exercise and we were the only warship left on duty. We were some way from the bigger ships but we could see them keel over and sink lower in the water. So we went at full speed towards them to try and stop the crews of the battleships or cruisers from abandoning ship. They took no notice of our words, so we fired a few rounds close to one of the cruisers and of course, quite naturally, the whole lot just jumped straight over the side! There was nothing you could do. We just stood there and watched this giant cruiser go down in front of our eyes."[7]

De Courcy Ireland continued his account by describing the aftermath: "Everywhere we looked we saw mast after mast sticking out from the water, it was an awesome sight. An entire fleet of 71 ships, ships that had fought at Jutland, all scuttled. We were the only warship to witness this extraordinary event and this made things a bit complicated."[8]

The young sub then describes what happened to the Germans after they scuttled their ships: "We gathered up the German crews from all the ships on to one island." "We were then left with these Germans as prisoners, but they weren't really prisoners."[9]

The reason for *Venomous'* presence at Scapa Flow was now apparent. Russell had been ordered to conduct salvage operations. *Venomous'* sailors were dispatched as salvage parties to the German destroyer, SMS *V82*, which had beached on the island of Fara.[10] Their work presumably involved the removal of ammunition, armament, brass fittings, and useful equipment but one could also assume the men took the opportunity to obtain a few souvenirs for themselves.

For the rest of the summer and the early days of autumn 1919, *Venomous* was engaged in drills, exercises and port calls along Britain's west and southern coasts. Returning to Rosyth, *Venomous* welcomed the return of her flotilla mates, HMS *Winchester*, *Wolsey* and *Whitley* on 9 October followed by HMS *Verity* and *Wanderer* on 10 October and HMS *Watchman* and *Valorous* on 12 October. With the Third Flotilla reformed, it awaited orders to the Baltic.

In 1918, the Treaty of Brest-Litovsk had terminated the war between Russia and Germany, but the political status of the nations bordering the eastern shore of the Baltic was chaotic. Russia was in the throes of revolution, counter-revolution and civil war. Finland, Estonia, Latvia and Lithuania had taken the opportunity to seek their independence from the defunct Russian Empire. The Russian Bolsheviks sought to recover these lost territories, while substantial German forces under Major General Adolf Joachim Rüdiger Graf von der Goltz were sent by the dying German Empire to assist the Finns.[11]

Goltz, an east Prussian by birth, had landed at Hanko, Finland in early April 1918 with a force of 12,000 German troops of the Baltic Sea Division. Goltz' force, together with Finnish and White Russian troops under General Baron Carl Gustav Mannerheim, quickly drove the Red Finns and Russian Bolsheviks from Finland and recaptured its capital, Helsinki. The success of the Allies' summer offensive on the Western Front led to Goltz and his troops being ordered back to Germany but in 1919 Goltz returned to the Baltic States under one of the provisions in the Armistice to prevent the Bolsheviks from taking over the region. Goltz interpreted his orders differently and commenced operations to bring the Baltic States under German control while repulsing Bolshevik advances.[12]

A British naval force had been supporting the Baltic States since the 1918 Armistice. This force comprised the Sixth Light Cruiser Squadron, together with nine V & W Class destroyers from the

Thirteenth Destroyer Flotilla, as well as seven minesweepers from the Third Fleet Sweeping Flotilla. They were under the command of Rear Admiral Edwyn Alexander-Sinclair RN.[13]

In January 1919, Rear Admiral Sir Walter Cowan, GCB DSC and Bar RN relieved Sinclair.[14] His orders were to show the British Flag and support the Estonian and Latvian governments in their opposition to Bolshevik aggression. He was instructed to treat all Bolshevik warships and auxiliaries operating off the Baltic States as hostile and to deal with them accordingly but not to land any of his sailors or marines except under exceptional circumstances. He was ordered to stay out of Estonian and Latvian internal politics, not to favour one party over another or raise any hope of military assistance other than the supply of arms.[15]

Cowan's flagship was the Caledon Class light cruiser HMS *Caledon* and his force included the Arethusa Class light cruiser, HMS *Royalist* and five of *Venomous'* sister V & W Class destroyers. Admiral Fremantle, the chief of staff to the First Sea Lord, briefed Cowan before leaving Rosyth. Cowan recalled that:

> "It seemed to me that there was never such a tangle, and my brain reeled from it. An unbeaten German Army, two kinds of belligerent Russians, Letts, Finns, Estonians, Lithuanians; ice, mines – 60,000 of them! Russian submarines, German small craft, Russian battleships, cruisers and destroyers all only wait for the ice to melt to ravage the Baltic. I felt that I had better get out there as soon as possible to get wise before the Gulf of Finland thawed out…"[16]

Upon arriving in the Baltic, Cowan established his forward operating base in Biorko Sound, Finland, deep in the Gulf of Finland. On the night of 18 August 1919, a daring raid by motor torpedo boats under Lt Augustus Agar RN, immobilised the Soviet Gangut Class battleships, *Andrei Pervozvanni* and *Petropavlovsk*, and severely reduced the capacity of the Bolsheviks to influence events at sea. Agar was awarded the Victoria Cross for this successful action.

The Royal Navy did not continue to operate in the Baltic unscathed. The Caledon Class light cruiser HMS *Cassandra* was sunk by a mine, killing 11 sailors; the sister ship of *Venomous*, HMS *Vittoria*, fell prey to torpedoes from the Bolshevik *Bars* Class submarine *Pantera* and HMS *Verulam* to British mines – 38 British sailors were lost in these two sinkings. The "war to end all wars" had not quite come to an end for the British sailor and nor was there tranquillity for sailors at home.[17]

Back at Rosyth on *Venomous*, the diary kept by Mid Renfrew Gotto RN, gives us a glimpse of what Britain and her Navy were experiencing. On Saturday 11 October 1919, Gotto wrote: "Several Engineer officers from the Destroyers, with care and maintenance parties, have gone to help running volunteer trains during the railway strike during the week." On 4 October "There has been some trouble with the men of the First Flotilla boats in here as they have been ordered out to the Baltic again and they have only returned a short whilst." The day *Venomous* left for the Baltic, Gotto wrote: "When we left Rosyth for Copenhagen...before leaving, three men broke out of ship." They had jumped ship and deserted. On 12 October he wrote that, "on hearing that they were about to return to the Baltic, 150 seamen broke out of their ships at Port Edgar, one losing one third of her crew."[18]

Desertion was not uncommon. Thousands of sailors were "hostilities only" and had expected to be quickly demobilised when the Armistice was signed while career navy men had expected more time ashore after four years of war. Pay was also a major issue. Barely adequate before the war, a sailor's pay was totally inadequate when inflation took hold of Britain's wartime economy. This led to sailors missing a ship's movement, deserting and, on a few occasions, refusing to perform their duties. Some were charged with mutiny and convicted. Admiral Cowen's Baltic force was not immune from such turmoil.

It was against this background that *Venomous* departed Rosyth just after sunset on 13 October 1919 in the company of another V & W destroyer, HMS *Whitley*. The two destroyers arrived at Copenhagen on the 15th, and immediately took on oil from the destroyer depot ship HMS *Sandhurst*, a former merchant ship. The next day Admiral Cowan signalled Russell to set his destroyer's course for the Latvian port of Libau.[19]

Russell took *Venomous* along the "Red Track", a channel swept clear of mines through the centre of the Baltic, and during the forenoon watch on the 16th *Venomous* entered the naval harbour of Libau. Russell was directed to refuel his destroyer and proceed that same afternoon on her first operational patrol under wartime conditions to the area off the Vlangen Lighthouse on the south coast of Sweden. *Venomous* patrolled the area for three days, stopping and checking merchantmen which might be trying to breach the blockade of German

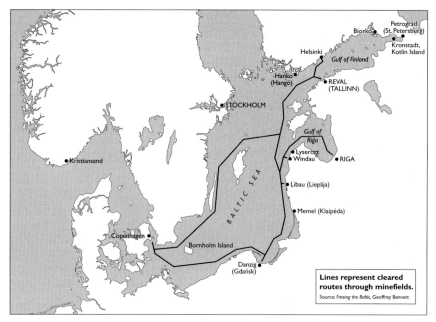

The Baltic theatre of operations, 1919 – 22.
Drawn by Kelly Erlinger based on map in Freeing the Baltic *by Geoffrey Bennett.*

ports and send supplies to General Goltz' forces. Russell had orders to send blockade-runners and their crews into Libau but drew a blank and at the end of the patrol he took *Venomous* back to Copenhagen to replenish stores.

Once alongside HMS *Sandhurst* Russell gave his ship's company a short spell of leave. Gotto was one of the officers taking advantage of the opportunity for a run ashore and this young man's impressions of post-war Copenhagen are worth recounting:

> "Tuesday, 21 October to Saturday, 25 October: Remained alongside Sandhurst and got leave each day. Copenhagen is a very fine city and one is very much struck by the clean and tidy appearance of all the streets. The shops too are exceedingly good and the shop windows are dressed very cleverly and the principal streets compare very favourably with any in London. The theatres are quite good and have all the latest English and American songs."

Venomous left Copenhagen on the afternoon of 25 October, spending the next two days patrolling off the Danish island of Bornholm, before proceeding to Reval (the city and seaport of Tallinn, Estonia) on 28 October. Gotto recorded some impressions of Reval in his journal:

"The Naval Harbour at Reval is uncompleted and looks as if it will remain so as the Estonians are taking no steps in the matter. The town gives one the feeling of desolation, the people seeming to take no interest in life at all. The *Maidstone* is in the inner harbour with four H class submarines. The exchange is fluctuating but the food is comparatively cheap."

During the morning of 30 October, *Venomous* carried out exercises with two of the H Class submarines before returning to harbour where she remained alongside until 3 November.

While four of her sister ships, together with the Danae Class light cruiser HMS *Dragon*, provided gunfire support for the Letts defending Riga, their capital city, from elements of Goltz's Freikorps, *Venomous* was ordered to be the mail boat. *Venomous* left Reval for the Finnish port town of Biorko, arriving on the morning of 4 November but returned to Reval the same day and was then ordered south to Libau in Latvia, steaming at a brisk 25 knots and arriving just after midnight on 5 November. Russell had been ordered to Libau to provide additional support to a Royal Navy cruiser/destroyer force that was helping defend the town against a determined German Army assault. The German attack began on 4 November, and the Arethusa Class light cruiser HMS *Phaeton* and the Danae Class HMS *Dauntless*, together with four of *Venomous'* sisters, HMS *Winchester, Whitley, Valorous,* and *Wryneck,* provided steady naval gunfire support to the small Letts garrison throughout the day.[20] The combined 6-inch guns from the cruisers and the 4.7-inch guns from the V & Ws proved too much for Goltz and his *Freikorps*. They fell back to escape the British gunfire but this was only a temporary respite as Goltz was determined to take the city.

When Russell arrived on 5 November he found the situation relatively quiet and *Venomous* was able to take on board a number of refugees before leaving the same day for Copenhagen with the mail and dispatches. *Venomous* missed the renewed assault by the *Freikorps* later that day and the naval gunfire support laid on by the Royal Navy. Many of those aboard *Venomous,* including Midshipman Gotto, must have been disappointed to have missed the first opportunity for their ship to fire her guns in combat.

Venomous left Copenhagen early on 10 November with mail and dispatches from the UK and arrived back in Libau on 12 November to find the port quiet except for jubilant Letts celebrating their latest but not yet final victory over the Germans. Admiral Cowan had ordered the newly arrived Erebus Class monitor, HMS *Erebus,* to Libau to strengthen the city's defences.[21] The sight of *Erebus* and her massive 15-inch guns must have raised the spirits of the British force. *Venomous* couldn't linger, she had mail and dispatches to deliver. Russell got her underway late on the 12th for her next run and *Venomous* again missed an opportunity to fire her guns in combat. On 14 November, *Erebus,* with her two 15-inch guns, provided naval gunfire support to the Letts, who not only kept a superior German force from taking the city, but successfully counter-attacked, killing approximately eight thousand. At times the British monitor, together with her cruiser/destroyer force, was firing at point-blank range – for 15-inch guns, point-blank range would approximate to one mile. The successful defence of Libau and Riga marked the high water mark for Goltz and his "Baltic Adventure."[22] From that time onwards, Goltz would be gradually forced to withdraw his forces from the Baltic States.

Venomous reached Biorko, where she secured alongside another V & W destroyer, HMS *Wallace,* on the morning of 13 November. The next morning Russell was ordered to weigh anchor and take up the Kaporia Bay patrol. Despite success against the Germans there was still a naval threat from the Bolsheviks at Kronstadt. The Kronstadt Naval Base on Kotlin Island in the eastern part of the Gulf of Finland was just west of the city of Petrograd (later renamed Leningrad and now St. Petersburg). The Bolshevik naval forces at Kronstadt had to pass through Kaporia Bay to reach the swept channel through the Baltic.[23] A Bolshevik naval offensive would threaten Cowan's line of supply across the Baltic from Denmark. Kaporia Bay provided an excellent vantage point for a picket ship to warn Cowan should the Bolsheviks sortie out from the Gulf of Finland. *Venomous* replaced another V & W on this patrol but after two days and with no sign of the Reds, it returned to Biorko arriving shortly after sunrise on 16 November.

Venomous returned to sea on the 18th and for the next two nights shared the boom defence duties of the port with her sister ship, HMS *Vanity*. Nothing of note happened during this local patrol and the next few days were spent back in Biorko.

Winter was approaching and there were deep snowdrifts ashore when *Venomous* resumed the Kaporia Bay patrols on 25 November. *Venomous* got under way just after sunrise in company with another sister ship, HMS *Viceroy*. They sailed into a stiff, bone-chilling breeze but apart from that the weather was good. Shortly after leaving Biorko *Venomous* experienced a serious engine problem, the result of a mistake by one of the duty stokers. A blown fire and defective bilge pump left *Venomous* dead in the water. Despite the rough seas that caused the ship to pitch and roll heavily, the stokers were able to quickly effect a temporary repair and the ship continued toward her patrol area. On 26 November, the weather deteriorated even further and *Venomous* took several "green seas", one of which came down the engine room hatches, drenching the duty watch with freezing water. The 27th found the ship back at Biorko. Further snowfalls were experienced when they went back on patrol on the 29th. For the first time there were thick patches of sea ice and when the ship returned to Biorko there was a thin layer of ice on the water in the harbour.

Venomous resumed the Kaporia Bay patrol on 2 December in company with another V & W destroyer, HMS *Wanderer*. During the afternoon there was a submarine alert when an anti-submarine trawler sighted a patch of oil near Siskar Island and dropped two depth charges bringing more oil to the surface but providing no positive evidence of a kill. *Venomous* and *Wanderer* continued depth-charging the last known position (datum) of the contact but without result.

Throughout 3 December weather conditions progressively deteriorated and as the ship closed up for night action stations, snow started to fall. *Venomous* and *Wanderer* anchored during the worst of the weather, while *Verity* remained under way. By daylight, the elements had relented and the force returned to harbour and soon afterwards was joined by the mail boat, HMS *Vanessa*.

Venomous enjoyed a welcome four-day break alongside at Biorko but resumed the Kaporia Bay patrol on 8 December with two sister ships, HMS *Vancouver* and *Vanessa*. Conditions at sea deteriorated even further, as Midshipman Gotto recorded:

"At about 11.00 p.m. on the 9th, it was blowing hard and the sea had got up. The 1st Lieutenant sent me onto the foc'sle to shackle up the cable again (when anchoring on patrol it is always broken at the sixth shackle ready for slipping). At 11.15 p.m. *Vanessa* dragged her anchor and had to get under way before anchoring again. By the time I went off watch, it was pitching considerably."

Gotto's words give a vivid impression of what it was like to be on deck during the late days of a Baltic autumn. Until now he had spent most of his time on duty (under instruction) in the warm confines of *Venomous'* engineering spaces, learning the finer points of the ship's propulsion system. It must have been a shock to transfer topside (under instruction) to learn the finer points of ship handling in bitter cold temperatures. With the arrival of the mail from *Vanessa*, Gotto learnt that his next appointment would take him to the Iron Duke Class battleship, HMS *Marlborough*, which, at that time, was in the Mediterranean. This news obviously warmed the young "snotty," who by now must have felt that he had spent enough time exposed to the numbing cold on *Venomous'* open bridge.

Venomous returned to Biorko during the middle watch on 10 December where she remained until the morning of 14 December when she left with *Vanessa* to patrol the Stiro Point area. By now temperatures were consistently below zero and as Gotto related:

"It is freezing hard and there is quite a lot of ice about. At 1530 got under way and proceeded on patrol. Went through a lot of pack ice on the way out, especially by the gate. During the night we were patrolling up and down through the ice all the time."

Back in harbour on 16 December, *Venomous* received the welcome news that she would be relieved on or about 20 December by a destroyer of the Fourth Flotilla. In any event, the increasing incidence of ice would close Biorko for the winter, forcing the Royal Navy to withdraw its presence in the Gulf of Finland.

On the morning of 18 December, *Venomous* got underway along with *Wanderer* on what would be her last patrol of Kaporia Bay. On 19 December Cowan and most of his force, including several store ships, an oiler and six destroyers left Biorko. As temperatures fell to minus 5 degrees Fahrenheit, *Venomous* spent an anxious day on 20 December in real danger of being frozen in by the rapidly building pack ice until Russell received orders to take his destroyer to Reval. Just before midday on 21 December she fell in with *Wanderer* and the Danae Class light cruiser HMS *Dunedin* on route for the Estonian coast. The next day both destroyers left for Copenhagen arriving in time for Christmas and the ship's company enjoyed a traditional Royal Navy Christmas.[24]

On Boxing Day, Russell steamed *Venomous* for home and the

Chatham Dockyard.[25] Midshipman Gotto described their unpleasant return voyage:

> "Proceeded out of harbour for Chatham. There was a very strong gale blowing. The seas were not too bad until we rounded the Skaw and then the seas were so bad we had to proceed at reduced speed. No one was allowed on the upper deck and for two days all watch keeping Officers slept and lived in the Chart House. We arrived at last on Sunday 28 December at Chatham after an extremely uncomfortable passage, our cabin being flooded with water about 1 1/2 to 2 feet deep."

For *Venomous*, this was the end to her first deployment away from home waters. These three months in the Baltic had been one hard slog, frequently in awful conditions and with the ever-present danger of mines, Bolshevik warships and submarines. Ships had been damaged or sunk and those in *Venomous* must have been relieved at their safe return. Midshipmen Gotto took up his new appointment in *Marlborough* but would renew his acquaintance with his old ship at a later date in circumstances of considerable danger.

The ships and men who served in the Baltic have become known as the forgotten fleet. With the end of the Cold War and the re-emergence of the Baltic States as free and independent countries, the accomplishments of the Royal Navy during the period after the Great War have become more widely known. Geoffrey Bennett wrote poignantly in the preface to *Freeing the Baltic* that:

> "I had the opportunity to visit the Estonian capital Tallinn…Walking around the charming 'old town' I entered the historic Church of the Holy Ghost and spotted a white Ensign at one end. Beneath this a new plaque, placed there in the year 2000, records Britons who have been honoured by Estonia for their contribution to freedom…Then, at the edge of the old town, there is a well appointed maritime museum in a castle tower known as 'Fat Margaret.' By the side of the entrance another clearly recent plaque, black marble topped with the silhouette of a destroyer, records in both English and Estonian:"

IN MEMORY
of the officers and seamen of the British Royal Navy
who served and gave their lives in the cause of freedom
in the Baltic during the Estonian War of Independence
1918-1920

The following Admirals were decorated
with the Estonian Cross of Liberty for their distinguished services:

Admiral Edwyn Alexander-Sinclair GCB MVO VRI/1
1865-1945

Admiral Sir Walter Cowan of the Baltic Bart. KCB DSC MVO VRI/1
1871-1956

Admiral Sir Sydney Freemantle GCB MVO VRI/1
1867-1958

Admiral Sir Bertram Thesiger KBE CB CMG VRI/1
1875-1966

On the 16 December 2005 the Duke of York unveiled a memorial in
Portsmouth cathedral recordings the names of fifteen Royal Naval
officers, 92 ratings, four Royal Air Force officers and one airman killed
whilst helping Estonia achieve its independence in 1918-9. It is a
replica of the memorial unveiled in Talinn, Estonia, in 2003.[26]

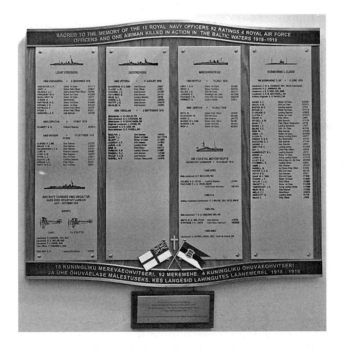

The memorial in Portsmouth cathedral to those who died in the Baltic campaign of 1918-9
Courtesy of Tim Backhouse of History in Portsmouth.

Venomous spent January 1920 dockside at its home port of Chatham and while the ship's company enjoyed some hard-earned leave the ship underwent routine maintenance. There were also changes amongst the ship's junior officers with Sub Lts Eric Gannon and Rob Nicholls replacing Edward Hurry and Henry Baker.

With the crew rested and routine maintenance completed Russell received orders to return to Scapa Flow. *Venomous* left Chatham on 9 February and arrived on the 17th after a slow passage having had the disquieting experience of passing through the Drifter Fleet on her way North. Many of the smaller units of the German High Sea Fleet had been refloated and were in the process of being towed to British ports for scrapping. Shortly after departing Scapa Flow for Rosyth on 24 February they overtook the former German light cruiser, SMS *Emden,* which was being towed by the tugs *Respond* and *St Cyrus*.[27] Russell saw the opportunity for some target practice. He cleared *Venomous* for action and as his destroyer passed the hapless cruiser, he directed the ship's secondary armament to commence firing. While the ship's company looked on and cheered, the ship's pom-pom guns poured dozens of rounds into the upper works of the ship, and hundreds of rounds from her Lewis machine guns peppered the bridge and riddled the once proud German cruiser's funnels.

After a week in Rosyth, *Venomous* headed back to Scapa Flow, arriving on 9 March, but on 12 March was ordered to return to Rosyth. Gannon ran into trouble. Russell recorded in his ship's log that he reprimanded Gannon, "In accordance with King's Regulations, AIN 685, ...for not keeping a good lookout as O.O.W. [Officer of the Watch], thereby causing the ship to come between and part the tow between the tug *Savly* and ex-German destroyer, *V100*." This left the former warship wallowing in the North Sea and it took several hours before *Savly's* crew could rig another towline to her charge and continue the journey south.

For Gannon the return to Rosyth was more than just a relief from being at sea, since another "snotty" reported aboard. Although Mid Robert H.S. Rodger [28] would serve just three months on board the destroyer, Gannon must have felt that in future he would not be the only target of his captain's wrath.

Throughout March *Venomous* participated in frequent gunnery exercises with her 4.7-inch guns, under both day and night conditions, either alone or as part of the Third Flotilla. On 30 March, Captain D of the Third Flotilla repaired on board to inspect the ship and ship's company at divisions, action and collision stations.[29] He also witnessed the ship's company being put through a series of physical fitness drills, including close order drill with rifles from the ship's armoury. This inspection was a precursor to renewed operations.

On April Fools' Day 1920, the entire Third Flotilla departed Rosyth for Ireland. The passage was far from straightforward, the weather was atrocious and all ships suffered minor damage, with *Venomous* losing fire extinguishers, fire hoses and other fittings secured to the ship's deckhouses. Upon arrival at Queenstown (Cork) on 14 April, the Commander in Chief (C in C) Western Approaches and his staff came on board to inspect the weather-beaten ships.[30]

Sub Lt Charles Robertson RN[31] joined the ship on 9 April and years later recalled the repetitive nature of post war operations:

> "I joined her when she was working on the odd sea activities around
> Ireland and thence at Harwich, from which the ship did various escort
> duties. It was all very dull and though I liked the ship and its crew I was
> quite glad to get appointed elsewhere after a few months."

Robertson's reference to *Venomous'* "odd sea activities around Ireland" is something of an understatement as Ireland was in the throes of urban and rural guerrilla warfare.[32] The smaller craft of the Royal Navy, including its destroyers, were directed to patrol the Irish coast to stop the smuggling ashore of weapons and to oversee the security of Irish harbours and ports. *Venomous'* contribution could only have been slight since she departed Queenstown on 22 April, steaming unaccompanied to Chatham for a month long upkeep. Arriving on 3 May, the ship was boarded by HM Customs Officers who inspected the ship for contraband. Once cleared, *Venomous* proceeded to the munitions wharf to unload her ammunition, before tying up alongside her sister ship, HMS *Verdun*.

Life aboard a warship during an upkeep period is a dull experience as can be seen from a typical day recorded in the ship's log:

0545 – Call the Hands
0615 – Hands fall in to clean ship
0715 – Breakfast

0800 – Hands fall in to clean Mess Decks

0845 – Hands employed as required

Noon – Dinner

1300 – Hands fall in. Employed as required

1600 – Tea

1900 – Supper

2100 – Rounds

With her upkeep completed, *Venomous* departed Chatham on 5 June in company with HMS *Verity*, *Wanderer* and *Verdun* for Invergordon Scotland at the beginning of a summer and autumn filled with drills and exercises, alone or with her flotilla mates and bigger ships of the fleet on Britain's east coast. This routine was broken by the occasional runs ashore or sortie in search of a dangerous relic from the war, floating mines that had broken loose from their moorings. Lt S.B. de Courcy Ireland RN, who joined the ship on 5 September 1920 described the routine:

> "Life in destroyers in those post war days had plenty of variety but it was dull variety. We operated far more as a Flotilla and gone were the days when you were on your own or one of a small force protecting a convoy or screening big ships. It took a bit of getting used to being one of a pack but on the whole I enjoyed the Fleet and Flotilla manoeuvres and the station keeping."

Christmas found *Venomous* moored in the Medway. Leave was granted to 110 of the ship's company but a combination of circumstances conspired to make the festive season bleak in the extreme for those remaining, as de Courcy Ireland remembered:

> "I spent my first Christmas in *Venomous* as duty on board with the Gunner (T) and 13 ratings. There was no berth available to us in the Dockyards at Chatham or Sheerness and we were stuck at moorings halfway between the two at a spot called Mud Acre Creek. The Messman went ashore to buy our Christmas dinner but the motorboat broke down. We couldn't collect him as we had no oars for the whaler and were several miles from anywhere. To cap it all, the Gunner (T) was having matrimonial difficulties and tried to drown his sorrows. I had to put him under open arrest in his cabin. I invited the sailors down to the Wardroom and we made the best of it, but it wasn't much of a Christmas."

De Courcy Ireland and his skeleton crew must have been relieved when *Venomous* moved into No. 3 Dock at Chatham on 30 December. At least they were dockside. The first week in January 1921 saw the return of the rest of the ship's company from Christmas leave and on 17 January Russell took his destroyer to sea. *Venomous* loaded stores at Torbay and on the 19th departed for a winter cruise in warmer waters.

Heading south through a wintry Bay of Biscay, her first port of call was Ferrol, Spain, on 22 January, then off to Areosa Bay, arriving on 1 February. *Venomous* then steamed for Vigo and entered its harbour on 9 February. Finally, *Venomous* arrived at Gibraltar and moored during the early evening hours on 22 February. In these warmer climes, there were numerous exercises including torpedo attacks on the *Tiger* Class battle-cruiser HMS *Tiger* and anti-submarine evolutions off Gibraltar. There were also lighter moments as de Courcy Ireland pointed out:

> "We visited various places in N.W. Spain – Ferrol, Areosa Bay, Vigo and Pontevedra – none of them wildly exciting, but quite interesting. Ferrol was a Spanish Naval Base and at a casino ashore we met up with a Spanish Naval Engineer who was a compulsive gambler. He admitted to us quite frankly that he was selling engine room stores and spare parts from his ship to raise money for gambling. There were several sardine factories at Areosa and nearby. Although the smell was appalling, we braved one and bought 144 tins of good sardines at 2d. per tin. Gibraltar was fun in those days for the sailors and Spain of course was wide open. There was a casino at the head of the bay at La Linea where they played roulette and gave you a free ride back to the Rock if you lost all your money."

With the cruise over, *Venomous* departed Gibraltar on the evening of 16 March and, after an uneventful voyage, arrived at Portland Harbour on 22 March.

After a few days alongside she put to sea for exercises on 30 March, after which she steamed for Chatham and thence with another V & W, HMS *Wild Swan,* to Port Edgar on the south side of the Firth of Forth, where the two destroyers arrived after sunset on 8 April. That month, two new officers joined the ship; Lt Reynold H. Alleyne, RN replaced Lt Willson on 12 April and Mid Reginald S. Young RN took up his duties on 1 May. Midshipman Young wrote of the activities undertaken during the ten days that *Venomous* remained in Scotland:[33]

The officers and ship's company of HMS *Venomous* at Hull in April 1921
Front row from left: Gnr (T) F.A. Dunn RN, Lt S.B. Courcy-Ireland RN, J.A.B. Wilson RN, Cdr S.P.B. Russell RN, Eng. Lt Cdr W.H. Pudner RN, Sub. Lt E.O. Adams RN, Sub. Lt G.H. Thompson RN, Mid. R.S. Young RN.

"Port Edgar was the main Destroyer Base consisting of a small harbour with wooden jetties. We spent our time doing exercises at sea. When with the Fleet, we Destroyers had to manoeuvre extremely quickly to get clear ahead, involving considerable seamanship by their Captains, owing to the numbers involved.

We only spent a short time there before the start of the first Railway and Coal Strike, *Venomous* was ordered to empty her ammunition magazines, proceed to Hull, guard the Docks and be prepared to transport flour in the empty magazines to the Port of London if London got short of food."

In response to the national coal miners' strike, *Venomous* left Port Edgar on Monday 18 April, passed the Bass Rock and St. Abbs Head that night, and came alongside Riverside Quay at Hull just after midday on the 19th before entering the Albert Dock before sunset to face an uncertain situation.[34]

During the eight weeks that *Venomous* was tied up at Hull, the ship's company experienced a drab, monotonous routine with few outside activities to occupy them. Lt de Courcy Ireland described how:

"We lay in one of the Dock Basins until June to combat any violence or vandalism that might arise in the Dock area. Many ships were laid up because of the strike, but all was peace and quiet. It was boring. The Captain got his wife up and they wangled accommodation in a laid up liner where the Purser and his staff catered for them very cheaply (he always counted the pennies very carefully). A number of the townsfolk were very kind to us and the sailors, but twelve weeks in a Dock Basin kicking your heels isn't much fun."

Midshipman Young described the occasional diversion from the usual routine:

"*Venomous* certainly spent a very dull two months guarding the docks with really nothing to do. No trains, no coal etc. and few cars in those days. We made friends with many people living around who were very hospitable. Lt de Courcy Ireland had a brother who was an actor in a travelling company who happened into Hull and got stuck there. The theatrical company spent much time on board and we enjoyed their company."

With the end of the strike, *Venomous* cast off and left Hull with another V & W, HMS *Whitshed*, on 13 June, arriving at Sheerness on the Isle of Sheppey at the mouth of the Medway, on the morning of the 14th and thence up the Medway to Chatham that afternoon.

Venomous spent the next month alongside at Chatham, departing on 14 July for Torbay as part of the Third Flotilla for exercises and torpedo trials. Cdr Russell was relieved on the day of departure by Lt Cdr Lewes G. Gardner RN. Gardner brought a different style of leadership which was quickly noted by the ship's company.

They returned to Chatham on 27 August and on 2 September, *Venomous*, together with another V & W destroyer, HMS *Wolsey*, departed for Port Edgar arriving just after midday on the 4th. De Courcy Ireland thought Port Edgar was a pleasant base:

"Oil, water and power were laid out and there were baths ashore one could use. Altogether a good base with facilities for sports and games. I ran the ship's Concert Party, which was very good considering we only had a compliment of just over 110. We gave a number of shows including one in Edinburgh before an audience of two thousand."

Perhaps the recent presence of professional players while they were at Hull had rubbed off on the ship's company.

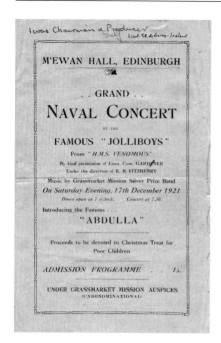

I was Chairman & Producer — Lieut SE de Courcy-Ireland

M'EWAN HALL, EDINBURGH

. . GRAND . .

NAVAL CONCERT

BY THE

FAMOUS "JOLLIBOYS"

From "H.M.S. VENOMOUS"

By kind permission of Lieut. Com. GARDNER
Under the direction of R. B. FITZHENRY

Music by Grassmarket Mission Silver Prize Band

On Saturday Evening, 17th December 1921

Doors open at 7 o'clock.   Concert at 7.30.

Introducing the Famous . . .

"ABDULLA"

Proceeds to be devoted to Christmas Treat for
Poor Children

ADMISSION PROGRAMME . . 1s.

UNDER GRASSMARKET MISSION AUSPICES
(UNDENOMINATIONAL)

A Merry Christmas

And

A Happy New Year

To You All

From the

"Jolliboys."

Lt Courcy-Ireland was chairman and producer of the concert in Edinburgh.
The "Jolliboys" put on a programme consisting of comic turns, duets, monologues tunes on a concertina and, of course, the famous "Abdulla", introduced by R B Fitzhenry.

The atmosphere aboard ship was not good as the officers sought to adjust to the more formal approach of their new commanding officer, described by one as "a man of uncertain temper". Gardner recorded in the ship's log of 4 October that he had cautioned Mr. F.A. Dunn, Gunner (T) for "exceeding his wine bill as laid down by King's Regulations." On 8 October, Gardner recorded that Sub Lt Thompson was reprimanded for "repeated disobedience of my orders in not completing the Deck Log when Officer of the Watch." This was followed on 14 October when Gardner wrote in the ship's log that he cautioned Lt Reynold Alleyne for "neglect of duty in taking no steps to ensure that liberty men are informed of orders affecting them, given by C in C Atlantic Fleet" and again on 19 October for "neglect of duty in frequently failing to carry out my orders personally and taking few if any steps to ensure that my orders are carried out by other Officers." It must be said that his fellow officers held Alleyne in high esteem as a capable and efficient officer and he went on to have a very successful career. Gardner again cautioned Gunner (T) Dunn, this time for "repeated disobedience of my orders in not completing the Deck Log when O.O.W. at sea." Within a three-month period it appears that Gardner had found many of his officers lacking.

The following month was spent in routine exercises and maintenance but on 9 December there occurred an unfortunate tragedy during "paint ship", when AB W.S. Easton lost his footing and fell into the cold waters of Port Edgar. Easton failed to surface, and divers recovered his body on the port quarter of the ship later that day. To lose a shipmate in such a way would have been sure to cast a pall over the ship, especially as Christmas approached.

The ship's log reported that on 31 December Capt Moir RN inspected the ship and on this, the last day of the year, Gardner further cautioned Gunner (T) Dunn for "repeated disregard for my verbal and written orders with regard to his wine bill."

Venomous remained at Port Edgar until the 26 February 1922 when Gardner received orders to take his destroyer south and *Venomous* steamed down the east coast for Chatham where she secured alongside a sister ship, HMS *Whitshed*. Lt de Courcy Ireland departed for an appointment with the Royal Australian Navy and was relieved by Sub Lt Philip Welby-Everard RN, described as a steady officer with a strong personality. He subsequently became Gunnery Officer in the Revenge Class battleship HMS *Resolution*.[35]

Venomous returned to Port Edgar and participated in exercises with the Sixth Destroyer Flotilla through March. From April through July, she conducted numerous exercises with various elements of the Fleet. With the end of the month, Gardner received orders that would take his ship back to the scenes of her operations in 1919. *Venomous* was due to depart for the Baltic on 22 August but before leaving the difficulty between Gardner and his Gunner (T), the officer in charge of torpedoes, came to a head. The previous day Gardner entered into the ship's log that he placed Dunn under close arrest and on the day of departure he was escorted ashore and a "pier head replacement" had to be found for the Gunner (T).

• • • •

Despite the internal commotion created by the arrest and dismissal of one of the ship's officers, *Venomous* got underway later that morning and headed for Kristiansand, Norway, where she secured pier side with her sister, HMS *Vampire* that evening. On 29 August she steamed for Riga, Latvia, with the Danae Class light cruiser HMS *Delhi*, arriving just before nightfall on 31 August. She remained in Riga until 4 September when she left for Memel.[36] During the next two days, *Venomous* participated in a series of formation exercises with other destroyers and cruisers. Their next port of call was the Free City of Danzig (now the Polish port city of Gdansk), and having passed the Hela Light near sunrise on 7 September, she arrived in Danzig and secured at mid-morning in the former German Imperial Navy Base of Kaiserhafen along with a sister ship, HMS *Vampire*, and the *Danae* Class light cruiser HMS *Dragon*.

One can imagine the reception her crew received when the ship visited the newly independent state of Latvia. The Baltic States never forgot Britain's support for them in their fight for independence in 1919. The following article is typical of those published when Queen Elizabeth II visited Estonia 87 years later in October 2006.

Estonians Honour Britain's Forgotten Fleet
Deutsche Presse-Agentur
Oct 20, 2006, 1658 GMT

Tallinn – Queen Elizabeth II joined Estonia's top civil and military leaders on Friday to honour a British naval detachment, which is almost forgotten in the UK.

'In Estonia, we place extreme importance on the (British naval detachment). It greatly assisted the birth of our country,' Vice-Admiral Tarmo Kouts, chief of the Estonian Defence Forces, said in an address from the deck of visiting British warship HMS *Liverpool*.

From late 1918 to early 1920, the newly declared state of Estonia fought a war of independence against the Soviet Union. Though able to defeat the Red Army on land, it had no answer to the former Russian Imperial fleet, which menaced its northern flank. In November 1918, at the Estonian's request, Britain's Royal Navy sent a squadron of light cruisers to the Baltic in a move, which is widely regarded as having turned the tide of the war.

'It would be wrong to say that without the British, the Estonians would have lost the war. But it would have been extremely difficult for them to win,' the Earl of Carlisle – an expert on the campaign – told Deutsche Presse-Agentur dpa.

The British ships blockaded the great Soviet naval base of Kronstadt, acted as floating gun batteries for the Estonian army, and supplied 5,000 rifles to the defenders of Tallinn.

Under the command of Rear-Admiral Sir Edwyn Alexander-Sinclair, the ships captured two Russian minelayers, the *Spartak* and *Avtroil*, in Tallinn Bay which were donated to the Estonians, becoming the foundation of the new Estonian Navy.

They also captured the Soviet Naval Secretary, the head of all Soviet naval forces. He was found hiding under a sack of potatoes on one of the ships.

And under Sinclair's successor, Rear-Admiral Sir Walter Cowan, the fleet managed to slip eight motor torpedo boats (MTBs) into Kronstadt, where they sank two dreadnoughts and a supply ship.

'We in the UK know about Horatio Nelson. Estonians know about Sir Edwyn Alexander-Sinclair and Sir Walter Cowan,' said Carlisle.

The victories were far from bloodless. The British lost over 100 sailors, six ships and eight MTBs during the campaign – losses now commemorated by plaques in both Tallinn and Riga.

'Our shared history, particularly during Estonia's struggle for independence, is something that we will never forget,' the Queen said in a toast to a state banquet on Thursday evening. And the naval link has now been brought up to date. Estonia recently purchased three mine-hunting ships from the Royal Navy – the first of which is to be called the '*Walter Cowan.*'

Estonia joined the EU and NATO in 2004, and its soldiers currently serve alongside British troops in Iraq and Afghanistan. The Queen met troops returned from those missions on Friday. And with both countries eager to highlight the warmth of their past and present defence cooperation, the 'forgotten fleet' looks likely to emerge from history's shadows at last.

Venomous and her consorts spent a week in harbour before proceeding to Stockholm and Copenhagen and then back to Sheerness where *Venomous* berthed during the late afternoon of 24 September. *Venomous* would not see the Baltic again.

The autumn of 1922 was spent at Port Edgar, but in December *Venomous* was ordered to Ireland. She slipped her moorings early on 4 December passing Swona, Stroma, Dunnet Head (the most northern point in mainland Britain) and Scrabster on the 5th and Cape Wrath just before daylight. On 8 December, *Venomous* commenced duties as Dublin's guard ship and Lt Francis Douglas-Watson RN joined the ship.[37] Another new officer, Sub Lt Richard Moore RN recalled that, "I joined *Venomous* as a Sub Lt on 1 January 1923. She was guard ship at Bantry Bay (Berehaven), The IRA were active at this time. We spent two days at anchor watch – appalling weather."

Venomous remained off Southern Ireland until 4 January when she steamed for Chatham. She spent the next three weeks on reduced status with the ship's company busy with routine maintenance and on shore leave.[38] On 5 February 1923, she paid off and recommissioned the following day into the Fourth Destroyer Flotilla of the Atlantic Fleet.

Her first commission had seen her being used to support the

quelling of social unrest in Britain and political unrest in Ireland whilst helping the Baltic States to gain independence from both Russia and Germany. The next chapter in the ship's life was about to begin.

Notes

1   Geoffrey Bennett, *Freeing the Baltic* (Edinburgh: Birlinn, 2002), p.4

2   In his e-mail, on 8 February 2009, Peter C. Smith wrote that the ship's name was changed from *Venom* to *Venomous* was "…because the name *Venom* was … too much like Vernon, the Royal Navy's Mine Base at Portsmouth and it was felt it would lead to confusion if that shore establishment was ordered to proceed to sea!"

3   An excellent summary of the class can be found at the Wikipedia website: http://en.wikipedia.org/wiki/V_and_W_class_destroyer.

4   HMS *Campbell* would have an eventful World War II service. One heroic event pitted the old destroyer against the German battle cruisers *Scharnhorst* and *Gneisenau* and the heavy cruiser *Prinz Eugen* when these ships and their destroyer escorts successfully dashed through the English Channel back to Wilhelmshaven on 12 February 1942. For a synopsis of her career visit Service Histories of Royal Navy Warships in World War 2 at http://www.naval-history.net/xGM-Chrono-10DD-03Scott-Campbell.htm

5   Refer to www.royalnavalmuseum.org/info_sheets_fleet_reviews.htm (the Royal Navy Museum website) for additional background about the Royal Fleet Review.

6   Capt Stanley Brian de Courcy-Ireland (1900-2001) was the last surviving naval officer present at both the Battle of Jutland and the historic event at Scapa Flow. In the course of a long and distinguished naval career, 'DCI' would attain the rank of Captain and the command of the cruiser *Ajax*, renowned for its part in the Battle of the River Plate, which led to the scuttle of the *Graf Spee*. See his obituary (*Independent* 29 November 2001) at http://www.independent.co.uk/news/obituaries/captain-brian-de-courcyireland-729545.html and his autobiography *A Naval Life* (Englang Publishing, 1990).

7   Private Papers of S B de Courcy-Ireland (Imperial War Museum Cat. Number 739 92/4/1).

8   Ibid.

9   Ibid.

10 SMS stands for *Seiner Majestät Schiff*, the German equivalent of HMS. Destroyers in the German Imperial Navy were numbered (like U-boats) hence SMS *V82*. The initial letter signifies the place of construction of the class; V was the AG Vulcan Yard at Hamburg.

11 Wikipedia: Gustav Adolf Joachim Rüdiger Graf von der Goltz was the commander of the German *Baltische Landeswehr*, which contributed to the defeat of Russian Bolsheviks and their local allies in Finland (1918) and Latvia (1919).

12 Count von der Goltz would claim in his memoirs that his goal had been to launch a campaign in cooperation with the White Russian forces to overturn the Bolshevik regime by marching on St. Petersburg and to install a pro-German government in Russia.

13 The force included four Royal Navy H Class submarines and several support ships, such as destroyer and submarine depot ships, colliers, and supply ships. There was also a significant fleet train that supported the Royal Navy's Baltic force.

14 Cowan entered the Royal Navy in 1884 and was a classmate and friend of another future admiral, David Beatty. In 1898, this small man – he stood just 5 feet tall – commanded the Royal Navy's river gunboat flotilla that supported Lord Kitchener's expeditionary force against the Khedive of the Sudan. At Khartoum, he received the Distinguished Service Order for his heroism. He was aide-de-camp to both Lord Roberts and Kitchener during the Second Boer War. In the years between the Boer War and the Great War, Cowan was the seagoing assistant to Admiral Roger Keyes who commanded the Royal Navy's fledgling destroyer command. With Keyes, Cowan developed new tactics for destroyers. Cowan was the first captain of the Indefatigable Class battle-cruiser, HMS *New Zealand*, and during the Battle of Jutland he commanded the *Lion* Class battle-cruiser, HMS *Princess Royal*. At the end of the war, Cowan, now a flag officer, received orders to the Baltic from the Admiralty.

15 Geoffrey Bennett, p.70-71.

16 Ibid., p. 70.

17 The strains on the social fabric of the nation were manifested through a succession of economic and political difficulties that came to the fore with the Armistice. The UK had to switch its large industrial base from war production to supporting a peacetime economy. The largest army and navy in its history had to be demobilised and integrated into an economy that was having considerable difficulty regaining its pre-war markets. There were simply not enough jobs for all the returning service men. National strikes by coalminers and railway workers ensued. Those on board *Venomous* would experience these unsettled times.

18 Geoffrey Bennett, p.198.

19 Libau is now Liepāja, Latvia. Its old fortress as well as the large former home of the Soviet Red Banner Baltic Fleet Naval Base can be seen on Google Earth.

20 *Freeing the Baltic*, p.189.

21 The monitor played a critical role by providing devastating gunfire support during the Normandy landings in 1944.

22 Geoffrey Bennett, p.191-192.

23 To protect his new capital of St Petersburg, Peter the Great, founded the naval base and fortress in 1704. St Petersburg was renamed Petrograd in 1914 at the start of the Great War.

24 As Christopher McKee wrote in his book, *Sober Men and True: Sailor Lives in the Royal Navy 1900-1945*, p. 160, "The lower deck (and officers as well) took Christmas seriously. Messes began stocking up on special foods and preparing puddings days in advance... The youngest boy in the ship put on the captain's uniform. At the conclusion of the Christmas morning church service, during which he had stood alongside the captain, the boy-commander took over and gave the ship's orders until ten o'clock 'lights out' that night." Christmas was one of those days in which roles were reversed.

25 All ships were assigned to one of the Royal Navy's three "home ports", Chatham on the Medway, Portsmouth on the Solent and Devonport near Plymouth. Ratings were posted to their ship from the naval barracks at its homeport and returned to barracks at the end of a Commission. Their families frequently lived nearby and a visit to the homeport was always welcomed. HMS *Venomous* was a "Chatham ship" from construction in 1919 to being placed in Reserve in 1930.

26 See http://www.memorials.inportsmouth.co.uk/churches/cathedral/baltic.htm for the names on the memorial.

27 HMS *Cryus* was a member of the *Saint* class and together with her sister ocean-going tugs performed rescue duties in addition to her role as a tugboat. *Cryus* was completed in 1919 and was mined off the Humber Estuary on 22 January 1941. See www.uboat.net

28 As for Rodger, he was to become one of the Fleet Air Arm's "Early Birds," gaining his wings on the second naval pilots training course conducted by the Royal Navy. Rodger would serve in the aircraft carriers HMS *Eagle*, *Courageous* and *Glorious*. He would also hold command of the gunboat HMS *Aphis*, serving on the Yangtze River patrol. As a commander, Rodger would serve in the Admiralty during the Second World War. A talented singer, Rodger often mimicked Noel Coward amongst his friends. For his war service, he was awarded the OBE in 1946 and retired to Dorset where he died in 1996 at the age of 95.

29 The Commander of a destroyer Flotilla was referred to by his rank, Captain D (Destroyers).

30 Queenstown (Cork) was a major naval base for the Royal Navy.

31 Robertson apparently longed for more excitement, because he served in submarines during the interwar years and commanded the submarine HMS *L 69*. He survived the war and retired as a Captain.

32 *The Rise and Fall of the British Empire*, by Lawrence James (New York: St. Martin's Press, 1994), p.375-80. In the spring of 1920, the British Government under Lloyd George passed the Government of Ireland Act that partitioned Ireland, creating two Irish parliaments, one for the Protestant north and the other for the largely Catholic south, which could collect taxes and enact laws, whilst foreign and defence policies remained in the hands of the British Government. Under its provisions, the Irish would hold general elections the

following spring. By that time, it was hoped that the British Armed Forces and the Royal Irish Constabulary (RIC) would be able to break the back of the Irish Republican Army (IRA). The Act was rejected by Sinn Fein and the IRA who supported a united Ireland, totally free from British rule, and by the summer of 1920, the pattern of guerrilla warfare became well entrenched.

33 Reynold Meynell Alleyne retired as a Commander in 1935. Through the war years he served ashore in Egypt, the Isle of Man and finally at HMS *President* (Accounting Section). Lt Cdr Young became a prisoner of war when Japanese forces captured Hong Kong. He survived captivity and retired as a Commander. For more information on this officer, visit http://www.unithistories.com/officers/RNofficers.

34 The coal industry was the lifeblood of the industrial revolution. Working conditions for British miners and their families were bad and relations between owners and miners were often confrontational. By the beginning of the twentieth century, miners were unionized and formed an alliance with the railway and transportation unions to obtain better conditions from the owners through joint union action. The war brought higher wages and nationalisation of the mines which, for the time being, avoided confrontation but at the war's end the boom ended and demand for coal dropped. The government announced that mines would be returned to private ownership at the end of March, and the owners stated they would drastically cut wages. The miners refused to accept these conditions, which led to a lockout of the miners. The strike lasted eleven weeks until they were forced to accept wage cuts of up to 40 per cent.

35 Philip Welby-Everard served throughout World War II. He obtained the rank of Captain after the war. He received his DSC as executive officer of HMS *Belfast* when his cruiser took part in the destruction of the German Battle-cruiser *Scharnhorst*. Welby-Everard received his Order of the British Empire on 1980. Visit http://www.unithistories.com/officers/RNofficers.

36 The German town of Memel and its surrounding territory was made a protectorate of the Entente States after the First World War but was taken over by Lithuania in 1923 and renamed Klaipëda in 1924.

37 Douglas-Watson continued his service through the early years of World War II. He was promoted to acting Commander in 1939. During the evacuation of Dunkirk, he received the DSO for his actions as commanding officer of the minesweeper HMS *Pangbourne*. He was killed in action when a British merchant ship blew up in the harbour of Piraeus, Greece on 7 April 1941 after being bombed by the Luftwaffe. For more on this officer, refer to www.unithistories.com/officers/RNofficersD2.html.

38 Reduced Status is a contemporary US Navy term meaning the ship is in commission, but it is not available for immediate operations. This could be measured in weeks.

CHAPTER THREE

THE MEDITERRANEAN YEARS
1923-9

"…Our Navy is no mere superfluity.
It is us." Ramsay MacDonald[1]

Although *Venomous* and the Fourth Destroyer Flotilla were considered part of the Atlantic Fleet, they would mostly operate with the Mediterranean Fleet for the next six years. The V & W Class destroyers formed the backbone of the Royal Navy's destroyer force after the war. *Venomous* and her sister ships would be dispatched to all parts of the world, with several being transferred to the fledgling Royal Australian Navy (RAN) and to China. The 1920s and 1930s were "…the heydays of the V & W boats…"[2]

The Royal Navy's destroyer force was re-organised during the immediate post-war period. The war had shown that the destroyer flotillas had too many ships to be effectively controlled operationally and administratively and that destroyers were much more than a pack of dogs, which simply responded to the fleet commander's tactical order to 'go get them' and then, 'come back.'

Capt Wayne Hughes, USN (Ret.) made the following observation in his book about destroyer battle tactics in support of the battle fleet:

> "Their role [destroyers] was to rush in a tight pack and seize a battleship's throat if they could or, as was more likely, to leap and claw and growl at the enemy's own mad dogs, which also charged into the fray at a single word from their master."[3]

Once the order was given to send the destroyer flotilla into the fray, the flotilla commander in his flagship had an almost impossible task to bring some sense of order out of the chaos that ensued during a fleet action. The Battle of Jutland had demonstrated that.

During the war the destroyer's role expanded beyond that originally envisaged. Destroyers were found to be an effective weapon for fending off attacking aircraft and submarines. Smaller calibre quick firing guns and automatic weapons were introduced to counter the air threat and depth charges, sitting atop mortar-type weapons, were added to counter the submarine. The operations in the Baltic demonstrated that destroyers were effective as artillery platforms against ground forces and as fast minelayers within coastal waters.[4] The V & W Class would acquire pom-pom guns for air defence and submarine detection equipment and depth charges for anti-submarine operations.

These new air defence and anti-submarine roles did not require the large number of destroyers needed to fire a barrage of torpedoes against an enemy battle fleet but this hardly mattered as the great battle fleets of the world's navies no longer existed.

One of the proposals to achieve greater operational and tactical efficiencies was to cut in half the number of destroyers in a flotilla, from sixteen ships and one leader (flagship) to eight ships plus a leader. The respected British naval analyst and historian Anthony Preston complemented Capt Hughes' observation when he noted, "...there had been a tactical problem of how to pass messages rapidly from the leader to sixteen destroyers, even with a half-leader heading a second division and sharing the burden of administration and paper-work."[5] Despite the introduction of wireless transmission to the Fleet, there was no tactical radio system between ships. Signal flags and flashing lights remained the primary signalling methods. The time delay inherent in these methods had to be taken into account during tactical manoeuvres between ships operating at close quarters.

These changes in the way the destroyer force operated were minor compared to those forced upon the Royal Navy by post-war austerity. The cost of the war placed incredible strains on the British economy and the civil servants at the Exchequer calculated that the Fleet was larger than was required.[6] The Exchequer "presented politicians with coherent strategic alternatives" to the Admiralty's position of maintaining a fleet large enough to counter any threat to the integrity of the Empire and Commonwealth. The economies proposed by the Exchequer were made possible by a series of treaties – of which the Washington Naval Treaty was the most important – that limited the total tonnage and the number of capital ships in the world's navies.[7]

The outcome of the war and revolution led to diplomatic initiatives and subsequent international treaties that would have a profound affect on the Royal Navy. The Paris Peace Conference and the Treaty of

Versailles ensured that a new Europe replaced the 'Old Europe.' Versailles formalised the collapse of empires, not only the Imperial German and Russian empires but also those bordering the Mediterranean. The Austro-Hungarian Empire that had the Adriatic Sea as its southern border was dissolved and the Ottoman Empire that dominated the eastern part of the Mediterranean was swept away as if it were desert sand. Power vacuums existed throughout the Mediterranean basin. The Treaty of Versailles and other treaties hoped to resolve these problems.

In Asia Minor, the demise of the Ottoman Empire and the rise of the modern Turkish state, together with the explosion of Greek nationalism, brought old rivalries to the boil. By the time *Venomous* arrived in the Mediterranean, the Greco-Turkish issue had erupted into open warfare, with thousands of civilian casualties, particularly around the port city of Smyrna (Izmir). The Royal Navy's Mediterranean Fleet was instrumental in restoring peace to the area.

Empires might collapse and the social fabric be ripped apart but the Royal Navy was slow to change. For those on the lower deck, life on board *Venomous* followed a routine that would have been familiar to those who served in Queen Victoria's Navy forty years earlier. This life can be seen through the eyes of an unknown rating, a stoker, who served in the engineering department on *Venomous* and her sister ships, *Wanderer* and *Woolston*, and kept a diary during his Mediterranean years.[8] *Venomous* was powered by oil burning steam turbines and the stokers trimmed oil burners instead of shoveling coal into a furnace. His clothing on watch at sea in the engine room was minimal, a boiler suit over underwear, and he could turn the boiler room into a laundromat by washing his kit in a bucket and drying it above the boilers. This stoker's daily routine centred on the needs of the ship. In port he carried out routine maintenance on the ship's boilers and engines and while on watch monitored the condition of the ship's engineering plant. At sea, routine watch-keeping alternated with combat drills and exercises and occasionally he would have to carry out maintenance and emergency repairs in rough weather.

A sailor's life, in port or at sea, revolved around his mess. Men of the lower deck were divided by branch and then by rank within each branch. In the case of our stoker, he ate, cleaned, laundered and slept with stoker messmates of his own rank within a cramped below decks compartment. The stokers mess deck was forward on the ship, down a round hatch about 36" diameter, which accommodated as many as twenty-two stokers but only half would be in the compartment at a time whilst at sea. They ate and slept in an area no bigger than an ordinary sitting room. Chief and senior petty officer stokers messed separately from ratings. Each sailor was expected to take his turn in preparing meals for his messmates.

Our stoker's account of this routine is intermingled with personal concerns and needs. He often described his meals on board, his longing for letters and packages from his wife and children back in England and his need to write daily letters to them. Dreams of home and a good bath were also recurring themes. His diary also provided an insight into his leisure activities – card games, music (he played a mandolin) and an occasional run ashore in Malta, including a visit to the canteen. A stoker's working life was hot and dirty, especially during the Mediterranean summer, and these distractions were essential to maintaining morale.

• • • •

On 8 February 1923, *Venomous* and the Fourth Destroyer Flotilla left home waters to steam into this new world. The flotilla arrived at Gibraltar on 12 February and *Venomous* secured alongside a sister ship, HMS *Worcester*. A brief stay below the Rock ended at noon on the 14th when the flotilla left the South Mole for Malta. Steaming in fleet cruising order, the ships passed abeam of Cape Bon, Tunisia, and entered the Strait of Sicily around midnight on the 16th. *Venomous* and the flotilla entered the Grand Harbour, Malta, at mid-afternoon on 17 February and tied up alongside the oiler, RFA *Boxol*. The flotilla made the near one thousand mile journey at an average speed of 14 knots – well within cruising speed and the budgetary constraints placed on the post-war navy.

After a brief two-day layover, Gardner received orders to take his destroyer to a major area of unrest – the Aegean. On 19 February, *Venomous* steamed for Mytelene (Mytilini) on the Greek island of Lesvos, arriving on the 21st, and continuing the next day to Smyrna, modern day Izmir, on the coast of Asia Minor, which it reached during the morning hours of the 22 February.

East Mediterranean theatre of operations, 1922-9.
Map graphic Kelly Erlinger. Map source Gordon Smith www.naval-history.net

Just six months earlier, the Greco-Turkish War was raging. The Turkish Army had entered the port city of Smyrna, the last Greek stronghold in Asia-Minor, and the Greek and Armenian parts of the city were set on fire with thousands killed and many more fleeing the city by boat. This marked the end of the war but it required the presence of the major powers to monitor the aftermath, until the Treaty of Lausanne finally formalised the outcome of the war in July 1923.

Venomous took over from her sister ship, HMS *Whitshed*, in monitoring the peace. The destruction of the city must have been very apparent to the ship's company, and a run ashore, even if possible, would not have been very pleasurable.

On 28 February she steamed for the Greek Island of Lemnos and its great harbour of Mudros. Lemnos and its harbour had served as the major staging base for the British during the disastrous Gallipoli Campaign. The island and its harbour remained strategically important to British interests throughout the tumultuous times surrounding the founding of the modern Turkish state, the frustrations of Greek nationalism and the revolutionary fervour of Bolshevik Russia. *Venomous* would find herself pulling into its harbour on more than one occasion.

Gardner soon received orders to take *Venomous* north into the Dardanelles, where she was on patrol until the end of March. April 1st found *Venomous* passing up the Narrows to Constantinople (Istanbul)

View of HMS *Venomous* leaving Valetta harbour taken from the bastions between 1923-8.
Photographed by Richard Ellis, Valetta, and reproduced courtesy of David Page who salvaged the print from a rubbish tip and published it on Navyphotos.co.uk

and she spent most of April on patrol and on exercises in the Sea of Marmara. On 29 April, *Venomous* steamed back to Mudros with the Insect Class River Gunboat HMS *Cricket*. Gardner brought his destroyer back up the Narrows on 23 May for another round of patrol duties but returned to Lemnos in time for the ship's company to take part in the Flotilla Regatta on 7 June. *Venomous'* log mentions the participation of the ship's whaler in several pulling races but it failed to win a trophy.

Venomous continued operating out of Lemnos and into Turkish waters until late August, on patrol and in exercises with her flotilla. Venomous' log often reported sighting US Navy warships including the destroyer of the Clemson Class, USS *Edsall*, and the destroyer of the

Sampson Class, USS *Sampson*, that were patrolling the same waters.[9] Our stoker met some of the crew of the American destroyers during his runs ashore and thought they were "Good Chaps".

While in Constantinople, Gardner received orders for *Venomous* to return to Britain with the Fourth Flotilla. On 24 August, the destroyers departed the ancient city and headed westward via Malta and Gibraltar. *Venomous* ended her first Mediterranean deployment when the flotilla arrived in Chatham on 8 September.

During upkeep in Chatham, *Venomous* and the Fourth Flotilla was officially reassigned to the Mediterranean Fleet. On 12 October, Gardner took his destroyer back to sea, heading for the Mediterranean arriving in Malta's Grand Harbour at sunset on the 21st. Malta would be her homeport for the next six years.

Malta had been a base for the Royal Navy and the home of its Mediterranean Fleet since the Napoleonic Wars. The support facilities for the fleet were extensive, and included dry-docks, and hospitals, as well as warehouses for storing ammunition, coal and fuel oil bunkering, spare parts and foodstuffs. Other amenities were available and they provided a welcome change in the sailors' daily routine – the canteen and of course the ladies of the night. During her six-year stay in the Mediterranean, *Venomous* and her crew would take advantage of all these facilities.

Although written more than a year later in 1925, the entries in our stoker's diary from 6 January to 3 February of that year, convey a good impression of Malta's ability to provide critical services to his ship:

> "Tuesday, 6 January: 'Had all of our guns lifted today by big crane for examination. We have been mooring all over the place today. Tug has been pulling us. Dinner of pork chops and bread pudding.' Thursday, 8 January: 'Moved again under the 150 ton crane to lift torpedo tubes.' Saturday, 10 January: 'Lying alongside the *Swan*.'[10] Sunday, 11 January: 'Entered Malta Dockyard.' Monday, 12 January: '*Valiant* went in dock.'[11] Friday, 23 January: 'Taking out bearings and stripping it down.' Tuesday, 27 January: 'Got own ship's galley in use again.' Thursday, 29 January: 'Malta dockyard. Lifted our starboard turbine. Several blades are broken. Lovely day, but three more tubes were taken out of boiler.' Friday, 30 January: 'More tubes out of boiler.' Saturday, 31 January: 'Lifted the turbine rotor this morning.' Monday, 2 February: 'Came out of dry dock. Went alongside gun mounting wharf. Got the last

of the tubes out of boiler, but had to cut out one extra.' Tuesday, 3 February: 'Finished my job on boiler. Dockyard boiler makers taking over. Went and saw tubes cut up and pricked.'

On 23 October, there was a change of command aboard *Venomous* when Lt Cdr Donal S. McGrath RN succeeded Gardner.[12] McGrath's previous command had been the S Class destroyer HMS *Sportive*. A solidly built Irishman, McGrath would eventually attain the rank of Captain, and during the Second World War he became the commander of the Attacker Class escort aircraft carrier HMS *Tracker*.

On 2 November, the ship's log recorded that every available officer and man was landed for inspection by the Commander-in-Chief of the Mediterranean Fleet, but apart from exercises with the Fourth Battle Squadron at the end of the month, the year drew to an uneventful close with *Venomous* moored in the Grand Harbour over the Christmas and New Year's holiday. Despite the holiday revelry and the arrival of letters and Christmas packages, our stoker would have had a lonely time away from his wife and children.

New Year's Day 1924 passed quietly for *Venomous* and the Fourth Flotilla but January brought a series of exercises to bring the ship and her squadron mates back up to fighting proficiency. As our stoker recalled in his diary "Torpedo and gunnery exercises commence with gunnery live fire."

Exercises did not always come without cost; our stoker wrote on 24 January, "On manoeuvres with HMS *Stuart* and *Veteran*. *Stuart* enters dry dock after collision." Collisions at sea during formation exercises were common occurrences. During his six years in the Mediterranean our stoker noted several major collisions involving cruisers, destroyers and merchant ships, as illustrated by the following entries in his diary during a single week in January 1928:

> "17 January: 'HMS *Viceroy* collided with HMS *Cyclops*. Pushed foremost watertight bulkhead back.' 20 January: 'Heard that HMS *Caledon* collided with a Greek steamer and cut her in two. *Caledon* being towed stern first by HMS *Ceres*.' 21 January: 'HMS *Vimiera* was in collision.' 25 January: "*Caledon* entered port. They had to blow part of the bow off to keep it acting as a rudder. Looked at *Vimiera* and she was upped pretty well. Quite an expensive day for the Navy.' 6 March: 'Skipper of *Caledon* court-martialled for collision.'"

With ship workups and squadron exercises completed, *Venomous* and the flotilla departed on 2 February for a fourteen-day cruise along the east coast of Sardinia, stopping off at Arania Bay and the Gulf of Terranova, and returning to Malta on the 16th.

On 10 March, *Venomous* and the Fourth Flotilla sailed westward for the island of Majorca, the largest of the Spanish Balearic islands, where the flotilla conducted night cruising formations and torpedo exercises. On the 12th the ship's log recorded the arrival at the port city of Palma from Villefranche-sur-Mer of the Flower Class (Anchusa sub-type) sloop, HMS *Bryony*,[13] with Admiral of the Fleet David Beatty aboard. At the time, Beatty was First Sea Lord of the Admiralty.[14]

Back in Malta on 18 May, *Venomous*' next deployment, in company with the Fourth Flotilla, except for *Vansittart* and *Witch*, was to Port Said, Egypt on the 24th. Mid Peter Barlow RN joined the ship on arrival and years later described his experiences:

> "On 26th May 1924 I was transferred from *Wanderer* to *Venomous*, then with the entire Fleet on the Eastern Mediterranean Cruise. On 28th May we were back in Port Said where we stayed until 2nd June. Then on to Haifa where we had a good opportunity to see quite a bit of the Holy Land as we were granted a few days leave. Thence to Famagusta, Mudros, Mauptia and back to Malta on 8th July, I left *Venomous* on 15th July."

Returning to Malta, Midshipmen Peter Dawnay (later Vice Admiral Sir Peter Dawnay KCVO, CB, DSC, DL) joined for an enjoyable few weeks:

> "We went on the 2nd Summer Cruise up the Adriatic, Yugoslavia, etc. which was the first time I had been to that coast. The Destroyer Pulling Regatta took place during the cruise, at Argostoli, where I had to substitute in the Officers' Race for an Officer who went sick at the last moment so I had to take part not properly fit for such a contest – very hard work it was too pulling the ship's whaler."

Nevertheless, the Regatta was a resounding success for *Venomous*. On 23 August its crew were supreme in the Fourth Flotilla pulling competition and three days later they repeated their performance, this time in competition with all the destroyers of the Mediterranean Fleet. Her crew won and flushed with victory *Venomous* returned to Malta on the 28th.

After a week back in Malta, McGrath received orders to return to the Western Mediterranean and on 8 September *Venomous* set out for

Barcelona where she spent four days before proceeding to Valencia on the 15th, on to Gibraltar on the 19th, before returning to Malta on the 30th. Her entrance to the Grand Harbour was not without incident as she rammed and sank a motorboat from the Caledon Class light cruiser, HMS Calypso. Fortunately, all hands were saved from the warm waters.

Venomous remained in Malta for the next three months, and only ventured out of Malta's Grand Harbour for local exercises, engineering and operational trials. On 6 December McGrath received orders to take *Venomous* to Port Said, Egypt, and arrived there on the 9th before moving on to Alexandria on the 14th, where she spent Christmas and the New Year's Day alongside. Here it was that Lt Cdr Lawrence Frederick Nelson Ommanney, RN assumed command from McGrath. Ommanney, known to his contemporaries as Jack, was a humorous and popular officer within the Wardroom whose previous appointments had included a commission in the Royal Yacht *Victoria and Albert*.[15]

Venomous began 1925 with Ommanney receiving orders to take his

HMS *Venomous* in the 1920s.

ship through the Suez Canal and into the Red Sea. This was in response to a flare-up of an age-old scourge that continues to plague humanity to this very day – the slave trade.

Four years earlier, the existence of the slave trade became a major public scandal. In December of 1921, while the Arabis Class sloop, HMS *Cornflower*,[16] was anchored in Jiddah Harbour, Saudi Arabia, its captain learned that slaves had been landed there. This information was relayed to Britain, and in January 1922 the news broke in the British press. The moral outrage stirred up by the press intensified when the British vice-consul in Jiddah confirmed the report "that Ethiopian slaves were being shipped from Obock and Assab to Maidi in Asir, where they were later transported by small sambuks (a type of sailing dhow) to Jiddah, disguised as free passengers."[17]

This was followed by a report to the Foreign Office by the British governor of Anglo-Egyptian Sudan expressing his vigorous dissatisfaction with Arab slavers. They were sailing across the Red Sea to capture

Photographed by Wright and Logan, Portsmouth. Courtesy of former AB Sydney Compston.

Sudanese Muslim pilgrims and take them back to Hijaz, at the time an independent state on the west coast of the Arabian Peninsula, where they were sold into slavery. The governor, together with the commander of the Mediterranean Fleet, strongly urged the Foreign Office to protest about this activity to King Husayn of Hijaz but, as Suzanne Miers recounts in her book, *Slavery in the Twentieth Century,*

> "...The king saw nothing wrong with slavery. The British did not want to alienate him, as they hoped he would agree to a treaty recognizing their mandates over Iraq and Trans-Jordan. Tactful protests, however, merely elicited the reply that slavery was recognised by the Qur'an, the trade was legal and, since the British had command of the sea, it was up to them to prevent slaves leaving Africa."[18]

It was one thing to have ships on station to prevent slaving but each ship's captain was faced with the dilemma that he could not seize vessels in Hijaz territorial waters and if a "suspicious" craft was stopped, "...it was difficult to detect slaves hidden among the legitimate passengers, particularly during the busy pilgrimage season."[19]

Little had changed when Ommanney took *Venomous* through the Suez Canal on 5 January 1925 and spent three weeks on anti-slavery patrols but, sadly, without tangible results. *Venomous* returned to Port Said on the 28th and two days later left for Malta, arriving at the entrance to the Grand Harbour on 3 February thus bringing the destroyer's only cruise East of Suez to an end.

The next six weeks were mainly spent alongside in Malta but on 17 March *Venomous* steamed for Palma, Majorca, on exercises, thence to Gibraltar where the ship's log records the discharge of an Able Seaman (AB) to the battle-cruiser, HMS *Hood* for passage to England on compassionate leave. Fleet exercises took up much of April, but with the AB back on board, she returned to Malta on 2 May.

On 2 June, Palma was again the destination and during the month further visits to Rosas Bay, Valencia and Pollensa Bay took place, before *Venomous* arrived in the Italian Naval Base of Spezia on 2 July where she witnessed the entry into harbour of the Italian Fourth Battle Squadron, before returning to Malta on 10 July.

On 20 August, *Venomous* steamed for the Eastern Mediterranean in company with four of her flotilla, HMS *Wryneck, Walrus, Wolverine* and

Wivern. They spent over a month in the Aegean, returning to the port city of Mytelene, back to Lemnos and then on 25 September to the port of Volos north of Athens on the east coast of Greece. On their way back to Malta they joined the aircraft carrier HMS *Eagle* in a series of exercises, which involved *Eagle* launching and recovering her aircraft. As well as providing an escort the destroyers conducted plane guard operations.[20]

Plane guarding requires a destroyer to take up position astern of the aircraft carrier during flight operations. If an aircraft crashed into the sea whilst taking off or landing, the destroyer would be in position to rescue the aircrew. This requires the destroyer to maintain a relatively close station – no more than a thousand yards astern. Since the carrier must keep heading into the wind to ensure enough wind is blowing over her flight deck whilst launching and recovering aircraft it was not uncommon for it to change course and to do so with little warning. A great deal of skill was needed if the destroyer was to maintain her station astern to give a downed aircrew a chance of survival. Flight operations are also risky for those on the aircraft carrier's flight deck. It was not unusual for flight deck personnel to misstep and fall overboard. The plane-guarding destroyer would then be in a position to pick up the unlucky sailor.

Venomous returned to Malta on 1 October and entered No. 3 Dock on the 9th for essential repairs and to paint ship. A routine day turned to tragedy with the discovery by the quarterdeck watch at first light that a Stoker, First Class, had taken his life by hanging himself from the searchlight platform. The funeral was held the following day and the young man's grave (he was twenty six) is in the Kalkara Naval Cemetery.

Suicide was not that uncommon and our stoker described a suicide earlier in the year whilst he was serving on board Venomous' sister ship, HMS *Woolston*: "Friday, 1 May – Great excitement this morning. Found Collins, one of our senior petty officers had hung himself in his storeroom. Found him around 7:30 a.m. Must have been dead for he was stiff. He made a decent job of it too." The next day he recounts: "Saturday, 2 May – Held inquest today. Suicide whilst of unsound mind was the verdict. Buried today." He mentioned another incident whilst serving on board *Venomous* in 1927: "26 December: …seaman on *Whitehall* tried to hang himself – unsuccessful. Too much alcohol – I have seen too much on this station."

Venomous moved to Sliema Creek, the main destroyer moorings, on the north side of Malta on 1 November and during the month undertook frequent firing exercises. On 1 December, *Venomous*, along with the heavy cruiser HMS *Frobisher* and the destroyers HMS *Broke*, *Vansittart* and *Whitshed* sailed for Corfu, where torpedo and gunnery target exercises were conducted. Christmas and New Year were spent in Sliema Creek alongside the oiler *Brambleleaf* and on 5 January 1926 she spent the day at sea with the cruiser HMS *Coventry* for gunnery and torpedo exercises. *Venomous* sailed to Palmas Bay on 17 January where a shocked stoker discovered the body of Chief Stoker Alfred Hatton who succumbed to a heart attack, aged 39, perhaps the result of years of exposure to the sweltering conditions prevalent in the engine rooms of that period.

The time for *Venomous* and her sister ships in the Fourth Flotilla to undergo a full refit was now approaching. On 19 February 1926 the Flotilla left Malta for Gibraltar where *Venomous* passed the night of 23 February under the Rock. The Flotilla slipped and departed Gibraltar the following morning, passing Cape Trafalgar to starboard some three hours later. As they entered the English Channel HMS *Volunteer*, *Vansittart* and *Wren* detached to Plymouth whilst HMS *Worcester*, *Witch* and *Whitehall* headed for Portsmouth leaving *Venomous* to proceed on her own up the Medway to Chatham where she arrived at first light on 2 March.

There now followed two months in refit until finally, on 30 April *Venomous* was paid off (decommissioned) and recommissioned later that day into the Fourth Flotilla of the Mediterranean Fleet. Most of the ratings would have returned to Chatham Barracks for leave and redeployment to other ships and a new crew would have joined the ship. Of the officers, only Ommanney and his executive officer, Lt F.R.G. Maunsell RN and Sub Lt Donald remained. Amongst the newcomers were Lt E.P.H. Pinckney RN, Gunner (T) L.C. de Voil and Engineer Lt L. Sims. Later that day Capt B.S. Bingham V.C. RN inspected the ship.

On 5 May it was back to the Mediterranean. She steamed for Gibraltar in company with the rest of the Fourth Flotilla and on 9 May *Venomous* secured alongside the South Mole. HMS *Broke* and half the Flotilla sailed for Malta leaving *Venomous*, *Volunteer*, *Vansittart* and *Whitshed* in Gibraltar. On 17 May *Venomous* made the four hour crossing to Tangiers for a six day visit where the captains of French and Spanish warships present in harbour came on board to pay their respects, the captain of *Venomous* being the senior officer. That afternoon *Venomous* dressed ship in recognition of the birthday of a member of the Spanish Royal Family.

Venomous returned to Gibraltar with a seriously ill British national on board on 23 May and left on 4 June with HMS *Volunteer* for Malta, arriving at the Grand Harbour on the 7th. At the end of June she took part in exercises with the Third and Fourth Flotilla at Argostoli in the Ionian Isles, off the west coast of Greece, together with the battleships of the Fourth Battle Squadron, the Revenge Class battleships HMS *Resolution* and *Royal Oak*, and with the Queen Elizabeth Class battleship, HMS *Barham*. The following day there were further manoeuvres with the First, Second and Third Destroyer Flotillas and the battleships of the Fourth Battle Squadron including the Queen Elizabeth Class battleship HMS *Warspite*.

Previous success in the Flotilla Pulling Regatta was not repeated in the Fleet Regatta at Sebenico on 19-20 July and after visiting Dragomesti Bay on the 27th *Venomous* was again at Malta on 10 August.

The autumn cruise in September took *Venomous* to Cape Matapan on the 26th, then on to Lassos Bay, Marmarice and finally Famagusta, before she returned to Malta securing alongside the oiler RFA *Brambleleaf* on 15 October.

After showing the flag in Greek waters, the remaining weeks of 1926 were taken up with essentially routine activities, including the granting of Christmas leave for the ship's company. In January 1927, command of the ship passed from Lt Cdr Ommanney to Lt Cdr Edmund G.N. Rushbrooke DSC, RN. Rushbrooke had considerable experience in destroyer service having been awarded his DSC "for distinguished service in destroyers of the Harwich Flotilla" during 1917.[21]

Our stoker didn't think much of the change of commanding officers. In his diary he wrote, "8 January – New skipper came in by mail boat today. The OD showed him around the ship about 11 o'clock. I haven't seen him yet & I ain't very interested." He seemed to have changed his opinion somewhat when he wrote the following day, "Saw the new skipper today & he didn't seem a bad sort of chap. But time will show us what he's like."

On 10 January, *Venomous* got underway from Athens with the flotilla leader HMS *Broke*, together with *Whitshed and Volunteer*. They arrived at Phalerium Bay on 13 January. HMS *Warspite* was at anchor in the bay and on 19 January the Greek Battleship *Kilkis* joined the assembled warships. The *Kilkis* was the former American Mississippi Class pre-dreadnought battleship, the USS *Mississippi*. The following day, the destroyers left for Navarin and thence to Malta where they moored in the Grand Harbour on the 29th.

Whilst in Malta, *Venomous* underwent a series of demanding engineering and operational trials. The ship's stokers worked feverishly to get *Venomous* ready for her steam trials as noted by our stoker in his diary, "5 February – plenty of work for we heard the news the Rear Admiral of Destroyers is coming on board tomorrow and steam trials when we go out on Monday. We are up to our eyes in it down below."

On 27 February the Fourth Flotilla got underway for Gibraltar, falling in with the Fourth Battle Squadron on 2 March. Rushbrooke took *Venomous* to her station astern of the Queen Elizabeth Class battleship

HMS *Venomous* with pendant number D75 probably taken in the Mediterranean in the 1920s.
From the W.R. Crick Collection at the IWM, Image Reference Q 58556. Courtesy of the Imperial War Museum.

HMS *Malaya*. Manoeuvres with the Fourth Battle Squadron continued through the 3rd, and *Venomous*, with the rest of the Fourth Destroyer Flotilla entered Gibraltar harbour on the 4th. *Venomous* secured alongside *Voyager* and between the battleships *Revenge and Royal Sovereign*. Two days later, *Venomous* departed Gibraltar to provide plane guard services for the aircraft carrier HMS *Eagle*. Our stoker noted this in his diary, "…followed the *Eagle* – fine sight to see about six planes go up one after the other and then come down about an hour afterward." *Eagle's* air operations concluded the series of spring exercises for the Mediterranean Fleet, and at its conclusion, *Venomous* and the rest of the Fourth Destroyer Flotilla returned to Malta.

It appears *Venomous'* steam trials off Malta did not go well as she spent March and April in engineering refit. Engine trials took place on 29 April and our stoker wrote in his diary: "29 April, Trials – Raised steam about 5.30 am. Steamed at 8 am for trials. Did an hour at 23 knots and 2 hours at 29. I was in my usual place in the boiler room. Everything went pretty well."

Before departing on a further series of cruises, *Venomous* received a new executive officer. Our stoker noted this, together with the return of Peter, the ship's mascot:

> "9 May: Our Peter the dog came back yesterday. He must have been a bad dog for he had a punishment sheet with him. Didn't know us at first, but he does now." 13 May: "Ship is different since the new First Lieutenant [executive officer] came. The lads are as happy as anything these days."

The next six weeks were spent in and around Malta before *Venomous* steamed for Navarin on 28 June, arriving on the 30th.

At Skiathos on 12 July she participated in anti-submarine warfare exercises with the battle fleet and the aircraft carrier Eagle, when her aircraft conducted aerial torpedo bombing exercises as described by our stoker, "…aeroplanes were dropping torpedoes and we were picking them up. They must have scored some hits too for the ones we picked up were smashed up. Our Peter enjoyed himself barking at the planes."

The Greek islands of Mudros, Dili, Syra and Argostoli were visited in company with *Eagle*, and the Coventry Class light cruisers HMS *Coventry*, and the Caroline Class light cruiser HMS *Conquest* before *Venomous* returned to Malta on 16 August. On the 31st the flotilla commander, Capt C.H.C. Bacon DSC RN, Captain (D), inspected the ship.

The autumn cruise began on 2 September and took *Venomous* to the Italian port of Genoa. Our stoker recorded this port visit in a straightforward way: "Had a good meal at the sailor's restaurant. Lots of ladies of easy virtue ashore. Came back at 10 pm."

On the 20th, *Venomous* departed for the Greek port of Salonika in company with the battleship HMS *Warspite* and the fleet auxiliary, HMS *Bryony*, which was carrying the C in C of the Mediterranean Fleet and his family. Entering the Ionian Sea via the Straits of Messina on the 21st, *Venomous* set a course for the Gulf of Corinth and the Corinth Canal on the 23rd. The transit through the canal was noted by our stoker: "Corinth Canal – It's about 3 miles long – took us about half an hour at 6 knots – but right through a hill with sheer sides to it. But it ain't half narrow. But, we didn't need a pilot as it's straight as a die." *Venomous* reached Salonika the next day.

This part of the cruise took *Venomous* back to the Aegean, to the island of Imbros and the Gallipoli Peninsula, a solemn moment for all on board. With the ship's company wearing their summer dress uniforms and arrayed along the ship's weather decks, *Venomous* slowly steamed past Anzac Cove and the other landing beaches. The Australian, British and New Zealand invasion force had suffered heavy casualties at Anzac during the disastrous Gallipoli Campaign.

The late summer cruise continued, when *Venomous* passed the Holy Mountain of Athos to port on the 25th and after a short visit to Kavalla in Thrace, steamed to Alexandria with 130 officers and men of HMS *Warspite* on board. An overnight stay on 2 - 3 October was followed by a call at Port Said on the 3rd, and Famagusta on the 6th when our Stoker recorded that, "the Captain [Rushbrooke] shoved off today – couple of days leave – took his golf clubs with him – very nice too. Lads had a good time in Nicosia yesterday."

The ship then steamed for Haifa on the 14th where shore leave was granted to all hands – an opportunity to visit the Holy Land could not be ignored. Our stoker wrote in his diary: "17 October – The RCs [Roman Catholics] went off this morning on 72 hours up to Jerusalem. Another party for 4 days tour round in motorcars. I went with the RCs." On the 18th, he visited the Sea of Galilee, "Went to the Sea of Galilee and had a ball. Tried walking on water, but no use." *Venomous* was back at sea on the 21st on exercises with the flotilla and the main battle fleet before her return to Malta on 14 November.

Venomous remained in port at Malta during December and, apart from local exercises, maintenance, and the start of Christmas leave for the ships' company, nothing out of the ordinary occurred. Our stoker remained aboard and wrote between 1 December and Boxing Day,

"Raining throughout and cold...missing my sweetheart and children...many of ship's company on leave...received Christmas package from wife on 9 December...Turned down Chief's offer for a run on shore – want to save money...weather breaks – very pleasant...16 December is my wedding day eight years ago...Sixth Christmas on station. Duck and pork for Christmas Dinner. Drinks all around. Captain and wife come aboard. Engineer gave me a bottle of beer...Received Christmas parcel on Boxing Day from wife."

Thus 1927 ended for *Venomous* and this lonely stoker.

New Year's Day 1928 brought the now familiar routine in and around Malta and this continued until April when *Venomous* began an abbreviated spring and summer cruise by steaming to Corsica and visiting Porto Vecchio, followed by a deployment back to Navarin in June. On 1 July she was ordered to return to Britain at the end of her commission, her voyage being broken by a short stay in Gibraltar. *Venomous* got underway on the 8th and moored at Sheerness on 13 July.

During refit, Lt Pinckney learned of his promotion to Lt Cdr and left the ship on 17 August to be succeeded by Lt I.T. Clarke RN. Recommissioned on 7 September, *Venomous* steamed for Gibraltar, arriving on the 11th where she remained until early the following month. Visits to Palma on 9 October and Algiers on the 17th preceded a return to Malta where *Venomous* spent the winter months on local duties.

New Year's Day 1929 saw the arrival of a new CO, Lt Cdr Cecil A.N. Chatwin RN.[22] Chatwin was a sharp, highly intelligent officer, with a strong personality who required high standards from both officers and men. He was married to the daughter of Admiral Sir Frederick Dreyer, a recognised gunnery specialist prior to and during the Great War.

On 12 March 1929 the ship was inspected by the C in C Mediterranean Fleet, Admiral Sir Hubert Brand, who came on board just after noon, remaining for one hour before departing for the new Nelson Class battleship, HMS *Nelson*. Considering who Chatwin's father-in-law was it is likely that Sir Hubert's time on *Venomous* involved more than the usual pleasantries.

The log records a visit to Rapallo Bay on 26 April and the discharge of Midshipman Viscount Jocelyn to HMS *Royal Oak* on 4 May. In June there were visits to Dragomesti Bay, Astokos, Skiathos and Argostoli Bay, giving *Venomous* a last view of the Greek Ionian coastline until her return almost fifteen years later under very different circumstances.

Fiscal restraints on the Royal Navy required further reductions to the fleet. *Venomous* was one of several V & W destroyers that would be 'Reduced to Reserve'. Chatwin got his destroyer underway for Sheerness on 28 August and she steamed past Gibraltar on the 30th, mooring in her homeport on 3 September 1929, exactly ten years to the day before the outbreak of a second world war. *Venomous* was only ten years old and her overall material condition was excellent but the need to reduce the Fleet was paramount.

Venomous was paid off at Sheerness and placed under dockyard control on 24 September, Chatwin having first handed over command to Cdr (E) P. Grieve RN on the 3rd. *Venomous* remained in reduced status through the rest of 1929 and the first six months of 1930. Following sea trials on 5 June 1930, *Venomous* was 'permanently' transferred to the Main Reserve Fleet. On 10 July 1930, this ship, with only ten years of service, became a tender to HMS *Pembroke*, the shore base at Chatham As for our stoker, his diary concluded with his return and his fate and identity remains unknown.

Venomous remained moored at Chatham until 1933 when she was towed to Rosyth and placed into the maintenance reserve. There now began years of virtual hibernation under a succession of officers of the engineering branch. It is a tribute to their skill that in 1939 *Venomous* was able to answer the call to arms.

Notes

1 Ramsay MacDonald (1866-1937) was twice Prime Minister of Britain, once as leader of the first Labour Government in 1924, which lasted less than year and again from 1929-35 as head of the National Government formed by a splinter group of the Labour Party with the Conservatives. This quotation is taken from Christopher M. Bell, *The Royal Navy, Seapower and Strategy between the Wars* (Stanford, Cal.: Stanford University Press, 2000), p. xv

2 The V & W destroyers were grouped into six flotillas. In addition to the Fourth Flotilla, they were the First, Second, Third and the Fifth, a total of 45 ships in all, with the Ninth Flotilla of ten ships laid up in reserve at Rosyth. *V & W Class Destroyers, 1917-1945*, Anthony Preston, p. 36.

3 Capt Wayne Hughes, USN (Ret.) *Fleet Tactics: Theory and Practice*, Naval Institute Press, Annapolis, Maryland, 1986, p. 76.

4 The decision to carry the modified British Army 4.7-inch field gun on these ships proved to be the correct one.

5 Preston, p. 35.

6 *The Royal Navy, Seapower and Strategy between the Wars*, p. 14.

7 The Washington Naval Treaty prevented an immediate post war naval arms race between the UK and the US. It also placed limits on the number of capital ships and aircraft carriers Japan, France and Italy could build and maintain. One consequence of this treaty was to

reduce the number of cruisers and destroyers needed to support the smaller battle fleets. The reduction in the number of cruisers and destroyers would come to haunt the Royal Navy when it went to war in 1939.

8   An unknown sailor wrote a collection of diaries between 1924 and 1928 which are now in the collection of the RN Museum, Portsmouth. Robert Moore died before he could positively identify the unknown stoker whose diary records the six years he spent in the Mediterranean on *Venomous*, and her sister ship, HMS *Wanderer* (RN Museum Ref. 2002.71/3 and 2002.71/5).

9   The *Edsall* was comparable to the Wickes Class described in Chapter 1. The *Edsall* transferred to the US Pacific Fleet and was sunk after a heroic action against superior Japanese naval forces during the Battle of the Java Sea, 1 March 1942.

10   The *Swan* was *Venomous'* sister ship HMS *Wild Swan*.

11   The *Valiant* was a Queen Elizabeth Class battleship that fought at Jutland and survived World War Two.

12   Donal McGrath would go on to command HMS *Vanquisher* in 1929. He was promoted to Captain prior to the war and placed on the retired list. McGrath served as commanding officer of several ships during World War Two. He was mentioned in dispatches on two separate occasion, for Operation Jubilee and for Operation Neptune the naval operation supporting Operation Overlord.
      See: http://www.unithistories.com/officers/RN_officersA.html.

13   HMS *Bryony* was completed in 1917. She and her sister ships looked very much like innocent merchant ships but had an array of concealed weapons that could be rapidly brought to bear against any German U-boat that surfaced, thinking it could dispatch such a ship with its gunnery, thus saving its torpedoes.

14   Admiral of the Fleet David Beatty was commander of the Grand Fleet's Battle Cruiser force during the Battle of Jutland. Sometime after the battle he assumed command of the Grand Fleet from Admiral Sir John Jellicoe.

15   Ommanney served throughout the war years and after the war became the King's Harbour Master at Chatham. http://www.unithistories.com/officers/RN_officersA.html. By a curious quirk of fate he passed away on the same date as his brother, also a serving naval officer, 22 February 1963.

16   HMS *Cornflower* continued her service through the mid-1920s but was then sold off to a commercial enterprise. The sloop was brought back into naval service during the war and was bombed and sunk by Japanese aircraft on 19 December 1941 during the fall of Singapore. *Conway's all the World's Fighting Ships 1906-1921*, p. 95.

17   Miers, Suzanne, *Slavery in the Twentieth Century: The Evolution of a Global Problem*, Alta Mira Press, 2003, p. 93.

18   Ibid, p. 93.

19   Ibid., p. 93.

20   It is important to recognise that at this time the Royal Navy was developing and perfecting the aircraft carrier flight operations at sea which have become standard operational procedures for all of today's navies. In this context, *Venomous'* role as a plane guard does not seem so mundane.

21   Rushbrooke would go on to command another V & W, HMS *Versatile*. He would command the aircraft carriers HMS *Argus* and HMS *Eagle* during the war, obtaineing flag rank and becoming Director of Naval Intelligence between 1942 and 1946, retiring as a vice admiral in 1948. See http://www.unithistories.com/officers/RN_officersA.html

22   Chatwin would command another V & W destroyer, HMS *Verity* prior to the war. He would go on to command other destroyers. See www.unithistories.com/officers/RN_officersC.html

CHAPTER FOUR

OFF TO WAR
September 1938 – June 1940

"Winston is back"... So is *Venomous*[1]

While *Venomous* was laid up at Rosyth fascism was taking a firm grip on Europe. Hitler's National Socialist party won 37.3% of the votes in the July 1932 election and in 1933 Hitler was invited by Hindenburg to become Chancellor. By 1935 Germany was openly rearming. In 1936 Hitler ordered his troops into the Rhineland, demilitarised under the Treaty of Versailles, and supported Franco in the Spanish Civil War whilst Mussolini demonstrated the ineffectiveness of the League of Nations by taking over Ethiopia.

Under the terms of the Treaty of Versailles the German Navy was only allowed six warships over 10,000 tons and no submarines. But in June 1935 the British Government signed the Anglo-German Naval Agreement, which permitted Germany to have one third of the tonnage of the British navy's surface fleet and an equal tonnage of submarines. Why did the British let Nazi Germany break the Treaty of Versailles? The government believed Germany would develop its navy anyway and that an official agreement would improve relations between the two countries but this policy of appeasement appeared to give the go-ahead to German re-armament.

By September 1938 Britain appeared to be on the brink of war. German troops had marched unopposed into Austria in March and when Hitler demanded that the Czechs hand over the German populated Sudetenland war seemed inevitable. British Prime Minister Neville Chamberlain flew to Berchtesgaden to meet Hitler and then, accompanied by the French premier, went to Munich on 28 September where they signed the notorious Munich agreement allowing Hitler to occupy the Sudetenland. Chamberlain returned to London waving the signed agreement and announced "peace in our time".

It was against this background that the Royal Navy's Reserve Fleet was mobilised. Mobilisation for *Venomous* commenced on the very day the Munich Agreement was signed, the 29 September 1938, when Lt James G.T. Western RN came on board to take temporary command.[2] He was joined later that evening by acting Sub Lt C.P. Ross RN, followed by Lt K.W.S. Buckel RN and 57 ratings from the Royal Naval Barracks (RNB) at Devonport. *Venomous* had been a "Chatham ship" but from now on its homeport would be the Royal Navy's Devonport dockyard at Plymouth.[3]

The following day found all hands stowing gear, cleaning the mess decks and taking the initial steps to bring the ship back into operational condition. During the afternoon, *Venomous* received an additional 49 Royal Fleet Reserve ratings to fill out her ship's company. During the morning of 1 October Western addressed the newly formed ship's company, and over the next five days a concerted effort was made to prepare the ship for sea.

By 6 October, *Venomous* had been brought back into reasonable shape, and Western, together with the reserve ratings, left the ship, leaving Buckel in command. For the next four days all hands continued working on maintenance issues and loading the ship's main magazines with 4.7-inch ammunition. On the 11th a chief petty officer stoker, two petty officer stokers and three unrated stokers arrived on board from HMS *Vansittart*, which had remained on active service through the 1930s, to prepare for basin trials the following day.

By 15 October they had made the ship's propulsion machinery ready for sea, and shrugging off the cobwebs *Venomous* passed through the lock of Rosyth and set course for North Berwick. During the morning the engines were subjected to quarter power trials and then to maximum power at a speed in excess of 30 knots. Gunnery trials with the 4.7-inch main guns and with the two pom-pom guns followed, and just after mid-day she returned to Rosyth and secured along the newer B Class destroyer, HMS *Bodicia* with another V & W, HMS *Volunteer*.

Ten days later, on 25 October, Buckel took *Venomous* back to sea for a second set of sea trials. After swinging her magnetic compass Buckel ordered full power trials to commence and *Venomous* reached her maximum speed of 32 knots. Upon return to Rosyth that afternoon Buckel conducted a brief re-commissioning ceremony.

However, war fears had subsided for now and with it the end of the fleet mobilisation of 1938. Buckel was ordered to place his destroyer back into reserve status and many of the ratings returned to Devonport Barracks. By 27 October the remaining ship's company were employed de-storing the ship, landing the pom-pom guns and returning the ship's barometer, gyrocompass and other navigational equipment to storage warehouses. By noon, all of the ratings repaired ashore and *Venomous* was officially returned to reserve. It would be just eight short months before *Venomous* was back in harness and by then the prospect of war would be all too real.

In March 1939 Hitler's troops marched into Prague and the signing of the Anglo-Polish pact in April ruled out any further concessions. As summer advanced and war appeared inevitable the Reserve Fleet was fortunate to have a highly capable officer as its commander in Admiral Sir Max Horton KCB. Horton had distinguished himself in submarines during the Great War but had left active service in 1936 after he clashed with the First Sea Lord. This apparently didn't hurt his career, for he was recalled to active service. Horton had overseen the mobilisation eight months earlier, and this forceful officer was accustomed to getting things done. The noted British historian, Correlli Barnett, provided an insight into his character when he wrote, "Horton drove his command hard, and his displeasure expressed in ways which reduced his less robust subordinates to nervous wrecks; and only the bravest dared approach him on days when he lost at his regular game of golf."[4] With the prospects of war with Germany increasing every day, someone like Horton was needed to bring the reserve fleet to a state of readiness for war.

The first appointment to *Venomous* for her second recall to active status was that of a Warrant Engineer, Mr. E.D. Tonkyn. He joined the ship on 1 July 1939 and his task was not an enviable one. *Venomous* had been the first destroyer fitted with what was then a new steam power system known as the "Closed Feed System", which became the basic steam system for all steam powered vessels. In theory *Venomous'* steam generating capability relied on using freshwater as feed water that was endlessly recycled to produce steam to turn the ship's turbine engines. In practice, actual operations produced significant corrosion within the steam fittings and loss of feed water through leaking valves, steam atomisation and evaporation. Losses were replaced by using evaporators to produce freshwater which was reintroduced into the system.[5] From the diary of the unknown stoker on *Venomous* during the 1920s we know that during its first decade of operational life this new type of steam plant required frequent repairs. It was now a decade older and was to prove a headache throughout the war.

On 24 July Commissioned Gunner Mr. W.F.H. Lewis joined the ship. Shortly after his arrival, an advance party of Chief and Senior Ratings, who were all regulars drafted from Devonport arrived on board. Their job was to organise the smooth running of the ship.

The ship's Coxswain (or Bosun) and senior rating was CPO Squibb. He was to be responsible for ensuring the ship's routine and maintaining discipline of the ship's company while serving as a link between officers and ratings. Amongst his many duties were: dealing with requests from the ship's company to the Captain; presenting those enlisted men with discipline problems (defaulters) to the Executive Officer and CO; and overseeing the daily issue of rum to the ship's company. As the senior special sea duty man, Coxswain Squibb manned the helm when the ship entered or left harbour and, as the most experienced helmsman, when *Venomous* was underway in heavy seas. As the ship's Coxswain, Squibb also supervised and ordered the routine issue of the basic foods to all ratings' messes.

Shortly after Lewis's arrival, PO Torpedo Instructor G. Hicks and PO Gunnery Instructor Billings arrived on board. They were charged with the training of their weapons crews and were responsible for the ammunition and explosives in the magazines, depth charges, torpedo pistols, rockets and flares. The care and maintenance of the ship's weaponry was the responsibility of CPO Ordnance Artificer Hugh H. McGeeney, who remembered:

> "My responsibility was the maintenance of all guns and mountings, Rangefinder (9 ft. optical) Director Control Tower and equipment in the transmitting station; also all small arms and binoculars. The equipment under my control was in surprisingly good condition although there were defects and items missing. Fortunately there were other ships not (at that time) being brought forward for service and so I was able to obtain duplicates of the missing items from them."

PO Michael O'Sullivan was responsible for the forward part of the ship. A large, well-built Irishman he was remembered by AB Harold Knapton as:

"A Petty Officer whom I admired although I was slightly scared of him, as I had previously served with him in the *Royal Oak* when I was a boy seaman. He was strict but fair and a man upon whom I tried to model myself when I made Petty Officer."

Both men had cause to be thankful for their transfer to *Venomous*. On 14 October the ship they served on together, the battleship HMS *Royal Oak,* was torpedoed at its mooring inside Scapa Flow by the daring U-boat commander Günther Prien and over eight hundred men perished in a few short minutes.

PO Cook Watts also made a vital contribution to the well being of the ship's company. Apart from a brief respite in mid afternoon he could be found throughout the day in the galley, situated across the ship at the break of the fo'c'sle. Canteen messing operated with each mess receiving a ration (by weight) of basic foods, such as meat, flour and vegetables. It was a mess cook's duty to present food to the galley ready to be cooked. Each mess caterer bought additional food from the victualling allowance, plus any extra finance provided by the mess members themselves. As McGeeney recounted: "It was not cordon bleu living but a pattern for survival and if we were honest it was our concern throughout the events that followed."

The messman for the Senior Rates was AB Lodwick. He was an interesting character who, in his mid-to-late forties, had been recalled to the service from the reserves. Lodwick had seen action in the Great War and been awarded the DSM for his part in the raid on Zeebrugge in 1918.

The appointment of the commissioned officers took effect from 31 July 1939. The new commanding officer, Lt Cdr Donald G.F.W. McIntyre RN, had recently returned from the Far East where he had been in command of the D Class destroyer, HMS *Defender*. He was to be the first in a line of distinguished wartime COs and, following a relatively short time in command, he would in later years earn the reputation of being an outstanding U-boat hunter. McIntyre would win a DSO and two Bars, and the DSC. In retirement, he became an author of distinction.[6]

His Executive Officer was Lt D.R. Duff RN, a tall man with a quiet, assured air. The Wardroom further accommodated two young regular Sub Lts, Walter Wells and John Vaughan-Lewis. Walter Wells was always sea sick and had to have a bucket by him on the bridge but was to be a great asset to the ship. The only reservist was Mid. Alan Esson RNR, an enthusiastic, wavy-haired Scotsman from Ardrossan.

By the beginning of August the ship's company was largely complete with men such as those mentioned above, who were mostly regular navy, pensioners, or time-expired reservists, who knew the ropes, some of whom had served in the last war and been recalled. *Venomous* was indeed a fortunate ship to have such a seasoned nucleus of officers and ratings to bring her back to life, unlike future crews, which would consist mostly of Hostilities Only (HO) ratings.

First impressions of *Venomous* were far from complimentary, postcards home reflecting the thoughts of many: "What a ship to look at," wrote AB Knapton, whilst AB Barnfield wrote on a postcard showing his ship, "This is the old tub." McIntyre also recorded his misgivings upon reaching Rosyth and seeing *Venomous*: "My gloom returned when I sought out from amongst the mass of old V & W destroyers lying in the dockyard basin the particular old warrior that had been selected for me."

The process of welding the ship's company into a competent fighting force began at once. *Venomous* was quickly made ready to get underway, and in early August McIntyre took his destroyer to sea for the first time in eight months. McIntyre remembered the moment:

> "Smoke began to pour from her funnels and machinery came to reluctant life giving the ship that vibration which is its soul. In due time we nosed our way into the Firth of Forth for trials and exercises."

Lt Duff recalled the occasion and one potentially dangerous situation:

> "The ship reached 29 knots on her steam trials and we managed one main armament firing before heading south for Weymouth. As 1st Lt and Officer of the quarter-deck of the after 4.7" mountings, I just prevented the loading of a shell which had been placed "arsey-versey" in the loading tray."

Passage down the East Coast was made without incident. In due course *Venomous* anchored in Weymouth Bay, where the Reserve Fleet Review was to be held. It was twenty years since *Venomous* took part in the Fleet Review at Southend to celebrate the end of the Great War and it was now to take part in a review on the eve of a new war against Germany. On 9 August King George VI inspected the 133 warships of the Reserve Fleet under Vice Admiral Sir Max Horton, flying his flag in the Glorious Class aircraft carrier HMS *Courageous*. During the course of the review McIntyre was presented to the King and noted the presence amongst the guests of the French Admiral Darlan. The six year old son of George "Arnie" Birkin, a gunlayer on "A" Gun, still vividly remembers being taken by his mother on a "boat trip round the Fleet" in the vain hope they would see his father on HMS *Venomous:* "the sea was very choppy, the boat was small, and the wind strong and gusty. I was so overawed by what I saw – those long, long lines of seemingly impregnable grey warships that seemed to stretch to the horizon – that the motion of the boat didn't register." AB James Eaton had vivid memories of the Review: "I can still see the lines of warships. What a great sight it was – we had a Navy in those days." The review at Weymouth was not as impressive as the Coronation Review at Spithead in May 1937 but it was the last Review when the Royal Navy was still the world's largest. Many of the ships and those who manned them would not survive the six years of war.

With the review over *Venomous* settled down to three weeks of intense activity. Stores and ammunition were taken on board, interspersed with ship handling and speed trials, gun and torpedo running. Lt Duff recalled they were then sent "to Portland for a crash course in anti-submarine training with the submarines there for HMS *Osprey*'s usual programme. It was a busy time as many ships companies were in an untrained state. *Venomous* was then ordered to join a flotilla of similar 'old timers' at Harwich." By the end of August McIntyre felt confident that *Venomous* was ready and that she would give a good account of herself.

Hitler's signing of the non-aggression pact with Stalin on 23 August had cleared the way for Germany's invasion of Poland on 1 September, which led to Britain and France issuing their ultimatum. *Venomous* sailed for Portsmouth where she arrived on 2 September, one day before the outbreak of hostilities. Anchored in Portsmouth harbour that Sunday morning at 1100 on 3 September 1939, the ship's company listened on the radio to Prime Minister Neville Chamberlain announce that Britain was now at war with Germany. Seventeen minutes later the Admiralty radioed a special message marked MOST IMMEDIATE to all His Majesty's Ships: "TOTAL GERMANY repetition TOTAL GERMANY."[7]

Shortly after receipt of the message McIntyre mustered all hands. He announced that Britain was now at war with Nazi Germany and then, as other captains had done before him when the Royal Navy went to war, he concluded his remarks by reading out the Articles of War. McIntyre then dismissed his officers and men.

Venomous and three of her sisters, HMS *Malcolm* (flotilla leader), *Wivern* and *Wren,* were based at Portsmouth as part of the Sixteenth Destroyer Flotilla.[8] Historians call the following six months "The Phoney War," but for *Venomous* and the Royal Navy it was anything but phoney.

That first night of the war found her with other destroyers of the Sixteenth Flotilla off the Nab Tower at the eastern approach to the Solent, preparing to escort a fast convoy of troopships to Cherbourg. This was the advance contingent of the British Expeditionary Force (B.E.F.), whose departure had been prepared in anticipation of the commencement of hostilities. Lt Duff remembers: "we spent the first two or three weeks escorting ships ferrying the British Expeditionary Force to France during the nights and returning the following day. These escort duties were good training in station keeping at the best speed the troop-carrying ships could make and without lights and, as yet no radar."

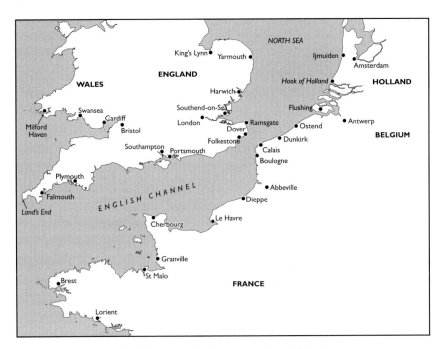

English Channel theatre of operations, 1939 – 41.
Map graphic Kelly Erlinger. Map source Gordon Smith, www.naval-history.net

Venomous escorted as many as five such convoys a week, either to Cherbourg or Le Havre, and occasionally accompanied slower convoys to Brest. Lt F. Twiss (later Admiral Sir Frank Twiss KCB DSC) was Flotilla Gunnery Officer in the destroyer leader HMS *Malcolm*:

> "Each night, ships of the Flotilla would form up with a small convoy of cross channel steamers full of troops and dash across the Channel to Le Havre or Cherbourg returning next day to repeat the process. Occasionally the task would be to escort larger and slower transports filled with tanks, guns and supplies to Brest. It was hard going leaving Harbour about 2200 picking up the troopships by the Nab Tower, where the boom vessel opened the gate to let us pass the nets and arriving about 0600 at Le Havre. Back to Portsmouth about 1500 fuel, rest and start again the same trip – and never a submarine or aircraft."

In fact, the greatest danger came from the risk of collision, as convoys would proceed at high speed whilst crossing the Channel at night. They would steam at right angles to the shipping lanes, showing no lights and without radar. There were, however, advantages to be gained from this regular cross channel activity. Often *Venomous* had an opportunity to pull into a French port such as Le Havre for a short stopover. McIntyre recounted:

> "We usually had an hour or two to wait before bringing back an empty convoy and could sometimes get ashore for a brief shopping tour – Guerlain's perfume for our girl friends, and wine. The former made us very popular ashore on our return and the latter soon gave *Venomous* a remarkably fine cellar at a modest price."

McGeeney described how "destroyers came and went frequently for repairs, boiler cleaning and various escort duties so there was no regular pattern and we never operated as a flotilla" and that:

> "Our fuel capacity was smaller than other destroyers and we were ideal for channel work. On entering harbour the priorities were for fuel, ammunition, water and mail in that order. Usually in harbours we were at 4 hours notice for sea and leave would be restricted accordingly. Urgent recalls to the ship were made by flashing notices on screens in cinemas and by naval patrols in public places."

Although the shuttle to France was generally uneventful, danger from mines was ever present as McGeeney remembered:

> "On our frequent trips in the Channel, at least during daylight, we
> saw the odd loose mine bobbing about having broken adrift from
> its mooring. Lookouts were always posted with binoculars and
> when a mine was sighted it was an opportunity for the marksmen
> of the ship, or the bridge Lewis Gunners, to 'hole' it and eliminate
> the danger. The mine would sink slowly but occasionally a hit on
> one of its horns would produce a big bang.
>
> Our own protection was the paravane which was "streamed"
> out each side from the bow and carried a serrated jaw that gripped
> the mine wire as it slid down the streaming wire with the speed of
> the ship keeping the paravane and mine well away from the ship."

With the BEF ashore in France *Venomous* returned to the Harwich
station and Duff described their role:

> "Our flotilla provided escort for east coast convoys, taking over the
> duty from escorts based in the Forth at a variety of rendezvous off
> the Yorkshire coast and handing over to Dover based escorts off the
> Thames. Occasional night encounters with German E boats gave us
> realistic training in the basics of night action. Any aircraft heard and
> occasionally seen were assumed to be sneak mine-layers and we did
> not advertise our convoy's presence by attempting to engage them
> with our negligible anti-aircraft capability, one three inch single
> mounting and a couple of machine guns.
>
> I do not recall any excitement on these runs except for false
> alarms occasioned, most frequently, by near misses with our
> darkened merchant ships finding station keeping at night very
> difficult. Two Polish destroyers, which belonged to the Harwich
> Force, could be relied upon to put some hair-raising night alarms,
> being very trigger-happy. They were *Blyskowica* and *Grom*."

In November, Duff left the ship for the gunnery course at HMS
Excellent, Whale Island, and was succeeded by Lt C.W.R. Milner RN.[9]
Shortly after Christmas, McIntyre also departed, assuming command of
a new H Class destroyer HMS *Hesperus*.

The new captain was Lt Cdr John E.H. McBeath RN, who took
command on 8 January 1940. McBeath was a South African, born in
Natal in 1907. He joined the Royal Navy as a cadet in 1923 and in 1939
was a Lt on HMS *Garland,* commanded by Cecil A.N. Chatwin, who
had been CO of *Venomous* in 1929. HMS *Venomous* was McBeath's
first command. As time would show, McBeath was a courageous naval
officer, possessing outstanding seamanship and tactical skills.

A determined man, he was to attain the rank of Rear Admiral, win the DSO and DSC, and in later years became High Sheriff of Surrey and Honorary Commodore of the Sea Cadet Corps, a position he held for twenty years.[10]

McBeath's seamanship skills became apparent from the very beginning. He held to an unusual way of securing his ship to a buoy. AB Knapton, who was a special sea duty man during this particular evolution, remembered his Captain's unique approach to mooring:

> "We never used a motor boat or whaler. The Captain would put the bow of the ship to the weatherside of the buoy and whilst an older rating held a bearing out spar to the buoy, I used to slide down the spar and put the picking up rope to the buoy before securing the cable to it."

On 26 February there was a new face in *Venomous'* Wardroom with the arrival of Sub Lt Peter Kershaw RNVR, who had just completed his basic training course at the training schools, HMS *King Alfred* and *Osprey*. This young officer would prove to be a valuable addition to the ship. His performance under fire would become an inspiration to all and he would be instrumental in helping his ship survive.

Venomous' first taste of action came on 2 March off the Isle of Wight when McBeath was ordered to discontinue his patrol and to stand by MV *Domala*, which had been bombed by a Heinkel 111 which machine-gunned the survivors as they took to the boats. The *Domala* was carrying passengers to India who had recently been released from Germany to be repatriated. One hundred of the passengers and crew were killed.[11] The fire was soon brought under control but its condition was critical and the *Domala's* captain beached his ship in the Solent to prevent her from sinking.

This was to be the last incident of note for some weeks for whilst leaving Portsmouth on the night of 5 March, *Venomous* collided with the tug *Swarthey*. The hull was stove in on the portside forward of the mess decks, fortunately above the waterline, but it still necessitated a spell in the dockyard at Portsmouth. Each watch was given three weeks leave but Sydney Compston remembers that he was aboard on his 21st birthday, the 16 March, and was given "sippers" from everyone's rum ration and was much the worse for wear.

Venomous had been in reserve for ten years and the spell in

Hole in hull of *Venomous* caused by collision with the tug, *Swarthey*, on 6 March 1940
Photographed by Lt Peter Kershaw RNVR.

dockyard hands repairing the damage done in the collision provided an opportunity for a refit to equip it for the action to come. It was to be nearly two months before *Venomous* returned to sea. To counter the submarine threat *Venomous* was belatedly equipped with Asdic, better known today as sonar, which had been widely introduced in the thirties whilst *Venomous* was in reserve. This required the cutting of a hole in the ship's hull and the fitting of an Asdic dome which emitted sound waves ahead of the ship which would be echoed back by a submarine target which could then be depth charged. The Asdic operators occupied a small cramped cabin on the starboard side at the break in the fo'c'sle. *Venomous* was now equipped with the technology needed to fight a modern war but traditions were strong in the Royal Navy and AB Sydney Compston recalled that a rack of cutlasses hung in a small fo'c'sle cabin, no bigger than a broom cupboard, under the bridge behind "A" gun ready for use should an attempt be made to board an enemy ship.

Whilst *Venomous* was in the yards, the war took a dramatic turn when, on 9 April, Germany executed Operation *Weserübung* – the invasion of Norway and Denmark. Hitler, fearing that Britain would occupy Norway and dominate Germany's northern flank, had directed the German General Staff in February to come up with an invasion plan. In less than two months they devised a complex plan that involved almost the entire Kriegsmarine, one thousand aircraft of the Luftwaffe, including five hundred transport planes and six army divisions.[12]

This bold move against the full strength of the Royal Navy appeared to fly in the face of prudence but *Weserübung* came as a total surprise. The Danes could only offer slight resistance and surrendered within hours. Key Norwegian ports, including Oslo, were captured within twenty-four hours but most of Norway continued to resist. Britain and France had planned to occupy Norway's iron ore ports and hastily threw their air, land and sea forces into the fight. The Royal Navy made the Kriegsmarine pay dearly for their affront but also suffered staggering losses showing its vulnerability to the overwhelming airpower of the Luftwaffe.

The British and French expeditionary force to retake Norway was hastily put together, poorly equipped, insufficiently trained, badly organised and not well led and after a two-month campaign it was forced to withdraw. The Royal Navy and Merchant Navy suffered heavy losses bringing off the surviving troops. Correlli Barnett placed the failure of the Norwegian campaign into perspective:

> "The Norwegian campaign cost the Royal Navy an aircraft carrier, two cruisers, seven destroyers, one sloop and four submarines. The German Navy suffered absolutely and relatively far worse...But this favourable balance could not disguise the fact that Britain, a great naval power, had suffered a strategic defeat at the hands of a continental power with a small navy – in considerable part because of flaws in the British command and control system and the errors of judgement and the vacillating purpose of the Navy's political and professional leadership."[13]

The Norwegian disaster would prove to be the prelude to an even a greater one – the collapse of France.

Venomous was still undergoing its refit in Portsmouth when the Norwegian debacle reached its conclusion. During this time there were also significant changes in the Wardroom. On 15 March Warrant Engineer A.E. Parkes replaced Mr. Tonkyn. An experienced engineer in his fortieth year, Mr. Parkes would later be awarded the DSC for his success in keeping the temperamental engines in running order.

Commissioned Gunner (T) R.K. Thomson succeeded Mr. Lewis and on 12 April Lt G.M. Cottam RNVR joined the ship. On 17 April, there was a further change of executive officers with Lt Angus A. Mackenzie RNR taking over from Lt Milner. A diminutive man with a ready wit and a partiality for a drop of Scotch, Angus Mackenzie came to the ship from pre-war service in the Merchant Navy. He became CO of HMS *Liddesdale* and *Undaunted*, left the Navy as Lt Cdr and went into business in Hong Kong and Japan before retiring to Menorca. He was a popular officer, even though he acquired the affectionate nickname of "Bloody Mackenzie."

Venomous was not back in service until the 2 May and had time for only one more run to Le Havre and two to Cherbourg before the "balloon went up" and Hitler's Blitzkrieg swept across France and the Low Countries, turning the defence by the French Army and the B.E.F. into a rout and making evacuation a priority. At 2330 on 9 May, *Venomous* left Portsmouth on her last convoy run to France. She arrived at Cherbourg at dawn and left at 0800 with the SS *Lady of Mann* for Portsmouth. As *Venomous* left Cherbourg McBeath received an all-Fleet broadcast signal stating that Germany had invaded France and the Low Countries and "We were not very surprised when, on coming in sight of St. Catherine's, the *Lady of Mann* was ordered back to Cherbourg and *Venomous* to Dover. We arrived at 1600 and found *Malcolm* and *Wyvern* alongside."

The Phoney War was over, and for *Venomous* and her crew desperate days were just ahead. The first indication of impending crisis came on 11 May when *Venomous* embarked a Dutch Military Mission consisting of two Generals and a number of other Dutch officers who would act as liaison to the B.E.F. and organise the last attempts to counter the German invasion of the Netherlands. McBeath described the assignment: "… we got a signal to leave our convoy and go to the northern part of Holland to pick up some Dutch generals and their staffs who had been cut off by the German breakthrough. We picked them up and took them down to another point further down where a small Dutch vessel, took them off our hands." They were taken to Dunkirk, and *Venomous* returned to Dover at 1740.

There was to be little respite. Late that evening, while *Venomous* was alongside her sister *Verity* at the Eastern Arm of Dover Harbour, McBeath received orders to embark one hundred Royal Marines, take them across the Channel and disembark them at the Hook of Holland. Compston recalled that they were Reservists, wearing the old fashioned uniform which was standard issue in the Great War. A large quantity of demolitions and stores was also hurriedly embarked, and *Venomous,* together with *Verity's* consignment of Marines and demolitions left harbour just before midnight on the 11th.

At sunrise on the 12 May *Venomous* and *Verity* fell in with *Wild Swan* off the Hook and were met by a pilot boat, which guided McBeath and *Venomous* into the Hook, covered by *Wild Swan.* While lying alongside during the mid-morning watch, the ship's company saw the first bombs dropped and then participated in a spirited defence with its pom-pom guns in which two German planes were shot down in flames. One of these planes came close overhead and the combined gunfire of *Venomous* and the H Class destroyer, HMS *Hyperion* helped in her destruction.

After landing his charges McBeath took his destroyer back out to sea at flank speed at 0815 but while still in the harbour entrance two bombers singled her out. The opportunity to sink a ship in the channel and prevent the use of the port was too much for them to resist.

Disembarking Royal Marines and their stores, Hook of Holland, 12 May 1940. *Venomous* is moored alongside a sister ship and the torpedo tubes of both are clearly visible.
Photographed by Lt Peter Kershaw RNVR.

McBeath reported what happened next: "Three aircraft (Heinkel XI) crossed the ship at about 6000 feet, proceeding north. Aircraft split up and two attacked HMS *Venomous* independently from the Port Quarter. Third aircraft attacked HMS *Verity*."[14] Two salvos of 250 lb bombs were released from a thousand feet and McBeath increased speed and went hard to port as *Venomous* used its close range weapons. McBeath continues his account of the action, "The aircraft machine-gunned the ship whilst retiring. One aircraft circled to deliver a further attack but was kept off by 4.7-inch barrage fire".[15] Fortunately, the bombs fell well astern. AB Knapton remembered this operation:

> "I remember the *Venomous* landing a detachment of Royal Marines at the Hook of Holland which was the same time as Rotterdam was being blitzed. It was during the morning watch and a very bright sun was rising over the land. On leaving we had the sun at our stern. We were attacked by Stukas, which came at us out of the sun. We had a few near misses but suffered no damage. As the Channel was so narrow we had no room to manoeuvre, so the Captain did the only thing open to him – he left harbour at full speed with all guns that could be brought to bear firing in our defence."

AB Sydney Compston added: "We saw our first dog fight at the Hook. Sorry to say two Blenheims shot down by Me-109s." AB Eaton remembered that first day when his destroyer was the target of the Luftwaffe: "Along with *Verity* we took on two hundred Royal Marines and landed them at Hook of Holland with all battle ensigns flying. We met German bombers on the way out but arrived O.K. at Harwich."

Queen Wilhelmina and the Dutch government were evacuated by British destroyers the following day and on the 14 May the troops were withdrawn.

On her return McBeath received new orders to take *Venomous* back to sea and take over the North Goodwin Patrol, a simple line of bearing that ran across the northern reach of the English Channel from the North Goodwin Sands to the coast of France and Belgium.[16] McBeath's mission was to steam along this line and intercept any attempts by the Kriegsmarine to conduct their own patrols, including mining operations, and to render assistance to any vessel in distress.

Whilst on patrol on 14 May *Venomous* met and escorted the Dutch merchant ship SS *Bussum*, which was being towed by the Halcyon Class minesweeper, HMS *Harrier*. The *Bussum* had been bombed and left dead in the water. The crew had taken to the lifeboats and were adrift and in distress. *Venomous* took them in tow to the port of Ramsgate where they were turned over to the guard ship. McGeeney recorded other errands of mercy:

> "The invasion of the Low Countries brought many small boats out into the North Sea with groups of escapees or refugees and we were involved with several from around the Ijmuiden area of Holland. Many were reported to be carrying diamonds from Amsterdam and it was important that the diamonds and the individual families should not fall into enemy hands."

While still on the North Goodwin patrol, AB Knapton remembered another incident involving fleeing refugees:

> "At first light, a boat was sighted coming towards us. Action Stations were sounded and we steamed to intercept. The vessel turned out to be a Dutch lifeboat similar to the type used by the RNLI [Royal National Lifeboat Institute]. The Captain had it brought along the starboard side. As it was filled with women and children we took them on board the *Venomous*. I was put in charge of the lifeboat and another AB and Stoker were sent to join me in the boat.
>
> The Captain called me from the bridge and asked me if I knew where Ramsgate was. I pointed in the general direction of England and said "Yes Sir". The Captain then said "take her there and rejoin the ship at Dover the following day". We arrived at Margate where we had a bit of trouble with identification as we were still flying the Dutch flag. We were then re-directed down the coast to Ramsgate. Again, we took a little time convincing the shore personnel that we were English – not German. As they had us covered with Lewis guns and rifles we were uncomfortable for a while and if our answers to their challenge had not carried credibility we were convinced they would open fire. However, we were well looked after and rejoined our ship the following day."

Venomous continued the North Goodwin Patrol and in the late afternoon of 15 May when she was escorting minesweepers her lookouts sighted a small motorboat and a tug, the *Atjeh*, both flying large Dutch flags. They were making distress signals and McBeath took *Venomous* alongside and took onboard forty-six Jewish refugees plus Cdr Goodenough DSC, RN and his demolition party of fifty that had

Dutch refugees from the tug *Atjeh* and a small motor boat are taken aboard *Venomous*.
Photographed by Lt Peter Kershaw RNVR.

been destroying the dock facilities at Ijmuiden. *Venomous* put back into Dover at 1800, disembarked her passengers, and eventually reached her buoy at just before midnight. She had spent four exhausting days on the North Goodwin Patrol. With her oil fuel down to twenty-five percent she spent the next day in harbour – a well-deserved rest for her crew.

The night of the 17-18 May was spent back on the North Goodwin Patrol. *Venomous* returned to port late in the morning of the 18th and her crew had a brief respite before McBeath took his destroyer out again, just after sunrise on 19 May, to resume her station but, taken completely by surprise, her luck almost ran out. McBeath wrote: "At

1203 on 19 May, a single enemy aircraft came down and let go a stick of bombs at us. The attack was unobserved and the bombs dropped 20 yards astern."

Later that afternoon *Venomous* joined up with another V & W destroyer, HMS *Whitshed,* to escort a bombed merchant ship to the Downs, a body of water off England's Kent coast. Upon arrival McBeath reversed course and headed his destroyer back out to her patrol area. *Venomous* was east of T buoy at 2200 when she was attacked by several mine-laying aircraft. Seeing *Venomous* at speed, trailing a bright wake in the late twilight, the Luftwaffe aircrews must have thought it was better to bomb an enemy ship with their mines instead of leaving it to chance that the enemy would hit one of the deployed mines. The aim of the enemy was improving, for the mines fell just ten feet away exploding on contact with the water. The venerable destroyer shook violently from the explosions but the hull remained intact and her temperamental engineering plant was undamaged – at least for now. AB James Eaton had vivid recollections of the incident: "Whilst on patrol we surprised mine-laying German planes. Had a bit of a fight with them, bombs bursting alongside. Thought we were a goner."

The score was soon evened. At 2325, in almost total darkness, a further mine-laying seaplane came within range and was quickly dispatched, the kill was claimed by young Mid Esson and his forward pom-pom gun crew. The wreckage was sighted the following morning, but there was no time to linger as *Venomous* was being subjected to regular bombing attacks. McBeath deftly manoeuvred his destroyer avoiding numerous bombs dropped by dive-bombing Stuka aircraft. Later that morning McBeath was directed to search for a lifeboat reported drifting in the Channel but it was aborted without success. *Venomous* returned to Dover harbour at 1300 on the 20th, having been relieved by HMS *Malcolm*.

By now the German advance had progressed from the Ardennes to the Atlantic with its left flank splitting the B.E.F. from the main body of the French Army. German panzers were forcing their way towards the channel ports. On 20 May they reached the coast at Abbeville on the Somme, about sixty miles south of Boulogne. Under the skilful command of Vice Admiral Bertram Ramsey, Britain quickly put plans into effect for evacuating the B.E.F.

At 1215 on 21 May, *Venomous* left Dover for Calais with orders to evacuate the ratings and equipment from the loop station at Sangatte. The loop station was a passive land-based anti-submarine detection system that relied on the natural magnetism of a submarine to produce an electric current while the submarine was passing over a series of looped wires lying on the seabed. The individual loop wires could run out several thousand yards from the cable hut located at the station. When a submarine passed over one of the wires it would send a signal to those manning the electronic detection equipment in the hut. If the submarine continued through the loop wire field, the station personnel could determine the approximate direction and speed of the submarine. With the course and speed determined, the station personnel would then send a signal to nearby patrol craft to attack the intruder. The station was similar to those built by the Royal Navy during the Great War and used as part of the defences for naval bases and harbours throughout the empire. The technology was made available to the US Navy when America entered the war.[17]

McBeath told what happened when *Venomous* pulled into Calais:

> "We arrived at 1315 and the STO asked us to take back a number of refugees who were at the railway station. 200 were embarked in addition to the Sangatte people. Whilst we were in Calais six high-level bombing attacks by formations of enemy planes were made on the harbour. About six bombs fell within 25 yards of the ship but luckily there was no damage or casualties."

The refugees, many of them British citizens, had suffered a harrowing time over the previous days and were in even more danger, exposed as they were on the docks, from repeated bombing attacks.

A young Scotsman named John Esslemont, whose father worked at Courtauld's factory at nearby Le Pont-du-Leu, wrote out his story of the day on arrival in England.[18] Upon being told to go to the docks:

> "We cut through the main streets, these being full of refugees and soon reached the Gare Maritime. It was now 1315 and the first thing we saw was all the British people from around Calais on the terreplein Paul Devos. The ship was lying at the quay of the station. It was the *Venomous*. The lock gates to the inner dock were opened so we could not yet reach her.
>
> There was an air raid in progress and those who had got there before us had to go into the trenches. Not long after our arrival we heard the German planes coming over the town, two of them circling half a mile away. Everyone rushed to the

trenches as the planes again came roaring overhead, followed by the crash of bombs on the other side of the Bassin Carnot, a few hundred yards away.

We remained in the shelters because other planes were heard approaching and for the first time whistling bombs hit Calais. The noise was dreadful and deafening and you had the feeling each bomb was coming straight at you.

Then we were left alone for a while. One lock gate was at last closed and we crossed over and safely reached the ship where we found others had been on the quay all the time during the raids. We went on board under the deck in the sailor's room. It was very hot. Everyone sat down round the tables and cups of tea were made available. We had been in a few minutes when Jerry came over again and dropped bombs on the quay and the water all round us. The AA gun of the destroyer was firing shots after the planes. The ship shook as if we were hit, but we were unhurt. People were on the quay as the planes came over and had to throw themselves under railway trucks."

AB Sydney Compston recalled the incident and the brave demeanour of the refugees: "During the air raids there were many women and children on deck, including two or three nuns. Although exposed to the greatest danger they were as good as gold – not a murmur."

Lt Taylor was directed by McBeath to organise the evacuation on the docks. He was responsible for the evacuation of fifty nurses from the Calais Base Hospital and the departure of a few employees of the Courtauld's factory, together with a highly valuable cargo. Mr. W.J. Allitt, Financial Director of the factory took up the story:

> "We had half an hour's advice to catch the destroyer that brought us away from Calais and that time was spent in getting all our platinum together and throwing it into ordinary sack bags. There was no time to count or check – we just ransacked the safes, jet cabins etc. and even the jets from spinning machines.
>
> On arrival at the dock I contacted Lt Taylor, the Officer I/C docks and arrangements were made with the CO of *Venomous* for the transfer on board of four sacks, containing the jets. It was quite a small load for all that money – £1.25 million – the Captain gave me a tin hat and a pistol in exchange."

Engine Room Artificer (ERA) Jim Irlam was ordered to take charge of the four sacks, and when told afterwards of his charge, observed: "This is the only time I have sat on a million and I knew nothing about it!"

The task was completed by 1430. With the gangways run back in, the ship cast off, and left Calais behind with all dispatch. Within the hour the ship was speeding by Dover at a speed approaching 30 knots,

Embarking refugees, including nuns and schoolgirls, at Calais on 21 May 1940.
Photographed by Lt Peter Kershaw RNVR.

before pulling into Folkestone. The reaction of John Esslemont was: "Amazement at finding everything so quiet and to see everybody going about as it was in Calais only a few days before."

Immediately after disembarkation McBeath brought *Venomous* back to Dover where she anchored at 1800 – a difficult and dangerous task safely accomplished.

Only then was it was realised that one of the ship's company was missing – the Able Seaman whose job was that of ship's butcher. Happily, he returned to the ship a few days later. Apparently whilst helping unload to quayside he took shelter during the bombing and when a lull occurred he discovered that the ship had sailed. He found shelter this time in a cellar with plenty of liquid refreshment and when he had recovered from his hangover he found some companions (not from *Venomous*) and together they took an abandoned boat out of harbour and so made their way back across the Channel.

The situation in northern France continued to deteriorate rapidly and by 21 May, Panzer Forces under General von Kleist were advancing virtually unopposed northwards along the Channel coast. That morning found the invading troops a few miles from Boulogne. The B.E.F. now faced the real possibility of being cut off from its only means of retreat and supply – Dunkirk and other French ports on the English Channel.

> "When the German armour broke through to the coast at Abbeville on May the 20th, Boulogne and Calais acquired a new importance for, apart from Dunkirk, they were then the only ports through which the British Army could be supplied."[19]

Late on 21 May the Imperial General Staff made the decision to send reinforcements to both Calais and Boulogne, the aim being to delay the German progress towards Dunkirk for as long as possible. The need to reinforce Boulogne was acute as the British Army had not garrisoned the town and it seemed that there was not much of an organised defence.

The force allocated to Boulogne was the 20th Guards Brigade consisting of the 1st Battalion Welsh Guards, 2nd Battalion Irish Guards and the Brigade Anti-Tank Company together with a Battery of the 69th Anti-Tank Regiment. Although intended as reinforcements there was no defence to reinforce as the French and British forces were out-manoeuvred by the pursuing Germans and were unable to occupy Boulogne. Orders were received at the last minute, the troops being taken on requisitioned civilian buses to board the cross channel steamers at Dover were delayed by massive traffic jams and much essential equipment was left behind. The main body of troops finally left Dover at 0530 on 22 May in the *Biarritz* and *Queen of the Channel,* escorted by *Whitshed* and *Vimiera,* followed shortly afterwards by *City of Christchurch* with *Vimy* and *Wolsey* as escorts.

The second contingent of the brigade did not leave Dover until 1000, and they were embarked in *Mona's Queen. Venomous* was charged with her safe arrival. The crossing itself was relatively

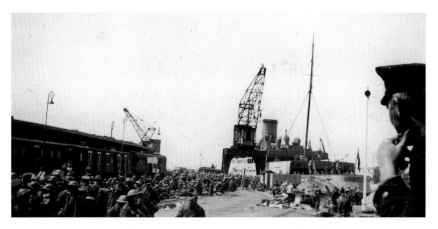

Mona's Queen landing troops at Boulogne, 22 May 1940.
Photographed by Lt Peter Kershaw RNVR.

Troops disembarking at the Gare Maritime at Boulogne, 22 May 1940.
Photographed by Lt Peter Kershaw RNVR.

uneventful, although Boulogne was under constant air attack. Disembarkation proceeded with urgency and without interruption. As with those ships that preceded *Venomous* and *Mona's Queen* into Boulogne, they took on board a full compliment of refugees, stragglers and non-combatants, both French and British, from amongst the milling throng on the quay.

Casting off their respective mooring lines at 1630, *Venomous* escorted *Mona's Queen* back across the Channel, arriving unscathed at Folkestone by 1820. *Venomous* off-loaded her passengers before returning to Dover where she dropped anchor just before 2000. Another strenuous day ended.

Venomous was in serious danger on numerous occasions during the war years, but the next day, 23 May 1940, stood out as the day when her existence hung by a thread. No matter how well the ship was fought, and

Venomous returning from Boulogne with refugees.
Photographed by Lt Peter Kershaw RNVR.

she was fought brilliantly and courageously, her survival on this day was probably due, in the end, to the skill, determination and luck of a young Royal Navy Reserve Sub Lt in a sister ship – HMS *Venetia*.

For *Venomous* that day started unusually late. In fact, she did not leave Dover until 1230, this time with a demolition party under Cdr Swinley RN, which McBeath was directed to take to Calais. CPO McGeeney explained their mission:

> "We were ordered to take a group of Royal Marines and Royal Engineers together with all their stores, explosives and demolition gear to Calais. They were to blow up the locks and docks, cranes and port facilities in general, and make their return as and when, on completion. The quarterdeck and after 4.7-inch gun deck were loaded with explosives and ammunition and many felt one hit would mark the end. The cross Channel dash was made at high speed and in daylight. We entered the port area without incident, in an uneasy quiet, and tied up to a quayside lined with railway trucks. Gangways out, and there were plenty of volunteers to help move everything ashore. Then the bombs started falling from high-flying planes, silhouetted silver in the sun. Some men took refuge under the railway trucks and the Captain, using the bridge megaphone, encouraged those unloading to greater effort – they needed no encouragement."

With the task swiftly accomplished, *Venomous* sped back across the Channel and McBeath had her back in Dover by 1500.

Meanwhile, in Boulogne, the situation was desperate, as the outnumbered, ill-equipped Guardsmen had been forced from their forward defensive positions outside the town and back into the lower portion of Boulogne's port.[20] The French garrison in and adjacent to the surrounding fortifications was also hard pressed, with many of their positions overrun by the assaulting German armour and infantry units. The position was hopeless and the decision was taken to evacuate the troops who had disembarked the previous day. By the time the first British destroyers arrived, surrounding hillsides were in German hands and fighting had spread to the steep, narrow streets of the lower town.

A brief description of Boulogne and its environs gives one an appreciation of what *Venomous* faced:

> "Boulogne lies at the mouth of the River Liane, which winds its way to the sea through a valley in the surrounding hills. The comparatively level ground near the harbour is small in area and congested by building; almost at once the town begins to climb the hill, and the roads up to the old walled town – known as the Haute Ville or 'the Citadel' – are steep. The river and the harbour basins cut the lower town in half..."[21]

Venomous left Dover at 1615 and shortly before sunset joined a French squadron of nine destroyers and five British destroyers, all V & Ws – HMS *Keith, Vimy, Wild Swan, Whitshed* and *Vimiera* – off Boulogne. They had been ordered to engage the German forces north of Boulogne and action was joined to good effect with all of the destroyers engaging enemy armour, artillery and infantry that began to amass on the shore north of the city. The 4.7-inch gun proved to be more than a match

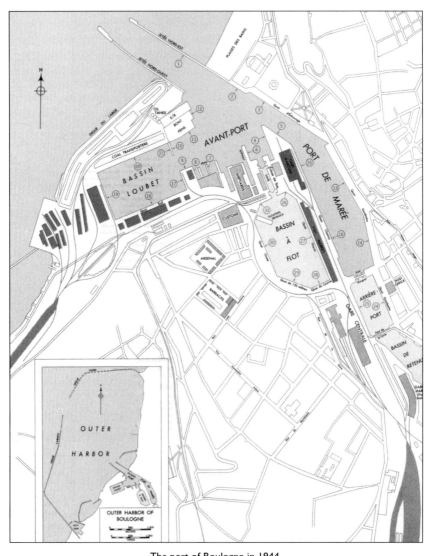

The port of Boulogne in 1944.
United States, Office of Strategic Services, Research and Analysis Branch.
Courtesy of the Lewis Map Library, University of Princeton. Reference MAX G5834.01.001.032.

against German panzers and accompanying artillery.

At 1900 *Keith* and *Vimy* were ordered into Boulogne to commence the evacuation and, almost immediately, the remaining destroyers were subjected to an intense dive-bombing attack by a force of about sixty Junkers 87 Stuka dive-bombers. Approaching at about seven thousand feet, the Stuka opened out and dived to attack, releasing their bombs at around one thousand feet. McGeeney described how the attack

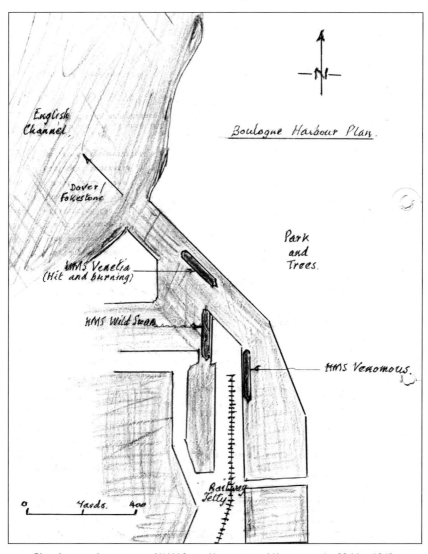

Plan showing the position of *Wild Swan*, *Venomous* and *Venetia* on the 23 May 1940.
Drawn by CPO Hugh McGeeney from his memory of events.
Courtesy of Monica Budden.

"resulted in the blowing up of the French destroyer, *L'Orage*; there was an explosion and the ship vanished and the torpedo boat, *Torpilleur,* was also lost." With all guns firing, at full speed, with McBeath ordering abrupt course changes, *Venomous* avoided the attacks and escaped with minimal damage from splinter hits. McBeath described the attack:

> "Ten attacks were made on *Venomous,* and in each case, salvoes of four 110 lb. bombs were dropped. The ship was closely missed on all sides; the nearest salvoes being only ten yards off and numerous splinters hit the ship's side and upperworks, in some cases penetrating. Mr. Thomson (Gunner T) and three other ratings were superficially wounded during the attack."

By 1915 *Keith* and *Vimy* had completed their embarkation, but they paid a horrific price for their daring with scores of crew members and their passengers killed or wounded. The officers on the open bridge were at great risk. In his book, *HMS Wild Swan*, Peter Smith described what happened:

> "*Keith* and *Vimy* lay alongside the quay and *Mona's Queen* was still loading inside the harbour. Two large formations of dive-bombers appeared over the harbour area and, brushing aside weak fighter patrol, commenced attacks on the town and shipping there. Simultaneously heavy mortar fire was opened on the two berthed destroyers in conjunction with another German assault. Bombs crashed into the quay close alongside the destroyers and shrapnel and splinters sliced through their thin bridge and upperworks plating causing heavy casualties, even though neither ship was actually hit. Cpt D.J.R. Simpson was killed by machine-gun fire on his bridge, and Lt Cdr C.G.W. Donald of the *Vimy* received fatal wounds."[22]

With the death of Cpt Simpson, the senior officer of the flotilla, command fell to the commander of HMS *Whitshed*. Cdr E.R. Conder was determined to continue the evacuation after *Keith*, *Vimy* and *Mona's Queen* had left the harbour. With the RAF providing temporary air cover, he directed HMS *Vimiera* to join his ship, and both quickly entered the harbour, tied up alongside the quay, and loaded hundreds of Guardsmen "without damage to ships or crew".

On leaving safely Conder directed *Venomous*, *Wild Swan* and *Venetia* into the harbour to take on the remaining troops. The position was perilous. German forces were now firmly in control of the high ground around the harbour, from which they were able to direct an accurate fire down on the defenders. *Wild Swan* was first in and berthed alongside the southwest side of the railway jetty. *Venomous* immediately followed and McBeath made an astute tactical decision: "Army officials called me to secure alongside *Wild Swan* but I decided to use the northeast side in order to keep all guns bearing on the left [east] bank." McBeath's decision was to have a decisive effect on subsequent events.

The berthing of *Wild Swan* and *Venomous* had taken place with relatively little reaction, but with the arrival of *Venetia* in the harbour entrance, the German intentions now became clear. *Venetia* was immediately subjected to heavy fire from the coastal batteries recently surrendered by the French, as the attackers used every means possible to sink her there and then, blocking the channel, thus preventing her two sister ships from leaving. The very first salvo struck a serious blow. The forward 4.7-inch gun mounts were disabled and their crews killed or wounded. *Venetia's* bridge received a direct hit, wounding the CO, Lt Cdr B.H. de C Mellor RN, killing the ship's navigator, and severely wounding the remaining bridge personnel.

With the bridge out of action, *Venetia* veered to starboard and ran aground – her engines stopped. Disaster was averted by the prompt gallantry of Sub Lt D.H. Jones RNR, the only uninjured officer left on board. Running forward from his action station with the after 4.7-inch guns, he climbed to the bridge and took over command of his ship. Jones was able to get her under way and, with difficulty, worked her out of the harbour stern first. Had Jones not been successful, there is little doubt that both *Wild Swan* and *Venomous,* and what was left of the 20th Guards Brigade, would have been lost.

By now *Venomous* herself was coming under concentrated fire from enemy forces concealed in the park adjoining the left side of the harbour. German infantry, equipped with machine guns and rifles, commenced firing. The Germans had captured Fort de la Creche on a hill to the north overlooking the town. They quickly manned the fort's artillery and, together with one of their own light field batteries, turned their attention to the two ships in the harbour and the Guardsmen manning the defensive positions within the town.

The decision by McBeath to berth on the northeast side was quickly vindicated as *Venomous* returned fire with all the guns that could be

HMS *Venetia* on fire leaving harbour stern first.
Photographed by Lt Peter Kershaw RNVR.

brought to bear, including members of the ship's company opening fire with their Enfield 303 rifles, Bren and Lewis machine guns. Further targets for her enthusiastic gunners soon appeared in the form of an enemy reconnaissance detachment on motorcycles and in armoured cars, which they observed proceeding down the hill between the houses along the main street. Action fell to Mid Alan Esson and his gunners on the port pom-pom. His first shots blew the side out of the leading car, setting it on fire, and scattering its occupants over the cobblestones. The same fate soon befell the other vehicles. The surviving Germans were picked off by a gallery of riflemen, led by Sub Lt Peter Kershaw and Mid Esson, who directed the fire of the torpedo men and stokers firing Lewis Guns and Enfield 303 rifles.

Action now switched to the former French battery situated in the hilltop fort from which the Germans were shelling the harbour. *Venomous* trained her four 4.7-inch guns on the fort and opened fire with Direct Action Impact Shells. The first salvo was over the target but the second produced a direct hit, blowing away the side of the fort and part of the hill. Pieces of guns and mountings were observed falling down the hillside. Several of the German field guns were shelled and destroyed as they were being placed into position.

AB Ian Nethercott, an anti-aircraft gunner (pom-pom) on HMS *Keith*, watched *Venomous'* 4.7-inch guns in action:

> "Nethercott watched as HMS *Venomous* fired her main 4.7-inch guns directly at a row of large houses and brought the walls of two hotels down on top of a German tank. Another tank took a direct hit from a naval shell and flipped over backwards. Yes a destroyer could be a pretty useful anti-tank weapon Nethercott thought."[23]

During this frantic action close to one thousand Guardsmen were sheltering on the quay from the heavy exchange of fire. Their predicament was described in the Irish Guard's Regimental Diaries:

> "The Battalion moved down to the quayside in sections and the bulk of it sheltered on the lower level of the quay on the inner (southern) side. The noise of the explosions above them and of the ship's guns below them deafened the Guardsmen. Straight in front of them they could see the tanks on the opposite quay."

The Welsh Guard's *War Diary* describes the situation from the vantage point of the survivors from its 2nd Battalion:

> "The French guns were firing at the Destroyers and the quay. Three French tanks had come down on the high ground just north of the quay and were also firing. Both Destroyers fired back with rapid fire from the 4.7s. The noise was very great and the situation a trying one. The men on the quay were absolutely steady and the embarkation took place without haste or confusion. The guns on the French fort were silenced and the naval 4.7 appeared to be the finest anti-tank weapon yet invented."[24]

The embarkation was not without its difficulties as, inevitably, the organised troops were preceded by the usual collection of undisciplined men seeking first place in the queue. McBeath described what happened:

> "The troops being unused to the noise of naval gunfire were difficult to handle and most of those who jumped on board the starboard side of the flag deck caused a temporary jam there. The Navigating Officer Sub Lt Vaughan-Lewis RN took charge of the flag deck and organised the troops so they were kept streaming down to the main deck."

Attention returned to the hillside where a column of some seventy German troops was observed advancing down a narrow wall-flanked pathway. Mid Esson, with AB Roy Stallard as his gunner, again swung the portside pom-pom gun into action, blowing down the wall and several houses on top of the luckless enemy.

HMS *Venomous* is firing its guns in the background of this painting.
Brigadier Fox-Pitt (centre) is checking troops across the Pont Marguet swing bridge with
Lt Colonel Stanier on his right and Major Jones-Mortimer on his left.
Courtesy of Welsh Guards Regiment

There was still no time to draw breath. An incendiary shell from a
light field gun pitched just short of *Venomous'* abreast "B" gun. An alert
Signalman, O.G. Mayland, had spotted the flash and reported that the
shell had come from the right of the fort in the garden of a house.
Venomous' guns immediately shifted to that point and the first salvo
blew down all the trees in the garden and set fire to the house beyond.
Those German gunners able to evacuate did so with utmost speed.

This proved to be the last major effort by the German forces and no
further large calibre gunfire was directed at the quay or at the two
destroyers. The gunners in *Venomous* had performed with skill and
courage, none more so than AB Roy Stallard, a Welshman from Llanelli,
whose initiative and the example he set to others had already been
recognised. AB James Eaton remembered Stallard's action as well as
those of many of his fellow sailors firing away with their rifles:

> "We entered Boulogne harbour *Wild Swan* first, *Venomous* second.
> We came under fire from gunmen, tanks and others. We opened fire
> with our 4.7s of which we had four and we on the 'Bandstand' fired
> 303 rifles. We only had one pom-pom, which was operational the
> other one had jammed. I will always remember AB 'Taff' Stallard on
> the good pom-pom. He received the DSM for that."

Whilst *Venomous* had much to thank her gunners for, the tide had also
played its part, as CPO McGeeney noted:

"We entered Boulogne harbour and began by turning our two-Pdr pom-pom guns onto the trees on our left to flush out any snipers. We were being fired on both from houses and tanks but the tide was well out and with the big drop from high water to low tide we sat well down in mid Channel and most enemy fire could not depress far enough to do any real damage. We, on the other hand, were able to fire both our forward 4.7-inch guns continuously to good effect."

It is appropriate to draw attention to the efforts of Sub Lt Walter Wells. On coming alongside the quay, McBeath had ordered the ship to be secured by a single spring wire forward from the bow. Wells dealt with the passing ashore, handling and securing of this wire. He remained on the exposed fo'c'sle throughout the battle, monitoring the strain on the cable and awaiting further orders from his CO, while McBeath gave continuous engine orders, using the ship's twin propellers and her rudder to counteract the strong ebb current flowing out to sea and the recoil from her 4.7-inch guns. Together, Wells and McBeath were able to keep *Venomous* alongside the quay wall, thus enabling hundreds of Guardsmen to climb over to her upper decks and down on to her main deck.

The troops were from the 2nd Battalion Irish Guards with elements of the 1st Battalion Welsh Guards. Lt Colonel Sir Alexander Stanier, the commanding officer of the 1st Battalion Welsh Guards, who embarked on *Venomous* with his men, was dismayed to find that many were left behind when mistakenly told by an army officer that the last destroyer had left.[25]

When McBeath gave the order to cast off at 2115 *Venomous* had been alongside for just 35 minutes. There was still one last problem to be overcome. As she went astern out of the harbour at 18 knots, the rudder jammed at "hard-a-starboard." McBeath quickly grasped the situation and by judicious use of the ship's two engines – ordering their respective engine telegraphs to either alter their speeds (rpm) or ordering one or the other forward or astern – *Venomous* continued to steam backwards through the very narrow channel.

It must have been an incredible sight to see this venerable destroyer, packed with five hundred guardsmen, many of them joining their hosts in firing their rifles and automatic weapons at the besieging Germans methodically closing in on the hundreds of guardsmen still holding on to their last piece of France. It was also a tragic scene as the men left behind

Burning truck on the quayside photographed from *Venomous* as it leaves Boulogne.
Photographed by Lt Peter Kershaw RNVR.

fought on, hoping another destroyer would return for them, or sought a way through the tightening German cordon round the harbour.

After *Venomous* had left the exhausted Germans withdrew to the perimeters of the town to rest and at 2300, when all hope seemed to have gone, HMS *Windsor* entered the harbour "with little interference from the Germans" to take off the naval demolition parties and six hundred men of the Welsh Guards. Finally, at 0140 HMS *Vimiera* entered and took on 1,400 men in just under an hour and slipped away without a shot being fired.

McBeath's masterful handling brought his destroyer out of the narrow harbour entrance and into the English Channel where he swung *Venomous'* head around and steamed back to England. A few miles from the French coast, *Venomous* caught up with the damaged *Venetia*, which was making slow progress with her forward guns and bridge wrecked and the dead and wounded strewn about her decks. She suffered twenty killed, one died of wounds, ten seriously injured (including the captain) and ten slightly wounded.[26] All those on *Venomous* must have counted themselves very lucky indeed to have escaped with only two men slightly wounded from the dive-bombing attacks. McBeath continued to steam *Venomous* alongside her wounded sister until *Wild Swan* came up astern to take over the escort duty. *Wild Swan* had also picked up several hundred Guardsmen and cleared the quay safely. Dangerously overloaded and with a jammed rudder, McBeath

Boulogne photographed from *Venomous* as it leaves the harbour.
Photographed by Lt Peter Kershaw RNVR.

couldn't linger to accompany *Venetia* on her agonisingly slow passage across the Channel. McBeath increased speed and headed for Folkestone, arriving at 2315, to disembark the evacuated troops.

McBeath then took his ship back to its homeport of Devonport for repairs to holes in the hull, some at the water line, and damage to the anti-submarine dome on the bottom of the hull. *Venomous* arrived in the dockyard on the 25 May and many of the ship's company were able to spend a few days leave with their families living nearby. Apart from the shell holes and the malfunctioning rudder, damage to the ship had been superficial. Part of the foremast had been shot away, the radio was out of action and the marks of rifle and machine gun bullets were everywhere but, amazingly, there were no serious casualties. The ship's reputation was established as McGeeney noted when he said:

> "This latest action had been fast and furious. Everyone recognised that, although by now we had an experienced crew and our new Captain had distinguished himself in action, we had been extremely lucky to survive and succeed."

McBeath recognised their good fortune in his report of 26 May when he singled out the following officers and men for special recognition:

> "Whilst the behaviour under fire of all my Officers and ship's company was exemplary, I particularly wish to bring to your notice the following Officers and men:

Lt A.A. MACKENZIE R.N.R. – the first Lt and G.C.O. who by his keen appreciation of the situation and accurate placing and control of the ship's gunnery armament under heavy fire, undoubtedly made possible the entire embarkations by both ships. It is also considered that the wholesale destruction of German field guns etc. was the main reason for the comparatively unopposed entry of subsequent ships.

Acting Gunner (T) THOMPSON R.N. – who although wounded in the bombing attack took charge of the after part of the ship whilst alongside, organising the supply parties and encouraging the Guns' crews. He was also responsible for controlling the after anti-sniper rifle party organised for the tubes' crews.

Midshipman ESSON R.N.R. – I particularly wish to emphasise the magnificent conduct of this young Officer. His courageous behaviour under heavy fire was an inspiration, not only to his pom-pom crews, but to all who saw him. His quick decisions and selections of targets were entirely responsible for the prevention of the German close range weapons being used effectively. Between giving orders to direct and control his guns, he was using a rifle to good effect against snipers in nearby cranes and houses.

Sub-Lt W.R. WELLS R.N. – This Officer courageously worked alone on the forepart of the F.X. under heavy fire and it was entirely through his efforts that the bows of the ship were secured alongside. He passed and secured the bow wire single-handed and his conduct in the most exposed position in the ship was outstanding.

Petty Officer M.J. O'SULLIVAN D/JX 132003 – for the cool and deliberate manner in which he performed his duties during both the dive-bombing barrage fire and the subsequent bombardment and destruction of enemy land forces. This Petty Officer normally performs his duties in an exceptional manner and his bearing in action, under heavy fire, was an inspiration to his director's crew and all who saw him. I particularly wish to bring this rating's conduct to your notice.

A.B. W. KNAPTON D/JX 151137 and A.B. J.G. HENDERSON D/JX 149499 – both these very young ratings performed their duties throughout the action in a manner which is deserving of the highest praise.

Signalman O.G. MAYLAND D/J 31638 – who kept the control informed of the positions of enemy field guns by observation of gun flash in an extremely able and efficient manner.

Ordnance Artificer H.H. MCGEENEY D/MX 47358 – quickly

rectified an electrical failure at "A" gun and after No. 5 of "B" guns crew had been wounded by shrapnel he efficiently performed the duties of that number – although he is a torpedoman.

A.B. E.R. STALLARD D/JX 142935 – gunlayer of the port pom-pom for extreme coolness and efficiency under heavy fire. This rating's handling of his gun was mainly responsible for the collapse of the enemy's close range opposition in Boulogne harbour. His bearing and manner during the air attack was exemplary. I strongly commend the conduct of this rating.

A.B. J. EDWARDS HD/X 2534 – port pom-pom loading number who efficiently performed loading duties at both guns after his opposite number had been incapacitated.

A.B. W.H. NICKLESS D/J 100855 – for coolness and efficiency in performing his duty as Telegraphsman during the action in harbour. He formed a link between the Commanding Officer and wheel to pass telegraph orders when the noise of action and embarking military prevented voice pipe orders being clearly heard."

Praise for *Venomous* was recorded in the Irish Guard's War Diary: "The Battalion was filled with a boundless admiration for the sailors manning their guns on the open decks. Their gunnery was splendidly effective." The Welsh Guards War Diary also mentioned that day: "The Navy had pulled the Brigade out of a very difficult situation and made possible an evacuation under most adverse conditions. Their skill and courage were a source of inspiration and the Brigade would never forget the part they played."[27]

A letter of appreciation received by Vice Admiral Ramsay from the Colonel, commanding the 2nd Battalion Irish Guards, was forwarded to McBeath and his fellow destroyer captains. It provided a fitting conclusion to this epic action:

"From: The Flag Officer Commanding Dover.
Date: 8th June 1940. No. G.1/3487/40
To: Commanding Officer, HMS *Venomous*.

The following letter from the Colonel commanding the 2nd Battalion Irish Guards is promulgated for the information of officers and ship's companies.

'Once again, within the space of a few days, I am writing to you on behalf of the Battalion to thank you and your Destroyers for all you did for us at Boulogne.

As you well know, the situation was really far more difficult and critical than it had been at the Hook and we are all of us agreed that those of us who saw the actions fought by the Destroyers whilst we were waiting to embark and whilst we were actually embarking at Boulogne are very unlikely ever to see anything more inspiring, gallant or magnificent.

We all felt that the Destroyers would have been completely justified in leaving the harbour and returning for us after dark. Had they done, so we should not have had the very smallest complaint for we should have well understood and appreciated the position they were in.

However, never for one second did there appear to be a thought of such a move, and the ships continued to embark wounded and unwounded and to continue their fight with the shore batteries as if the whole affair was perfectly normal and humdrum.

I cannot tell you the depth of the impression which has been made upon us all but I can assure you that there is no doubt of it and that the whole Battalion is filled with an affection and admiration for the sailors who have on two occasions done so much for them.

I wish you could sense the feeling that exists here. I believe it would make you more proud than ever of the men and the ships that you command.

Would it be possible to let the Captains and crews know how clearly we realise the dangers they ran for us, and how clearly we realise too that it is due to their courage and conduct that we are here now.'

B.H. Ramsay,
Vice Admiral"

The next week would hold fresh dangers for *Venomous* and her crew, and their actions would contribute to the success of Operation *Dynamo* and what historians have called "The Miracle of Dunkirk." The evacuation of the troops had begun on 27 May and the inner and outer harbours were soon partly blocked by ships sunk by German planes. Two of the steam ferries which had taken the Welsh and Irish Guards to Boulogne were sunk. The Dover ferry, *Queen of the Channel*, was bombed and sank on the 28 May and the next day *Mona's Queen*, the Isle of Man Steam Packet Company's ferry, hit a mine outside Dunkirk and sunk within two minutes with great loss of life amongst the Manx crew. Between 31 May and 4 June when the evacuation ended *Venomous* was to make five trips to the outside mole and the nearby beaches.

Desperate times aboard HMS *Venomous* under Lt Cdr J.E.H. McBeath DSO RN

Lt Angus "Bloody" MacKenzie & Lt Cdr John McBeath

Warrant Engineer A.E. Parkes RN

AB Roy Stallard DSM

Lt Peter Kershaw RNVR

AB Sydney Compston

CPO Hugh McGeeney DSM

Mr R.K. Thompson (left) & Sub Lt A.F. Esson RNR

Venomous left Plymouth at 1200 on 30 May for Dover, where she arrived shortly before sunset at 2100. Within four hours McBeath received orders to proceed to Dunkirk, leaving harbour in company with her sister ship HMS *Whitehall* just after midnight on 31 May. McBeath's instructions on this first morning were to head for the beaches of Bray Dunes, near the border of France and Belgium east of Dunkirk. Both destroyers arrived just before daylight, and with the morning light the difficulties of evacuating the waiting troops became immediately obvious: there was no provision for the transfer of men to the waiting ships. In an effort to overcome the deficiency, *Venomous* launched both her motorboat and whaler, but by 0515 there were still only forty-five soldiers on board.

McBeath was now ordered to take *Venomous* berth alongside the Mole at the entrance to Dunkirk. He discussed the problem of berthing alongside the Mole with "Bloodie Mackenzie", his outspoken No 1, who amused the ship's company by saying "there is only one way you would ever get alongside, and that is to go straight through the *** jetty and come out the other side." In more restrained language McBeath described the problem and the approach he adopted:

> "... part of the embarkation had to be eventually done from the mole, that was really a sort of skeleton concrete breakwater which stuck out on the north side of the harbour entrance and it was never intended for ships to berth alongside and if there was a strong tide running as there frequently was, it tended to make it difficult to secure alongside, you had to nose out and then stick wires and ropes through parts of the concrete and secure yourself and of course the

HMS *Malcolm* approaching the entrance to Dunkirk.
Photographed by Lt Peter Kershaw RNVR.

easiest way to go alongside was with a bit of a bump to make sure
you got there and you often got a large chunk of concrete weighing
two or three hundred weight arriving on your deck."[28]

Once the destroyer was secured alongside the breakwater, she began to
receive on board a full complement of troops.

Many of them had been on the move continuously for three weeks,
and their description by one officer as being "really beaten up" was
hardly surprising. Private D.J.W. Marr remembered well that day:

> "My first sight of her was at the end of a jetty, and she was a welcome
> sight, as I and my pals had been on the beaches for four days. As we
> reached her, the AA guns she carried were firing at Jerry aircraft.
> Most of the soldiers were sliding down poles to her deck. I thought
> this was a little bit dangerous so I threw my rifle to a crewmember
> and jumped, as she came close, the 20 odd feet to her deck. The
> thought in my mind was that if I break my legs at least I am safe.
>
> After finding a place to sit down on two deck, I was given a
> mug of tea and was happy to sit there for the journey to Dover. It
> took about two hours and they did fire at Jerry on the way, but
> other than that, it was uneventful. It was Friday 31 May. I always
> had a soft spot for *Venomous* after that."

Private Marr's apprehension about boarding *Venomous* was well
founded. Shortly after Marr's experience, PO Dagley, who was manning
Venomous' railing to help bring on board the soldiers, remembered
with considerable sadness, how he tried to help a British soldier trying
to come on board with his full kit. "I tried to haul a soldier onto the deck
but the poor man slipped down between the ship's side and the jetty

HMS *Basilisk* alongside the Mole at Dunkirk on the 31 May. HMS *Basilisk* was bombed and sank
off La Panne the following day.
Photographed by Lt Peter Kershaw RNVR.

Troops boarding HMS *Vanquisher*, a sister ship of *Venomous*, at the Mole.
IWM Image Reference HU 1153. Courtesy of the Imperial War Museum.

and couldn't be recovered."

A quick turn round in Dover and *Venomous* headed back to the beaches at Bray Dunes. McBeath described how "... we very often used to tow them [the small boats] three or four at a time and then they'd slip their tow when they got nearer." They were back at Bray Dunes by 1300, where the afternoon and first dogwatch were spent getting troops aboard and dodging bomb attacks. McBeath said, "we never got closer to the beach than a couple of hundred yards at the most, because being a destroyer one drew more water than the mine sweepers and the small craft that were going in." He also described how the soldiers approached the water from the beach: "… the troops came down in a sort of 'V' shape to a crocodile semi-single file as they got near the water's edge…"

There was obvious concern for the ship's safety. Kershaw remembered, "The worst job was to pick up rowing boats from the sand dunes. They only came at intervals and we could in the meantime be bombed." Wells was frustrated with both the method of recovery and the antiquated equipment of his ship: "Troops arrived only in half dozens from the ship's whaler or the motorboat fitted with a 1903 engine which rarely worked." Some help was available. The 51-ton yacht *Gala*, commanded by Sub Lt J.A. Dow RNVR, towed boats laden with troops from the beaches to *Venomous* and HMS *Vivacious*.[29]

CPO McGeeney gave an extraordinarily concise and vivid depiction of what he saw that afternoon:

> "We arrived in daylight and moved fairly slowly up and down parallel to the beach. To the west, fuel oil tanks were on fire and dense black smoke dispersed as it drifted across the scene. We saw occasional snatches of dogfights by our own and enemy fighters in breaks between the clouds. Also groups of soldiers formed in queues on the beach but not in any great numbers that first day."

McBeath described how although "the army were very tired … they certainly had their tails right up … 90% of them left with weapons …" and "many of the army helped us, they volunteered to go in some of our boats when we were anchored off shore going in and getting them off the beaches. We had several sergeants and they would go and sort of speak pongo language to the other soldiers and help our embarkation …"

Because of the air attacks the ship was frequently on the move and while on this occasion transport from the beaches was more effective, only two hundred troops had been taken on board before *Venomous* received orders to return to Dover. McBeath found the small boats were unwilling to give up their troops to *Venomous*:

> "One quite often offered to take their crews of soldiers off them so that they could go back for another load and they said no fear we've got our twelve pongos and we're going back to England with them, you go and get your own."

As *Venomous* turned for home yet another fierce air attack developed and it was now that she won her second confirmed anti-aircraft success of the war. It was a spectacular one at that, with the enemy aircraft

HMS *Venomous* off the beaches at Dunkirk with small boat alongside.
From the collection of Cdr R. Bill RN, the CO of the minesweepers off Dunkirk.
IWM Image Reference HU 56091. Courtesy of the Imperial War Museum.

being brought down by a direct hit from a 4.7-inch shell. With this final flourish to the day McBeath returned *Venomous* to Dover with just eight rounds of H.E. ammunition for her 4.7-inch guns.

McBeath described how a few of the exhausted troops made a return trip:

> "We had several cases where when people had got on board they went to sleep in some out of the way place. We'd arrive back in England discharge everybody and then [on returning to Dunkirk] you'd find a soldier suddenly reappear and ask where are we … you see he'd made a trip back to the continent again without knowing it."

Thus the day ended for *Venomous* and her crew. Admiral Ramsey's report of 31 May gave a concise, matter-of-fact assessment:

> "Operation Dynamo was pressed on with all energy and by noon/31st approximately 164,000 men (including 14,000 Allied troops) had been landed in England. The day was a repetition of previous days in almost every respect, except that it was thought that the night would see the conclusion of the operation, and plans were made accordingly for the greatest possible number of ships to be available for the last trip…it was decided that it would be possible to continue the evacuation for another 24 hours."[30]

The all-out effort of 1 June was met by an equally determined German aerial blitz of Stuka dive-bombers flying in beautifully clear and sunny weather. The first attacks claimed the B Class destroyer HMS *Basilisk* and her sister ship, HMS *Keith*. *Basilisk* lost over 100 men, whilst

Keith lost 36 men. The Halcyon Class minesweeper HMS *Skipjack* was also lost to air attack, together with most of her crew and all of the 275 soldiers she had rescued. Her sister ship, the minesweeper HMS *Salamander,* was damaged and the Admiralty tug *St Abbs* disappeared with a huge flash when it received a direct hit from a dive-bombing Stuka. This little tug had just taken on board 100 survivors from *Keith* – there were very few survivors.

The attacks continued with the loss of the new H Class destroyer, HMS *Havant*, whilst another H Class destroyer, HMS *Ivanhoe* and *Venomous'* sister ship, *Vivacious* were both badly shot up. The newly completed Dragonfly Class river gunboat, HMS *Mosquito* was also hit and set afire and eventually sank before noon with heavy loss of life.

The forenoon of 1 June found *Venomous* still berthed in Dover replenishing her depleted stocks of ammunition. She had missed the morning's carnage but at 1200 McBeath set out once again for Dunkirk. On her way across the Channel *Venomous* passed the crippled destroyer HMS *Ivanhoe* being towed, and McBeath and his men saw in the distance the second wave of dive-bombing attacks. These sights must have made them wonder whether their luck would hold but as McBeath steered *Venomous* onto her final approach into Dunkirk, a signal was received from Ramsay's headquarters ordering all destroyers home. McBeath immediately reversed course and *Venomous* was back in harbour at 1600.

The scale of the damage to the destroyers operating to and from Dunkirk in daylight hours justified the decision to concentrate evacuation on the hours of darkness. McBeath echoed his men's thoughts when he recorded: "I think everyone was thankful that we were no longer required to evacuate troops by day."

Although the continuous air attacks had proved costly to the destroyers, the ships fought back gallantly, frequently with a collection of weapons acquired from their temporary guests. Lt Kershaw remembered:

> "We were subject to a good deal of air attack in our trips to Dunkirk. Although our 4.7 guns were not able to elevate high enough for aircraft, we did get one direct hit. Many of us had our own machine guns, Bren guns etc., which we had taken off the Army after the evacuation of Boulogne and Calais and we had plenty of ammunition. It was a great relief to be able to fire back but in due course we were asked to return them."

At 1900, after a short break, McBeath took *Venomous* out on her first night run to France. This time the destroyer was carrying a party of ten Royal Navy officers and ninety ratings sent out in an effort to organise and speed up the evacuation of troops from the beaches and the port of Dunkirk. The senior officer was Cpt Renfrew Gotto RN, who was renewing his acquaintance with *Venomous*, having last served on board her as a Midshipman twenty years earlier on the frigid waters of the Baltic. Off the beaches, one officer and six ratings were sent ashore from the whaler and the ship then moved into Dunkirk. Whilst off the beaches she came under artillery fire, with shells falling within 30 yards of the ship, but had picked up no troops.

By 0215 on 2 June McBeath had berthed his destroyer alongside the Mole at the entrance to Dunkirk and immediately the ship's company began taking men on board. Captain R. Lockerby of the Second Ordnance Field Park remembered: "I was brought back from Dunkirk in *Venomous* on lst/2nd June. We embarked by sliding down on swaying poles. If you lost your footing you were crushed between the boat and the jetty." PO Dagley was on deck assisting with the boarding: "We continued to haul people over the gap until we almost collapsed. Everyone but everyone served so hard to save our lads." Kershaw also took part in this evacuation:

> "It was my job to climb on the jetty and push the soldiers on board. It was a 6-8 foot drop and they were very tired. We of course did not wish to stay any longer than we had to. For some reason we had quite a bit of grapeshot fired which we heard go whistling by."

With a full load of troops aboard McBeath cast his destroyer off from the mole and slowly manoeuvred *Venomous* out of the wreck-strewn harbour, and brought the old destroyer up to speed. As she approached the North Goodwin Light she was spotted by an enemy seaplane and strafed by its machine guns but, fortunately, no one on the crowded decks were hit. Without further incident, McBeath brought *Venomous* into Dover's harbour with hundreds of exhausted soldiers around sunrise that morning.

Venomous spent the day in the safety of Dover Harbour giving those on board a chance to get a few hours sleep between taking on stores, storing ammunition and eating a hot meal. At 1900 on 2 June, McBeath took *Venomous* out again and headed once more for Dunkirk, which she reached just before 2200. However, she had to take her turn to berth as McBeath described:

> "They decided latterly only to do night operations … and one used to sail just before dark from Dover or some port on the English coast and a whole heap of ships would go in and they would sit off Dunkirk in a big sort of crescent shaped formation waiting to go in. There was no particular order in the race to get in … if you saw a hole that somebody had just come out of you'd rush your way in and I being a particularly junior officer, of course, was liable to be left right out to the end and so many times we resorted to little tricks by making a signal saying, make way, we've got Rear Admiral Dover or Captain (D) aboard and quite often it worked and we'd get in get our load and get out again. The idea was not to be the tail end Charlie of the party because that meant you more or less came back in daylight and perhaps get a bit of a dusting on your way back."

Once again she tied up alongside the Mole, and immediately began taking on board members of the Green Howards, one of the British Army's famous light infantry regiments. Corporal Douglas King was one of eleven remaining members of 5th Battalion's D Company.[31] They were all members of the Territorial Army, called up immediately after the declaration of war, and sent to France as part of the BEF. They had left a crack French infantry unit they had been fighting alongside and marched through the previous night along the beach from Bray Dunes, under constant fire from German aircraft, only to find the last destroyer had left. The 4th and 5th Battalions of the Green Howards, plus a few stragglers from other units, assembled around their standard on the beach and spent 2 June awaiting nightfall and the arrival of the destroyers at the Mole. A Hurricane flew low over the beach and dropped a handwritten message, "Good luck, we can do no more". Sergeant L. F. Warn described how the officers ashore "organised a bayonet cordon to police the embarkation that evening and avoid the chaos of the previous night" when panic stricken French conscripts who had abandoned their weapons struggled to board the waiting destroyer. Sergeant Warn was "one of a hundred ranks and four officers controlling embarkation."[32] When *Venomous* arrived Colonel W. E. Bush led his men along the Mole to the waiting destroyer.

McBeath had orders not to take back more than nine hundred men but it was difficult to keep track of numbers and in thirty minutes two depleted battalions of over fourteen hundred men were embarked, a remarkable achievement given the darkness, potential confusion and damage done to the Mole from German aerial bombing and artillery fire. CPO McGeeney remarked that:

> "Organisation of a high order in the larger vessels was required in addition to much ad hoc work by small ships of every description. A good deal of control was also required ashore in marshalling the troops and ensuring they were at embarkation points in large numbers during the hours of darkness."

Kershaw, who was once again on the Mole, explained that, "It was my job to count the troops and on this occasion we had over 1,300 of them. Counting was difficult and you could do better when they walked onto the jetty at Dover." From his position on *Venomous*, McGeeney observed what had become a sort of routine for his ship:

> "There was a long narrow jetty running out from the western end of the beach. Gaps existed as a result of bombing or gunfire but temporary repairs having been carried out. Destroyers and other vessels of similar size could secure alongside. Ships were secured in succession and doubled up when necessary. Once the routine was established, one trip was very much like another but refinements were made.

Sergeant Warn and the others on the cordon had been told that they must expect to be left behind and become prisoners of war but he described how the cordon:

> "worked so well that, just after midnight, we were told that all troops had passed through the cordon onto the Mole, and had been picked up by the naval boats waiting in the dark. We were told there was also a chance that we could get away and we should proceed to the Mole at once as there was a destroyer ready to pick us up. The Mole itself had been badly damaged which made getting a hundred men along it quickly and in the dark a very daunting task. I remember seeing the shadowy shape of the destroyer at the side of the Mole and thinking 'Thank God I've made it.'
> However, there was no time to think as two crew members took charge of me and one said 'Now Jump!' I jumped. It was dark and seemed so very unreal as the deck seemed to come up to meet me. Then another crewmember told me to put my rifle on a pile of others, and led me down to a mess deck. I did not know it at the time, but I was on board HMS *Venomous*. Members of the crew came round with pails of water, which was very welcome as

> we had not shaved, washed or even eaten for several days. I could
> hear the engines and gunfire, and feel the motion of the ship, but
> I had no idea whether we were at sea or still at Dunkirk."

Towards the close of the thirty minutes alongside, a voice from the
jetty addressed McBeath, asking him if he was able to accommodate
some senior officers and staffs. Having checked the beaches for
stragglers, General Harold Alexander, commander of the First
Infantry Division, together with General Arthur Percival, and their
staffs were finally leaving France. Not aware of the identity of his
potential guests, McBeath told them to come aboard starboard side
aft. "We've got a couple of Generals, Alexander and Percival aboard
now," reported Lt Angus Mackenzie and added, "I have put them with
a few aides in your cabin but I am afraid one of the Colonels has
hopped into bed with his spurs on."

Afterwards Kershaw was faced with reporting to his Captain the
bad news that his eiderdown had been ripped apart by the offending
spurs. In fact, the officer was General Alexander himself as Kershaw
relates: "I was told there was a high ranking officer in the Captain's
cabin. I found an officer lying on the bed, booted with spurs, which had
made a hole in the counterpane. It was General Alexander and he was
very friendly." General Alexander was invited to join McBeath on the
bridge where he was seen by Sydney Compston on "B" Gun.

Having passed the daylight hours of the 3rd back in harbour,
McBeath set *Venomous* on her final sortie toward Dunkirk at 2030.
Upon arrival outside the harbour it became apparent that the
organisation of the port had finally broken down. It was some three
hours before she was finally able to pull alongside the Mole shortly
before 0200 on 4 June. It was during this time that she sustained her
only significant damage, being rammed by a tug in the harbour
entrance. The collision resulted in a deep dent in her port side,
breaking the steam pipe casting to the port dynamo. Enveloped in
steam, her stokers were able to affect temporary repairs to the
ruptured steam pipe.

Once alongside, *Venomous* took on board, with considerable
difficulty, hundreds of French troops. McGeeney remembered:

> "On our last night we embarked a good number of French
> soldiers who had been guarding the perimeter or part of it, and

thus ensuring the success of the evacuation. Many appeared
with Michelin inner tyres inflated around their shoulders and
waists. Our gangways and ladders were narrow and negotiating
them, dressed as they were, was virtually impossible. The
frustrations and the language difficulties were evident. A few
blows were struck."

Parkes recalled, "I remember most of the French crowding the upper
deck seeming to refresh themselves with perfume after sleeping
wherever they could find a space."

Venomous bade farewell to Dunkirk for the last time at 0235 with
1,100 French troops on board. Their insistence upon staying on the
upper deck created one final hiccup. As AB Compston explained:
"There were so many troops on board that we had to stop and trim ship
as we were in danger of overturning." One of the French soldiers
offered him a swig from his water flask which he accepted and found to
his surprise it contained a rough red wine, the first time this young
seaman had ever drank wine. One could not blame these French
soldiers for wanting to stay on the upper deck for if *Venomous* was
bombed and sunk those below would have little chance of escape.
McBeath ordered Compston and his fellow sailors to forcefully send
many of the Frenchmen below decks. There was considerable knocking
about between Englishmen and Frenchmen before order was restored
and McBeath felt comfortable enough with his ship's trim to order the
engine room to resume full speed ahead.

Arriving back in Dover at 0610, the French soldiers disembarked,
and the crew set about repairing the damage. Even this had its
advantages, as McGeeney recalled: "The damage was sufficient to
support a plausible story that a cask of rum was split in the spirit room.
The Cox'n persuaded the Captain that he could 'splice the mainbrace'
and issue an extra tot all round by writing it off. 'Up spirits' was
therefore piped again." Sydney Compston remembers that they were all
totally exhausted by the end of the week.

And so *Venomous* survived a hazardous operation, which had cost
some nine destroyers with many more damaged and requiring
extensive repairs. "Out of the thirty-eight British destroyers involved in
'Operation *Dynamo*' sixteen were 'V & Ws' or old leaders. One was
sunk and six damaged."[33] In his book about the V & W Class destroyers,
Anthony Preston paid tribute to *Venomous*, her sisters, and the men

Alongside the Mole on the last night.
Photographed by Lt Peter Kershaw RNVR.

Evacuating French troops from Dunkirk on the last night.
Photographed by Lt Peter Kershaw RNVR.

Distant view of Dunkirk skyline.
Photographed by Lt Peter Kershaw RNVR.

Giant plume of smoke from exploding oil tanks as *Venomous* leaves Dunkirk for the last time.
Photographed by Lt Peter Kershaw RNVR.

who manned them during this critical period:

> "There is something appropriate in the way that the old destroyers gave of their utmost in the hour of crisis. Having missed the opportunity of distinguishing themselves in a previous war, they more than made up for this by their efforts in 1940, like veterans recalled to the colours. The 'V & W' destroyers can count Dunkirk as their finest hour; for all their work in the Battle of the Atlantic, nothing can compare with their labours in May and June 1940. In nine days they did more fighting and steaming than they had throughout their lives, and their aged hulls were equal to the challenge."[34]

In his preface to "The Evacuation from Dunkirk," the historian of the Naval Historical Branch, Mr. W.J.R. "Jock" Gardner, wrote succinctly about the reality of Dunkirk:

> "Operation *Dynamo* was not a victory; no evacuation can be ever considered as such. What it did mean, however, was that a substantial body of troops in dire difficulty on land and pressed from the air were firstly sustained, then delivered from the situation because of the utility and flexibility of sea power."[35]

Venomous and sister ships wait to berth at Dover.
Photographed by Lt Peter Kershaw RNVR.

French troops disembarking at Dover from *Venomous*, 4 June 1940.
Photographed by Lt Peter Kershaw RNVR.

The last word rests with McBeath who had guided his ship and crew safely through those difficult days: "We were very lucky. The whole party was over and we had come through it without serious damage and without a single casualty."

At 1300 on 5 June *Venomous* left Dover, bound for Devonport, Plymouth's naval dockyard, with the knowledge of a job well done. A record 4,410 soldiers had been safely returned to fight another day. *Venomous* and her sisters had performed duties beyond the expectations of their designers.

Notes

1   "Winston is back" was the signal sent by the Admiralty to its ships and stations in response to the news that Winston Churchill had been selected by Prime Minister Neville Chamberlain to become the First Lord of the Admiralty on 3 September 1939. HMS *Venomous*' return to active service coincided with Churchill's return.

2   Western served throughout the war as a gunnery officer with several postings at various shore-based facilities. See www.unithistories.com/officers/RN_officersW3.html for his service record

3   The Royal Navy had three main manning ports: "Guz" was the Navy's name for Devonport, with "Pompey" for Portsmouth men and "Chats" for Chatham men.

4   Correlli Barnett, *Engage the Enemy More Closely: The Royal Navy in the Second World War,* (New York: W.W. Norton & Company, 1991), p. 592. Horton would command the Western Approaches and Venomous would fall under his exacting leadership.

5   The Historic Naval Ship's Association Website has a copy of the US Navy's Bureau of Ships Operational Manual for the Main Propulsion Plant for the DD 445 and 692 Classes. See www.hnsa.org/doc/destroyer/steam/index.htm for a discussion of the closed feed system.

6   Cpt Donald McIntyre wrote the following books on the war at sea: *U-boat Killer* (New York: Avon Publications, Inc., 1956); *The Battle of the Atlantic*, (London: William Clowes and Sons, Ltd., 1961); *The Naval War Against Hitler* (London: B.T. Batsford, Ltd.,1971).

7   Cpt Steven W. Roskill RN, *Naval Policy Between the Wars, Vol. II, The Period of Reluctant Rearmament*, p. 483.

8   Preston, p. 59. The appendix contains the organisational breakdown of the destroyer flotillas and individual ships assigned to the Channel Force.

9   After *Venomous* Duff served in HMS *Manchester*, was torpedoed twice and when she sank was imprisoned by the Vichy French in North Africa until the Allied landings. He was Staff Gunnery officer for the naval force at the D Day landings where he directed naval gunfire support. He was Gunnery Officer on the carrier, HMS *Formidable*, sent to the Far Eastern theatre to assist the Americans and later carried released POWs back to UK. Cdr Duff was invalided out in the mid fifties as a result of Gunfire induced deafness. See http://www.unithistories.com/units_index/default.asp?file=../officers/personsx.html for further details of his career.

10 John Edward Home McBeath (1907-82) fell out with his parents whilst in his teens and went to live in Massachusetts, USA, before joining the navy as a 16 year old cadet in 1923. During his twenty years as Honorary Commodore of the Sea Cadets he gave the McBeath Trophy which is awarded annually to the best Sea Cadet Unit in the country. For further details of his naval career see http://www.unithistories.com/officers/RN_officersM2.html#McBeath_JEH and his obituary in *The Times* on the 2 April 1982.

11 The passengers were mainly lascar seamen who had been serving on German ships before the war. Churchill had to answer a question in the Commons about the failure of the escorting destroyer to provide an adequate defence for the *Domala*.

12 Barnett, p. 103.

13 Ibid, p. 139.

14 *Enemy air attacks. From The Commanding Officer HMS Venomous to Captain (D) 16th Destroyer Flotilla; dated 21 May 1940*. In: *1940-42 Enemy air attacks on RN and Merchant shipping* (NA Ref: ADM 199/100).

15 Ibid

16 The North Goodwin Sands, a treacherous part of the English Channel, is the grave of many a sailor and ship. Please refer to www.whitecliffscountry.org.uk/heritage/goodwins.asp

17 Dr. Richard Walding, a Research Fellow at the School of Science, Griffith University, Australia, has reported on his research into indicator loops at www.indicatorloops.com.

18 Courtauld was one of the world's largest manufacturers of rayon and one of the firm's English directors, Tommy Davies, who also worked for British Intelligence, "…went over to Calais shortly before the Germans arrived there and removed several hundred thousand pounds' worth of platinum from Courtauld's factory." Patrick Howarth, *Undercover: The Men and Women of the Special Operations Executive* (Routledge & Kegan Paul Ltd., 1980), p. 10.

19 *History of the Second World War: United Kingdom Military Series*; edited by J.R.M. Butler. *The War In France And Flanders 1939-1940*; by Major L.F. Ellis C.V.O., C.B.E., DSO, M.C. (London: HMSO, 1954), p153.

20 See http://www.historyofwar.org/articles/battles_boulogne_1940.html for a brief account of the battle for Boulogne. A more detailed account by Jon Cooksey was published as a volume in the series on *Battleground Europe: The Channel Ports* titled *Boulogne: 20 Guards Brigades Fighting Defence – May 1940* (Leo Cooper, 2002) ISBN 0 85052 814 3.

21 Ibid, p. 154.

22 Peter C. Smith, HMS *Wild Swan* (London: William Kimber & Co, 1985), p. 69.

23 Tim Clayton and Phil Craig, *Finest Hour*, (Hodder & Stoughton Limited, 1999), p. 80.

24 According to the combat report of the Welsh Guards three French tanks had been captured by the Germans and were used against the Allied forces but Peter Smith in an e-mail to the author on the 8 February 2009 claims they were actually German tanks.

25 Sir Alexander Stanier described the action at Boulogne in his memoirs and in a recorded interview in the Sound Archive of the IMW, Reference 7175. His son, Sir Beville Stanier, wrote the introduction to the book by Jon Cooksey cited above.

26 *Boulogne: Damage reports to Venomous and Venetia* can be found at the National Archives in ADM 267/101 Shell and bomb. The unemotional factual description contrasts with the devastation shown in the accompanying photographs.

27 Welsh Guards *War Diary*, NA Ref. WO 166/4113

28 This description was taken from a 1972 recorded interview with Rear-Admiral McBeath produced by Thames TV. It is now in the IWM Sound Archive, Ref. 2808.

29 See: http://www.adls.org.uk/t1/node/601

30 Peter C. Smith, *Hold the Narrow Sea* (Annapolis: United States Naval Institute Press, 1984), p. 53.

31 Corporal King fought with the Eighth Army in North Africa and escaped capture when Tobruk fell. He was commissioned and left the army after six and a half years as Cpt D. King. During a successful career in banking Sergeant Lou Warn, now 97, was one of his customers.

32 Sergeant L. F. Warn's account was originally published in *Hard Lying*, the magazine of the V&W Association in June 1999, but an extended version appeared later in *Hard Lying: The Story of the V & W Class Destroyers and the Men Who Sailed in Them*: by Cliff Fairweather (Avalon Associates 2005). ISBN 0952944049.

33 Preston, p. 77.

34 Ibid, p. 77-8.

35 *Whitehall Histories: Naval Staff Histories, The Evacuation of Dunkirk 'Operation Dynamo', 26 May - 4 June 1940*, Senior Editor: Cpt Christopher Page, RN Retired and Editor, Mr. W.J.R. Gardner, Frank Cass Publishers, London 2000.

CHAPTER FIVE

THE NORTH SEA AND BEYOND
June 1940 – December 1941

"And of the three armed forces, it was upon the Royal Navy
that the greatest burden and the greatest strain was to fall,
for its role was all-pervasive and its service in
the face of the enemy unceasing." [1]

The twelve days *Venomous* spent in Plymouth's dockyard provided a welcome break for the hard-pressed destroyer and her ship's company but with enemy troops massing in northern France and invasion soon to be expected, the race was on to restore *Venomous* and the other damaged warships to battle-worthy condition.

During the Dunkirk evacuation the V & Ws had suffered from the lack of an effective defence against enemy planes. Their main armament, the 4.7-inch guns, could not be elevated to fire at planes and their only other weapons were twin Lewis guns on the bridge wings and the two 2-pdr pom-poms which "rapid improvements in aircraft design had rendered obsolete, as it had a low muzzle velocity, lacked a satisfactory explosive shell and no tracer ammunition was provided".[2] Steps were taken to provide *Venomous* with a more effective defence against enemy aircraft. The after set of torpedo tubes was removed and a 3-inch high angle (H.A.) dual purpose (D.P.) gun and mounting was installed together with magazine stowage for its ammunition. As McGeeney remarked, "until the 3-inch HA 18 cwt gun was fitted the ship had very little HA defence and whilst the gun was no real threat to the enemy it did give some satisfaction to the Ship's company who felt that an attempt was being made to hit back." Sydney Compston, a sight setter on "B" Gun, was given the same job on the 12 pounder.

It was also intended that *Venomous* would receive a technology that was already having a substantial effect on the ongoing Battle of Britain and would change how the war at sea was fought. This new technology was called Radio Direction Finder or RDF for short. It would later be called RADAR.[3]

'Freddo' Thomas was sent to Devonport to join *Venomous* as the ship's first RDF operator. Thomas was a student at a teacher training college when he received his call-up papers. After volunteering for the navy he was sent on an RDF course at HMS *Ganges*, a shore establishment in Suffolk. On arrival at the dockyard he looked up at the masthead on *Venomous* expecting to see an RDF antenna but the RDF equipment was still in crates on the dockside. There was nobody at the dockyard with the skill to fit and set the equipment and Thomas only knew how to operate it once that was done. Fred spent his first few months attached to the deck department as an ordinary seaman with very little to do when action stations were called.

While *Venomous* was in the dockyards the evacuations of the B.E.F. and elements of the French Army continued. Between 9-11 June Operation *Cycle* successfully evacuated eleven thousand British troops from the bomb-shattered port city of Le Havre but the evacuation of the 51st Highland Division, trapped in St. Valery-en-Caux, was a bitter disappointment with only two thousand (plus a thousand French troops) brought back across the channel. The main body of this splendid division that included some of the British Army's greatest regiments (The Black Watch, Cameron Highlanders, Gordon Highlanders and the Seaforth Highlanders) were forced to surrender. Over six thousand men would spend years in prisoner of war camps in Germany.

On 15 June Operation *Aerial* began the evacuation of British, Canadian, French and Polish forces from Brest, La Pallice, St. Malo and St. Nazaire. The First Canadian Division was evacuated from St. Malo on 16 June and by the 18th over 182,000 troops had been brought home. This 'mini-Dunkirk' was marred on 17 June by the bombing of the British liner *Lancastria* with nearly six thousand troops on board. The exact number lost will never be known but over three thousand went down with the ship.[4]

On the 25th the Royal Navy was ordered:

> "...to carry out the melancholy task of evacuating 22,656 people of military age, women and children from British territory soon to be abandoned to the enemy – the Channel Islands. Once seapower had protected the islands against Bonaparte; it could not preserve them against Hitler in the face of the Luftwaffe..."[5]

Britain had not been so isolated from Europe by a hostile power since the Napoleonic Wars. Matters were made worse by Italy's declaration of war on Britain and France on 10 June. The Italian Navy and Air

Force were a serious threat to the main sea route that connected Britain to her Empire and Commonwealth – the Mediterranean. Britain adopted a strategy it had relied on in the past, a 'Blue Water' strategy that depended upon the Navy for defence, which would lay the foundation for eventual victory.

The Admiralty prepared for the invasion, which everybody expected:

> "It was at the end of May, whilst '*Dynamo*' was in full spate, that the Admiralty sent a directive to all home Commanders-in-Chief outlining its anti-invasion strategy; one little-altered in the course of the summer and autumn, and which broadly followed the precepts laid down by the Admiralty in 1803-05, and, for that matter, by Lord Howard of Effingham, Raleigh, Drake and Hawkins in the 1580s. Believing that the enemy would choose the shortest crossing and be prepared to accept 'catastrophic losses' in order to land an army in England, the Admiralty stressed the importance of 'attack before departure' …which therefore demanded 'early indication of assembly by our intelligence and reconnaissance."[6]

The first priority was to make good the heavy losses suffered during Operation *Dynamo* and to reorganise her surface forces in the Channel and the North Sea to provide a strong defence against invasion by sea. This mainly relied on thirty-two destroyers, which were now organised into four flotillas operating out of Harwich, Dover, Portsmouth and Plymouth.[7] *Venomous* would be one of the destroyers based at Harwich.

The desperate events of the previous month had drawn attention to the absence of a medical presence in the ship and Surg. Lt Woodyatt RNVR was appointed to the ship with effect from 15 June 1940. For Peter Woodyatt events had indeed moved at a bewildering pace:

> "I joined the Royal Navy on 13th June and two days later was posted to *Venomous*. She was in Devonport dockyard having just been fitted with a 3" high angle gun in place of her after set of torpedo tubes. Three days later we sailed up Channel and joined the Harwich Fighting Force".

McBeath took *Venomous* out for sea trials and to practice firing her new 3-inch H.A. D.P. gun at airborne-towed targets on 16-17 June. With the successful completion of her trials, *Venomous* left Plymouth that afternoon, steaming up the Channel to Dover, and after a short layover, through the Dover Straits to Harwich arriving just after daybreak on the

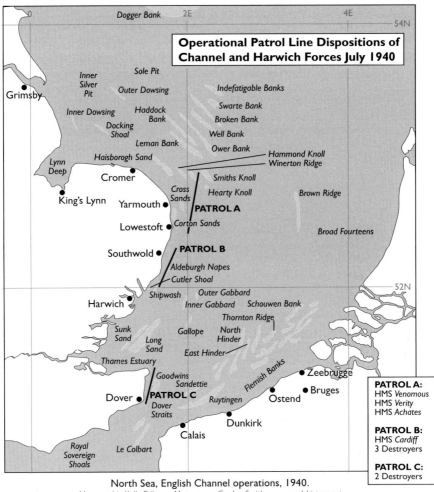

North Sea, English Channel operations, 1940.

Map graphic Kelly Erlinger. Map source Gordon Smith www.naval-history.net

20th. She was assigned to the Eighteenth Destroyer Flotilla with her fellow V & W Class destroyers, HMS *Montrose* (leader), *Verity*, *Veteran*, *Whitshed*, *Wild Swan*, *Wivern* and *Worcester*.

For the next eleven days *Venomous* and the Eighteenth Flotilla were on 'O' and 'T' Patrols, steaming a set course between two fixed points, one on the English coast and the other adjacent to enemy territory. The eastern extremity was invariably approached with some degree of trepidation as the German presence began to assert itself. CPO McGeeney recalled these patrols:

> "German E-Boats began to patrol the southern end of our coastal ship routes at night. On several occasions we were not far away

when a skirmish began to develop but the presence of Destroyers on our side probably ensured the breaking off of the encounter and their withdrawal at high speed."

With much of the Kriegsmarine's destroyer force on the bottom of Norwegian Fjords, the E-Boats (*Schnellboote*) had taken over their role on England's eastern and southern coasts. Operating mostly at night, they proved to be very successful tactical craft, well suited to such narrow seas. British losses were considerable but E-Boat losses were also high, especially as radar was introduced throughout the Royal Navy and the enemy began to be targeted by the RAF.

A diversion from the usual round of night patrols arose on the evening of 1 July when an attempt was made to intercept German vessels engaged in mine-laying operations. At 2200 *Venomous* left harbour in company with HMS *Malcolm* and the A Class destroyers, HMS *Achates* and *Ambuscade*, to rendezvous with the Town Class 6-inch gun cruisers HMS *Manchester*, *Newcastle* and *Sheffield*, escorted by the modern J Class fleet destroyers, HMS *Jackal* and *Jaguar*. This impressive force patrolled the central and eastern reaches of the Harwich command sector of the North Sea until 0600 on the 2nd but without results and, with daylight approaching, the Harwich-based ships returned to port, leaving *Newcastle* to head for Plymouth, the remaining cruisers to Sheerness and the destroyers to the Humber.

HMS *Venomous* in the Thames estuary on the 2 July 1940.
The new 12 pounder HA gun which replaced the rear torpedo tubes is clearly visible,
Photographed by Lt Cdr J.K. Neale DSC RNVR from the minesweeper HMS *Speedwell*.
IWM Image Reference HU 67084. *Courtesy of the Imperial War Museum.*

The challenges that *Venomous* had faced had produced a spirited fighting unit. Lt Frank Twiss RN (later Admiral Sir Frank Twiss K.C.B., DSC) serving on *Malcolm* as Sixteenth Flotilla Gunnery Officer remembered with respect both *Venomous* and her Captain: "John McBeath was a delightful person, full of zing and hammer and of course his ship reflected him. *Venomous* was one of the best ships in the Eighteenth Flotilla."

As June gave way to July the Royal Navy intensified its offensive operations, within the designated English Channel and North Sea patrol areas during the short summer nights. Across the Channel events appeared to be moving towards their climax. Reconnaissance aircraft revealed the build-up of barges in the Channel ports and all indications were for an early invasion. Operational dispositions for the Channel and Harwich forces were duly allocated with the Harwich force being allotted three patrol areas to take effect from 2-3 July:

> PATROL A
> Harwich-based Destroyers to patrol between Smith's Knoll
> and 54B Buoy in position 52° 27' N, 2° 6' E.
>
> PATROL B
> Cruiser *Cardiff* plus 3 Destroyers to patrol the swept Channel
> about 7 miles each side of the Aldeburgh Light Float.
>
> PATROL C
> 2 Destroyers from the 21st Flotilla based at Plymouth to
> patrol below North Foreland.

Initially *Venomous* was assigned to Patrol A (in the Harwich Command Area), together with the destroyer *Achates* and *Venomous'* sister ship, *Verity*. She and her consorts were at sea on six successive nights from 6-7 July until 11-12 July but without contact with the enemy.

Officers and men had to snatch what sleep they could after many daylight hours had been taken up with routine but essential maintenance and storing provisions. McGeeney's role involved the guns: "When we returned to harbour my first task was to strip and refit the gun breeches and firing mechanisms, plus carrying out various checks and tests generally known as 'Preparation for Firing'."

As dusk fell McBeath would take his destroyer back out of harbour for another tense night at sea. AB Compston recalled the routine: "Out over the other side most nights. Back at dawn. Usually three at a time.

Sometimes the old Cruiser *Cardiff* would accompany us. Called out occasionally to assist an East Coast convoy."[8]

These convoys assembled at Southend-on-Sea and headed north hugging the coast behind the East Coast Mine Barrier which extended from the Thames to Scotland. One such call for assistance came on 11 July from southbound Convoy FS.218 under attack off Southwold. After joining up with the convoy, *Venomous*, in company with *Wivern*, was in position 52° 10' N 1° 52' E at 1140 when the first of four separate attacks occurred. The attack concentrated on the escorts with all the bombs directed at *Wivern* but she escaped unscathed, as did the ships in the convoy. Not so lucky was northbound Convoy FN.223. Just after 1100 on 15 July the Egret Class escorting sloop, HMS *Stork*, reported a shadowing aircraft, and at 1400 when the convoy was passing the Aldeburgh Light Float, it was attacked by ten aircraft. *Venomous* and *Wivern* were directed to close with the convoy and found the merchant ship SS *Heworth* hit and on fire (it sank later).

On 17 July *Venomous*, this time in company with the A Class destroyer, HMS *Arrow*, was ordered to assist the southbound convoy FS.224, which had come under air attack at 1330 in the danger zone close to the Aldeburgh Light Float. A further attack came just after midday on the 18th when the trawler HMS *Stella Leonis* was bombed and machine gunned in position 52° 4' N 1° 56' E. The *Stella Leonis* suffered two killed with one wounded and was in danger of sinking. At 1600 *Venomous* signalled that the trawler had been taken in tow by the trawler HMS *St. Olive* and was making three knots. She not only made port but survived the war to be returned to her owners in May 1945. Shortly afterwards, whilst escorting Convoy FN.225 from Southend, a Polish steamer, SS *Zagloba*, was damaged and out of control. The attackers were driven off by fighter aircraft, and *Venomous* and *Valorous* stood by whilst *Zagloba*, was taken in tow by the trawler *Vidonia* and returned safely to harbour. Lt Peter Kershaw observed that: "I thought being bombed by JU87s was the worst. They came straight for you at a very steep angle and we virtually hadn't much to attack them with. It was particularly unpleasant in moonlight as we couldn't see them."

Occasionally there was a chance for shore leave and not unnaturally, as Kershaw recounted, the men made the most of the opportunity:

> "When we were in Harwich on one occasion we were given shore
> leave on the Shotley side. Then we were ordered to sea in a hurry

and the Captain sent for me, told me to take his motorboat and collect them. Fortunately there was only one pub but I was mystified when I found no one in the public rooms, the pub being empty as it should have been at 4.30 p.m. So I called for the Landlord and he led me to the cellar. There were about twelve of our sailors lying on mattresses and each had a pint pot, which they were filling up, from the barrel. I asked the Landlord if he wanted payment but he said 'no' and I soon had them back on board."

Lighter moments such as these were few and far between as the nightly patrols continued through 27 July. *Venomous* was then ordered to Chatham for a boiler clean, arriving early in the afternoon on 28 July. This voyage was, however, not without danger. For some months German aircraft had been laying mines in the approaches to the Thames and the area was considered somewhat hazardous. As Kershaw noted, it proved particularly hazardous for Sub Lt Wells:

"We were going to Chatham for a boiler clean when a magnetic mine went off close to her stern. Walter Wells was having a glass of beer in the Wardroom. He rushed on deck and was soaked by the water coming down. Beer was hard to come by and he took it with him to no avail – his glass was half full of water and beer."

With her boiler cleaning completed *Venomous* returned to Harwich on 2 August. She joined Force H comprising the light cruiser HMS *Cardiff*, together with *Verity*, *Wild Swan* and *Wivern*, plus the Kingfisher Class patrol vessels, HMS *Puffin*, *Shearwater* and *Sheldrake*. This force conducted ten additional patrols during August but without contact with the enemy.

During the month Winston Churchill visited Harwich to inspect the force, and the crews of destroyers, minesweepers and trawlers were drawn up on the jetty to await their distinguished visitor. Lt Kershaw witnessed the event:

"The Admiral and his staff didn't seem to know whether he was arriving at Shotley or on the Harwich side. Suddenly there was a shout 'perhaps the old devil will arrive by parachute.' The Admiral was furious and told his staff to investigate. They got nowhere but in fact we all knew it was a sailor from one of the Trawlers who were always a law unto themselves."

On 28 August 1940 *The London Gazette* published a lengthy list of awards for good services in operations off the Dutch, Belgian and French coasts during the Battle for France. Included in the list were the following officers and ship's company of *Venomous*: Lt Cdr John Edward Home McBeath RN was awarded the DSO whilst the DSC was given to Sub Lt Walter R. Wells RN (who was promoted to full Lieutenant the following month). For the ship's company, the DSM was given to Ordnance Artificer 3rd (Chief) Class Horace Hugh McGeeney, PO Michael Joseph O'Sullivan, Acting PO Leslie William Dagley, AB Harold Knapton and AB Ernest Roy Stallard. The absence of Mid Alan Esson from the announcement in the *London Gazette* was surprising to say the least. His outstanding courage and effectiveness during the action in Boulogne was especially noted in McBeath's after action dispatch. There was, however, some consolation for the young Scotsman, for his promotion to sub lieutenant was announced that day.

The next day found *Venomous* back at Chatham for a further boiler cleaning and the opportunity to observe the desperate battle in the skies over Kent – the Battle of Britain was reaching its peak. *Venomous* returned to Harwich on 2 September and the routine of nightly patrols – the nights were getting longer and so were the patrols.

An invasion attempt was still anticipated before the onset of winter. On 12 September, after the receipt of reconnaissance information that barges were heading down the Channel for Boulogne, the following signal was made at 1750 to Captain (D) Sixteenth Flotilla:

> "*Malcolm, Wild Swan* and *Venomous* are to sail at 1900/12 and to proceed to the vicinity of Boulogne, then sweep towards Cap Griz Nez.
>   Object is the destruction of any shipping or barges met off the French coast.
>   Prisoners required if possible.
>   If practical sweep to 50° 51' N and then return to Harwich. Course to pass south of Le Colbert would seem desirable if shore batteries are troublesome. Reports indicate barges may be making for Boulogne during the night."[9]

No action was joined that night, but a repeat patrol the following evening resulted in intermittent action with enemy trawlers off Boulogne during the early hours of the 14th but without damage to either side.

After a 24-hour respite *Venomous, Veteran* and *Wild Swan* executed a further patrol sweep to intercept enemy craft near the East Coast Mine Barrier but without opposition. A similar patrol on 17 September, also without results, was enlivened by the activation of a magnetic mine between three and four cable lengths from *Wivern,* which had on this night replaced *Veteran.* She was lucky to escape as magnetic mines proved an extremely difficult weapon to evade.

On Sunday 22 September *Venomous, Veteran* and *Wild Swan* were again out in the North sea patrolling the Dogger Bank in position 55° 47' N 2° 55' E, as part of the covering force for an operation to lay mines off the Dutch coast near Oost Gat. This hazardous operation was completed successfully and without loss, all ships being back in Harwich by dawn. A further sortie occurred the next evening after receipt of the following signal from Commander in Chief Nore ordering:

> "*Mallard, Sheldrake, Venomous, Veteran* and *Wivern.* Proceed through Gap E reaching 51° 47' N, 2° 55' E at 2315/23. Destroyers to patrol there. Corvettes to 51° 30' N, 3° 12' E at 0115/24. Lay mines. 037° completed by 0215 and will depart Gap E."[10]

The operation was concluded successfully with both corvettes, *Mallard* and *Sheldrake*, laying their mines as ordered off the Scheldt and returning safely with their three escorting destroyers.

Venomous was chosen to take part in an imaginative new plan to counter the expected invasion. Capt Augustus Agar, whose daring raid on Soviet battleships at Kronstadt in 1919 won him the VC, was charged with the execution of Operation *Lucid*. Two old oil tankers were to be filled with a highly flammable liquid mixture and towed across the Channel toward the French coast and ignited at the entrance to the key ports that were being used to assemble the German invasion force.[11] It was hoped that these 'fire ships' would explode and set fire to the port facilities and the amphibious craft within the harbour. Operation *Lucid* was authorised for the night of 25-6 September. *Venomous, Veteran* and *Wild Swan* were to be part of the covering force. Engine defects in both oil tankers caused delays and adverse winds conditions finally resulted in postponement of the operation. Two further attempts were made but the weather remained unkind and Operation *Lucid* was finally scratched for good.

The Thames Estuary was a prime target for German mine-laying aircraft and in the early afternoon of 27 September, whilst steaming close to the Mid Barrow Light Vessel, *Venomous* narrowly avoided joining the list of victims. Two magnetic mines exploded some seven cable lengths from her beam.[12]

Shortly after midnight on 1 October three enemy destroyers were reported off South Foreland. *Venomous*, *Wild Swan* and the new Hunt I Class escort destroyer HMS *Eglinton* were ordered to sea by Commander in Chief Nore: "Proceed to South Falls Buoy along QZ5117. Remain near there to be ready to reinforce four destroyers patrolling off Dover if necessary. Return to harbour by daylight." The potential adversaries were not destroyers but four Raubvogel Class 'Torpedoboote', part of the Fifth Torpedo Boat Flotilla. KMS *Falke*, *Greif*, *Kondor* and *Seeadler* were conducting one of their regular mine-laying operations but, as happened so frequently, *Venomous* and her consorts did not make contact.

There were intermittent runs ashore for all hands, and now that the hunting season had begun, members of the Wardroom decided to attempt to supplement their rations by shooting pheasants. The parish of Shotley, upriver from Harwich on the triangle of land between the Orwell and Stour, was mostly farming land and woodlands. Parkes and Kershaw set out with guns in hand and a box of raisins. Parkes recalled what happened: "Peter Kershaw and myself soaked some raisins in Naval Rum (proof) and laid them out for the birds hoping these would be consumed. The theory was that the birds would become intoxicated and thus easy prey" but as Kershaw confirmed, "the birds appeared to have a strong head and this hunting expedition was to be as barren as others later in the war."

Routine patrol work continued until the end of the month, interrupted only by a further boiler clean, but by now it was evident there would be no invasion that year and more important tasks awaited *Venomous* elsewhere.

• • • •

In March 1940 the Admiralty had begun to reorganise its Mediterranean Fleet under the command of one of England's great fighting admirals, Admiral Sir Andrew Browne Cunningham. Any hopes that the French Fleet would control the western Mediterranean whilst the bulk of Cunningham's revitalised fleet in Alexandria would protect the east were dashed by the fall of France only days after Italy's entry into the war on 10 June. The First Sea Lord, the Chief of Naval Staff, Admiral of the Fleet Sir Dudley Pound, and the Director of Naval Plans all favoured withdrawing the Mediterranean Fleet to Gibraltar. They believed, rightly, that Britain's survival depended on keeping the Atlantic open to British shipping and that this could not be achieved whilst keeping a fleet in the Mediterranean. The Joint Planning Sub-Committee of the Imperial Joint Chiefs of Staff, together with Admiral Cunningham saw things differently. Cunningham's personal letter to Pound summed up a strong countervailing opinion:

> "...the effects of this withdrawal would mean such a landslide in territory and prestige that I earnestly hoped such a decision would never have to be taken. As already pointed out, the Commander-in-Chief, Middle East considered Egypt would become untenable soon after the departure of the fleet. Added to that Malta, Cyprus and Palestine could no longer be held, whilst the Moslem world would regard it as surrender...The Italian battle fleet had so far shown no signs of activity...I was of the opinion that the battleships we had were sufficient to contain the Italian heavy ships...and that the route to Malta could be opened when required."[13]

Churchill supported Cunningham and vetoed the proposal. There was no doubt in his mind that the Mediterranean Fleet had to stay and that the Mediterranean would become a major theatre of operations.

Both sides had a common aim: the running of supply convoys to support their ground operations in Egypt and Libya. The Axis sent convoys to North Africa from Italy whilst Britain planned to run convoys to Malta, which lay across Italy and Germany's supply routes. It was hoped that Malta would become a thorn in the side of Axis ambitions in North Africa. *Venomous* participated in these operations to support Malta from the outset, returning to the waters that her keel had plied in 1929.

Pre-war economies had left the island with little by way of defence and as it came under increasing pressure from Axis air attacks it urgently needed fighter reinforcements. The proposed solution was Operation *Hurry* – the ferrying of fixed-wing aircraft in the old aircraft carrier, HMS *Argus,* to within flying range of Malta. *Venomous, Vesper,* and *Windsor* were to be part of the large escorting force and were ordered to get underway for the Clyde. The three ships left Harwich just after sunrise on 31 October, proceeded up the east coast and reached Greenock, Scotland during the afternoon of 3 November. After joining up with *Argus*, the Royal Navy's first aircraft carrier, and her escorting Danae Class light cruiser, HMS *Despatch*, the force sailed from the Clyde during the forenoon of 7 November with the intention of passing *Argus* through the Straits of Gibraltar after dark on 13 November.[14] Since the operational range of all three destroyers was limited their orders were modified as follows: "Route for *Argus* and *Despatch* from Clyde to Gibraltar. Destroyer escort *Venomous*, *Vesper* and *Windsor* to remain in company as far West as endurance permits and then fuel at Londonderry and Nore via Rosyth."[15]

They steamed westward beyond Ireland before heading south to attempt to stay beyond the reach of Luftwaffe aerial reconnaissance planes and marauding U-boats.[16] The outward passage was uneventful but during the early morning hours of 9 November, shortly before the V & W destroyers parted from *Argus* and *Despatch*, McBeath received the following signal from C in C Western Approaches:

> "SS *Nalon* (bombed 6/11) with valuable cargo was bombed and abandoned at 1145/6. Estimate approximate position 1200/9 – 53° 50' N 15° W. When returning to harbour, endeavour to locate this vessel."

No trace was found of the ship and, after refuelling in Londonderry, *Venomous* was back in the Clyde on 13 November.

There was to be no early return to Nore Command as a further reinforcement of Malta's air defences was required. The number of aircraft that *Argus* provided was woefully inadequate. The dozen Hurricanes that took off from its deck on 17 November were launched too far from the island and only four landed safely, the rest ran out of fuel and were lost when they crashed into the Straits of Sicily.[17]

The follow-up operation would be carried out by HMS *Furious*, which had been designed as a battle-cruiser but while still under construction in 1917 had been given an open deck for flying-off with a hangar underneath and had undergone a series of modifications through the 1920s that eventually converted her to a full-fledged aircraft carrier.[18] Even before *Venomous* returned to the Clyde, McBeath received a signal from C in C Western Approaches telling him what to expect: "To escort *Furious*, with *Havelock* and *Hurricane* from Liverpool, *Vesper* and *Venomous* from Clyde, *Velox* from Londonderry."[19]

Venomous and *Vesper* left Greenock on 15 November to join the escort force and once again the operation passed off without incident but because of their limited range they had to break away from the other escorts before *Furious* reached Gibraltar and they returned to the Clyde on the 21st.

The return of *Venomous* to the Nore was again delayed whilst it escorted an aircraft carrier. *Venomous, Vesper* and the H Class destroyer *Hesperus* provided close escort for the new Illustrious Class aircraft carrier HMS *Formidable* during her sea trials in the Irish Sea between 21 and 26 November (with a quick return to port to be commissioned on 24 November). *Venomous* then followed *Formidable* into Belfast for a post-commissioning refit and McBeath was able to provide his crew with a short break. On 29 November *Venomous* and *Vesper* escorted the new carrier to Scapa Flow where it joined the Home Fleet.

With *Formidable* safely at anchor McBeath refuelled his destroyer and returned to Belfast on 2 December. She remained in port until after sunset on the 10th when *Venomous* headed out into the storm-tossed North Atlantic to round up and escort Convoy SL56 that had been scattered by severe Atlantic gales:

> "SL56 – Estimated position from aircraft of a portion of SL56 at 0001/12 i.e. 55° 50' N 0900 steering 100°. Estimated position of

Venomous at full speed (30.5 knots) escorting the aircraft carrier HMS Formidable on her trials in the Clyde, December 1940.
Photographed by Lt Peter Kershaw RNVR.

HMS *Formidable* on its sea trials in the Clyde estuary with HMS *Venomous*.
Photographed by Lt Peter Kershaw RNVR.

Burnham in company with 2 ships at 0001/12 i.e. 55° 50' N 12° 10'
W. Course 90°. Position of remainder of convoy is uncertain. Aircraft
assisting to locate."[20]

Later that day the orders to *Venomous* were amended, "Proceed to
search for SC.14 – 21 ships. Commodore is Master of *Athenic*."[21] The
whole of 13 December was spent in a fruitless search:

"SC.14. Since 2200/12 have swept westward along the route of SC.14 i.e.
55° 20' N 14° 30' W thence N for 25 miles and eastwards 55° 20' N 8° 40'
W. From latter position at 0415/14 am steering mean course 320° at 15K
until 0800 then 157°, 160°, 263°, 263°, 270°, to continue search."[22]

McBeath continued the search through the 14th until receiving a signal
from Western Approaches Command ordering *Venomous* to return to
Belfast where she came alongside just after sunrise on the 15th.

• • • •

On 18 December *Venomous* was formally transferred to Western
Approaches Command, along with sister ship HMS *Watchman*, their
places at the Nore being taken by the brand new Hunt I Class escort
destroyers, HMS *Exmoor* and HMS *Pytchley*.

Venomous joined the First Escort Group, based at Londonderry,
Northern Ireland. Despite lacking the ship repair facilities of
Birkenhead the westerly location of this small port had made it the

main naval base for the escort groups accompanying the Atlantic convoys. Captain Philip Ruck-Keene, Captain (D) at Londonderry, was known as "Ruckers", and was a charismatic strong willed individual

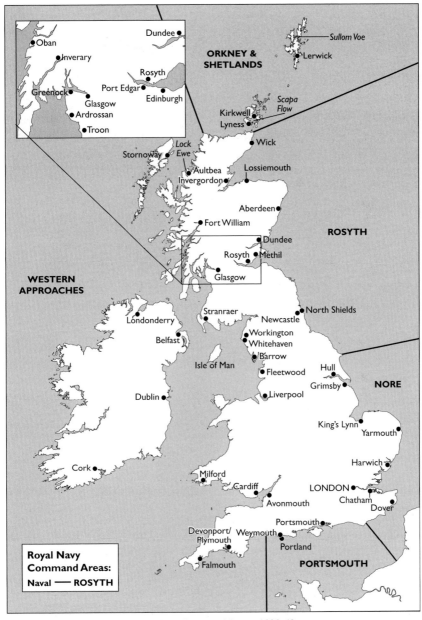

Royal Navy Command Areas, 1939-42.
Map graphic Kelly Erlinger. Map source Gordon Smith www.naval-history.net

who had mainly served in submarines but was later to command HMS *Formidable*, the aircraft carrier *Venomous* had accompanied on its trial on the Clyde. The First Escort Group included *Venomous'* sister, *Wild Swan*, two Flower Class corvettes, HMS *Fleur de Lys* and *Gardenia* as well as the destroyer HMS *Rockingham*. *Rockingham* was the former US Navy destroyer USS *Swasey*. She was one of fifty Great War era US Navy destroyers given to the Royal Navy in exchange for 99 year leases to establish US military bases on British island possessions in the Caribbean.[23]

Capt P. Ruck-Keene RN, Captain (D) at Londonderry (on left), with Cdr Howard-Johnson (second left) and two junior offices visiting HMS *Venomous*.
Photographed by Lt Peter Kershaw RNVR.

The operation began inauspiciously. Both Lt Cdr McBeath and Lt Wells had been taken ill and were not on board when *Venomous* put to sea. AB Compston remembers what happened next:

> "The Captain was taken ill and as we were sailing that day "Jimmy The One" (Lt Mackenzie RNR) had to take charge and we went aground in the Belfast River. That was the only time I heard the pipe 'Hands to dance and skylark on the upper deck'. All the ship's company

> jumping up and down on the quarterdeck to try and lift the bows off
> the sandbank. But it was no use – we had to have a tug, and because
> we sustained some damage it meant Christmas in harbour so the lads
> were quite happy. Cdr McBeath was ashore sick and was replaced by
> Cdr Henderson."

Under John McBeath *Venomous* had distinguished herself and he left
behind a happy ship with a reputation that stood as high as any destroyer
in service. Happily, he was soon to recover and able to resume active
service in command of the new O Class destroyer, HMS *Oribi*.

Cdr H. Pitcairn Henderson RN assumed command on Christmas
Eve. He was a large bluff character with a dry sense of humour,
frequently to be seen puffing his pipe. Henderson, who prided himself
on his standard of dress, was reputed to be a descendent of the
Henderson who met the *Bounty* Mutineers on Pitcairn Island.

Christmas celebrations were enjoyed in the safety of Belfast Harbour
and yet it was here that *Venomous* suffered one of her few wartime
casualties as Lt Kershaw recalled: "On Christmas Day 1940 a very well-
liked sailor died on board through drinking rum (proof) and I was
informed as I came on board. I asked how old he was and was told '45 –
a great age Sir.' He was right as we rarely had anyone of that age." Sydney
Compston remembered how "poor Lodwick, a WW1 veteran who had his
Christmas dinner and his tot, went to sleep and never woke up."

The loss of this well-liked shipmate sent morale plummeting and
presented a challenge on Henderson's assumption of command but
Henderson's agreeable personality and fair and firm command style got
the ship's company through it. Henderson would prove to be popular
with both officers and the ship's company as illustrated by this story
told by Kershaw:

> "On one occasion when coming alongside there was a problem with
> the bow rope and it was only after some pressure on my part that
> matters were eventually put right and the ship berthed. I apologised
> to Cdr Henderson whose reply was 'Don't be too hard on them; we
> shall have a better dinner than they will tonight.'"

With her new commander *Venomous* got underway mid-morning on
27 December in company with the destroyers *Rockingham* and *Wild
Swan*, and the corvettes *Fleur de Lys* and *Gardenia* of the First
Escort Group. They were to meet Convoy HX.96 from Halifax, Nova
Scotia, and escort it into the Clyde. With this task successfully

accomplished on 29 December, *Venomous* steamed for Liverpool.

Disaster struck the following day at 1120 as she passed abreast of B2 Buoy near the mouth of the Mersey. *Venomous* activated a mine despite degaussing being in use. Despite extensive damage on the starboard side there were no casualties or serious leaks. Rivets were loosened, the seams to the oil tanks and engine room bulkhead were distorted, and the bulkheads to the Cabin Flat (the officers' accommodation) plus the Captain's Day Cabin, Wardroom, Pantry and Wardroom Galley were badly bulged. The H.P. turbines, auxiliary machinery and starboard dynamo would also need repair. Only one

Venomous "out of control after hitting a mine on 30 December" (left) and under tow.
Note the crow's nest, a "large bucket" (AB Harry Haddon), the two black balls flying from her port signal halyard
signalling she is under tow and the absence of an RDF aerial from the mast head.
Photographed by Lt Peter Kershaw RNVR.

member of the ship's company was wounded, a stoker who was scalded on his hands and arms when one of the ship's steam pipes burst. Another casualty was a substantial portion of the Wardroom's wine store but a sympathetic inspector was persuaded to write off the loss, thus saving the members' pockets. She was not the only vessel damaged as the SS *Dorcasia*, a tanker of 8,053 tons, and the coaster *Calcium*, also struck mines. *Dorcasia* made port but *Calcium* sank with one fatality, a stoker. *Venomous* was soon taken in tow and berthed in Liverpool's Gladstone Dock around 2100. On New Year's Day 1941, *Venomous* was towed into Cammell Laird,

Birkenhead, where she was to remain for close on two months.

New Year's Day also brought the announcement of the award of the DSM to Chief ERA Don Passmore "For outstanding zeal, patience and cheerfulness and for never failing to set an example of wholehearted devotion to duty without which the high traditions of the Royal Navy could not have been upheld." The award was made on the recommendation of Warrant Engineer Parkes, in recognition of Passmore's tireless work keeping *Venomous'* engineering plant operational. The condition of the ship's engines and boilers (which needed frequent cleaning) would continue to deteriorate under the remorseless demands of wartime service.

Whilst in dock a number of the ship's company were posted to other ships and the remainder were given the opportunity to take leave. The Wardroom entertained itself with periodic runs ashore, frequenting an establishment going by the dubious name of "The Bear's Paw." On 28 January Sub Lt Arthur D. McPhee RN, and Temporary Mid. J.T. Knight RNR augmented *Venomous'* officer strength. "Homer" McPhee was a tall raw-boned Canadian, well liked by his colleagues, who had joined the Royal Navy as a boy sailor in 1936, was promoted to Petty Officer and commissioned shortly before joining *Venomous*, whilst Knight added a youthful cheerfulness to proceedings.

By the time these officers reported on board, the increase in complement of both officers and men on board *Venomous* was becoming a strain to the berthing and victualling arrangements, a situation shared by all of His Majesty's Ships during the war. The cramped overcrowded accommodation combined with the arduous conditions of the cold North Atlantic and Arctic Seas made conditions on *Venomous* and her sister V & Ws almost unbearable.

On the 26 January Henderson reported to Flag Officer in Charge Liverpool the belated discovery of a crack in the turbine foot which further extended the time *Venomous* spent at Cammell Laird's shipyard. During this protracted time in dockyard hands steps were also taken to better equip *Venomous* for her role as an escort for the Atlantic convoys. The removal of "Y" Gun at the stern made it possible to fit port and starboard rails for launching depth charges off the stern and increase the number of depth charges carried.

Despite having had an RDF operator for more than six months *Venomous* still had no RDF equipment due to lack of skilled artificers to fit and set this unfamiliar new technology which was to have such a decisive effect on the war at sea. During the two months *Venomous* was in the Cammell Laird shipyard she received the Type 286 RDF, a radar system originally designed for RAF aircraft to detect surface vessels, which could only track surface targets 45 to 60 degrees on either side of the ship's bow. This primitive early radar system would eventually be replaced by the Type 271, the first effective surface warning microwave shipboard radar set operated by the Royal Navy. Thomas described his role as the ship's radar operator:

> "The radar cabin was on the superstructure above, and abaft the bridge, and very exposed to the cold, bullets and shrapnel…it was a few months until I was given an assistant. Before his arrival, I was always on call – no regular watch-keeping for me, and very little sleep! R.D.F operators …were rare specimens, but this shortage was gradually remedied…"

On the 21 February, the day repairs were completed, *Venomous* commenced her sea trials. But almost immediately difficulties arose when the pump to the starboard dynamo engine failed. Disappointed, Henderson brought his destroyer back into the yards. It took three days to install and test the new pump and on 24 February *Venomous* appeared ready to return to Londonderry and rejoin the First Escort Group, but the departure did not go smoothly, as Lt Kershaw described:

> "On at least two occasions the dockyard maties announced that she was not fit to go to sea and we had to wait for a further two days. On the third occasion Cdr Henderson asked Lt Parkes whether he was ready and he said "yes". We immediately went out stern first and by the time we reached the Liverpool Light Vessel the dockyard maties were extremely worried. It was my first task to ask them whether they wished to proceed to Ireland or be landed on the Liverpool Light Vessel. They wisely chose the latter".

Hitler had not given Dönitz the number of U-boats he asked for but the fall of France and the building of U-boat bases on the Atlantic coast had greatly extended their range. The Royal Navy escorts were unable to accompany the convoys beyond the Mid Ocean Meeting Point (MOMP) where the ill-equipped and inexperienced Royal Canadian Navy took over the escort of the westbound convoys, the "empties", and handed over to the Royal Navy the escorting of the eastbound convoys. The convoy system was complex with:

> "more than 200 convoy routes in existence during the war of which 94

routes were under attack by U-boats. Each convoy was known by two or more letters designating the route and a consecutive number added in chronological order. Additionally, the letter 'F' was sometimes used to identify fast convoys (9 knots) and 'S' for slow ones (7 knots). The convoys received the number when they left harbour. Vessels that could make 13 knots or more could qualify for independent sailing but the losses amongst this group were three times higher than for those travelling in convoy."[24]

Sub Lt John C Tucker RNR who had been commissioned on leaving the training ship, HMS *Worcester*, at the outbreak of war and joined *Venomous* from the E Class destroyer, HMS *Escort*, in June explained the practical problems of escorting a large number of merchant ships. There were often more than fifty ships in a convoy and each ship had a diagram showing its position in the convoy and flew a signal flag identifying it to the other ships. The convoys assembled at Liverpool and Loch Ewe and to maximise their operational range the escort groups based at Londonderry would usually meet them in the Atlantic or the Minches between the Hebrides and the west coast of Scotland.

The Commodore of the Convoy, a senior ex-naval officer, possibly a retired admiral, would be on one of the merchant ships with a couple of signalmen. He would communicate with the CO of the escort group with signal lamps (Aldis lights) or flag signals and form up the ships in the agreed pattern. The escort group rarely had more than three or four destroyers and the numbers would be made up with armed trawlers (with a single 4-inch gun or 12-pounder on the fo'c'sle) and sloops or Flower Class corvettes. They would take up their positions with two escorts ahead, one each on the port and starboard sides and one astern.

There were all kinds of practical difficulties. Although ships in a convoy were supposed to be of a similar type and speed this was not always the case. Some could only manage 5 or 6 knots due to poor quality coal or low steam pressure and lagged behind. These stragglers were signalled to speed up and if that didn't work an escort would be detached to nag them until they caught up with the convoy. Some skippers were just "bolshie" and resented being shepherded along in a convoy. The convoys were blacked out, dead lights screwed down over portholes and the crew were forbidden to smoke on deck. Strict radio silence was observed.

Merchant ships were often sunk by attacking U-boats but the convoy never stopped to pick up survivors. Some convoys were accompanied by a slightly faster rescue ship with more life boats and better sick bay facilities. The primitive Type 286 RDF in use at the time was not a great deal of help in detecting U-boats attacking on the surface at night. *Venomous* had to circle in a figure of eight to do a complete sweep with her RDF and whilst doing so risked losing contact with the convoy. At this

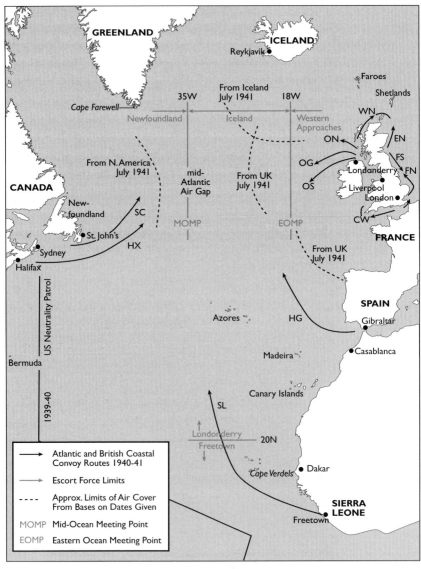

Atlantic theatre of operations with convoy routes designators.
Map graphic Kelly Erlinger. Map source Gordon Smith www.naval-history.net

stage of the war counter attacks were rarely effective.

In command of the First Escort Group was Cdr J.E. Broome DSC RN in the destroyer HMS *Keppel*.[25] By this point in the war "Jackie" Broome had acquired a reputation as an anti-submarine specialist. *Venomous* had joined a crack unit. *Venomous* arrived in Derry on the 25th and hardly had time to settle back into her base before orders came to escort Convoy OG.54, a convoy of 45 ships bound for Gibraltar With *Venomous* and the rest of the escort group the convoy proceeded untroubled by U-boats or aircraft and *Venomous* returned to Londonderry on 5 March with the prospect of a few days alongside.

Her next assignment began on 13 March. *Venomous* and the First Escort Group departed Londonderry for Loch Ewe on Scotland's north-west coast. Loch Ewe, a large deepwater loch with a narrow opening to the sea on the west coast of Scotland, had been selected as an alternative and more secure base for the Home Fleet after the sinking of the *Royal Oak* at Scapa Flow in 1939. It was also an assembly point for convoys to North America and from February 1942 for Arctic convoys to Murmansk and Archangel in north Russia. *Venomous* would call in at Loch Ewe on many future occasions. After topping up with fuel she and the other ships of the group joined Convoy OB.297 for North America. In what would become standard procedure *Venomous* and her group would escort the convoy westward to the limit of their endurance before transferring to an eastbound convoy, in this case Convoy HX.113 with 27 ships from Halifax, Nova Scotia.

Back in harbour at Londonderry on the 21st there was a brief three-day respite before *Venomous* let go once more to join OB.302, a 32-ship convoy out of Liverpool. This was to be an important occasion, as in the absence of Broome and *Keppel* Henderson would be in command of the group and *Venomous* would become the flotilla leader.[26]

For the next few months *Venomous* would lead the First Escort Group consisting of the old S Class destroyer HMS *Sabre*, and the former US Navy destroyers, HMS *Reading* and *Wellington*. The Flower Class corvettes, HMS *Dianella*, *Kingup*, and *Ausma*, reinforced the destroyers. They and the anti-submarine trawlers HMS *Man O'War*, *Lady Elsa* and *Northern Dawn* would become familiar names to the men of *Venomous*.

No losses were incurred by Convoy OB.302 until 29 March when the escorts left on reaching their maximum range and the convoy dispersed. At this point the SS *Liguria* was sunk, a victim of U-46 whose CO, Lt Engelbert Endrass, was an officer of U-47 when that boat penetrated the defences of Scapa Flow to sink the Battleship *Royal Oak*. After leaving OB.302 Henderson and the First Escort Group met incoming convoy HX.115 of 34 ships from Halifax to Liverpool. The SS *Hylton,* carrying a cargo of timber from Vancouver to the Tyne, and the SS *Germanic* were both torpedoed by U48. Sydney Compston described how they took onboard the survivors from the *Germanic*, many coughing up the fuel oil in which they had been swimming. The SS *Hylton* refused to sink giving plenty of time for the entire crew to be rescued before it was despatched by *Venomous* with gunfire and depth charges. Its last moments were captured by Lt Peter Kershaw.

The frustration that Henderson and his men felt at having to leave the convoys unprotected in the mid Atlantic gap was somewhat relieved as newer escort ships with greater cruising range started joining the escort groups. In his book, *Atlantic Escorts*, David K. Brown categorised this period as "A Gleam of Hope."

"There were more escorts; gone were the days of only one or two per

HMS *Venomous* with Atlantic camouflage and minus "Y" Gun at stern.

convoy. They were better trained too; both individually and as groups...Operating bases in Iceland and Newfoundland helped in making good use of the ships. It became possible to run more fast convoys, enabling the minimum speed of independents to be raised, with a marked drop in losses."[27]

The position deteriorated drastically in the spring of 1941, when Grand Admiral Dönitz changed the operating areas of his U-boats and their tactics. The heavily defended concrete submarine pens being built at Lorient on the French Atlantic coast enabled the U-boats to push farther into the Atlantic, out of reach of RAF Coastal Command air patrols. Despite the presence of more long-range escorts, a significant gap existed in the middle of the Atlantic Ocean that left convoys without air cover – and airpower was critical for convoy protection. Dönitz also re-organised his submarines. Instead of hunting alone in specified patrol area, his U-boats would hunt in 'wolf packs' which would strike a convoy together, overwhelming the escorts, and bringing chaos and destruction.

By April Anglo-Canadian naval and air forces countered this new

Photographed by Lt Peter Kershaw RNVR.

threat by operating out of bases in Iceland. Earlier in 1940, fearing a German invasion, Britain sent a large contingent of Royal Marines to occupy strategic points on the island. RAF Coastal Command now established airfields on the southern coast whilst the Royal Navy established an advanced fuelling base at Hvalfjord on the southwest coast of Iceland near Reykjavik, Iceland's capital. In July 1941, without any prior announcement to the American people, President Roosevelt agreed to take over the defence of Iceland. US Navy "Neutrality Patrols" began escorting convoys from ports in North America to the Mid Ocean Meeting Point (MOMP) south of Iceland.

The escort groups could now switch over – the relieving group from Hvalfjord would take up the escort back to Britain or on to North America, whilst the group being relieved would head to Hvalfjord to replenish and catch a short rest. The Royal Navy's official historian of the Second World War, Capt Stephen Roskill RN, put the Icelandic environs and the opportunity for the men of the escort groups to have a break from their gruelling work in perspective:

> "The treachery of the Icelandic climate…the inhospitality of its harbours and the virtual certainty that little rest or relaxation would be possible in them soon aroused the British sailor's intense dislike for the place. To come in from fighting the enemy and the elements only to find that the fury of the latter had followed him with intensified malevolence awoke all his wide capacity for sardonic humour."[28]

Venomous followed this new operational routine. On 8 April she and the First Escort Group accompanied the westward-bound Convoy OB.307 of 24 ships to a designated area south of Iceland, where an escort group from Iceland relieved it. The relief force escorted the convoy until it reached its North American destination whilst *Venomous* and her consorts headed to Iceland for refuelling. Once refuelled, *Venomous* and the group steamed back south to pick up a convoy heading east toward Britain, in this instance Convoy SC.27, which was brought safely into the Minches and thence to Liverpool.

For the ships' companies engaged in the Battle of the Atlantic this was a time of unremitting hardship. AB James Eaton records the grim conditions then prevailing:

> "We received six old pennies for hard lying per day. It was pretty rough washing. We had no hot water, just a steam geyser – a metal drum with steam pipes inside it. We filled up with cold water, turned the

Atlantic convoy OB.302 with Flower Class Corvette, March 1941.
Photographed by Lt Peter Kershaw RNVR.

Convoy HX.115, note aircraft on deck.
Photographed by Lt Peter Kershaw RNVR.

SS *Germanic* sinking, 29 March 1941.
Note gun at stern, typical of DEMS ships.
Photographed by Lt Peter Kershaw RNVR.

SS *Hylton* stayed afloat after being torpedoed on 29 March 1941 until sunk by *Venomous*.
Courtesy of Fred Thomas.

145

steam on, and there was our hot water. Washing facilities were situated starboard side at the break of the foc'sle – pretty grim trying to bathe at sea with a stern sea running, but we managed it."

'Freddo' Thomas recalled the messing arrangements on *Venomous* under these conditions:

"...Messes had about 14 or 15 seaman each, and the meals were prepared and served and cleared away by the system of 'mess-deck catering.' Two men from each mess served as 'cooks of the mess.' Their job for a day was to prepare the ingredients of the meal, take it up to the galley, and hand it over to the galley cook.

The galley cook's job was merely to see that the various meals did not burn or dry out. In small ships...weekly duty as 'cook of the mess' was in addition to all other duties. When the pipe 'cooks to galley' was sounded about midday, the two sailors on duty went to the galley to pick up the mess meal – usually contained in a large metal tray with two very hot handles which were wrapped in dish-clothes. One cook of the mess carried the meal to the hatch leading down to his mess-deck. His partner went ahead and descended halfway down the metal ladder to take hold of the tray when it was lowered. When the sea was rough, a third mess-mate was required to steady the one on

AB "Freddo" Thomas, RDF operator (left).
Courtesy of F.N.G. Thomas.

Cdr Henderson and the officers and men on *Venomous* escorting Atlantic convoys in 1941.
Photographed by Lt Peter Kershaw RNVR.

Lt Walter R. Wells, "No. 1" in 1941.

Cdr H.P. Henderson RN, CO from
December 1940 to June 1941.

Sub Lt Tucker seated on depth
charges on quarterdeck.

Warrant Officer Parkes RN with ship's crest.

Surgeon Lt P.B. Woodyatt RNVR.

Munro, Yeoman of Signals.

Lt "Homer" McPhee, a Canadian
officer, on bridge.

Visiting RAF officer with HMS *Sabre* behind

From left Chief Engineer Parkes, Cdr H.P. Henderson, Lt W.R. Wells,
Gunner Thomson with Sub Lt Esson in front, 3 May 1941.
Photographed by Lt Peter Kershaw RNVR.

Gunner Thomson and Lt Walter Wells on the bridge firing at a mine (left) and
Maylands on signalling lamp (right).
Photographed by Lt Peter Kershaw RNVR.

the ladder by placing his hands firmly on his mate's buttocks.

It was a dangerous procedure, which sometimes ended with the very hot contents of the tray falling on the head of the men. To suffer bodily harm from the constituents of a meal was not always accidental for the 'cook of the mess,' as my own experience testified. The leading seaman of the mess decided on pancakes for 'afters.' Neither I, as cook, nor my mate, had the slightest idea how to make them. We experimented with a stiff mixture of flour, milk and butter and tossed the hard round rubbery disks! When these were served they were quite inedible, so our shipmates pelted us with them – very forcibly! Shrove Tuesday always brings back memories."

There was an unexpected respite for the ship's company on 28 April, following a collision with the submarine H31 in the approaches to Derry. *Venomous* was dry-docked on 2 May and repairs took until the 19th when Henderson received orders to depart for Aultbea on Loch Ewe, to join Convoy OB.323 of 35 ships from Liverpool. Because of the improved programme of warship construction the number of escorts for this convoy had increased to fourteen, of which no fewer than six were destroyers. Once again the cover provided was effective with only one ship lost and this after the escorts had departed.

After leaving Convoy OB.323 *Venomous* and her consorts entered Hvalfjord, Iceland, on 21 May and secured alongside the new Depot Ship, HMS *Hecla*, to refuel and recover. There were usually three or four destroyers moored alongside *Hecla* and *Venomous* was to be a regular visitor. *Hecla* was not popular with the destroyer crews. It could carry out most repairs depriving the crew of shore leave whilst their ships were being repaired in Londonderry or on the Clyde.

The return journey was made with Convoy HX.126, which had suffered heavily, having lost nine of its 31 ships. Fortunately, the later stages of the journey were accomplished without further loss but AB Sydney Compston recalled one haunting moment: "There had been the

HMS *Hecla* at Iceland (Hvalfjord), 1941.
HMS *Oribi*, G-66, with John McBeath commanding, alongside *Hecla*, with a Town Class destroyer (former USN destroyer) and a possible V Class leader outboard of *Oribi*. *Courtsey of George Male.*

occasional U-boat contact but no kill. Homeward bound with a 30-ship convoy we met the Fleet out after the *Bismarck*. The next day (24 May) *Hood* was sunk." *Venomous* must have been among the last to see HMS *Hood* as she and the newly commissioned King George V Class battleship, HMS *Prince of Wales*, together with their escorting destroyers, steamed past on their way to engage the battleship KMS *Bismarck* and the Hipper Class heavy cruiser, KMS *Prinze Eugen*.[29]

The west bank of the River Foyle marked the border of the neutral Irish Republic and, during the brief sojourns in port, there were frequent opportunities to row the ship's whaleboat across to the other side for the purpose of replenishing stocks of supplies that were not readily available in Northern Ireland. As Lt Kershaw remembered, this could also lead to amusing incidents:

> "Before going to convoy, we used to go into the Free State and they would row out to us in small boats and we would barter for eggs (usually about 2 shillings a dozen). On one occasion going to Iceland, the weather was very bad and fortunately I had the morning watch. I went straight to the galley to find Bloody Mackenzie (No.l) with 2 eggs he had just boiled by holding the pan against the top of the coal galley (it took a long time). I started mine off only to find Bloody Jack with his hands covered in egg (he had fallen down the ladder to the Wardroom) and wanting to take my place, I suppose on the grounds of seniority. But I would have none of it and told him to take more care (the Stewards always seemed to be sick on these occasions)."

Sub Lt John Tucker reminisced "I recall leaving our caps behind and donning raincoats (to cover uniforms) and going ashore to the pubs in Buncrana for a little 'relaxation' whilst in Derry". Buncrana, an attractive small town on Loch Swilly in the Irish Republic six miles from Derry, was 'out of bounds' to naval officers but the pubs' landlords were happy to have them as customers.

Following a few days' break the destroyer was back at sea on 2 June spending five days with Convoy OB.330 and refuelling alongside HMS *Springbank*, one of five Armed Merchant Cruisers (AMC) manned by the Royal Navy. *Springbank* had been converted from an old banana boat and carried two catapult-launched Fulmar aircraft flown by Fleet Air Arm (FAA) pilots to intercept enemy planes.[30]

Venomous returned with Convoy HX.129 of 61 ships with additional cover provided by the battle-cruiser HMS *Repulse* and the County Class heavy cruiser HMS *Suffolk*.[31] Yet again there were no U-boat attacks, the main enemy being the uncompromising Atlantic. On 17 June Sub Lt J.C. Tucker RNR joined the Wardroom at Londonderry in time to accompany the ship to sea with Convoy OB.336 of 24 ships, returning with Convoy SC.34 of 35 ships covered by the battleship HMS *Revenge*.

The capture of U-110 and with it the German Enigma machine and codes on the 9 May was kept secret but by the end of June the code breakers at Bletchley Park were able to decipher the messages sent by

Venomous alongside HMS *Springbank*, an Armed Merchant Cruiser (AMC), to refuel on 6 June 1941.
Springbank was torpedoed by U-201 on 27 September 1941 and then scuttled by gunfire.
Photographed by Lt Peter Kershaw RNVR.

The CAM launched Fulmar aircraft on *Springbank*.
Photographed by Lt Peter Kershaw RNVR.

Dönitz to his U-boat commanders and convoys could be ordered to change course to avoid interception. The failure of the U-boats whilst the Group was on station is recalled by Surg. Lt Woodyatt:

> "Convoys were reasonably peaceful – we made attacks from time to time on U-boat contacts and on one occasion we were almost certain we had sunk one of them. However, there was no positive evidence and we could not claim a definite success."

Woodyatt also remembered the vulnerability of the unescorted merchantmen in the mid Atlantic, brought about by the limited range of the old destroyers, sloops and corvettes:

> "Owing to fuel restrictions we could only stay with the outward bound convoy to a point about half way across the Atlantic. We then had to break off and dash up to Iceland to refuel and then return to meet the next lot of ships from the U.S.A. It was at this point of course that most merchant ship losses occurred and on several occasions we had the sad task of having to sink our own crippled but still floating ships to prevent them being a danger to other shipping."

The officers of USN ships accompanying convoys from North America to the MOMP had no experience of anti-submarine warfare (ASW) and responded to Royal Navy Asdic contacts by depth charging at random which made it impossible to continue tracking the attacking U-boats. Sub Lt Tucker remembered an American "Admiral" joining *Venomous* on a convoy to learn how the Royal Navy did it. Judging from the amount of "scrambled eggs" on the peak of his naval cap he was certainly a senior officer but probably not an Admiral.

Gunner Thompson, Mid R.J. Knight, Cdr H.P. Henderson and unknown USN officer.
Photographed by Sub Lt J.C. Tucker.

After refuelling at Loch Ewe *Venomous* returned to Londonderry at midnight, on the 27 June with Henderson navigating Loch Foyle and the river at its head in the dark without the help of navigational aids – not an easy task, as Broome recalled in his book *Convoy is to Scatter*:

> "Navigating up and down the River Foyle between Derry and Moville at the mouth of Lough Foyle could be exciting. I remember a small derelict lighthouse, uninhabited with neither light nor foghorn, but a very helpful dog which always barked when ships came too close."

On the 29 June U651 was forced to the surface south of Iceland by repeated depth charging whilst attacking convoy HX.133 from Halifax.[32] Captain Lohmeyer and his crew of forty-five were photographed by Lt Peter Kershaw as they were brought ashore at Londonderry. The sinking of U-651 and the first sight of the enemy they were fighting made a huge impression on the crews of the escort vessels. Every member of the crew of U-651 was interrogated at great length and the confidential report of their interrogation is very revealing.[33]

Captain Lohmeyer of U-651 watches his crew come ashore at Londonderry.
Photographed by Lt Peter Kershaw RNVR.

On the 2 July a party was held by the wardroom of *Venomous* to bid farewell to Cdr Henderson who was replaced as CO by Cdr Hugh Falcon-Steward RN. Falcon-Steward was widely respected as a fine destroyer captain, particularly in the anti-submarine field, in which he had specialised since 1931. He had served as anti-submarine officer on HM *Escapade* and HM *Echo* and with the Nineteenth Destroyer Flotilla and his last appointment before joining *Venomous* was at HMS *Osprey*, the anti-submarine school at Portland. He would remain with

Venomous until the end of 1942, apart from a short spell whilst she was in dockyard hands. Falcon-Steward would see *Venomous* safely through dangerous situations, and although a somewhat private man, he was known affectionately to his officers as "Freddie Sugar" (from the phonetic alphabet in use at the time).

Cdr H.P. Henderson RN posing with army Bren Gun (on left) was very different from his successor as CO, Cdr Hugh Falcon-Steward RN.
Photographed by Lt Peter Kershaw RNVR.

Five days later Falcon-Steward took *Venomous* to sea as part of the escort for Convoy OB.343, a large convoy of 72 ships, which had left Liverpool on 6 July. All went well until 11 July, when *Venomous* broke down south of Iceland. Falcon-Steward signalled: "Both extraction pumps broken down. Proceeding in tow of *Sabre* to Reykjavik. My position is 62° 06' N 22° 04' W." There now began a tense period for those in both destroyers. The S Class destroyer HMS *Sabre* was as old as *Venomous* and progress was agonisingly slow as Woodyatt described:

> "On one occasion we had just left a convoy when we had some sort of engine room breakdown and had to be towed about 200 miles into Iceland by *Sabre* – one of the oldest Destroyers in the Navy at that time. This was a very slow process and we would have been powerless to do anything about a U-boat attack. However, *Venomous* was always a lucky ship and all was well."

Emergency repairs to *Venomous* were carried out alongside HMS *Hecla* before she departed under her own steam on the 14th, arriving in Derry two days later. This was the first of many occasions when the tired engines would protest, a tendency not appreciated by the Escort Group Commander as recounted by Warrant Engineer Parkes: "On one occasion Cdr Broome took me aside and pressed me regarding our temperamental engines. I explained the problems we faced but he did not seem to appreciate the difficulties." Nevertheless, Parkes was shortly to receive the DSC for his prolonged and largely successful efforts as engineering officer.

Venomous put out from Moville on 21 July and, in line with usual practice, topped up with fuel at Loch Ewe before joining Convoy OB.349 of 44 ships on the 23rd. By now Woodyatt had departed and been succeeded by Surg. Lt Robert Browning RNVR who recalled a typical convoy operation:

> "The ships forming the convoy came mainly from Liverpool and the Clyde. After leaving Moville we would set out for a rendezvous point at one of various places off the West Coast of Scotland. Sometimes we would call at Loch Ewe in Wester Ross for more oil before joining the convoy."

By this time it was apparent that more extensive engine repairs were urgently required. Accordingly, *Venomous* entered Derry on the 1 August for her first refit since April 1940 and with it the opportunity of leave for her crew. The priority during the three weeks she spent in dock was, of course, her temperamental and unreliable engineering plant. During the refit Mr. Thomson (Gunner T) departed *Venomous* and was replaced by Gunner Arthur Simms RN and "Homer" McPhee was promoted to full Lieutenant with seniority from 16 May.

Venomous being towed to Hvalfjord by HMS *Sabre*, 11 July 1941, and alongside HMS *Hecla*.
Photographed by Lt Peter Kershaw RNVR.

Germany had invaded Russia on the 22 June and Britain was no longer fighting alone but its new ally desperately needed supplies to resist the rapidly advancing German forces. The first convoy round Norway's North Cape to Arctic Russia left in August. Many more were to follow. That same month Finland, supposedly neutral, invaded Russia with German support to regain the territory seized by Russia in the Winter War of 1939-40 and Churchill came under pressure from Stalin to join its ally in fighting Finland. Lt J.C. Tucker wrote to that "whilst based in Derry I have a recollection of loading ladders and filled oil drums all on deck ready to support an invasion of Finland. This was called off before we actually sailed." With the Baltic firmly in German hands this was not a realistic option and was wisely abandoned.

Following torpedo exercises *Venomous* rejoined the First Flotilla Group at Loch Ewe on 29 August as part of the escort for westbound Convoy ON.10 of 73 ships and after refuelling at Iceland on 1 September she and the group returned to the UK with Convoy HX.146 of 71 ships. By now the mid-Atlantic gap was being bridged, with long-range escort ships and anti-submarine patrol aircraft, although many convoys transited the gap without air support. Browning remembered that *Venomous* hosted RAF officers keen to discover how best to provide air cover:

> "Convoys consisted of a large number of merchant ships (60-70 or more) of all shapes and sizes. We pursued a zigzag course and after 5-6 days handed over the convoy to another group. On two occasions we had on board an RAF Officer (Observer) from Coastal Command, who came to find out about the problems of escorting convoys, with a view to giving assistance from the air."

Lockheed-built Hudsons with ASV Mark II radar were used by RAF Coastal Command on anti-submarine patrols from bases in Iceland and Northern Ireland.
Photographed by Lt Peter Kershaw RNVR.

The relieving escorts were usually ships of the Royal Canadian Navy and over the next few weeks the names of the Flower Class corvette HMCS *Spikenard*, the C Class destroyers HMCS *St. Laurent* and *Restigouche*, and HMCS *St. Croix* (the former US Navy destroyer *McCook*) would become familiar to those in *Venomous*.

Protection of Convoy ON.15, an important convoy of 42 ships, mainly large oil tankers, was the next assignment. On the 13 September there were more engine problems, which forced her to abort after two days at sea and eventually led to her being towed back to Moville on Loch Foyle, in the supposedly neutral Irish Republic, twenty miles from Londonderry. The repairs required were obviously of a minor nature as *Venomous* was at sea the following day to meet Convoy SC.43, which she stayed with until the 20th.

From time to time, the convoys were detected and shadowed by the long-range, 4-engine Focke-Wulf 200 Kondor reconnaissance bombers. This was a frustrating experience as Browning recalled:

> "Not infrequently we had a visit from the Luftwaffe in the form of a spotter plane which circled the convoy at a safe distance for hours on end. Presumably he would be passing on details of a convoy – size, speed, direction, number of escort vessels etc. There was nothing we could do about it."

Having returned from escorting Convoy SC.43 on 20 September, *Venomous* and her crew were able to enjoy a brief respite before Falcon-Steward took his destroyer back out to sea on the 24th to escort Convoy ON.21 of 33 ships. *Venomous* and the group covered the convoy until 5 October, when they picked up Convoy HX.152 of 60 ships, and brought them back to the UK intact – but not without loss of life. Sydney Compston remembers that "It was very rough weather out in the Atlantic, Teddy Weeks always wore heavy leather sea boots, and was washed overboard and was lost. He was a reservist from Oxfordshire." Falcon-Steward turned the ship sharply round but with little hope of finding him in these huge seas. The same giant wave which washed this young seaman to his death broke the arm of the officers' steward. The personal belongings of a dead seaman were auctioned and the money raised sent to his family. Arnie Birkin, a friend of Teddy Weeks, bought his bosun's pipe (also known as a "call") and his son still has it. Teddy Weeks was swept overboard on the 8 October and the following day another escort, an old S Class destroyer, HMS *Shikari,* lost most of her bridge after a large wave crashed over her bow.

The conditions which led to such accidents were recalled by Freddo Thomas, the RDF operator:

> "In the North Atlantic winter the wind and the enormous waves were a great problem, especially for the west-bound convoys (i.e. the "empties"). The convoys followed an agreed route, thought to be the safest from U-boat attacks but this route was not always the best in relation to the huge waves that had built up over hundreds of miles. A ship, large or small, generally steers into the storm. Small escort ships like *Venomous* (only one-fifth the size of the average merchant ship), were unable to do this, without breaking the escort defence pattern. The result was that *Venomous* often steered into the waves at a slanted angle, causing dangerous side to side rolling, as well as the pitching motion, when the bows protruded almost vertically above the sea before crashing down into a deep hollow.
>
> Water raced the full length of the upper deck, making it

AB Sydney T. Charles, Bosun's Mate (on left), with his 'pipe'.
Courtesy of Arthur Charles.

extremely dangerous for crew members to move about. To reduce the danger of being swept overboard a steel wire was secured from one end of the deck to the other with thick sliding hand-ropes but on at least one of the escort ships, a seaman moving to his station was washed overboard. To the dismay of his shipmates, and particularly of the captain, the ship had to move on. To stop and attempt a rescue would have been futile and exceptionally hazardous. On several occasions the sea was so rough that almost everyone on board, including the old "salts" were seasick."

The frequently hazardous duties of a Medical Officer under these condition are remembered by Browning:

"On a destroyer, sea duties are not very heavy unless the ship is in action and there are a lot of casualties. Consequently, I had a lot of time on my hands, which I filled by deciphering W.T. Signals. To help me, I had one sick berth attendant [SBA]. The Sick Bay was situated on the forward deck just below the bridge. It had two bunks, but these were seldom occupied except by the SBA as his normal resting place. Illness at sea was rare as there are few germs in the North Atlantic, but on coming into port the coughs, colds, tummy upsets and other infections started up again. On one occasion when the ship was on escort duty, I had to be taken in the whaler to see a sick man on a large merchant ship. This I found quite exciting as the ship was not allowed to stop and I was very relieved when I was able to grab the ladder over her side and climb up."

Surgeon Lt Browning (left) and the "Doc" being taken in the ship's whaler to a sick seaman on a merchant ship.

After the turbulent conditions of the previous few days the First Escort Group enjoyed a welcome break in Derry before sailing on 20 October to meet Convoy ON.28 of 42 ships. *Venomous* was not amongst them, being delayed because of a malfunction in her port condenser. It was shortly before midnight on the 21st before she finally left Lough Foyle on passage to Loch Ewe to refuel. Even before she arrived, the defects again manifested themselves and further repairs were required before she left Loch Ewe at 1930 on 22nd to join the convoy the following afternoon. *Venomous* took over from HMS *Westcott* as SO Escort (Broome on *Keppel* was absent). Suffering a severe shortage of feed water, she was forced to leave the convoy at noon on the 25th, before the arrival of the US escorts, securing the following day in Reykjavik, and she was soon back alongside the repair ship *Hecla* where examination revealed cracked and holed tubes in her boilers.

Also in Hvalfjord under repair was USS *Kearny*. With "Neutrality Patrols" of US Navy ships escorting Atlantic convoys it was inevitable that one of them would eventually become a target for a German U-boat. On the 17 October whilst escorting Convoy SC.48 USS *Kearny* was hit on the starboard side by a torpedo fired by U-652 and was photographed at Hvalfjord, listing heavily and lying alongside the repair ship USS *Vulcan*. Two weeks later on the 31 October USS *James Reuben* was torpedoed and sank whilst escorting Convoy HX.156. Everyone aboard *Venomous* must have known that American entry into the war had been brought much closer.

With *Keppel* absent Falcon-Steward was supposed to have been leading the First Escort Group but recurrent mechanical problems had resulted in *Venomous* being late to join Convoy ON.28 and having to

USS *Kearny* alongside USS *Vulcan* at Hvalfjord after being torpedoed on 17 October 1941.
Photographed by Sub Lt J.C. Tucker RNR.

leave it early. Cdr Broome attached a covering note to Falcon-Steward's report to Captain (D), Londonderry, making clear his concern:

> The internal difficulties of *Venomous* are brought to your notice. During the last three trips, defects have developed which have necessitated her leaving the convoy. Her fuel consumption is excessive. The defects may be a run of bad luck but they are putting an extra strain on her engine room staff and may point to the ship becoming more a liability than an asset this winter. *Venomous* was the lame dog of my division at Harwich last summer.[34]

Repairs to the boiler were completed in time for *Venomous* to leave Hvalfjord on the 31st to meet the 41 ships of Convoy SC.50 and arrived back in Derry on 4 November.

Venomous spent five days alongside before proceeding to Loch Ewe, where she took station with two columns of merchantmen scheduled to join Convoy OS.35. Departure of the Loch Ewe section was delayed, however, and there was some doubt whether they would fall in with the Liverpool section of six columns before nightfall. *Venomous* joined at 1800 on 11 November, taking up her usual position astern of the convoy. Shortly afterwards Falcon-Steward was directed by Cdr Broome to pass, by visual signal, two important messages to escort ships on either side of the convoy. Conditions worsened as the convoy left the shelter of the Minches and having completed his task Falcon-Steward found that he had lost touch with the convoy, which by then had executed three changes of course.

Having regained contact with the convoy, Falcon-Steward realised that *Venomous* was now in the van, leading the convoy, instead of being on her correct station astern. The lead merchant ship of the port column was now on *Venomous'* starboard quarter. Visibility was at best variable with low cloud and intermittent squalls. Adding to this navigational challenge was a moonless night. Broome described what happened next on the bridge of the *Keppel*:

> "At 2343, Midshipman B.H.G.M. Baynham, sweeping on the port bow with his glasses, swept past what he thought was a disturbed patch of water but on sweeping back he identified a ship. I immediately identified *Venomous*, ordered full speed astern, sounded three blasts on the siren and switched on navigation lights. Mercifully with almost all way off we struck *Venomous* on her starboard side almost abreast of the torpedo tubes".

In *Venomous* the sighting was almost simultaneous. PO J.F. Crowley recounted what he saw from his position on *Venomous'* bridge:

> "Roughly about 1145 I was looking out to port with binoculars. It was blowing a bit and slightly dark. I took the binoculars from my eyes and happened to glance out to starboard where I saw a dark object, which I reported to the Captain as a ship. I heard two blasts from *Keppel's* siren."

Falcon-Steward takes up the sequence of events:

> "Petty Officer J.F. Crowley, 2nd Officer of the Watch, reported a ship bearing 30°. *Venomous* went hard a port and switched on navigation lights. The other vessel sounded one short blast. I then ordered full speed ahead to increase turn movement".

The confusion over the number of blasts from *Keppel's* siren undoubtedly contributed to the collision. Another member of the watch on *Venomous'* bridge, Leading Seaman J.A. Newton, stated: "I was certain I heard *Keppel* give two blasts and although I could have mistaken this for three, I don't think so." The significance attached to the number of blasts is explained by the steering rules for power-driven vessels:

> One short blast – I am altering my course to starboard
> Two short blasts – I am altering my course to port
> Three short blasts – my engines are going full speed astern

ERA James Irlam was on duty in the engine room and he remembered what happened next:

> "We were steaming at 71 revs. I was just making up the register. I got an order 'full speed ahead both'. I immediately replied to the bridge. I telegraphed the boiler room 'full speed'. I went down to start the main feed pump. Then I got the order 'stop both'. I stopped both. I went off to have a look round and to see if anything was the matter. I saw water coming in."

With considerable damage done to her starboard side *Venomous* ran clear of the convoy and stopped. With the ship at action stations damage control parties swung into action. *Venomous* was in real trouble. Falcon-Steward recounted in his report:

> "Engineer Officer, Mr. A.E. Parkes DSC RN attended to the pumps and arranged the shoring up of the bulkheads with great efficiency. The placing of the collision mat and preparation for towing were carried out under the charge of Lt W.R. Wells DSC RN."

Sub Lt J.C. Tucker was in the cabin he shared with Homer McPhee when the collision occurred. They found the round bolt down hatch, their only access to the main deck, was blocked by the torpedo tubes which had swung over the hatch to the starboard side. Once they had been swung clear by the men on deck they clambered out to find they could hardly see *Keppel* due to thick fog.

The steps taken to save the crippled *Venomous* can be determined from the signals that reported the collision and the response to them. Cdr Broome sent the first signal: "Have been in collision with *Venomous* in position 280°, Cape Wrath 14 miles. *Venomous* holed starboard side. Engine room flooded. *Kingcup* has taken in tow. Require salvage tugs immediately."[35] In the signal from NOIC Greenock, a tug was immediately dispatched to assist the crippled *Venomous*: "Sail *Marauder* with dispatch to assist *Venomous*."[36]

After checking the damage done to his ship Broome decided that *Keppel* could not continue as escort leader and he remained with *Venomous* and her tow, the Flower Class corvette, *Kingcup*, until dawn. Broome then took over the tow from *Kingcup* which rejoined the convoy. Broome sent the following signals:

> "My 0110/12 *Venomous* in tow of *Keppel* reports bulkheads holding, pumps working. No immediate danger apparent. Course and speed 193° 5 knots. *Keppel* has stem buckled above and below waterline. Forepeak flooded No. 5 collision bulkhead undamaged. Am standing by tow until daylight."[37]

> "*Venomous* in tow of *Marauder* 58° 16' N 05° 41' W. 193° 5 knots. *Venomous* reports water level approximately sea level in engine room. Can keep steam for about two more hours, after which water will gain but should not be dangerous if bulkhead holds. *Kingcup* rejoin convoy. *Keppel* still standing by tow. Consider more advisable repair bow damage then continue."[38]

The seriousness of the situation was made very clear by this last signal.

Broome and Falcon-Steward received a signal from C in C Western Approaches that *Venomous* should be towed directly to the Clyde, but this was considered by both officers to be too hazardous. The following arrangements were made: "Rescue tug *Mastadonte* will be sailed from Loch Ewe about 1830 today with divers' equipment and salvage personnel. *Marauder* is to stand by *Venomous* until relieved by *Mastadonte*."[39] *Mastadonte* was described by Sub Lt Tucker as "a pretty ancient vessel and an extraordinary sight with one huge long funnel ...

higher than the mast". It towed *Venomous* back through the Minches (between the Outer Hebrides and the Scottish mainland) to Loch Ewe where it arrived for essential repairs at 1444 on 12 November.

It took two days for *Mastadonte's* divers to render *Venomous* seaworthy and on the 15 November orders to get underway were received: "Require you will sail *Venomous* in tow of *Mastadonte* for Greenock p.m. tomorrow. Fighter co-operation will be arranged by FOIC Greenock."[40] A rapid deterioration in the weather delayed the sailing and it was not until the evening of the 17th that *Venomous* was towed to Rothesay, on the Isle of Bute at the mouth of the Clyde not far from Greenock, arriving on the 19th.

Shortly after her arrival the Flag Officer in Charge at Greenock convened a Board of Enquiry "to investigate the circumstances attending the collision between HMS *Keppel* and HMS *Venomous* on

HMS *Venomous* at Loch Ewe on the 15 November 1941 after the collision with *Keppel*.
Note the absence of "Y" Gun.
Photographed by Lt Peter Kershaw RNVR.

the night of 11/12 November 1941."[41] In his letter accompanying the report of the board, the C in C Western Approaches, Vice Admiral Sir Percy Noble RN wrote: "A good look-out was being kept in both ships. But, owing to the ever efficient camouflaging, *Venomous* was unable to estimate accurately the inclination of *Keppel*."[42] He agreed with the Board's conclusion when he wrote: "It is considered that blame is attached to the Commanding Officer of HMS *Venomous* in that having lost the convoy, the use of R.D.F. in order to regain touch was a seamanlike precaution which he omitted to take."[43] Both HMS *Keppel* and HMS *Venomous* were fitted with the Type 286M radar but, under questioning, Broome said he did not detect a "rapidly closing echo" whilst Falcon-Steward admitted that his radar was not in use "because I thought I knew where the convoy was".

Falcon-Steward was not penalised for his lack of judgement in failing to use his RDF and remained in command of *Venomous*. Such incidents are treated differently in times of war, especially if they do not involve the loss of the ship or the death of any of the crew. Combat experienced officers were in short supply and this was a learning experience for all involved. A year to the day later, during a "very long night" off the coast of Morocco, Falcon-Steward was to demonstrate that he had learned his lesson on the importance of using radar.

Notes

1   Barnett, p. 167.

2   See http://www.navweaps.com/Weapons/WNBR_2pounder_m8.htm. *The Gunnery pocket book* available online at http://www.hnsa.org/doc/br224/index.htm on the same web site is a valuable resource.

3   The key texts on the adoption and use of RDF in the Royal Navy are: *Radar - the Development of Equipments for the Royal Navy 1935 - 45*; edited by F.A. Kingsley (Basingstoke: Macmillan Press Ltd, 1995). ISBN: 0-333-61210-8. *The Applications of Radar and Other Electronic Systems in the Royal Navy in World War 2;* by F.A. Kingsley (Basingstoke: Macmillan Press Ltd, 1995). ISBN 0-333-62748-2. *Radar at Sea - The Royal Navy in World War 2*; by Derek Howse (Basingstoke: Macmillan Press Ltd, 1993). ISBN 0-333-58449-X.

4   Ibid, p. 163.

5   Ibid, p. 163.

6   Ibid, p. 187.

7   Smith, *Hold the Narrow Sea*, p. 75.

8   The light cruiser HMS *Cardiff* belonged to the *Ceres* Class. Completed in 1917, *Cardiff* led the entire German High Seas Fleet in to surrender and internment at Scapa Flow on 21 November 1918. She survived the war and was sold for scrap in 1946. *Conway's All the World's Fighting Ships 1906 – 1921*, p. 61.

9   C in C Nore signal sent at 12/1755/9/40.

10   C in C Nore signal sent at 23/2013/9/40.

11   Operation *Lucid* was inspired by Drake and Nelson's use of fire ships against the Spanish Armada and Napoleon's invasion flotillas.

12   Degaussing reduces the magnetic signature of a ship so that it can not be detected by a magnetic mine. Degaussing equipment must have been installed on Venomous since the damage report on the evacuation of troops from Boulogne on the 23 May mentioned that it

was damaged (NA Ref. ADM 267/101) but de-gaussing was not always effective as *Venomous* found to its cost when it hit a mine in Liverpool Bay on the 30 December 1940 despite the degaussing equipment being in use (NA Ref. ADM 267/91).

13 Barnett, p. 211-12.

14 *Argus* had been loaded with a dozen Hurricane fighter aircraft and was met by heavy units at Gibraltar and escorted to a point west of Malta where the Hurricanes would take off and fly straight to the besieged island.

15 C in C WA to NOIC Greenock sent at 12/1651/11/40.

16 Only the Luftwaffe's four-engine Focke-Wulf Kondor reconnaissance bombers, with a range of over 2,000 miles, were able to intercept the *Argus* force and the few U-boats available concentrated their efforts to the north and westward of Ireland (the Western Approaches).

17 Barnett, p. 241.

18 On 2 August 1917 Squadron Commander Edwin Dunning successfully landed a Sopwith Pup on *Furious*, the first person to land an aircraft on a moving ship. On 7 August he made another successful landing but he was killed on his third attempt when the rotary engine choked.

19 Signal from C in C WA to FOIC Liverpool at 11/1643/11/40.

20 Signal from C in C W.A. sent to *Highlander*, *Venomous* and *Ambuscade* at 12/0158/12/40.

21 Signal from C in C W.A. sent to *Venomous* at 12/1914/12/40.

22 Signal from C in C W.A. sent to *Venomous* at 14/0445/12/40.

23 HMS *Rockingham* was one of the US Navy's *Clemson* Class destroyers referenced in Chapter 1.

24 See http://www.convoyweb.org.uk/extras/index.html?code.php~exmain (on *Convoy Web*) and *Convoy System 1939-45: its organization, defence and operation* by Andrew Haigh (Vanwell Publishing, 2000).

25 HMS *Keppel*, the destroyer leader, was a member of the *Shakespeare* Class and a contemporary of *Venomous*. She was completed in 1920.

26 *Keppel* would be in long-term refit to be converted to a Long Range Escort (L.R.E).

27 David K. Brown, *Atlantic Escorts: Ships, Weapons & Tactics in World War II*, Naval Institute Press, Annapolis, Maryland, 2007, p.67.

28 Roskill, *War at Sea*, Vol. 1, p. 452.

29 During the Second World War KMS (*Kriegsmarine Schiff*) replaced the SMS (*Seiner Majestaet Schiff*) used in the German Imperial Navy as the standard designation for surface warships.

30 The other four AMC were HMS *Patia*, HMS *Ariguani*, HMS *Maplin* and HMS *Pegasus*. Their planes were flown by Fleet Air Arm pilots. In addition to the five Royal Navy manned AMC there were 35 CAM (Catapult Armed Merchant) ships with planes piloted by the RAF.

31 HMS *Repulse* and *Suffolk* had been sent to protect the convoy from a possible attack from *Bismarck* and *Prinze Eugen*.

32 See http://www.cnrs-scrn.org/northern_mariner/vol12/tnm_12_3_43-50.pdf for a detailed account of the attacks and counter attacks on HX.133 originally published as *The battle for Convoy HX.133, 23-9 June 1941*; by David Syrett in *The Northern Mariner* 2002 12(3) 43-50.

33 The report can be seen at http://www.uboatarchive.net/U-651INT.htm. In addition to the names of all crew members, technical details of U651 and its operations it contains details such as the statement "that the prostitutes of Lorient knew more about past and present plans than many German officers."

34 HMS *Venomous, Convoy ON28, Report of Proceedings*. In: *1941 – 42 ON, HX, SC Convoy Reports*, Case 8078 War History (Admiralty Record Office) NA Ref. ADM 199/1147.

35 Signal sent from *Keppel* to C in C WA at 12/0110A/11/41.

36 Signal sent from NOIC Greenock to NOIC Stornoway at 12/0223A/11/41.

37 Signal sent by *Keppel* to C in C WA at 12/0330A/11/41.

38 Signal sent by *Keppel* to C in C WA at 12/1047A/11/41.

39 Signal sent by NOIC Greenock to *Venomous* and *Keppel* at 13/1230A/11/41.

40 Signal sent by NOIC Greenock to NOIC Aultbea at 16/1314A/11/41.

41 *Collision between HMS Keppel and HMS Venomous and Findings of the Board of Enquiry. NA Ref.* ADM 1/12015(29)

42 Ibid.

43 Ibid.

CHAPTER SIX

REFIT, RECOMMISSIONING AND RUSSIA
January – June 1942

The cold and ice equalled the enemy's ferocity

The damage to the hull was not catastrophic but the starboard engineering space was extensively damaged when the compartment flooded up to the ship's waterline. The repair work was allocated to Messrs. Scotts of Greenock but later transferred to The Ailsa Shipbuilding Company of Troon on the Ayrshire coast. *Venomous* entered the dry dock at Troon on 2 December 1941 and was still there on Christmas Day. That was good news for all on board. It was better to be in the hands of the dockyard "maties" during Christmas than at sea.

While *Venomous* was in the dockyard at Troon the war took a dramatic turn. Britain's declaration of war on Finland on the 6 December was completely overshadowed by the Japanese attack on the American fleet at Pearl Harbour (Hawaii) the following day and Germany's declaration of war on the United States four days later on the grounds that "vessels of the American Navy, since early September 1941, have systematically attacked German naval forces" (the USS *Kearny* and USS *James Reuben* were both mentioned). These few days changed everything. The demoralizing loss of the battleship HMS *Prince of Wales* and the battle cruiser HMS *Repulse* off Singapore on the 10 December was a terrible blow to the Royal Navy but Britain now had a powerful ally in the war against Germany and the war against Japan.

Whilst repairs were underway the Admiralty directed Falcon-Steward to prepare *Venomous* to be taken in hand for a major overhaul to convert his destroyer into a Long Range Escort (L.R.E.), a similar conversion to that of two of her sister ships, HMS *Vimy* and *Viscount*. This work was going to take time and, as the ship would be reduced to Care and Maintenance, only essential personnel would be retained. In the days following Christmas there would be a number of departures.

First to leave was Lt Walter Wells, who had joined *Venomous* as a seasick young sub lieutenant in 1939, won the DSC at Boulogne and left as "No. 1" on Boxing Day.[1] After him went Lt John Vaughan Lewis, the popular Canadian officer Lt "Homer" McPhee,[2] Sub Lts Alan Esson[3] and John C Tucker and "Chiefie Parkes". Last to go was Lt Peter Kershaw, but at least he would be on familiar territory, his next appointment being to the even older S Class destroyer, HMS *Sabre*, a chummy ship of the *Venomous*.[4] At the turn of the year Lt S.J. Parsons DSC RN experienced a fleeting association with the ship: "I joined *Venomous* at Troon on 31st December 1941 and left again on 2nd January 1942 – my shortest ever appointment. I was sent to assist in paying off the ship at the commencement of her refit". Of the officers, only Cdr Falcon-Steward and Mr. Simms the Gunner would still be on board when *Venomous* next put to sea.

Repairs to the ship's hull were completed by 29 December. Up to this point only minor modifications had been made to *Venomous* but conversion to an L.R.E. would require major modifications which would change her combat capability and greatly alter her appearance. These would convert *Venomous* from an elderly but fast greyhound to a sheepdog, whose primary mission was to provide anti-submarine warfare capability in defence of merchant convoys. The modifications to her engine room would reduce her maximum speed but improve her endurance whilst changes in her armament would transform her from a general-purpose fleet escort to a dedicated sub-hunter. The tall thin front funnel, widely known as the "Woodbine" after a popular brand of cigarettes, would be removed and the forward boiler room ripped out. The lower part of the boiler room would be replaced with fuel tanks and a larger mess deck for the ship's company would be fitted out above the fuel tanks. Additional changes included improved electronic equipment, the re-wiring of the ship's electrics and the installation of electric heating.

There is, however, conclusive evidence that the original conversion plans for *Venomous* were not implemented. In his classic book on the V & Ws Anthony Preston lists the nineteen V & Ws converted to L.R.E.s giving the date when each ship entered the yards and when it left.[5] According to Preston *Venomous* entered the yard for its refit in January 1942 and returned to service in August 1942 but in fact it left for Londonderry on the 6 April after only three months. If as Preston states it took at least four months to convert a V & W to an L.R.E. (with the average being five months) then it would have been impossible to convert *Venomous* to an L.R.E.

A signal from C in C Western Approaches to C in C Home Fleet in April 1942 after *Venomous* left the yards stated that *Venomous* would be transferred to Home Fleet to support Convoy PQ.15 and that she had 'short legs', an indication that *Venomous* was still a Short Range Escort (S.R.E.). By the time July rolled around, instead of still being in the yards as claimed by Preston, *Venomous* was supporting Operation *Pedestal* and in his history of *Pedestal* the naval historian, Peter Smith, wrote that on 4 August 1942, "The short range escorts were refuelled during the day: *Wolverine, Venomous, Derwent* and *Wishart* from the *Nigeria* and *Kenya, Amazon, Malcolm* and *Zetland* from the battleships."[6]

A photograph taken in the Mediterranean after the landings in North Africa early in 1943 showing *Venomous* crossing astern of the fleet aircraft carrier, HMS *Formidable,* provides conclusive evidence that it was not converted to an L.R.E. (see page 256). As previously mentioned, the most distinctive feature of an L.R.E. was the short stubby single funnel, the tall thin front funnel, the "Woodbine", having been removed. In this photograph, one immediately sees that *Venomous* still had two funnels. We are also fortunate to have been lent an album of photographs taken by Lt Leslie Eaton, who joined the ship after its overhaul and refit, in which both funnels are clearly visible. The photographic evidence for *Venomous* not having been converted to an L.R.E. at Troon is overwhelming.

The photograph taken from HMS *Formidable* in 1943 also shows that although *Venomous* was not converted to an L.R.E. at Troon its armament was altered along similar lines to those V & Ws that were converted. The armament visible in this photograph is very similar to that described by Preston in his book:

> "In their final guise the 'V & W' escorts would have a typical armament as follows:
>
> "A" position – 'Hedgehog.'
> "B" position – 4-inch or 4.7-inch gun (original weapon)
> Bridge wings – single 20-mm guns port and starboard
> Abaft funnels – two single 2-pounders or 20-mm A.A., port and starboard, one set triple torpedo tubes, additional depth charge stowage, and possibly depth charge throwers.

"X" position – 4-inch or 4.7-inch as "B"

"Y" position – two depth charge racks discharging over the quarterdeck, and two depth charge throwers on each side, with associated stowage and davits for reloading; additional 20-mm A.A. gun in some ships."[7]

It can be seen in the photograph that the 4.7-inch gun in "A" position has been removed and replaced by the Hedgehog Anti-Submarine mortar, partly concealed under a canvas cover. Anthony Preston described the Hedgehog:

"This was a spigot which fired twenty-four bombs ahead of the ship; each bomb had a war-head with 32 pounds of Torpex, a new powerful explosive, fused to burst only on contact. The 'Hedgehog' was the first weapon introduced to counteract the problem … of loss of Asdic contact as the ship ran over the target. By firing a salvo of twenty-four bombs ahead, the escort could remain in contact longer, and increase the chances of a 'kill'…The name was derived from the rows of bombs resting at an angle on their spigots, like the spines of a hedgehog."[8]

Venomous and *Keppel* were amongst the first of the V & Ws to be fitted with this still untried new anti-submarine weapon which had its sea trials on *Westcott* at the end of 1941. *Venomous* was fitted with the Mk 10 version of the Hedgehog. When fired, the bombs fell in an elliptical pattern about 250 metres ahead of the ship and a well-trained weapon's crew could fire a 24-bomb salvo every three to four minutes.

The 2-pounder anti-aircraft guns on Preston's list of armaments were the outdated pom-poms and the 20-mm guns the more effective Oerlikons which eventually replaced them. The photograph shows that the 4.7-inch gun remains in the "B" position and a single 20-mm gun (an Oerlikon) is positioned on the port wing just below the bridge. The pom-pom guns can be seen between the funnels and the remaining triple torpedo tube mount between the after funnel and the searchlight platform. The 4.7-inch gun remains in the "X" position atop the aft deckhouse and the 3-inch H.A. (High Angle) D.P. (Dual Purpose) gun on the quarterdeck (forward of the aft deckhouse) where it had replaced the aft triple 21-inch torpedo tube mount at Plymouth in June 1940. Collister recalled that changes were made to the fore torpedoes: "the top or No. 1 21-inch torpedo was replaced with one having a one ton depth charge head with very strict rules covering the firing thereof. It was nicknamed 'the brute' and we never fired it."

The 4.7-inch gun in "Y" position had already been removed at Cammell Laird a year ago to make way for twin rails for dropping depth charges off the stern as described by Preston. When *Venomous* went to war she had four Mark II depth charge throwers, a single spigot-type mortar that fired a Mk VII depth charge which rested on a crescent-shaped cradle on top of a stalk. "The carrier and stalk were thrown with the charge, which was wasteful in weight and storage space. It was later replaced by the Mk IV in which the carrier and the stalk were retained."[9] There would have been sufficient time during the three-month refit and overhaul to upgrade the depth charge throwers and their support equipment as seen in the photograph.

Venomous was fitted with the Type 286 Radar at Birkenhead but she now received the improved Type 271M radar with a rotating aerial, "...the British introduced the Type 271M 10-centimetre radar from September 1941, which gave an all-round picture of the convoy and surfaced U-boats. It could even pick up a periscope in calm seas."[10] The detection range of the Type 271 was between ten and twenty-five nautical miles. It proved to be a very successful system and hundreds were built.[11] It was much heavier than the Type 286 and Collister recalled that it required the fitting of new pole mast to support the weight:

> "The latest RDF was fitted and a new pole foremast to accommodate the extra weight. When we had the addition of a very heavy radar set we did stability tests in a very choppy Clyde. It was very wet and uncomfortable and considerable extra solid ballast had to be shipped. We could not afford to use tank space as both fuel and water space were at a premium."[12]

The radar's rotating aerial was mounted on a small pedestal behind the bridge and forward of the mainmast. A circular wooden lattice cage encased the aerial, which was covered by canvas whilst in port to prevent it being identified. It would be easy to determine the performance characteristics of the system from the size of the antenna. An after-action report, produced by the Anti-Submarine Warfare Division of the Admiralty in 1943, confirmed that *Venomous* had the more advanced radar system in November 1942 but still carried the ASV radar described by Fred Thomas; its aerial can also be seen sitting atop the masthead.

In conclusion, it appears that after Falcon-Steward handed *Venomous* over to Ailsa the Admiralty decided that it was to receive the armament and sensors of an L.R.E., but her engineering plant would not be changed and *Venomous* would remain an S.R.E. No explanation has been found for this decision, but one could speculate that it might be because of the unreliability of its boilers and engines, which Cdr Broome drew to the attention of Captain (D) Londonderry shortly before the collision with *Keppel*.

Although non-operational during the first three months of 1942 there was one event of real significance, the results of which would ensure that the name of *Venomous* would live on long after the old ship passed into history. In the midst of many combat reverses and little success the Government looked for ways to sustain morale and at the same time raise funds to support the war effort. One of the morale boosting and fund raising efforts was Warship Week, which began on 5 February 1942 when Royal Navy ships were affiliated to cities, towns and villages throughout the country.[13] *Venomous* found herself linked with the town of Loughborough, at that time a community of some thirty thousand inhabitants, in the East Midlands triangle between the cities of Nottingham, Derby and Leicester. Notwithstanding its distance from the sea, the town had an active Sea Cadet Unit, which officially assumed *Venomous'* name as the title of their training ship, TS *Venomous*, the name the Sea Cadet Unit retains to this day.

The response from the town was overwhelming as the following article from the local newspaper, the *Loughborough & Shepshed Echo* indicates:

"Warship Week At Loughborough Feb 5th to 14th"

Warship Week begins at Loughborough and the target to reach is £210,000

This is the representing cost of a new hull for the Destroyer *Venomous*

"Many fund raising things were done to collect in the £210,000 needed for the *Venomous*. The paper put in news appealing to small investors to help raise money for the Destroyer. It had an immediate effect and Loughborough Warship Week ends with a grand total of £300,116, £90,116 more than needed. The total of the last day was the highest all week with a grand total of £73,474 followed by the next highest being a total of £63,000 on the banks day. Since commencement of the war, Loughborough with 33,000 has invested £1,790,000 (Feb. 19th 1942). A lot of the sum has come from saving certificates and deposits in the Post Office and Trustees Savings Bank which shows that a lot has definitely come from the small men because without this the target would have never have been reached.

The Mayor received telegrams of congratulations when the target was found out, these were sent from Sir Noel Curtis Bennett and Capt MacDonald. The Brush played a major part in Warship week as they set out to raise £1,200 for the purchase of 87,000 rivets to mend the hull of *Venomous*. They actually raised £12,000. The firm kept its promise and the total was eventually £37,000.

The County Council, Loughborough Permanent Building Society and the Pearl Insurance Company, invested £5,000 and the Loughborough Co-Operative Society with the C.W.S. invested £3,000."

The bronze plaque presented to HMS *Venomous* by the town of Loughborough (left) is now the proud possession of TS *Venomous*. "Climbing to Victory" sign on Loughborough's Town Hall (right) raising money for the war

The Mayor of Loughborough, Alderman George Hill, recorded his appreciation in the *Loughborough & Shepshed Echo*:

"Sir,

As the leading citizen of this Borough and as President of Warship Week, I should be glad if you would insert this letter to expose my deep appreciation to all the members of our community who, by their efforts, have so successfully contributed to the splendid results achieved. Lack of space prevents me from mentioning by name, as there are so many workers who for weeks have been preparing the way for this happy result. The value of this work can to some extent be measured by the large sum of £90,000 raised in excess of the community's target of £210,000. The reputation of this Borough for

good service and efficiency has been fully maintained.
George Hill
MAYOR

Town Hall
Loughborough."

The *Loughborough & Shepshed Echo* duly recorded the letter of appreciation that the Mayor received from Falcon-Steward:

"**Commander of H.M.S** *Venomous* thanks the people of Loughborough"

Ardent Congratulations

It will be remembered that during the Loughborough Warship Week the people of Loughborough invested the magnificent sum of £300,000, thereby adopting HMS *Venomous*. The secretary of the Loughborough Warship Week has now received the following letter from the Commander of HMS *Venomous*:

"It is with great pleasure that I learn that His Majesty's Ship *Venomous* under my command has been adopted by Loughborough.
    On behalf of the Officers and Ship's Company will you please convey to His Worship the Mayor, the most ardent congratulations on the magnificent results obtained by the citizens of Loughborough during Warship Week.
    In these times it is indeed a matter of great moment to achieve one's aims and greater still to exceed them. With the example of the citizens of your Borough before us, I hope that we too may as readily hit the target wherever we may find it.
    With regard to your kind enquiry in what way you may be of assistance to us, may I suggest that the supply of comforts, with the exception of woollen garments for which an organisation already exists, would be most gratefully received by the Ship's Company. Books, cards, games or gramophone records would be very much appreciated on the Mess Decks.
    I hope the link now forged with Loughborough and 'your' ship may ever be a strong one.

    Yours truly,
    H.W. Falcon-Steward (Commander)

One of the casualties of the refit was the ship's crest, a massive bronze casting which was attached to the base of the bridge at the back of "B" Gun. It was removed by the dockyard workers and lay on the deck with a pile of timber waste until it was rescued by "Freddo" Thomas, the

RDF operator, who placed it in his locker in the mess room. It is now the proud possession of TS *Venomous* at Loughborough.

Towards the end of February while *Venomous* was still undergoing her repairs and refit, Falcon-Steward left the dry-docked ship to attend a course at C in C Western Approaches Headquarters on anti-submarine tactics and technology for commanding officers of escort vessels. It is reasonable to assume that in addition to becoming familiar with using his ship's new weapons and sensors as an integrated weapon system, he also received the latest tactical insights on the command and control of an anti-submarine escort group to protect convoys against the U-boat threat.

During Falcon-Steward's absence, Lt Cdr the Lord Teynham was appointed to command *Venomous*. Christopher John Roper-Curzon,

Lord Teynham and his officers during the refit at Troon, Spring 1942.
From left: Lt M. Cashman RN, Lt Leslie C. Eaton RNVR, Lt H. Pead RN, Mid J T Knight RNR, Lt Cdr Lord Teynham RN, unknown, Gunner (T) A N Simms RN.

Nineteenth Baron Teynham, would stay with the ship until *Venomous'* refit was completed in April. Teynham would go on to command another destroyer before, as a Captain, he would be appointed Senior Officer (S.O.) of all Royal Navy minesweepers in the English Channel during Operation *Neptune,* the assault phase of Operation *Overlord.* He would become reacquainted with *Venomous* at the end of the war.

Lt Michael Cashman RN, the new Executive Officer of *Venomous* took up his duties on 5 March 1942:

> "Having spent from November 1939 to 1942 in the destroyer *Westminster,* I was in March 1942 appointed No. 1 of *Venomous.* She was at that time refitting in the small dockyard at Troon. The Commanding Officer when I joined was Lt Cdr Lord Teynham. He had been CO of the destroyer *Campbeltown.* However, when she was taken into Portsmouth to be made ready for the raid on St. Nazaire, it was not considered to be a very good idea to hand the enemy a piece of propaganda by putting a senior Peer of the Realm into a situation where the betting was odds-on he would be captured."

A further newcomer on 24 March was Sub Lt Proes RNVR. Proes had been in the Navy before the war but was invalided out with an injured arm. He rejoined as a Volunteer Reserve Officer on the outbreak of hostilities. Warrant Engineer H.R. Pead, age 42 also reported on board. 'Chief' was a real character, dark, short and saturnine. A continual smoker, he held his cigarette hidden below the palm of his right hand, a habit acquired through smoking on watch before he became an officer. Lt A. de E.T. Sangster RN and Lt L.C. ('Slogger') Eaton RNVR joined during the next few days along with Mid. R.C. Elliott RNR and finally Surg. Lt G.C. Milner RNR.[14]

By early April work on *Venomous* was completed and with Falcon-Steward back in command and her new ship's company embarked, *Venomous* departed Troon on 6 April 1942. She spent just four days on trials and work-ups off Ayr before returning to Derry where *Venomous* became leader of the Twenty-First Escort Group with Falcon-Steward as the group commander.

Venomous sailed from Derry on the 16th for Loch Ewe and several days on local escort duties but these operations were soon brought to a close when Falcon-Steward received the following signal: "Require you sail *Venomous* to arrive Seidisfjord a.m. 27/4. On arrival *Venomous* to act under orders of C in C Home Fleet."[15]

HMS *Venomous* alongside HMS *Sandhurst*, the depot ship for the escorts at Londonderry.
Photographed by Lt Leslie Eaton RNVR.

View for'ard from above the bridge with the Type 271 RDF in foreground (left) and looking aft showing the triple torpedo tubes and projectile depth charges.

Venomous is inboard (recognisable by its prominent RDF dome) with two Hunt Class escorts (left) and view of mail being transferred from HMS *Sandhurst*.

Venomous was familiar with Icelandic waters but her next operation would take her much further into northern latitudes than she had been before. *Venomous* was to be part of the escort for Convoy PQ.15 to north Russia. The Royal Navy began escorting convoys to Murmansk and Archangel in August 1941, "Britain quickly began to despatch aircraft, tanks, trucks and other war supplies which she could ill spare at this time of her own weakness."[16] Within five months of Germany's attack on Russia on the 22 June 1941 German panzers were at the gates of Moscow but the successful Red Army counter-offensive during the winter of 1941 showed that the vaunted Wehrmacht could not only be stopped but shredded. Despite this the outcome was very much in doubt and convoys to north Russia had to fight their way through in the face of increasing opposition from enemy aircraft, ships, and U-boats based in occupied Norway. *Venomous* could expect a hazardous deployment.

Arriving at Seidisfjord (Seydisfjordur) on the east coast of Iceland on the 27 April, *Venomous* took on fuel and passed the night alongside

HMS *Venomous* with zig-zag camouflage at Seidisfjord, Iceland, prior to start of Convoy PQ.15
Courtesy of Chris Eaton.

A US Navy Brooklyn Class Light Cruiser (foreground) with a US Navy Wyoming/Texas Class Battleship (background) at Akureyri Fjord.
Courtesy of Chris Eaton.

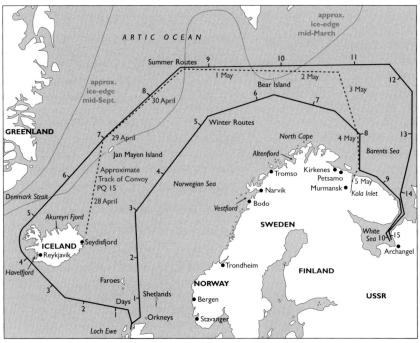

The route taken by *Venomous* from Loch Ewe to Iceland and north to Murmansk in Arctic Russia.
Map graphic Kelly Erlinger. Map source Gordon Smith www.naval-history.net

an oiler before steaming to the main anchorage at Akureyri Fjord on the north coast the following morning, in company with HMS *Nigeria* and HMS *Somali*. The assembly of ships of the Home Fleet made a big impression on those on deck, most of whom were more accustomed to the company of weather-beaten escorts. Lt Sangster remembered:

> "Being part of the Western Approaches Command we all had a slight inferiority complex when in company with the Fleet and you can imagine how chuffed we were when Admiral Burroughs in the Cruiser *Nigeria* sent a signal to *Venomous* congratulating the ship on her appearance."

The convoy consisted of twenty-five merchant ships, fifteen of which were American, plus a close escort comprising the large destroyer of the Tribal Class, HMS *Somali*, the B and I Class destroyers, HMS *Boadicea*, *Badsworth* and *Inglefield*. The new M Class destroyer, HMS *Matchless*, and the Norwegian destroyer HMNS *St. Albans* also joined the escort group. Rounding out the group was *Venomous* together with the auxiliary anti-aircraft ship *Ulster Queen*, the submarine HMS *Sturgeon* and the Catapult Armed Merchant (CAM) ship *Empire*

Morn. As its designation implies, this ship had a catapult fitted on its fo'c'sle upon which rested a Hurricane fighter which was boosted to takeoff speed by rockets. The introduction of the CAM ship was an emergency measure until small escort aircraft carriers could become available in greater numbers. In the past year convoys had suffered from the appearance of enemy reconnaissance aircraft and the CAM fighter was a means of destroying the intruder. With nowhere to land the pilot would either ditch his aircraft or bale out, hoping to be picked up before he succumbed to the freezing ocean.

The heavy cruiser, USS *Wichita*, one of the USN warships which provided support for Convoy PQ.15.
Photographed by Lt Peter Kershaw RNVR.

Close cover would also come from the Colony Class light cruiser, HMS *Nigeria,* and the County Class heavy cruiser, HMS *London.* In the case of a foray by major units of the Kriegsmarine based in Norway, more distant support would be provided by Admiral Sir John Tovey flying his flag in the battleship HMS *King George V*, the US Navy Washington Class battleship, the USS *Washington*, the Illustrious Class aircraft carrier HMS *Victorious*, plus three cruisers and four destroyers. Two of these cruisers were also American – the Wichita Class heavy cruiser USS *Wichita,* and the New Orleans Class heavy cruiser USS *Tuscaloosa.* The US Navy task group had been attached to the Home Fleet in April.[17] *Venomous* would be part of the first major Anglo-American naval operation of the war.

The distant cover would accompany the convoy at a distance of some hundred nautical miles to protect it from an attack by the Deutschland Class Panzerschiffe "pocket battleships" KMS *Admiral*

Scheer and KM *Lützow*, which together with four large destroyers were based in Narvik, Norway, and the battleship KMS *Tirpitz* (*Bismarck's* sister ship) and the heavy cruiser *Admiral Hipper*, which along with six destroyers were based at Trondheim.

Convoy PQ.15 departed Akureyri Fjord late on 28 April. From his position on the bridge of *Venomous* Cashman clearly remembered his thoughts at that moment: "I experienced a feeling of growing isolation. We were steaming away from the last friendly nation and for the rest of the journey the nearest land would be occupied territory."

By 1942 the Royal Navy had the equipment and expertise to refuel at sea and Royal Fleet Auxiliary (RFA) Oilers from Force Q, based in Iceland, met the outgoing and returning arctic convoys to refuel their escorts most of which lacked the fuel capacity to make it to Murmansk without underway refuelling. *Venomous* in particular had become notorious for excessive fuel consumption. RFA *Grey Ranger* escorted by HMS *Ledbury* joined PQ.15 on the 29 April and after refuelling *Venomous* and the other destroyer escorts awaited the arrival of incoming convoy QP.11 to refuel its escorts before returning to Iceland.

The uneasy calm was broken shortly before midnight that evening when the inevitable spotter aircraft appeared, a sure warning that an attack would soon follow. Poor visibility and frequent snow squalls delayed the expected attack, and it was not until late on the 1 May that the first planes appeared, six twin-engine JU-88 bombers. One was shot down whilst attacking HMS *London* whilst the others were driven off by heavy fire whilst attacking an unarmed trawler, one of four rescue ships. Capt Harvey Crombie RN on the minesweeper, HMS *Bramble*, the senior officer after the departure of the close covering force, wrote in his report that: "the aircraft on the CAM ship were not flown off as no suitable opportunity appeared to present itself since the convoy was seldom being shadowed by less than two aircraft and since it was desired to keep it in reserve for the final attack before entering the Kola Inlet where it could have landed."[18] Fortunately, this attack failed to inflict any damage to the convoy.

Disaster struck earlier that day when there was a collision between elements of the distant covering force. In thick fog the battleship, HMS *King George V*, collided with the large Tribal Class destroyer, HMS *Punjabi*, and cut it in two. In his illustrated history of the Russian convoys, Paul Kemp described the incident:

With Cdr H.W. Falcon-Steward to Arctic Russia.

Cdr Falcon-Steward on bridge.

Lt Leslie Eaton RNVR.
Courtesy of Chris Eaton.

A young Sub Lt RNVR with Cdr
H.W. Falcon-Steward RN on left.
Courtesy of Chris Eaton.

AB Cyril Hely, who took many of the
photographs in this book, in Iceland.
Courtesy of Dorothy Hely.

Shipmates: Able Seamen Shepherd, Cyril Hely, Hayes
(Hargreaves ?) and Hopwood, all of 3 Mess.
Courtesy of Dorothy Hely.

Ratings normally wore dungarees aboard ship.
From left: Yelland, Orwell and Shepherd, in September 1942.
Courtesy of Dorothy Hely.

> *"Punjabi's* forward half remained afloat long enough for 206 men to
> be rescued but the stern half, on which *Punjabi's* outfit of 30 depth
> charges was stowed, sank rapidly. The DCs had not been set at 'safe'
> and exploded, increasing the damage the battleship had suffered in
> the collision."[19]

Soon afterwards the distant cover turned back on coming within range of
German aircraft based in Norway and by midnight on 1/2 of May it was
time for the close cover to take its leave. HMS *London* turned to the west
to be followed ten hours later by Vice Admiral Burrough in HMS *Nigeria*.
The two cruisers fell in with Convoy QP.11 returning from Russia.

The defenders were now left to depend upon their own resources
and appeared to meet with almost immediate success when a
submarine contact was detected and depth charged to the surface by
the *Halcyon* Class minesweeper HMS *Seagull* and the Norwegian
Destroyer, HMNS *St. Albans*. Upon closing, the escorts were mortified
to discover they had disabled the Polish submarine *Jastrzab* (Polish for
Hawk), the former British submarine, P551, received from America
under the "Lend Lease" programme. *Jastrzab* had strayed one hundred
nautical miles from its area of operation. She was machine-gunned on
the surface with five killed and six injured, including the commander.
The remainder of the crew were saved but their boat, rendered
unseaworthy, had to be sunk.

By now the crew of *Venomous* were experiencing their first taste of
conditions in the high Arctic, which, even during late spring, were
particularly harsh, as Sangster remembered:

> "The weather was happily not rough but bitterly cold. A cup of cocoa
> went cold in about one minute and the dregs in the cup would freeze
> solid after about five minutes. *Venomous* had an open bridge and the
> sides were just canvas with an outer protection of canvas covered
> sandbags. As we progressed eastwards, the pack ice forced us further
> and further south towards the German air and U-boat bases. Officer
> of the Watch duties were very strenuous, particularly at night when it
> was difficult to sight and avoid the large pieces of pack ice."

Collister recalled that the temperatures fell so low "that ploughing
through the icepack gave us twelve-inch ice fingers from the deck head
at all times at sea." Every morning the ship's railings and supporting
stanchions at all deck levels had three inches of ice on them. The ship's
weapons and exposed deck fittings also had thick layers of ice. This had

to be chipped off every morning or it would drastically alter the ship's stability, interfere with her manoeuvrability and the operation of her weapons. This was an extremely laborious and dangerous work for the seaman of the deck department. Robert Back, an art student at Edinburgh who volunteered for the navy in 1940 and was a gunner on *Venomous,* told his family that the forward mess deck was constantly awash and during one air attack every gun on the ship had frozen.[20]

As the convoy approached northern Norway to make its passage around North Cape the Luftwaffe took advantage of the longer daylight hours and the nearness of the convoy to its airfields to force home its attacks. At around midnight on the 2- 3 May, three ships of the convoy were lost in quick succession. At 2327 six torpedo-carrying Heinkel He111 aircraft from I/KG 26 (1 Coastal Group 26), attacking in formation at low level so that "sea clutter" helped them evade detection by RDF, penetrated the protective screen and released their torpedoes. The outcome was described by Capt Crombie RN in his report on PQ.15:

> "SS *Botavon,* SS *Jutland* and Cape *Corso* were hit by torpedoes. *Cape Corso* blew up and *Jutland* sank very quickly. *Botavon* settled down by her bows and sank more slowly and I ordered *Badsworth* to sink her by gunfire. The Commodore (Capt Anchor RN) and one hundred and thirty seven survivors were picked up by HMS *Badsworth,* trawlers and HMS *Chiltern.*"

There were pitifully few survivors from the *Cape Corso* – just three – whose rescue Lt Sangster described:

> "There was a vivid flash and a violent explosion. One merchantman carrying ammunition had blown up and another sunk. Surprisingly the rescue Trawler picked up and passed to us three of the D.E.M.S. crew off the poop deck gun of the ship which had blown up. We slept these three survivors in the Wardroom."[21]

The gunners were fortunate men indeed, having survived both the explosion and immersion in the icy seas. In reply the defenders had accounted for three of the Heinkel He111. As for the German aviators, there is no account of survivors.[22] For the next two days "the convoy was constantly shadowed by submarines abaft either beam and there were seldom less than two at a time."

By now Convoy PQ.15 had rounded North Cape and was nearing the protection of the Kola Inlet and Russian defences. The enemy mounted one final attack at 2330 on 3 May when an escorting A/S trawler was damaged, and one of the attacking aircraft shot down. On the morning of the 4 May they were met by two Russian destroyers which were placed five miles on the starboard and port beam of the convoy. Taking advantage of the low cloud ceiling and frequent snow squalls, the convoy's twenty-two surviving merchant ships steamed into the Kola Inlet and toward Murmansk, arriving on 5 May. Captain Crombie concluded his report on PQ.15 by recording:

> "the excellent conduct of the convoy, the majority of which were American ships unused to convoy work. Their steadiness when the torpedo attack took place and leading ships, including the Commodore and Rear Commodore's ships were sunk, their speed of opening fire and their excellent station keeping made the task of the escorts very much easier. It was largely due to the good conduct and discipline of the convoy that twenty two ships out of twenty five arrived at Murmansk undamaged."[23]

Venomous followed an icebreaker into the Naval Base of Polyarnyy and was directed to come along side the damaged Colony class light cruiser HMS *Trinidad* to refuel. Collister described how a gale was blowing when they cast off from *Trinidad* and "a bigger destroyer ploughed into us" and they ended up with the mooring wire wrapped round their screw. The *Trinidad*'s divers failed to clear it due to the cold and Ordinary Seaman Harry Haddon remembered how the Russians had to send over some of their own divers including a woman in a worn out diving suit to do the job.

HMS *Trinidad* had only been commissioned in October 1941 but was an unlucky ship. While defending Convoy PQ.13 against marauding German destroyers she had fired a salvo of torpedoes, one of which had

HMS *Trinidad* at the Russian naval base of Polyarnyy.
IWM Image Reference HU 43945. *Courtesy of the Imperial War Museum*

a faulty gyro, which caused it to circle back on itself, striking the cruiser and killing 32 of her crew. She was able to reach Murmansk under her own power but had to stay for emergency repairs. On the 13 May she made a second attempt to return to the UK but was dive-bombed and rendered dead in the water. After her survivors were rescued she was sunk by HMS *Matchless* with a single torpedo.

Polyarnyy, the Russian naval base where *Venomous* berthed, 1942.
In the background is a Russian destroyer with a smaller torpedo boat alongside.
Courtesy of FNG Thomas.

Venomous and her crew were stranded in Polyarnyy for sixteen long dreary days. The 790 survivors of the cruiser, HMS *Edinburgh*, which had been lost whilst carrying five tons of gold bullion back to Britain as part of convoy QP.11 were also stranded, short of food and desperate to get home.[25] They and the men of *Venomous* found the shore facilities spartan and good food very scarce. Robert Craddock, the "tankie" (butcher) recalled the black bread and tough "yak meat" they were given by the Russians, and occasionally being allowed ashore to see a film show in the Russian naval base[26] They all grew beards: it was too cold to wash and shave. When the Russians placed a sentry on the gangplank to prevent the seamen going ashore they gave him some scraps from the mess which he wolfed down and, after glancing cautiously to left and right, called out "Churchill" and gave the 'V Sign'.

Harry Haddon recalled the amusement of the ship's company when the medical officer went for a dip every morning to harden himself in case he had to abandon ship.

AB Leslie May remembered how they tried to supplement their rations: "I remember the run ashore to a wooden shack for pictures and of course the duck shooting expeditions." The duck shooting forays were an attempt to supplement the meagre rations by shooting birds from the great rafts of eider duck, which congregated close to the ship. Sangster was a participant in one hair-raising and abortive expedition:

> "We set off, five of us, in the whaler under sail. We tacked up to where the water was brown with duck and when we were about 40 yards away they all took off. None of us owned a shotgun but the ship had 'won' from the army a Bren gun when Calais had been evacuated. This vicious weapon was cradled in the arms of Gunner (T). 'Guns' achieved a 20 second burst without hitting anyone in the boat, which, considering the gun was without tripod, showed great restraint. Two birds fell from the sky but then the wind dropped completely. We resorted to oars but by the time we reached the estimated area no birds could be found."

During the two weeks *Venomous* spent in Polyarnyy, she took her turn conducting night patrols on the Kola Inlet, but, thankfully, nothing happened during her forays, and no one was sorry to say goodbye to northern Russia when orders came to steam for home. *Venomous* along with *Inglefield, Escapade, St. Albans, Boadicea, Badsworth*, the anti-aircraft ship *Ulster Queen* and the CAM ship *Empire Morn* formed the escort for the return convoy, Convoy QP.12, of fifteen merchant ships. The convoy departed Kola Inlet on 21 May and the weather again favoured the homebound ships. As Lt Cashman recalled: "The return journey was without particular incident. We were shadowed on a number of occasions by a four-engine Focke-Wulf, but a heavy fog after we got through the Bear Island Strait kept us from being attacked." The Luftwaffe concentrated its attacks on the 35 heavily laden merchant ships of north bound Convoy PQ.16 which lost six ships during a running five day battle. The failure to attack QP.12 was also in some measure due to the expertise of Pilot Officer J.B. Kendal, the CAM pilot aboard *Empire Morn,* as described by the Flight Direction Officer:

> There were now four enemy aircraft circling QP12 independently. The Hurricane engaged a Junkers 88, which was still circling the

convoy at a height of about 1,000 feet. When the 88 was astern of the convoy the Hurricane was seen to attack opening fire at short range. It was a perfectly timed attack and must have caught the enemy by surprise.

Kendall reported by RT that he had found the wreckage of the aircraft and a rubber dinghy but with the weather closing down there was the problem of picking up the pilot. The Fighter Direction Officer concluded his report:

> "Some seconds later the Hurricane was seen to dive perpendicularly, into the sea, followed immediately by Kendal, his parachute opening some 50 feet before he reached the water. *Badsworth* raced to the scene some half a mile ahead of her and within a few minutes had a boat out and picked him up at 1004. They signalled that Kendal was alive but very seriously injured and later that he died."[27]

RFA *Black Ranger*, part of the Force Q oiling group in Iceland, met the convoy on 25 May, and refuelled *Venomous* and the Hunt Class destroyer, HMS *Badsworth*. The two destroyers detached from the convoy on the 27th and headed to Iceland arriving on the 29th. Convoy QP.12 reached Iceland later that same day, fourteen ships strong, one having turned back to Russia.

Venomous returned to Londonderry via the Clyde on 3 June. Lt Sangster probably reflected the views of all on board when he said: "Without being wildly patriotic, one could not help feeling what an elegant place was Gourock and what a sublime climate it had after Polyarnyy."

• • • •

The men who served on the convoy escorts and the merchant ships formed the North Russia Club (1985) and the Russian Convoy Club (1988) to keep in touch with former shipmates. They went on to campaign for wider recognition of the contribution the Arctic convoys made to winning the war. That was slow in coming. No campaign medal was issued for veterans of the Arctic convoys and they were only eligible for the Atlantic Star if they had served in the western Atlantic for at least six months.

In 1986 the USSR showed its gratitude by awarding the commemorative medal celebrating the fortieth anniversary of the war's end to veterans of the Arctic convoys and 270 attended an investiture and reception at the Russian Embassy. In 1991 the Russian Federation invited veterans to reunions in Murmansk and Archangel and on the 31 August, the frigate HMS *London* sailed into the White Sea and up the Dvina River to Archangel to commemorate the arrival fifty years earlier, on that exact day, of the first convoy bringing aid to our new wartime ally. Further reunions were held and medals were awarded on the fiftieth and sixtieth anniversaries of the end of the war but these cannot be worn by the Arctic veterans alongside their British campaign medals.

In June 1995 Fred Thomas, the RDF operator on *Venomous*, was amongst a party of fifty Arctic veterans led by Rear Admiral A.B. Richardson, the Patron of the North Russia Club, who visited St Petersburg and Murmansk on the fiftieth anniversary of the end of the war.

In 1997 the Queen Mother and the Russia Ambassador attended a memorial service in the crypt of St Paul's Cathedral and unveiled a memorial tablet to the three thousand men who lost their lives on the Arctic convoys. Finally, in 2005, at a reception for Arctic veterans the Prime Minister announced that an Arctic Emblem would be awarded to those who served on the Arctic convoys with no minimum service requirement. Applications can be made by family members of those who served on Arctic convoys as well as the veterans.

By 2008 both the Russian Convoy Club and the North Russia Club had been dissolved but on the 9 October a reunion of veterans was held at Pool House, the former command centre for the convoys, which is now a hotel on the shore of Loch Ewe. The Loch Ewe memorial commemorating the sacrifice of those who lost their lives on the convoys stands nearby. Some branches of the two clubs are still active and the Russian Arctic Convoy Club Scotland issues a quarterly newsletter and meets twice annually, at Loch Ewe and in Edinburgh where the Russian Consulate is very supportive. Jock Dempster, its Chairman, will be glad to answer enquiries from veterans of the Arctic convoys and their families.[28] There are also branches in Australia (Fremantle) and New Zealand (Wellington).

Notes

1   Lt Walter R. Wells RN (1919-86) would serve on a new P Class destroyer, HMS Panther before going to signal school in 1943. He commanded the 525th Landing Craft Assault (LCA) flotilla at Normandy. He returned to signals for the rest of the war and continued his service in signals until his retirement as a Captain in 1966. He served during the Korean War and received the Order of the British Empire (OBE) in 1966.
See also: http://www.unithistories.com/officers/RN_officersW3.html for more information.

2   Lt Arthur D. McPhee RN (1919-2006) was born in Vancouver, entered the Royal Navy as a boy sailor and after promotion to Petty Officer was commissioned in 1940. He commanded HMS *Belvoir* in the Mediterranean in 1942 and served on HMS *Formidable* in 1944. He transferred to the Royal Canadian Navy in 1947, was promoted to Captain in 1958 and when he retired in December 1974 he was the longest serving officer in the RCN. He died at Sechelt, British Columbia, on the 27 January 2006 aged 86. His obituary was published in the *Vancouver Sun* on the 2 April 2006.
See also: http://www.unithistories.com/officers/RN_officersM3.html#McPhee_A

3   Alan Flockhart Esson trained at HMS *Conway* and, sometime after leaving *Venomous*, became a submariner and as Lt A.F. Esson was CO of HMS *Ultimatum* from 11 June to 4 September 1945 and was mentioned in dispatches on the 15 June. According to CPO Hugh McGeeney (writing around 1990) "he was blinded later in the war and lived in the care of a Scottish War Blinded institution. He died some years ago after a long period of poor health."

4   *Sabre* and *Venomous* had worked together whilst operating out of Derry, and Kershaw would have had several opportunities to visit *Sabre*. After the war he ran the family business, a brewery and pub chain, and named two of his pubs "The Frigate" and "The Sabre" but decided it would not be appropriate to name a pub after HMS *Venomous*.

5   In addition to HMS *Vimy* and HMS *Viscount* seventeen other V & Ws were similarly converted. See Anthony Preston's book, *V & W Class Destroyers 1917 – 1945*, p. 120.

6   Peter C. Smith, *Pedestal: The convoy that saved Malta*, 5th Edition, Crécy Publishing Limited, Manchester, 2002, p.

7   Anthony Preston, p. 90.

8   Ibid. p. 88.

9   David Brown, p. 38.

10 Ibid. p. 90.

11 The events leading to the widespread adoption of the Type 271 Radar by the Royal Navy in 1941, were outlined by John Wise in an e-mail to the author on the 3 September 2009. "The first trials of Type 271 took place on HMS *Orchis* on 25 March 1941, in the Clyde, using a small Norwegian B1 submarine as a target. Such was the success of this trial, and the following days in a rough North Atlantic, that the original order for 24 sets was increased to 150 in April then to 350 in May 1941. Unfortunately there is no indication as to how long it took to install all the 350 systems, but 50 were at sea in the North Atlantic and used successfully against German submarines by Christmas 1941."

12 Ibid. "There were many system failures with early installations, some suggest because this set was rushed into service, but the bigger problem was the system weight. To overcome potential turtle situations in high seas, other upper deck equipment had to be removed to reduce the top weight."

13 "The aim was for cities to raise enough to adopt battleships and aircraft carriers, while towns and villages would focus on cruisers and destroyers. The number of warships adopted was over 1,200, and this number included the battleships, cruisers, destroyers and trawlers. The total amount raised for the war effort was £955,611,589." Wikipedia.

14 Lt Tony Sangster had been torpedoed whilst en-route by liner from South Africa to England, took to a boat, befriended a young woman passenger whilst on the boat and corresponded with her from his next posting. On joining *Venomous* he faced a charge of "disclosing information which could be of use to the enemy" but was cleared (Stephen Barney).

15 A signal sent from C in C W.A. to *Venomous* at 24/0100/4/42.

16 Correlli Barnett, p. 693.

17 The USN task group would continue to operate with the Home Fleet through August 1942. United States Department of the Navy Naval Historical Centre's website: www.history.navy.mil.

18 Report by Capt H. Crombie RN of HMS *Bramble* on Convoy PQ.15 from the departure of HMS *Nigeria* on 2 May to arrival at the Kola inlet on the 5 May 1942. NA Ref. ADM 199/721. See also: http://www.halcyon-class.co.uk/Arctic/pq15.htm

19 Paul Kemp, *The Russian Convoys 1941-1945*, Arms and Armour Press Ltd., Link House, West River, Poole, Dorset BH15 1LL, 1987, p. 25

20 Robert Trenaman Back (1922-2004) had a distinguished career as a marine artist. His paintings hang in galleries and private collections in the US and in Britain. His obituary in the *Independent* can be seen at http://www.independent.co.uk/news/obituaries/robert-back-550082.html Unfortunately, no sketches or paintings of HMS *Venomous* have been traced.

21 D.E.M.S. stands for Defensively Equipped Merchant Ships. For more on DEMS and the experience of their sailors see: www.bbc.co.uk/ww2peopleswar/stories/90/a2056790.shtml.

22 To be shot down in the Norwegian Sea and Arctic Ocean was certain death.

23 Ibid

24 This photograph shows a probable *Type VII* Class destroyer against the quay wall, whilst the ship sitting outboard is a probable *Shtorm* Class torpedo boat. Polyarnyy can be found by using Google Earth. The buildings seen on the hillside and in the background of the photograph still exist.

25 The survivors were stranded in Polyarnyy for some weeks and 39 were killed when the ship taking them home, the minesweeper, HMS *Niger*, strayed into an allied minefield off Iceland and blew up on 5 July 1942. The gold, payment for allied aid, was salvaged in 1981. The sinking of the *Edinburgh*, the controversy surrounding the award of the salvage contract and the salvage of the gold is described by Barrie Penrose in *Stalin's Gold, HMS Edinburgh and its treasure*. St Albans: Granada, 1982.

26 Craddock was mistaken. The Yak is found in Tibet, not northern Russia. The tough meat given them by the Russians may have been reindeer but was most certainly not Yak.

27 *The Catapult fighters*; by Alan Payne. *Navy Historical Review* December, 1975. See http://www.navyhistory.org.au/the-catapult-fighters/

28 Write to: Jock Dempster, Chairman Russian Arctic Convoy Club Scotland, 40 Bellevue Court, Queens Road, Dunbar EH42 LYRE.
E-mail: dempster646@btinternet.com Telephone: 01368 866 825

CHAPTER SEVEN

BACK TO THE MEDITERRANEAN
June – November 1942

The Verdun of the Maritime War: Malta, 1942[1]

Venomous and her crew had barely enough time to thaw out from the Arctic before they were ordered to sea on 8 June to rendezvous with the Danae Class light anti-aircraft gun cruiser HMS *Delhi* and the equally old S Class destroyers, HMS *Saladin*, *Scimitar* and *Sabre,* to escort RMS *Queen Elizabeth* into the Clyde.[2]

The two luxurious Cunard liners, RMS *Queen Mary* and the *Queen Elizabeth*, the largest in the world, transported troops between North America and Britain. They often carried over ten thousand American or Canadian troops and steamed unescorted, relying on their speed and information provided by the Admiralty's Operational Intelligence Centre, to avoid the U-boat menace.[3] It was only when these majestic ships reached the Western Approaches that the Admiralty provided a close escort.

There were more dangers to face than U-boats. A simple breakdown in communications between the escorts and these massive trans-Atlantic liners was enough to cause a major accident. Three months later RMS *Queen Mary* struck the Ceres Class light cruiser, HMS *Curacoa,* slicing it in two and, fearing an attack by U-boats, didn't stop. Only 99 men out of the ships company of 437 were rescued.

Harry Haddon remembered that *Venomous* had problems keeping up with the *Queen Elizabeth*. This may have been in the minds of the C in C Western Approaches when they closed their signal by stating, "no risk of weather damage is to be taken". The operation was prematurely terminated as Lt Cashman recalled:

> "We were coming in at full speed on the starboard bow of *Queen Elizabeth* when one of our oil lubricating pumps stopped. We pulled out of the screen but before we could do anything there was

> white metal all around the system. We limped into Londonderry on one engine and had to spend some time in the dockyard having the system put right."

This was not a good start after her major refit and it would be nearly a month before Falcon-Steward was able to take *Venomous* back to sea.

On 28 June she was ordered to escort the newest addition to the Fleet, the King George V Class battleship, HMS *Howe*: "*Venomous* and two destroyers of Twenty-First Escort Group are to be sailed to rendezvous as requested by NOIC Greenock with *Howe* early a.m. 1st (July) and escort to Rosyth, subsequently to return to Londonderry."[4] *Venomous* and the S Class destroyer HMS *Shikari* got underway by midday on 30 June, followed by another S-class destroyer HMS *Sardonyx*. The Colony Class light cruiser HMS *Kenya* joined them later. The force arrived at Rosyth with HMS *Howe* without incident on 3 July.

Falcon-Steward was next directed to escort the liner RMS *Llanstephen Castle*, but before *Venomous* could deploy she again developed engine problems and on 5 July, Captain D of the Greenock-based escort destroyers signalled Home Fleet and Western Approaches Command: "*Venomous* reports the presence of oil in all boilers and leaking tube ends causing serious loss of feed water. I consider the ship is in an unsafe condition to proceed on present duty. Propose to examine all boilers and take required remedial action."[5]

These latest problems necessitated a further lengthy spell in dockyard hands, this time on the Clyde. By now it was clear that *Venomous'* decline could not be arrested – only delayed. There would come a point when she would no longer be able to carry out her duties as an escort. She was still needed and it was imperative that the ship should be in good shape for the critical operations that lay ahead. As July ended *Venomous* was again restored to fighting condition, ready to face action in the warm waters of the Mediterranean.

German and Italian forces were advancing inexorably towards the Egyptian border. As more of the Libyan coast fell into their hands, the running of supplies into Malta became ever more hazardous. By July the island was down to a few weeks of supplies and it became essential that a major operation should be mounted to break the siege. As Correlli Barnett observed, "Throughout much of 1942 the island of Malta served less as a British strategic asset than as a hostage to the enemy."[6]

The answer was Operation *Pedestal* – a convoy of fourteen fast merchantmen escorted by major units of the Home and Mediterranean Fleets. "Operation *Pedestal* (or '*Middle August*' as the resulting battle was known by the Axis) was the last victory of the Axis in the aero-naval war in the Mediterranean."[7] Although Operation *Pedestal* would be a tactical victory for the Axis it was a strategic success for the British. The Maltese considered it a victory and called it "The Santa Marija Convoy."[8]

The story of Operation *Pedestal*, the most powerful and complicated naval operation executed in the Mediterranean by the Royal Navy up to this point, has often been told and this book will largely confine itself to the part played by *Venomous* but some background to the operation is needed to understand the role played by *Venomous* and the other V & W destroyers.

Force Z was the main covering and escort force for the convoy prior to its entrance into the Sicily Straits between Sicily and the Tunisian port of Bizerta. The new Illustrious Class aircraft carrier, HMS *Indomitable* steamed from her Indian Ocean station to reinforce Force Z. The battleships *Nelson* and *Rodney* travelled north from South Africa via Freetown in the British colony of Sierra Leone to join Force Z. Home Fleet units, consisting of the light cruisers HMS *Nigeria* and *Kenya*, together with the light cruiser HMS *Manchester* and the Dido Class anti-aircraft gun light cruiser, HMS *Sirius,* also joined the main covering force. From Home Fleet came the aircraft carriers HMS *Eagle* and *Victorious*, which with HMS *Indomitable* would provide a hundred aircraft for the aerial defence of the total force. The aircraft carrier *Furious*, carrying aircraft for the defence of Malta (Operation *Bellows*), and escorted by *Venomous* and her consorts would accompany the force.

On arrival at the Straits of Sicily the merchant ships (Force F) would continue to Malta escorted by the close covering force of light cruisers and destroyers (Force X). HMS *Furious* and her escorts, including *Venomous*, would proceed as far eastward as possible to ensure that the Spitfires carried on *Furious* would have the best chance of reaching Malta once launched.

While this was taking place Force Y, which consisted of two battered empty merchant ships and two damaged destroyers, the Hunt II Class escort destroyer HMS *Badsworth* and the modern destroyer HMS *Matchless*, would attempt to leave Malta and make their escape to

Gibraltar (Operation *Ascendant*) whilst the Germans and Italians concentrated on the ships of Operation *Pedestal*.

Force R, consisting of two tankers, five corvettes and the ocean-going tug *Jaunty*, would support the operation by providing refuelling service to the force. The corvettes and the tug would escort the valuable tankers and provide a rescue and towing service for damaged ships.

In addition, units of the Mediterranean Fleet at Alexandria, together with four empty merchant ships, based in Port Said and Haifa would rendezvous and head westward. It was hoped this dummy force would draw off some of the Luftwaffe squadrons based in Crete as well as units of the Italian Navy.

The Malta-based submarines were directed to lie in wait outside Italian naval bases on either side of the Straits of Messina in the hope that they would be able to warn *Pedestal* when the Italian ships departed as well as being in a position to attack them.

Force Z	Aircraft Carriers: *Indomitable, Victorious* and *Eagle* and 100 aircraft. Battleships: *Nelson* and *Rodney* Light Cruisers: *Sirius, Phoebe* and *Charybdis* Destroyers: *Laforey, Lightning, Lookout, Quentin, Somali, Eskimo, Tartar, Ithuriel, Wishart, Westcott, Vansittart, Wrestler, Wilton, Zetland*
Force F Convoy WS.21S	Merchant ships: *Ohio, Santa Elisa, Almeria Lykes, Rochester Castle, Deucalion, Clan Ferguson, Empire Hope, Wairangi, Waimarama, Port Chalmers, Dorset, Melbourne Star, Brisbane Star, Glenorchy*
Force X	Light Cruisers: *Nigeria, Kenya, Manchester* and *Cairo* Destroyers: *Ashanti, Intrepid, Icarus, Foresight, Fury, Bicester, Pathfinder, Penn, Derwent, Bicester, Bramham, Ledbury*
Operation *Bellows*	Aircraft Carrier: *Furious* with 36 Spitfires for Malta[9] Destroyers: *Venomous, Vidette, Keppel, Malcolm, Wolverine, Amazon*
Force Y Operation *Ascendant*	Destroyers: *Matchless, Badsworth* Merchant ships: two damaged ships
Force R	Tankers: *Brown Ranger, Dingledale* Corvettes: *Jonquil, Geranium, Spirea, Coltsfoot, Salvonia* Tug: *Jaunty*
Alexandria Decoy Force	Warships: several cruisers and destroyers Merchant ships: four empty merchant ships
Malta	Submarines: HMS *Safari, Unbroken, Uproar, Ultimatum, Unruffled, Utmost, United, Una, P.222*

Operation *Pedestal* Order of Battle[10]

The Admiralty was only able to put together this powerful force because of three major events in the global war at sea: the Convoy PQ.17 disaster, the Battle of Midway and the decision by the Allies to invade French North Africa (Operation *Torch*).

The heavy losses suffered by Arctic Convoy PQ.17 forced the Admiralty to stop sending convoys to Russia until it was better able to protect them, a difficult political decision when the Red Army was hard-pressed by the Wehrmacht's summer offensive. The stunning American victory at the Battle of Midway blunted Japanese expansion and reduced the pressure on the Royal Navy in the Indian Ocean. As a result the carriers, cruisers and battleships from the North and South Atlantic and the Indian Ocean theatre could be released to form the powerful heavy covering force for Operation *Pedestal*. Operation *Torch*, the seaborne landings in Morocco and Algeria to attack Rommel from the rear, required Malta to become a base for offensive operations to hinder Axis efforts to counter the invasion and the offensive of Britain's Eighth Army at El Alamein.

The convoy, designated WS.21S, assembled off the Clyde on 3 August, with *Venomous* and the destroyers HMS *Keppel, Malcolm,*

"Oiling alongside battleship at sea" (left) photographed by Cyril Hely and "Flotilla in line ahead with ships offset" photographed by Lt L. Eaton RNVR.
"In fog marker buoys were trailed to further minimise danger of collision", Stephen Barney.
Courtesy of Chris Eaton and Dorothy Hely.

197

Taken from the quayside or from *Venomous* with HMS *Rodney*
framed by "B" gun of another V&W.
Courtesy of F.N.G. Thomas.

Wolverine, Amazon and *Vidette*. Lt Cashman described the rendezvous: "I have never seen so many warships gathered to protect fourteen merchant ships. We sailed out of the west of Ireland with battleships, carriers, cruisers and many destroyers."

Amongst the assembly was the Flagship of Force X, *Nigeria*, flying the flag of Rear Admiral Burrough, the Carriers *Argus* and *Victorious*, plus the battleships *Nelson* and *Rodney* and the aircraft carrier, HMS *Furious*. The next day, *Venomous*, together with *Wolverine, Wishart* and *Derwent* were refuelled from *Nigeria*, whilst the other short-range destroyers, *Amazon, Zetland* and *Malcolm* refuelled from the other light cruiser *Kenya*.

Rear Admiral Burrough began drilling the merchant ships and escorts in a series of complicated tactical manoeuvres, which, it was hoped, would improve their chances of surviving the aerial, submarine and surface attacks that would surely come once the convoy neared Sardinia.

On the 5th Burrough put his force through the same set of drills, including anti-aircraft gunfire drills by the escorting cruisers and battleships, while the entire force executed numerous emergency course changes due to U-boat alerts.

Taken during Operation *Beserk* whilst en route from the Clyde to the Straits of Gibraltar.
Nearest the camera is HMS *Eagle,* then HMS *Indomitable* and HMS *Victorious.* IWM Image Reference A 11155.
Courtesy of the Imperial War Museum.

On the same day the carriers and their escorts commenced Operation *Berserk*. This exercise, the first of its kind for the Royal Navy, required the three fleet carriers *Indomitable, Victorious, Eagle* and their air groups to co-ordinate their air defence operations.[11] This involved tactical air-to-air combat training in which carrier fighters would be directed by air controllers using radar tracking to intercept incoming enemy aircraft and the escort ships practiced radar-directed barrage anti-aircraft gunfire. *Venomous'* limited anti-aircraft capability would have restricted her contribution to firing at low flying torpedo-carrying aircraft.

At the conclusion of the exercise the convoy proceeded unhindered towards Gibraltar where, just before midday on 9 August, *Venomous* and the A Class destroyer, HMS *Amazon* (Lt Cdr Lord Teynham commanding), together with *Wolverine* and *Malcolm* accompanied *Furious* into Gibraltar where its Spitfires were fitted with extra fuel tanks to extend their range. Cashman takes up the story:

> "We left the Fleet and went into Gibraltar. Our job from now on would be, whilst the convoy was going through, to act as close escort to the Aircraft Carrier *Furious* who would deliver two loads of land based Spitfires to Malta. We waited at Gibraltar whilst

Furious loaded 36 Spitfires fitted with extra fuel tanks. We left Gibraltar and soon caught up with the convoy, tucking ourselves into the middle, closely guarding a very valuable cargo.

As soon as we got within range the air raids started. During one of the raids I saw a bomb hit the flight deck of one of the carriers, fail to explode, bounce along the deck and over the stern".

At mid-day on 11 August with Malta within range, and *Furious* about to begin flying-off her Spitfires, disaster struck. *U-73* under the command of Lt Helmut Rosenbaum penetrated the destroyer defensive screen and fired four torpedoes at HMS *Eagle*.[12] All four found their mark, slamming into the venerable carrier's port side.[13] Cashman was an eyewitness to the loss of *Eagle*, and recalled these dramatic events:

"Before we flew off the first lot of Spitfires from *Furious,* a submarine penetrated the screen and hit the carrier *Eagle*. It was an awesome sight to see that great ship turn slowly over to port and to sink with the planes which had no time to take off sliding off the flight deck."

HMS *Eagle* sinking, with merchant ship in foreground; photographed by Cyril Hely.
Courtesy of Dorothy Hely.

In the water, struggling for survival was AB Bill Loades. His story was typical for those surviving *Eagle's* sinking:

"My recollection is receiving four hits along the port side and the ship going over to starboard. I was on the bridge on the starboard side and we were in great difficulty getting down to sea level to swim for it. As the ship sank in eight minutes it didn't give too much time, although it seemed ages. We waited until she was at an angle of 45° or so to starboard and then slid down the port side – not so easy as there were numerous openings into the waist of the ship. When we did get down, we then had the problem of climbing up the torpedo bulges which were also at 45° but the other way, thus forming a V, and very slimy. Once in the sea we faced fuel oil and patches of aviation fuel, and with no buoyancy, you needed to swim under these patches. Then to help matters the Destroyers were dropping charges trying to get the U Boat. After about 4 hours we, or some of us, were picked up by the *Jaunty* and later transferred to *Venomous* where we were given some dry clothes and a tot – most welcome."

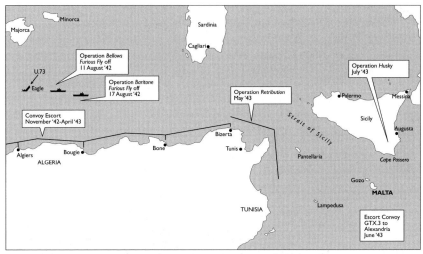

Mediterranean theatre of operations, 1941-3.
Map graphic Kelly Erlinger. Map source Gordon Smith www.naval-history.net

Venomous, *Wolverine* and *Wrestler* were detached to hunt for Rosenbaum's submarine but *U-73* slipped away. *Venomous* was then ordered to join *Keppel* and *Malcolm* in taking on board *Eagle*'s survivors from the L Class fleet destroyers, HMS *Lookout* and *Laforey*, and the tug *Jaunty*. Despite *Eagle*'s rapid sinking, 929 men from the ship's company of 1,160 were saved.

Cyril Hely, who photographed HMS *Eagle* sinking beneath the wave from his action station on *Venomous'* starboard 20-mm Oerlikon, describes the transfer of the survivors to *Venomous*:

"The task of getting them all aboard whilst underway meant that the other ship had to steam alongside us, both travelling at about fifteen knots we had to secure, with the aid of heaving lines, a gang plank between the two ships for the lads to be able to walk aboard us. It

HMS *Laforey* coming alongside during Operation Pedestal to transfer survivors of HMS *Eagle*.
Courtesy of Chris Eaton.

Eagle survivors being transferred from HMS *Laforey*.
Note the Vickers Quadruple 2 pdr Pom-Pom gun mount, not fitted on *Venomous*.
Courtesy of Chris Eaton.

"Eagle survivors on HMS *Venomous;"* photographed by Cyril Hely.
Courtesy of Dorothy Hely.

all went rather smoothly taking on board some three hundred ratings. The fine weather was appreciated as most of them had to stay on the upper deck, there not being enough room below decks."

Venomous took on board 48 Officers and 487 men including the Commanding Officer, Capt L.D. MacKintosh DSC RN, from *Laforey*. The large number of survivors on deck hindered the ship's ability to manoeuvre and threatened her stability. Lt Sangster remembered: "500 extra men in a 1,100 ton ship does alter your performance somewhat and we had to avoid violent rudder movements." Memories of Dunkirk, when *Venomous* found herself with well over five hundred extra men on board, would have been on the minds of some of the ship's company.

With the transfer of survivors completed, *Venomous, Keppel* and *Malcolm* rejoined *Furious* and the rest of her destroyer screen. Just before nightfall, *Furious* completed Operation *Bellows* – all 36 Spitfires were on their way to Malta. The group turned back for Gibraltar at high speed. With an unstable ship Falcon-Steward had to take extra care to maintain a steady helm despite *Furious'* zigzag manoeuvres.

HMS *Furious*, the elderly aircraft carrier which *Venomous* escorted taking Spitfires to Malta.
Photographed by Telegraphist Air Gunner Arthur Eric Jones, Fleet Air Arm, whilst serving on HMS *Furious*.

The *Wolverine's* commander, Lt Cdr Peter Gretton, remembered that the return journey to Gibraltar was not without incident:

> "Whilst we were escorting *Furious* back from this operation we were Senior Officer of the three Destroyer screen. *Furious* always relied on speed for her protection and rumour had it that her old battle-cruiser turbines could still wind her up to 33 knots. Anyway it was dark as pitch and we were straining away to keep ahead of *Furious* on her port bow. She was doing a standard zigzag and we were rather cutting out the deeper turns to stay ahead. On the starboard wing of our screen was *Wolverine*."

One hour past midnight on 12 August, *Wolverine* spotted the Italian submarine, *Dagabur*. The submarine was operating on the surface. Without hesitating, Gretton ordered his helmsman to steer straight for *Dagabur*. *Wolverine* rammed the luckless Italian. Lt Sangster remembered the aftermath:

> "We got to Gibraltar the next day and the day after that *Wolverine* entered harbour with her foc'sle down in the water – an extraordinary sight – her waterline from the stem had been turned back for about 35 feet. She had hit a submarine at right angles at over 30 knots and cut it in two halves."

Despite the success of Operation *Bellows*, there was still a need for additional fighter aircraft to assist in the defence of Malta and Operation *Baritone* was implemented. *Furious* would once more be used and this time she would launch 32 Spitfires. Just before sunset on a warm 16 August, Falcon-Steward got his destroyer underway from Gibraltar in company with a heavy escort led by the Dido Class anti-aircraft gun light cruiser HMS *Charybdis*, together with the destroyers HMS *Laforey, Lookout, Lightning, Antelope, Wishart, Derwent, Keppel, Malcolm, Bicester, Eskimo, Somali* and *Venomous*. Steaming at high speed, the force reached its fly-off point the next day. One Spitfire was lost on take-off, while two more had to be ditched when their undercarriages failed to retract. All of the pilots were recovered safely. The remaining aircraft landed safely on Malta. The force returned intact on the 18th – Operation *Baritone* was a success.

These two successful operations to fly off aircraft from HMS *Furious* enabled Malta to defend itself against the Luftwaffe. The besieged island would no longer be a strategic liability. News of the breaking of the blockade and Malta's renewed security would have reached all on board *Venomous*, and it can be assumed a certain sense of satisfaction would have prevailed.

This was the last action *Venomous* would see in the Mediterranean for the immediate future, her presence being needed in home waters prior to further deployment on the Russian convoys. She was ordered home from Gibraltar: "Intend sailing Force F – S.O. in *Nelson* with *Furious, Argus, Kenya* escorted by *Keppel, Malcolm, Venomous, Tartar, Fury, Eskimo, Somali, Bicester* at 0300B/20th."

Approaching the UK after an incident-free passage, HMS *Kenya* proceeded to Scapa Flow via the Minches, HMS *Nelson*, *Furious* and

Argus to the Clyde with *Venomous* and *Keppel* entering their homeport of Derry on 25 August. While in port there was a change of Wardroom officers. Surg. Lt Maxwell replaced Surg. Lt Milner and Lt John Coleman RNR joined the ship. Coleman replaced Lt Proes who had remained in Gibraltar before his appointment to the Hunt III Class escort destroyer HMS *Aldenham*. Six young CW (Commissioned Warrant) candidates also joined *Venomous* at Londonderry to serve for five momentous months as ordinary seaman before returning to Britain for officer training. Although assigned to different departments they messed together. As with other CW candidates in ships throughout the Fleet, they were given a hard time by the senior ratings, who knew they would soon become officers.

On 5 September, within a fortnight of their return from the Mediterranean, orders arrived for Falcon-Steward to take *Venomous* back to Iceland to join her second Russian convoy, Convoy PQ.18. Convoy PQ.17 had been a disaster. It had been ordered to disperse in the mistaken belief that a German surface force led by the battleship KMS *Tirpitz* had sailed to intercept it and as a result was severely mauled with twenty-one of its thirty-five merchant ships being sunk.[14] It would have been natural for those on *Venomous* to wonder whether their convoy would suffer a similar fate to that of Convoy PQ.17.[15]

There would be plenty of time to mull over what lay ahead as *Venomous* was ordered to proceed to Scapa to escort the battleship HMS *Howe* to Hvalfjord. They returned to Hvalfjord safely but not without discomfort as Lt Coleman recounted:

> "Soon after I joined *Venomous* at Londonderry we proceeded to Hvalfiord just above Reykjavik encountering some of the worse weather I have known, not helped by the fact that we had to make all possible speed. Almost everybody aboard was seasick, except Cdr Falcon-Steward himself. He sat on the bridge smoking his pipe and refraining from seasickness by sheer willpower. How the old ship stood up to that fearful battering I shall never know."

But survive she did, arriving off Iceland on 7 September. Falcon-Steward took her around to Akureyri Fjord on the north coast the following day and Coleman described what happened next:

> "Off Reykjavik with the weather more or less calm, I remember meeting up with other members of the escort group and steering in line ahead. As Officer of the Watch at the time, I realised at one stage that we were creeping up on the next ahead so I ordered a reduction

in revs. Nothing happened so I ordered a further reduction, still without response; therefore I had to pull off to starboard. I eventually ordered the engines stopped but that didn't happen either. Finally the engineer came dashing up to the bridge to say that he could not stop her until he had carried out some repair or adjustment. This made a change as it was not sometimes so easy to get her to start."

Venomous was compelled to return to Hvalfjord and Coleman recalled that: "We put alongside a repair ship where we had to attend to over 200 boiler tubes. This took several days which resulted in our being too late for PQ.18 and necessitated our return to Londonderry."

The extent of the repairs required to *Venomous'* boilers can be seen in the exchange of signals from Admiral Commanding Iceland Command to C in C Home Fleet: "Serious boiler defects. Will not be ready before 16/9. If satisfactory will join W.A.2."[16] This was followed by the signal to Rear Admiral Cruiser Squadron 18: "Details work necessary to repair boilers…further fire row tubes certain to fail."[17]

The urgent need for *Venomous* to make this convoy is evident from a signal sent by C in C Western Approaches to Rear Admiral (D) Home Fleet: "Request A.M. (Admiralty) be informed by signal estimating extent fire row tubes needed that can be spared before T.I.H."[18] Realising the full extent of the damage, the Admiralty signalled back, "Your 1853/16. Do not intend using 'V' anymore as 'EV.' Request you issue instructions."[19]

On the completion of temporary repairs *Venomous* left Hvalfjord at 1920 on 19 September, arriving at Derry on the 21st. In his signal of 23/1210/9/42, Commodore Londonderry detailed the extensive repairs required: "All A & B fire rows of all boilers of *Venomous* require re-tubing and boilers, containers and full systems will require degreasing. Propose to send ship to Belfast for this work."

Venomous arrived in Belfast on 24 September where she was taken in hand on the 28th by the dockyard 'maties.' Upon completion of the repairs Falcon-Steward got her underway for the Clyde on 17 October. On board was a recently promoted midshipman, Stephen Barney, who had joined *Venomous* from the Hunt I Class escort destroyer, HMS *Atherstone*, in which he had participated in the St. Nazaire raid.[20] His initial acquaintance with the ship would be brief:

"I joined *Venomous* as a Midshipman RNVR in late 1942 when Cdr H.E. Falcon-Steward was in command. We shortly sailed for the

Clyde where we arrived in typical Scottish pouring rain. I was immediately sent off on a short Radar and A/S Course with a view to becoming Anti-Submarine Officer of this old V & W destroyer with very basic Asdic equipment.

When I returned to Gourock, *Venomous* had sailed for the Mediterranean, so I was sent across to Londonderry to await passage in a suitable ship for Gibraltar. Eventually I sailed to the Med. in *Rother*, a *River* class Frigate, where I rejoined *Venomous*."

In the atmosphere of the time almost anybody could be suspected of being a spy and Robert Back recalled sitting in the lounge bar of the Bay Hotel in Gourock "doing a pencil sketch of an armed merchant cruiser anchored in the Clyde when a voice from behind him said 'That's nice, can I have a look?' 'In a minute' I replied, 'I will just finish it off'. I was aware all eyes were on me, and there was a deathly hush. The two gentlemen were plain clothes police." He was escorted out of the hotel, his sketchbook confiscated and warned he would hear further from his ship's captain. Eventually his sketchbook was returned, each drawing having been stamped and passed by His Majesty's Censor.[21]

The reason for *Venomous'* presence in the Clyde was to accompany Convoy KX.4A as far as Gibraltar, as ordered by C in C Western Approaches:

"*Malcolm, Broke, Wrestler* are to arrive Greenock p.m. 20th. They are to proceed to Londonderry after convoy conference and are to join convoy at rendezvous to be arranged by NOIC Greenock. *Venomous* (Senior Officer) to do likewise if ready."

A typical wartime painting by Robert Back of a Captain Class frigate.
Courtesy of his daughter, Alison Travis.

Venomous was indeed ready and, after a farewell party in the Bay Hotel, she left with the convoy the following afternoon, passing the Clyde Boom at 1600 on Trafalgar Day, 21 October 1942.

Lt Sangster remembered the sight which greeted *Venomous* on her emergence from the Clyde.

> "Off the Mull of Kintyre, where all the elements of the convoy assembled, were passenger ships, fast liners with troops crowding them. Cdr Falcon-Steward was Senior Officer of the Escort, and there was the usual extended climax of signalling by lamp and flag to the Commodore and the escort to arrange ourselves in the appropriate pattern. After all the usual grind of protecting trade, at last it looked as if we were going on the offensive."

There were nine escorts for the twenty merchant ships, including four tankers, in Convoy KX.4A and Falcon-Steward aboard *Venomous* was the senior officer in charge. Sangster and all those on *Venomous* knew that this convoy was different. *Venomous* was to escort a component of the first major amphibious operation against the Axis powers, Operation *Torch*, the invasion of Morocco and the Vichy controlled colonies in North Africa. Lt Cashman continues the narrative:

> "Our route took us well out into the Atlantic before turning towards Gibraltar to rendezvous with the faster ships. It was the most uncomfortable time as we wallowed in heavy seas with gale force winds for days and days unable, because of the slowness of the merchant ships and large landing craft, to increase to a speed which would be comfortable for a destroyer."

The following signal from *Venomous* confirms the difficulties of keeping the convoy together in such adverse conditions: "Running before gale, *Bachaquers* unable to make good convoy course. *Wrestler* escorting."[22]

Nevertheless, the weather conditions were overcome. *Malcolm* and *Venomous* detached from the convoy during the evening of 30 October and proceeded into Gibraltar to take on fuel on 1 November. Both ships got underway 24 hours later to rejoin the convoy and remained with it until 4 November, returning to Gibraltar later that day.

The next 36 hours provided a brief respite before Falcon-Steward received orders on the 6th, to take his old destroyer south to meet a small convoy and escort them into Gibraltar. The next seven days would be amongst the most demanding *Venomous* had ever faced.

Notes

1   Barnett, p. 491.

2   HMS *Delhi* had been sent to America to be refitted as an anti-aircraft gun cruiser. She was unique in having an all-American main gun armament and fire control system. *Delhi* shipped a powerful anti-aircraft armament of five of the very successful 5-inch 38 calibre dual-purpose guns, 8 x 40-mm Bofor guns and 12 x 20-mm Oerlikon guns.

3   The intelligence provided by the Admiralty's Operational Intelligence Centre was based on information obtained from signals intercepted from German U-boat command radio transmissions, intelligence provided by convoy escorts and patrolling aircraft, as well as from the U-boats themselves. As for the former, the British were able to successfully break the German Enigma codes.

4   Signal from C in C WA to NOIC Londonderry sent at 28/1227B/6/42.

5   Signal from Capt D Greenock to C in C WA sent at 5/1414B/7/42.

6   Barnett, p. 491.

7   Greene, Jack and Alessandro Massignani, *Naval War in the Mediterranean 1940-1943*, Chatham Publishing, Great Britain, 1998, p. 242.

8   Ibid, p. 231.

9   Various accounts give the number of Spitfires carried by *Furious* as being from 36 to 42.

10 Operation *Pedestal* Order of Battle derived from Peter Smith's book, *Pedestal: The convoy that saved Malta*, p. 251-256.

11 Ibid., p. 64.

12 On 13 December 1943, two US Navy destroyers in the Mediterranean near Oran would sink *U-73*.

13 Barnett, p. 518.

14 This disastrous decision by Admiral Sir Dudley Pound was taken at a time when naval intelligence had not been able to provide positive information that *Tirpitz* and her battle group had sailed. All he had to offer was 'negative intelligence.' For more on the role of intelligence and Pound's decision-making process that led to the order to scatter Convoy PQ.17, refer to *Very Special Intelligence*, Patrick Beesly, p. 124 – 141.

15 Convoy PQ.18 would consist of forty-four merchant ships. By the time it reached Russia, the convoy had lost thirteen merchant ships of which six were American.

16 Admiral Commanding Iceland Command's signal sent to C in C HF at 11/2109A/9/42.

17 Signal sent from HMS *Blenheim* to Rear Admiral CS 18 at 14/2127/9/42.

18 Signal from C in C WA sent to Rear Admiral (D) HF at 16/1853A/9/42.

19 Signal from C in C HF to Rear Admiral (D) HF sent at 17/1017/9/42.

20 The objective of the night raid on the French port of St. Nazaire was to destroy the outer gates of the large dry-dock and associated pump works to prevent the Kriegsmarine from using the facility to support its large ships. Royal Marine commandoes disembarked from several motor torpedo boats and destroyed the pump works, whilst the former US Navy 'Four Pipe' destroyer, HMS *Campbelltown* rammed the gates of the dock. When the explosives stored in the bows finally exploded, it destroyed the gates flooding the dry-dock.

21 This story is from an interview with Robert Back, by then a highly respected marine artist, published in the arts journal *Prints,* March/April 1984.

22 Signal sent from *Venomous* to C in C WA sent at 28/2017A/10/42.

CHAPTER EIGHT

A VERY, VERY LONG NIGHT
11 – 12 November 1942

"Do not go gentle into that good night." [1]

Venomous was not a major participant in Operation *Torch*, the British-American invasion of French North Africa, but was to play a key role in countering part of the German response to this, the first great Allied amphibious expedition of the Second World War. The 11 to 12 November 1942 would be a very, very long night.

On 6 November while the ship's company enjoyed a brief respite in Gibraltar, Falcon-Steward received the following signal: "Sail at 1700Z/6 to RV with convoy CF.7 in 29° 03' N 21° 48' W at 1200Z/9 to escort *Vindictive* and *Hecla* to Gibraltar. *Marne* will be sailed later to join you." [2]

The former Hawkins Class heavy cruiser, HMS *Vindictive*, had joined the fleet in 1918 but had been converted to an experimental aircraft carrier in 1919 and served in the Baltic shortly before the arrival of *Venomous*. She was converted back to a heavy cruiser in the mid 1920s and in the thirties to a training ship for cadets before becoming a fleet repair ship in 1939. *Vindictive's* commanding officer and the senior officer of Convoy CF.7A was Capt Herbert G.D. Acland, DSC, RN (Ret.). Acland had received his DSC in 1920 whilst the gunnery officer of the First Destroyer Flotilla, Baltic. His last command at sea before joining *Vindictive* was with the Royal Australian Navy seaplane carrier HMAS *Albatross* in 1938. [3] He would play an important role in the events of 11 November.

HMS *Hecla* was a new ship but an old friend to *Venomous* and her crew. She had repaired the ship's troublesome engineering plant while the destroyer was operating out of Iceland. She also provided some relief from the tight quarters of the old destroyer's overcrowded mess decks that constantly smelled of unwashed bodies and tobacco smoke. *Hecla*, a 10,850-ton destroyer depot ship of the *Tyne* Class, had spent several months in South Africa's Simonstown dockyard after striking a mine whilst en route from Freetown to the Royal Navy's Far East Fleet.[4] With repairs completed, and under the command of Capt Stephen Arliss RN, she was redirected northward to Gibraltar, to join *Vindictive* in supporting the fleet engaged in Operation *Torch*. Admiral Cunningham called her a "…valuable and useful ship…"[5]

Venomous' rendezvous with Convoy CF.7A took place as planned, approximately 200 miles west of the Canary Islands on 9 November, the day after the successful landing of British forces at Algiers and Oran and the American attack on Casablanca. The large convoy and its heavy escort soon drew away as they continued to Liverpool whilst *Venomous* and *Marne* escorted *Hecla* and *Vindictive* toward Gibraltar. The brand-new 'M' Class destroyer HMS *Marne* and her shabby and outdated consort, *Venomous* took up position on either bow of the lead ship, HMS *Vindictive*. The return journey passed without incident until the evening of Armistice Day, 11 November, when they were approximately 250 miles west of Gibraltar.

The eastern and western approaches to the Strait of Gibraltar was one of the most strategically important areas of the world's oceans, an area always at high risk from U-boat attacks but never more so than now after the landings in north Africa. At sunset Capt Acland ordered the four ships to commence a zigzag course, a decision supported by warning signals received from the Admiralty's operation centre, via the Naval Intelligence Division's secret Operational Intelligence Centre (O.I.C.).[6]

They were now part of a game of deception and intricate planning and a test of wills between Gross Admiral Dönitz and his U-boat commanders and the Allied planners and officers executing Operation *Torch*.[7] "The Germans remained in blissful ignorance of *Torch* right up to the moment that the landings began" but they responded very quickly to the Allied offensive.[8] When the amphibious landings began on 8 November Dönitz diverted many of his U-Boats from the critical Battle of the Atlantic to counter them. The dozens of U-Boats that streamed into the relatively confined sea space west and south of Gibraltar and in the Western Mediterranean would be roughly handled by the mostly British anti-submarine forces. But, through the iron determination and brilliant tactical skills of its U-Boat commanders, the Kriegsmarine would score some notable successes against the Allied naval forces of Operation *Torch*. *Venomous* would find itself pitted against one of Dönitz' most able U-Boat commanders.

The after action report to the Naval Commander Expeditionary Force (Operation *Torch*) by *Hecla's* commanding officer sets the stage for the events of the night and early morning of 11/12 November. Capt Arliss wrote:

> "H.M.S HECLA was on passage from FREETOWN to GIBRALTAR and was stationed 3 cables 270 degrees from H.M.S. VINDICTIVE (Capt H.G.D. ACLAND, DSO, R.N., (Retd.), who was Senior Officer, with escorting destroyers MARNE (Lieut. Cdr H.N.A. RICHARDSCN, DSC, R.N.) and VENOMOUS (Cdr H.W. FALCON-STEWARD, R.N.) in Screening Diagram No. 2 VENOMOUS being in position (a) and MARNE in position (0). The mean course was 090 degrees to which it had been altered from 043 degrees at 2230. The force was zigzagging in accordance with Diagram No. 15. Speed through the water was 14 knots, Wind – N.N.E. force 3. Moderate northerly swell. The night was dark, but starlit, the moon having set at 2200. Heavy cumulus clouds low down on the horizon had the effect of rendering silhouettes difficult to see, although the ships' wakes were plainly visible."[9]

A radar contact was made by *Venomous* fifteen minutes prior to Capt Arliss' account, when the formation's heading was 043 degrees at 14 knots, with *Venomous* positioned off the port bow of *Vindictive*: "At 2215 *Venomous* obtained R.D.F., contact bearing 215 degrees, range 4,000 yards. Falcon-Steward turned his destroyer to investigate, but as *Venomous* approached the radar contact, it was lost at a range of 2,200 yards."[10]

Venomous' Executive Officer, Lt Sangster, recalled what happened when they reached the area of the last radar contact,

> "I had the First Watch that night (2000-2400), the Asdic operator reported a contact 60° on the starboard bow. We did not drop any depth charges because contact faded and disappeared and 'non-sub' eventually classified. So the Captain hoisted up the speed to 24 knots and withdrew the Asdic dome in order to regain station on our convoy, which had now got ahead of us by about 8 miles."

The official report failed to mention this Asdic contact, but stated that, "...at 2228 *Venomous* made a search in the area and at 2250 having found nothing, set course to rejoin." Plate II in the Anti-Submarine Division's report shows *Venomous'* manoeuvres in response to the radar and Asdic contact.

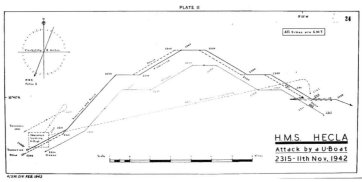

Tracking plate showing position of HMS *Hecla*, HMS *Vindictive*, HMS *Marne* and HMS *Venomous* during the attack.
Analysis of U-boat attacks: HMS Hecla, 11 - 12 Nov.1942.
Report of Anti-submarine Warfare Division (NA Ref. ADM 199/2013).

Capt Arliss' failure to mention *Venomous'* radar contact might be attributable to reporting procedures. *Marne's* radar didn't detect the contact either, possibly due to the type of radar the destroyer operated. At this point it would be helpful to examine the radar equipment available to Convoy CF.7A.

Vindictive had no radar and *Hecla's* radar was designed for gunnery and not for surface-search. Only *Venomous* and *Marne* had surface-search radar and their sets varied in capability. *Venomous'* Type 271M radar antenna was electrically rotated, whilst *Marne's* Type 286 antenna was either fixed or was manually rotated. A fixed aerial would have required *Marne's* CO to manoeuvre his ship at least 20 degrees on either side of the base course of the formation but the track plate shows *Marne* maintaining a steady course until reaching the end of each leg in the zigzag plan. It appears that the Type 286 radar on *Marne* was, therefore, manually rotated. The next question to be asked is how would Lt Cdr Richardson have employed his radar? The answer may be found by re-examining the tactical situation at the time.

Convoy CF.7A was a "high-speed" convoy (14.5 knots was considered fast for a convoy) and a zigzag course was being followed which reduced the likelihood of a U-boat being able to obtain a firing solution from a position ahead of the convoy. It would have been even more difficult for a U-boat to obtain a firing solution from astern of the convoy since the U-boat commander would have had to surface (its submerged speed was much too slow) and pursue the speeding ships at close to its top speed. Most U-boat commanders would consider the risk of detection far too great.[11]

The convoy's course and speed would have partly determined how *Marne*'s radar would have been operated. *Venomous* and *Marne* were positioned ahead and on either side of the bows of the larger ships, with *Venomous* off the port bow of *Vindictive* and *Marne* off the starboard bow of *Hecla*. Since it was thought that a U-boat attack was more likely to come from ahead of the convoy, it would have made sense for the antenna of *Marne*'s Type 286 radar to be manually rotated 40 degrees either side of the formation's course. This tactic, combined with *Venomous* 360-degree electrically rotated radar antenna, would have been considered the correct tactical use of both ships' radar and probably explains why *Venomous* made a radar contact astern of the convoy, whilst *Marne* did not.

Could the radars have been employed differently by altering the position of the destroyers in relation to the larger ships? This may have been in Admiral Cunningham's mind when he wrote that there was a lack of coordinated radar operations.[12]

It is clear from his report and that of the Anti-Submarine Division that Capt Arliss on *Hecla* was not notified of *Venomous*' radar contact:

> "VENOMOUS' signal, reporting the contact, was received by VINDICTIVE only, and not until 2230. It has been verbally stated by the Commanding Officer, H.M.S. VENOMOUS that a signal, cancelling his previous one, was made at about 2250, when the search was abandoned. This latter signal also was only received in VINDICTIVE and not until 2320, when it was too late to be of any value, HECLA by that time having been torpedoed."[13]

Why was Falcon-Steward's signal reporting a radar contact astern of the convoy only received by *Vindictive*? Falcon-Steward would have reported direct to Capt Acland on *Vindictive* as the senior officer present. Acland's reporting requirements may explain why *Hecla* and *Marne* did not receive the signal. Or perhaps the other ships were simply unable to receive the transmitted signal.

Acland's lack of experience in the use of radar and anti-submarine warfare, especially when compared to Falcon-Steward and *Marne*'s commanding officer, Lt Cdr Richardson, might have contributed to the disaster.[14] If Falcon-Steward had been responsible for the anti-submarine defence, would he have signalled the entire formation of his contact, and the subsequent signal indicating he was breaking off the search? Would he have set up the destroyer escort screen (formation) differently to take advantage of the radar capability on the three ships? It is possible that a different formation, one that took advantage of the radar capability of the convoy, could have detected a stalking U-boat travelling on the surface. Would the outcome have been different if Falcon-Steward had been made responsible for the tactical command of the anti-submarine screen? Then again, could anything have prevented a very determined and skilled U-boat commander from carrying home his attack?

Venomous was away from her station following the Asdic contact for nearly an hour. As Sangster noted, at 2250 Falcon-Steward stopped the Asdic search and steered *Venomous* back to the convoy at 24 knots. *Venomous* could have raced back faster but she was not an L.R.E. and had to conserve fuel for what may lie ahead. Gibraltar was still someway off and further radar or Asdic contacts could be expected.

At 2311 the formation was on a course of 120 degrees when *Vindictive* sighted a wake bearing 260 degrees. The officer on watch took this to be *Venomous* rejoining the convoy but it was *U-515*, commanded by Korvettenkapitän Werner Henke, beginning his attack.[15] Capt Arliss recorded what happened next in his report:

> "At 2316 [11:16 p.m.], when in position latitude 35 degrees 42 minutes North longitude 9 degrees 55 minutes West, VINDICTIVE was just turning to the mean course 090 degrees from 120 degrees at the end of the starboard leg of the zig-zag. HECLA had not commenced to turn when two torpedoes struck the ship on the starboard side abreast the Boiler Rooms. The tracks were not reported, and I had no previous indication that enemy submarines were in the immediate vicinity."[16]

After the two torpedoes struck *Hecla*: "Action alarm rattlers were sounded, and the hands proceeded quickly and quietly to their stations. The ship paid off to starboard, lost way, listed rapidly to 7 degrees and then slowly to 11 degrees starboard, where she hung."[17] This was radioed to Gibraltar and communicated by signal lamp to *Marne*.

Venomous was still some distance off and Arliss ordered *Marne* to commence a circular anti-submarine patrol around his stricken ship. Lt Cdr Richardson swung his new destroyer toward the direction from which the torpedoes were fired and lit up the moonless night sky with a star shell.

Arliss received the first damage report and casualty list, "both boilers rooms flooded and all steam lost, but ship in no immediate danger of sinking."[18] He ordered counter flooding of the portside outboard compartments abreast of the ship's boiler rooms to reduce *Hecla's* starboard list.

Lt Herbert Hastings McWilliams of the South African Naval Force (SANF) was asleep when the first torpedoes struck. McWilliams had joined *Hecla* at Freetown. The ship was to transport him to Gibraltar and from there he had orders for North Africa. His description is taken from a letter he wrote within a week of the incident:

> "The first torpedo struck us at 11.16 practically underneath my cabin. My first reaction was one of annoyance at being awakened so violently but as the ship immediately took on a considerable list, and the air was filled with the stink of burned oil, explosives and steam, I realised at once what had happened and leaped out of bed."[19]

Also asleep, swinging gently in his hammock, was 2nd Class Stoker Norman Johns. Johns had joined *Hecla* in Iceland in January 1942. Awakened by the explosion, Johns went to his action station, "which was the port forward damage and fire control party on the fo'c'sle." As Johns recounted:

> "Nobody else mustered, and I could see that the whaler was hanging out of the davits and by the list that the ship was severely damaged. I called up damage control on the telephone that was there, asking for orders and permission to go below and put on more clothing as I was only dressed in underpants and singlet. This was granted and I went down to the mess-deck to find my jersey and overalls…"[20]

Lt Sangster picks up the story from his vantage point on *Venomous*: "As we got close, we could sight the nearest ship and she was obviously stopped. Fearing the worst, the Captain reduced speed to 15 knots, lowered the Asdic dome and ordered 'Action Stations'."

By the time Falcon-Steward steered *Venomous* into a position to begin searching for the submarine, *Vindictive* had already departed the scene.[21] The former cruiser headed toward Gibraltar at flank speed, leaving Arliss on *Hecla* as the senior officer with the two destroyers to ward off further attacks.

At 2342 *Venomous* closed *Hecla* with the intention of passing a tow, but Arliss declined and directed Falcon-Steward to resume his anti-submarine patrol. No immediate contact was established as Henke had cleared his submarine northward to reload his forward torpedo tubes and return for another attack.

And so he did. Henke manoeuvred his submerged submarine against *Hecla's* port side. At 22 minutes past midnight on the 12th the plight of *Hecla* became even more desperate when a third torpedo ripped home, followed by a violent explosion. Arliss reported that:

> "At 0022/12 a torpedo track was observed to be approaching from the port quarter, and the ship was struck at a position estimated to be exactly on 82 bulkhead. The explosion of the torpedo, which appeared to be more violent than the others, threw up large quantities of water, oil, and debris, which covered personnel on the bridge...The ship listed very rapidly from 5 degrees starboard to 17 degrees to port...and that the ship's condition was critical."[22]

Fred Lemberg, one of eleven New Zealand ratings on *Hecla,* was a lookout on the port side of the bridge when the torpedoes struck:

> "On the night of 11 Nov I was on watch as lookout on the port side of the bridge when a torpedo struck the starboard side [in fact two torpedoes struck almost simultaneously]. I remained in my position as it was also my action station, preparations were being made for the *Vindictive* an escorting cruiser to take us in tow, but scanning the darkness with binoculars I saw a white line approaching. I immediately informed the bridge with as much volume as my vocal cords would allow, the torpedo arrived directly below me. I was blown back into the W.T. caboose, fortunately, because when I came to the wing of the bridge was littered with debris from a whaler which was swinging from davits below."

Before the third torpedo hit McWilliams found his way to the boat deck to take up his position as the ship's second boat officer along with a friend and fellow officer:

> "...we spotted the phosphorescent track of another torpedo coming for the port side, apparently due to hit the ship just below us. We ran inboard, covered our heads with our arms and ducked under one of the motorboats. This torpedo struck just abaft of the bridge, some distance forward of where we stood. The actual shock of the explosion was less than I expected and I imagined we should be thrown to the deck. There was a terrific orange flash, shooting up as high as the mast, above which rolled a huge billowing cloud of ruddy smoke studded with flying debris. Then a great column of water went up and presently bits of steel and wood began raining down all round with fearful clattering sounds. We shrank against the overhanging boat until this was over, then ventured out to be caught in a shower of water coming down like rain."[23]

218

All the ship's boats had been destroyed but thirty Carley floats, each capable of supporting twenty men, had been lowered into the sea and an enormous quantity of rough planks and baulks for repairs which could support a swimmer were cut loose.

Stoker Johns was still on the mess-decks trying to find his clothes when the third torpedo struck, "I abandoned my search for more clothes and went up again to the well-deck where a lot of the crew gathered. I found my friend George Fortey from Gloucester."[24]

The ship's port list increased to 25 degrees and Capt Arliss asked *Marne* to standby to assist with picking up survivors from his ship. He then ordered all hands to Carley Raft and float stations. This order was followed by the order to abandon ship. Ten minutes later at 0032, just after midnight, with men entering the water, a fourth torpedo struck her port side abreast of *Hecla's* "X" gun. The end was now very near.

Fred Lemberg "tied a rope to the guardrail on starboard side and slid down over barnacles into the briny, blew up the life belt and made my way out into the darkness".[25] McWilliams with his two friends and fellow officers, Spring and Cox, made their way to the highest point of the shelter deck, next to the after funnel.

> "I was not scared – certainly not at this stage – much to my surprise, but after the last torpedo I felt that perhaps it would be wise to leave. The wireless aerial fell down in leaping coils and as the ship took on a greater list there were ominous rumblings and crashes between decks as heavy objects broke loose and slid to port…The water, owing to our great list, still seemed a long way down and as I peered over I saw the enormous hole made by the first torpedo (it turned out afterwards that two struck us simultaneously) which gaped in the ship's side immediately below. I noticed some chaps being sucked into it and decided this was no place to go overboard so I worked my way further aft. Reluctantly I laid aside my overcoat. I thought my scarf might be in the way so I took that off, too. Then I scrambled over."[26]

George Male, a sick berth attendant, was not so lucky:

> I went up the starboard rail, I could almost walk down the side it was so far keeling over. The rope ended and I let go and found myself back in the ship. I'd gone into a hole made by the torpedo. I was a good swimmer and there was a destroyer HMS *Marne* standing by to pick up survivors. I was swimming towards her and amongst others in the water I saw the Master at Arms (Johnny Harbour); he was standing

upright in the water with his hands on the reading desk of the ships lectern with his feet on the cross bar at the bottom. What are you doing I said? He said, "If I'm going to heaven boy I'm going in style".[27]

By this time Richardson had positioned *Marne* about four hundred yards on *Hecla's* port quarter, and was preparing to take survivors on board when a swirl of phosphorescent water was spotted about a thousand yards off *Hecla's* starboard beam. Richardson ordered full speed astern to clear *Hecla* and proceeded to investigate but countermanded that order when *Marne* found herself amongst many of *Hecla's* survivors who were floating about in Carley Rafts or bobbing in the water supported by their life jackets. In lieu of pursuit Richardson ordered another star shell to be fired. This decision almost proved fatal when one of Henke's torpedoes struck *Marne*.

What Richardson saw was Henke's *U-515* on the surface, moving clear of the area, having just fired two more torpedoes. "Almost at once, at 0105, *Hecla* was hit again, for the last time, on her starboard side right aft by a torpedo that was fired from the beam. A few seconds later *Marne* sighted a wake of a torpedo one cable away and was hit aft and had her stern blown off."[28]

HMS *Hecla* with torpedo striking HMS *Marne* in background; drawn by Herbert McWilliams.
IWM Image Reference ART LD 002612. *Courtesy of the Imperial War Mueum.*

The moment when HMS *Marne* was torpedoed in the stern by U-515; drawn by
Herbert McWilliams after his rescue by HMS *Venomous*.
Courtesy of George Male.

Herbert McWilliams was swimming towards *Marne* when:

> A torpedo struck the stern of the destroyer and blew it sky high.
> Two sections of the quarterdeck rolled up like bits of stair carpet,
> flinging some men into the air, and the vertical spurts of orange
> flame showed up jagged pieces of metal hurtling upwards.
>
> It wasn't long before the depth charges [which had been on the
> quarter deck] began to go off. I can't describe the terrible
> sensation, just like a giant squeezing me in his fist.

McWilliams grabbed a lifeline hanging from the gunwale of a 27-foot
whaler lowered from *Marne* shortly before it was hit. He was
eventually allowed in the overcrowded and part flooded whaler, where
everybody was baling desperately to keep it afloat.

Stoker Johns was still on *Hecla* when the torpedo struck *Marne*:

> "It was about this time that one of our escorts, the destroyer HMS
> *Marne* was hit. George and I were standing on the port side of the
> well deck and saw the explosion. She was hit aft and the ready use
> ammunition that was stored in lockers on that part of the ship went
> up like a firework display."[29]

Johns recounted what happened when he and his shipmate abandoned ship:

> "George wanted to go over the port side as by this time the deck was only a few feet from the water, but in the end we thought that the ship would roll over that way, and if we were still near would roll on us so we decided to go for the starboard side. We went over together, the side of the ship was almost horizontal. We slid down the bottom and into the water. I didn't see George after this. As I hit the water I went down. Then the buoyancy of my lifejacket brought me up to the surface and I started to swim away from the ship, I then realised that I was being sucked back towards the ship's side, and then saw the hole that the 1st torpedo had made, and as much as I tried I couldn't stop myself from going in. I thought 'this is the end.' As far as I recall I must have grasped a rope that was hanging, and I could hear screams and shouts from others that had also been sucked in. At that time I must have struck something hard and I must have become unconscious, and when I came to I was well away from the ship."

In his after action report, Falcon-Steward described what happened next:

> "At 0100 hours *Marne* was standing by to pick up survivors from *Hecla* who were in the process of abandoning ship, having already been torpedoed four times. At 0105 both *Hecla* and *Marne* were hit by further torpedoing on the starboard side, *Hecla* sank and *Marne* had her stern blown off but remained afloat. *Venomous,* who was at this time on the port bow of *Hecla,* closed *Marne*'s starboard quarter at full speed, illuminating the area with starshell. Shortly after, a U-boat was sighted on *Venomous* port bow, crossing from port to starboard at about 1500 yards range. *Venomous* was proceeding at 24 knots.
>
> On sighting *Venomous,* the U-boat altered course and steered a zigzag course at high speed. *Venomous* overhauled slowly. When the range was about 1000 yards the U-boat fired a torpedo from the stern tubes, which was avoided.
>
> At a later stage of the chase, *Venomous* opened fire with her main armament but claimed no hits. The U-boat did not dive until the range had been closed to 200 yards and the periscope was observed to pass down the port side of *Venomous* about 10 yards away.
>
> A pattern of five depth charges set to 50 feet was fired by eye when the last feather from the disappearing periscope was passing astern. *Venomous* and the U-boat were still on approximately parallel courses when the attack was made.

> With the last charge, there was a much heavier explosion than
> normal and a much higher column of water. The last charge did not
> appear to fire shallow."[30]

Lt Sangster gave his view of what happened:

> "We had just started a square search of two mile sides when our
> Asdic operator yelled 'Torpedo, Torpedo, Torpedo, Green 40-70'
> (40-70 degrees on starboard bow).
>
> 'Hard a' starboard, steady on 110°,' ordered the Captain quite
> quietly. On the Asdic loudspeaker dwarfing the 'ping' of our own
> transmission, everyone could hear the tube-train roar picked up
> from the torpedoes. There was a horrible thud in our own ears and
> the loudspeaker roar decreased, there was another horrible thud
> and the roar ceased altogether. *Marne's* stern had been blown off
> and the other torpedo had hit *Hecla* again.
>
> Immediately a lamp started flashing us from *Marne*: 'U-boat on
> my starboard quarter.'
>
> 'Hard a' starboard, full head both engines' and off we went,
> cutting past *Marne's* stern. After a minute with no report from
> radar the Captain cried, 'Fire a snowflake.' With a swish, the rocket
> ascended and far above, the magnesium burst into light and floated
> down on its parachute and there at Red 10 was a submarine
> powering away on the surface, 400 yards away.
>
> At full ahead, *Venomous* had sunk her stern as her screws bit
> into the water. There were lots more orders. B Gun (4.7") got off
> two rounds whose charges were supposed to be non-flash for night
> fighting but we on the bridge were all blinded. The port Oerlikon
> opened up and tracer crowded round the [submarine's] conning
> tower gun. By the next time a snowflake went up there was no
> submarine, just our white bow wave spoiling the calm dark sea.
>
> And then we saw it, just near our bow, the still bubbling swirl of
> a submarine's dive. The A/S Bosun broadcast, 'Stand by emergency
> pattern – shallow setting. Fire 1, 2, 3.' *Venomous* careered on and
> immediately the five explosions were over the Captain reduced
> speed to 15 knots so as to use his Asdic.
>
> Square searches followed around the last known spot of 'swirl'
> for an hour and a half but we did not get contact with the Asdic."

The explosion of the depth charges put one of *Venomous'* dynamos
out of action, resulting in an electrical failure. Although this was soon
put right neither Asdic nor Radar contact was regained, in spite of a
thorough search.[31] Falcon-Steward continued the search until 0240. Lt
Coleman takes up the story:

> "That was the night that was – a night in my life which I could not

possibly forget. I spent ten hours in the Chartroom below the bridge with the chart or plotting sheet before me, with the Chernikoff Log clock, the Gyro compass repeater and a chronometer watch adjacent. I could hear through the voice tube all that was going on up top, everything that was said or ordered, the Asdic pinging, the lot.

A surface target was reported by a lookout bearing Red 40. This sighting turned out to be a U-boat with conning tower out of the water. We opened fire with the forward 4.7-inch and headed straight for it. We passed the diving submarine close down the port side within feet actually, and planted depth charges on top of it as it passed astern."[32]

The two RDF operators at their action stations in the radar shack above and behind the open bridge had a clear view of the action and 'Freddo' Thomas described the scene lit up by a star shell: "almost under our bows, it seemed, was the U-boat, like a monstrous black whale its wet side glistening in the yellow light". His dramatic account is very vivid but he was over optimistic when he described the result of their depth charges "one actually striking the submerged conning tower … astern the sea shuddered, boiled and up-heaved itself into a gigantic water spout. By the light of our ten inch searchlight we saw a huge, black cigar shape appear, to break slowly into two, both parts disappearing almost immediately."[33]

In *U-515* that night was Hans Hahn. He described the action and its aftermath:

"It was our second raid. We left Lorient at the beginning of November. Because of the landing of Allied armies on the coast of Morocco we, along with other boats, were ordered into this particular area. On the 12th we sighted a group of warships with two Cruisers and three Destroyers. After several hours of shadowing, partly below water, partly above, we managed to get in front of the boats. Despite the actions of the Destroyers to secure the safety of the group, we managed to break through successfully, went to action stations at dive position and attacked. About midnight we fired a spread of four torpedoes at a Cruiser – two torpedoes hit amidships and she started to list. We left below water! About 0100, a new assault towards a destroyer was started, the ship which lay alongside the cruiser. With the Heck-torpedoes we shot another salvo of two torpedoes and both were hits. We heard explosions on the Destroyer but could not ourselves make observations because we were under depth charge attack and forced out of the area. We left to reload torpedoes.

A new assault on the damaged Cruiser began and more hits were recorded. This was followed by more depth charging and we were forced to give up our attack due to heavy damage to our boat.

> "About 0500 we became aware that the heavily damaged ship had been towed away. We could not carry out further actions because of massive air activity and the great damage sustained by ourselves.
>
> Official reports later confirmed that we had in fact assaulted and damaged and sunk not a heavy cruiser but the repair ship *Hecla*."[34]

This was indeed the case and at 0116, *Hecla* finally succumbed to the fifth torpedo, heeling on her beam-ends and sinking stern first.

HMS *Hecla* sinking as survivors struggle in the water; drawn by Herbert McWilliams.
IWM Image Reference ART LD 002611. *Courtesy of the Imperial War Mueum.*

Venomous returned to the scene with *Marne* helplessly adrift and hundreds of men struggling in the water for survival. It was clear to Lt Cashman what had to be done. It was something that *Venomous* had been called on to do before:

> "*Vindictive* did the very sensible thing, used her superior speed, tucked her stern down and went flat out for Gibraltar. Shortly afterwards *Marne* had her stern blown off by the outside 'Fish' of a spread. This left us with the triple task of protecting *Marne*, lying helpless without screws, picking up survivors and looking after ourselves."

As the end approached Capt Arliss realised there was nothing else to do but to try and save himself and those around him. He made his way down the starboard side of his sinking ship and into the water where he was joined by some of his officers and ratings.

Edward Coleman, an Electrical Artificer (EA), was part of a damage control party working below decks to restore emergency power whilst all this was going on:

> "The ship had become ghostly quiet and unusually motionless. I didn't like it and suggested we move to the upper deck. There was no response." When the forth torpedo struck and nobody made a move: "Bugger this I'm going to have a look up top."[35]

The main deck was awash and he barely had time to inflate his life jacket before the *Marne* was hit. Soon afterwards a fifth torpedo hit *Hecla:*

> "It hit us on the port side near where I and my shipmates had been working … what had happened to the other lads? Did they perish as a result of that fifth torpedo? I saw not another soul on board at that time. I believed that I was …the last man to leave *Hecla.*"

Coleman scrambled over the guardrail on the port side, fearful that it would roll over him. He saw a Carley float with sixty men trying to clamber aboard, gave up on it, and swam for a while talking quietly with a younger man until "he suddenly said 'Oh, fuck this for a lark' and with no more ado threw up his arms and disappeared". He was horrified, realising he could not have had a life belt, and felt he had let down a shipmate. He remembered sadly that:

> "I heard men singing. But they were not drunk. As I cast around me in the darkness, I suddenly realised they were still on *Hecla*, now settling by the stern. They had gathered on the foc'sle singing hymns. 'Abide with me' and 'Eternal Father strong to save' carried clearly cross to me. I willed them to abandon ship; I prayed that they would join me in the drink but to no avail."[36]

Before *Hecla* finally sank Coleman found an empty Carley float without a wooden platform inside the steel iron tube body. He hung onto the rope loops around its outer edges and was soon joined by others but to their horror they discovered it was attached to the sinking ship by a three-inch rope. Chief E.A. Brown, who had been vague and withdrawn in South Africa after having been sunk two or three times, was now completely calm and rational and called out: "Hang on a bit you lads, let me get my knife out and see if I can cut it". He could, and he did and with joy we saw the distance between us and the ship increasing minute by minute."

Meanwhile, Norman Johns "heard voices and I made my way to a group that was on a carley raft … I hung onto one of the lines on the edge for I don't know how long until our other escort, HMS *Venomous*, came alongside to pick us up":

> "There were scrambling nets over the side and many of the carley raft occupants left to grab the nets. I was on the far side so didn't attempt any move. The suddenness of all the men leaving meant the float capsized. At that moment, orders came from the *Venomous* to get back on the raft as she had got 'a ping.' The destroyer moved away, some of the men had managed to get aboard the nets but many dropped into the water and were probably killed by her propellers."[37]

This was not the end of Johns' ordeal as he was amongst those left behind when *Venomous* moved away.

McWilliams was luckier – but only just. The whaler launched by *Marne* before it sank capsized as *Venomous* approached and the Bosun, Henry Button, dived in to help those trapped underneath. McWilliams managed to reach the scrambling nets and hung on "as others trod on my shoulders and head and climbed over me" and "as she gathered speed I braced myself for the last spurt and just managed to scramble high enough for someone to grab me". He heard "the cries and curses of those who had to be left behind, a horrible sound."

Ordinary Seaman Harry Haddon remembered the bravery of Wharton, a scouse from Liverpool, who was nearly left behind when he jumped in to help, but at the last minute grabbed a scrambling net at the stern and was pulled back on board. As *Venomous* pulled away Haddon saw a shark near one of the men floundering in the water and an officer fired at it from the bridge (the man was rescued the following morning).

Cashman explained why the rescue operation by *Venomous* was suddenly stopped:

> "During the night whilst we were stopped, boats and floats tied on both sides, men on the scrambling nets and a sitting target, the Asdic operator reported 'torpedoes approaching.' We were going ahead fairly fast before we cut the last boat or float adrift. The C.O. turned to starboard to comb the tracks and we watched, relieved, as the torpedoes passed, close on either side of us.

Almost immediately afterwards we picked up a firm contact and attacked with depth charges several times. Without definite evidence, we could not claim to have sunk the submarine."

Stoker Johns vividly remembers the affects of *Venomous'* depth charges: "…whilst I was hanging on the ropes of the raft, *Venomous* had made several depth charge attacks on the U-boat. These were felt by me, and I expect all the others that were in the water. It was as if I was being put through a wringer and being squeezed from the legs upward."[38]

This third alarm of the night began at 0402 when *Marne* sighted a dark object and a swirl in the water some thousand yards on her starboard beam. She opened fire with her forward 4.7-inch gun and star shell. *Venomous* moved in to attack, Hydrophone effects were heard on the bearing and firm echoes obtained at a thousand yards. Range decreased to 150 yards as *Venomous* dropped two depth charges, but contact was lost. The target had passed under the helpless *Marne*.

The respite was short as before the rescue could be resumed a further contact was obtained. Falcon-Steward in his report described the sequence of events:

"At 0530 *Venomous* made R.D.F. contact moving right at a range of 3600 yards and closed to investigate. A U-boat was then sighted on the surface moving towards *Marne* on an approximate course of 260°. Speed was increased to ram and fire opened with a 4.7-inch and Oerlikon, by which time the U-boat had reached a position 1000 yards – 30° on *Marne*'s port bow. *Venomous* considered she had been unobserved until this moment. Fire was also opened by *Marne* with B gun but was broken off as *Venomous* came in.

Venomous scored hits with her Oerlikon on the conning tower and the Boat dived 300 yards fine on her port bow. Asdic contact was obtained with opening Doppler and counter attack was carried out at 0554 with a five-charge pattern set at 50 feet. After the fifth charge had detonated, a sixth and heavier explosion was heard. Immediately after the attack, *Venomous* had to alter to port to avoid *Marne*."

Arthur J. Mervyn Mansell saw the brief surface action from his action station with the depth charge party: "We saw a U-boat on the surface…and saw tracer bullets [20 mm Oerlikon] ricochet off the conning tower as the U-boat submerged."[39]

Falcon-Steward continues:

"Contact was regained with closing Doppler and hydro effect and it was decided to carry out another counter attack without waiting for

> a full charge pattern to be reloaded, as the U-boat was dangerously near the disabled Destroyer. The second attack at 0603 was therefore made with five heavy charges set to 140 feet. Contact was not regained and a search was carried out until daylight when rescue operations were resumed at 0730.
>
> The impression of various witnesses was that the U-boat was considered larger than the one previously attacked at 0139."

This impression may have been accurate given the account of Hans Hahn, who did not mention any attacks after 0240. The contact that *Venomous* pursued remained undetermined but was later established not to have been a U-boat.[40]

One of those hanging onto a Carley float whilst *Venomous* followed up Asdic contacts was Les Rowles:

> "The raft was overladen and had people hanging on the sides. Every so often we would get tossed off and had to swim back. Every time we got back we would be less in numbers as we sat through the night.
>
> We had little lights plugged into our life-belts and you could see them bobbing about in all directions. A sight never to be forgotten. During the night a Destroyer slid close by us and threw us a line. We missed it and she sped off, much to our disappointment".

'Freddo' Thomas, the RDF operator, wrote "we made four depth charges that night but with inconclusive results. Between these attacks, we would make periodic sweeps around the *Marne* then stop and pick up more men." Even under these circumstances there were occasional humorous incidents. Harry Haddon remembered abandoning one poor fellow, stubbornly still wearing his sailor's hat, to follow up an Asdic signal and when they reassured him that they would soon be back he replied "I won't be going anywhere". When they finally picked him up Harry was amused to find that he was weighed down by a heavy spanner in the narrow slit pocket in his dungarees.

Fred Woods remembered "seeing the mast of *Venomous* like a needle on the horizon when daylight broke through, weaving her way, gathering those that could climb the scrambling nets, some blokes just hanging on." Craddock sadly recalled that there were "hundreds of dead bodies floating in the water with one or two feebly waving arms". Prominent among the rescuers was Bosun Herbert Button, a strong swimmer who, on a number of occasions, swam out with lines to rafts

Hecla survivors on Carley floats photographed in the early morning light by AB Cyril Hely (left) and Lt Leslie Eaton RNVR (right).

and pieces of loose timber and other wreckage to which exhausted survivors clung. George Male was unconscious by the time he was rescued that morning and believes he may have been one those Herbert Button saved. He came to lying on the galley flat with corned beef being spooned out of a six-pound tin into his mouth. Greg Clarke, the youngest officer aboard *Hecla,* only recovered consciousness days later in Gibraltar hospital.[41]

Les Rowles recalled the moment when he was rescued:

> "We were picked up by *Venomous*. I remember trying to climb aboard but was slipping back. Someone said, 'grab him,' and I was hauled aboard where I just flaked out. Standing over me was a couple of *Venomous* lads with a tot, which was pushed down me. I had no choice. Then cigarettes, following by corned beef straight out of the tin with fingers – not enough knives to go round. It tasted good."[42]

Collister recalled in his memoir written in 2006, a few months before his death, that, "when full daylight dawned it just left *Venomous* and a few survivors on bits of wood. He and Leading Seaman Bush "who dived in with a line between his teeth" helped rescue four survivors but reflected that "had I known the number and size of sharks I might have had second thoughts." The survivors made no mention of sharks but many of those on *Venomous* were convinced that there were sharks. Cyril Hely took advantage of the morning light to photograph the last few survivors awaiting rescue.

It was late morning when Edward Coleman's little group hanging onto the damaged Carley float was picked up. This was the first time he had been aboard a destroyer, and he found that "there was no public address system on these ships. The bosun's mate went round the ship giving a short shrill blast on his pipe and shouted out his message like a town crier: "The Captain has ordered splice the Main Brace, all hands may collect a ration even if they are 'temp'.""

Norman John's overloaded Carley float had capsized as *Venomous* came alongside and he was left behind when *Venomous* got a "ping" and moved off. "When light came there were only two of us on the float." They were spotted by an American Catalina flying boat and "were the last to be picked up". "Our Master-at-Arms [Johnny Harbor] had made a list of all those that had been picked up by *Venomous* but my name is not on it as I expect he thought there were to be no more survivors recovered and was busy in *Venomous*' office typing it all out."

"It was not until 1250 that *Venomous* finally completed the rescue, by which time she had on board 17 Officers and 476 Ratings. A further 64 survivors were in *Marne,* still wallowing helplessly in the swell.

In response to the news of the attack three escorts were sent to help. The Canadian Flower Class corvette, HMCS *Prescott,* and two Hunt III Class escort destroyers, HMS *Glaisdale* and *Albrighton* together with the tug *Jaunty*, were dispatched from Gibraltar. By late afternoon they had still not been sighted which presented Falcon-Steward with a series of difficult decisions.

Venomous was running short of fuel. Efforts to take on oil from *Marne* were unsuccessful because of the heavy swell during the late morning hours. Falcon-Steward knew that if he waited much longer *Venomous* would not make it back to Gibraltar. The nearest port was Casablanca which, according to reports, was now in Allied hands but not yet to be confirmed. Falcon-Steward didn't really know what reception he would receive when his ship approached the Moroccan coast.

And he couldn't leave *Marne* while there was a chance of her being saved. As senior officer present he could decide to scuttle *Marne* but he already had five hundred survivors on his ship, many seriously wounded. Adding a few hundred more would have been impossible without further risk to the stability of his ship. Falcon-Steward held on. Together with patrolling anti-submarine aircraft, *Venomous* continued protecting *Marne* throughout the day, knowing relief was on its way. At

1600 salvation appeared in the form of the Flower Class corvettes, HMS *Jonquil* and *Louisburg*. They had been steaming to reinforce Convoy JGF.2 but had been diverted to assist. It was now imperative that if *Venomous* was to make harbour under her own power she should proceed immediately. As the senior officer present, Falcon-Steward directed *Jonquil* to stand by *Marne* until the arrival of the ships from Gibraltar. The ten officers and fifty-four ratings aboard *Marne* transferred to *Jonquil*.

As the ship's navigator Coleman summed up the situation facing *Venomous* and the decision Falcon-Steward reached:

> "I was summoned to the bridge to assist in making the decision. We were desperately short of fuel – not enough to get back to Gibraltar. From signals received we knew the Americans had invaded and taken over Casablanca the day before. Having calculated our fuel, no zig-zag and maximum economical speed, we found we could just make Casablanca, so off we went."[43]

At 1615 Falcon-Steward set *Venomous* on course for Casablanca. The ship was crammed with survivors and Cashman recalled how they affected the ship's stability: "We had them stowed everywhere, as far down below as possible. Even so we could only use about 5° of wheel to turn, otherwise we would keel over to a crazy angle."

Lt Sangster recalled the journey – and the problems faced by the "Chief":

> "We steamed at the most economical speed on one boiler only at 11 knots. The least cheerful chap in the Wardroom was the Warrant Engineer. He, by all the gauges had no fuel left at all, and yet he had to coax 120 miles of steaming to Casablanca."

The stokers had been busy with a very critical but dirty job, transferring the fuel oil residue from the empty tanks into just one tank and through their efforts and Falcon-Steward's skilful ship handling, *Venomous* made it to Casablanca with just four tons of fuel remaining.

While the stokers were busy transferring the oil, the ship's company were taking care of both the living and the dead that were taken from the oily and wreckage-filled sea. Surg. Lt S.L. Hetherington, one of those rescued from *Hecla*, did the best he could for the wounded. The dead were sown in weighted hammocks and placed on the fo'c'sle. They would be buried at sea when time allowed.

Exhausted survivors of HMS *Hecla*.
On port side looking towards stern from funnels (note whaler and pom pom gun).
Courtesy of Chris Eaton.

As for the living, the ship's company was busy passing out their own rations of hot tea, biscuits, spare blankets and tots of rum to *Hecla's* survivors who were strewn all over the decks. Many were wounded, some very seriously. All were black with oil. They lay cold, exhausted, shivering and vomiting, expelling the oil that had until recently filled the tanks of their ship. The tot of rum that Stoker Johns received immediately acted upon his stomach. Up came the oil that he had swallowed. Johns was glad to be alive and pleased to see that George had also made it and had not been sucked into *Hecla's* gaping hole. They sat together, leaning against the starboard side of *Venomous'* torpedo tubes.

Edward Coleman had some difficulty in finding somewhere to sleep on the overcrowded ship but eventually settled down for the night near "B" gun, "taking care not to cause a riot by treading" on the four or five

HMS *Venomous* berthed alongside the heavy cruiser USS *Augusta* at Casablanca.
Image Reference NARA-80-G-30471. *Courtesy of the National Archives and Records Administration, USA.*

The *Hecla* dead sewn in canvas hammocks ready for burial are moved on
the deck of *Venomous* at Casablanca.
Image Reference NARA-80-G-30105. *Courtesy of the National Archives and Records Administration, USA.*

already there. He "slept like a log … but was awake early next morning and got quite a shock. The four or five chaps I had stepped over the night before were sewn up in hammocks awaiting burial!"

Venomous had signalled her intentions of proceeding into Casablanca late on the 12th, and as she was passing the breakwater a signal from Gibraltar was received, "Under no circumstances proceed Casablanca." *Venomous* had already made contact with the American Task Force (TF) 34 commander, Rear Admiral Hewitt, on his flagship, the Northampton Class heavy cruiser, the USS *Augusta*. Hewitt directed Falcon-Steward to enter Casablanca's harbour and secure alongside his flagship.

Hecla survivors on *Venomous* at Casablanca, carrier is USS *Chenango*.
Looking towards stern, note Aldis lamp on rear platform. *Courtesy of Chris Eaton.*

The day before, Hewitt's task force had defeated the Vichy naval units that had sortied out against the Americans and overcome the coastal defences of the port city. The amphibious assault had successfully secured a beachhead and taken the city after some intense fighting but conditions in the port were still chaotic when *Venomous* entered Casablanca's harbour.

Upon securing alongside the *Augusta*, the American capacity for help and generosity was immediately put into motion. Lt Coleman remembered the assistance given to *Hecla's* survivors: "The Americans took us alongside, took off all our survivors and dished out 500 showers, four-course breakfasts, complete kits of clothing". George Male remembered how the movie cameras filmed them as they climbed the scrambling nets to board *Augusta* and that within ninety minutes they had showered, been issued with US sailors' clothing, fed and were back on *Venomous*.

At first light on the 13th, Admiral Hewitt directed Falcon-Steward to take *Venomous* alongside one of the US Navy's escort aircraft carriers, which had been directed earlier by Hewitt to enter the harbour and provide fuel for the destroyers operating with the task force. Lt Sangster described what the men of the American carrier did for the survivors:

> "An Officer arrived to say, 'Please send over your survivors 20 at a time, every twenty minutes.' *Boxer*'s Commander had organised a line of goodies on a scale of one minute per man. Issue of new sailors' kit, shaver, thank you very much and off you go back."[44]

Les Rowles described his reception on board: "They gave us a cafeteria style meal, as much as we wanted, a cinema show which most of us were too tired to watch, and kitted us out like Yankee sailors. The Yanks were very good to us." They bedded down with mattresses and blankets in the huge hanger of the aircraft carrier and rejoined *Venomous* the next morning.

Having refuelled, *Venomous* secured alongside one of Casablanca's quays for another day. The fight for the city was over and they witnessed its return to Allied control and the transformation of its port into a major logistics centre for the Anglo-American Army that would fight its way across North Africa. Herbert McWilliams spent part of this day making the vivid sketches for the paintings of *Hecla* sinking and *Marne* being torpedoed which he later presented to the Imperial War Museum, London. They were made on the reverse of old charts and coloured with iodine using a throat brush from the sick bay.

Venomous departed Casablanca early on the morning of 14 November. Lt Coleman remembered the voyage: "We left for Gibraltar, the open deck covered with survivors, the Wardroom, the Captain's Cabin – every available space crammed. We cruised up the Atlantic to Gibraltar safely, arriving next morning."

The darkness of that long night still cast a pall over *Venomous*. On

Venomous on her way to Gibraltar with Hecla survivors.
Courtesy of Mervyn Mansell.

Hecla survivors on passage to Gibraltar 14-15 November.
Note seaman with US sailor's hat and elderly seamen, not uncommon on depot ships like Hecla.
Courtesy of Chris Eaton.

"Burial at sea [whilst en route to Gibraltar] of the unlucky ones", Cyril Hely.
An unknown officer is reading from the Bible whilst survivors of the Hecla crowd round.
Photographed by Cyril Hely. Courtesy of Dorothy Hely.

The dead were sewn in weighted hammocks.
"The officer in foreground is the one that died a few days afterwards, he was a fine bloke too", Cyril Hely.
Almost certainly Chief Petty Officer Herbert Button, the Bosun.
Photographed by Cyril Hely. Courtesy of Dorothy Hely.

her return passage to Gibraltar the bodies of nine men who died after rescue were buried at sea, sewn in hammocks weighted at the foot. The survivors crowded round and one of the officers read the last rites as the bodies were slid into the sea from boards resting on the depth charges at the stern of *Venomous*. CPO Herbert Button, the Bosun, to whom many *Hecla* survivors owed their lives, had been totally exhausted by his efforts and retired to his bunk, but despite being unwell he was present as the dead were committed to the deep. Cyril Hely photographed the scene. Their burial was noted as 34° 30' North / 7° 30' West. Most of the 273 on *Hecla* who died (out of a total ship's complement of 838) were recorded as "missing presumed killed".[45] On arrival at Gibraltar they found the badly damaged Marne in the harbour. After temporary repairs it was towed to Britain where a new stern structure was fitted. The *Hecla* survivors on HMS *Marne* and *Venomous* were passed from one ship to another before finally returning to Britain on an old liner, the *Reina del Pacifico*.

HMS *Marne* at Gibraltar, November 1942.
Courtesy of George Male.

During that very, very long night, the performance of Falcon-Steward and the ships company was nothing less than outstanding. Those on the lower deck, as well as those in the Wardroom, still remembered it fondly and with pride many years later. AB R.A. Craddock's opinion was typical:

"In my mind, the Captain of *Venomous* was one of the great Captains of our time. He saved the *Venomous*, picked up survivors from *Hecla* and fought U-boats at the same time. I still think of him now." Lt Coleman reflected the view of the ship's company when he said: "This was a terrific accomplishment and the fact that not a single mention or decoration was awarded seemed a bit hard."

The absence of such recognition appears the more surprising when considered in the context of the letter accompanying the report on the loss of *Hecla* written by Admiral Andrew Browne Cunningham, the C in C Mediterranean Fleet and also the Naval Commander Expeditionary Force (NCXF):

> "A satisfactory feature of this incident was the sound appreciation, initiative and determination of the Commanding Officer of *Venomous* who coped admirably with a most difficult situation making two highly efficient attacks on U-boats, recovering survivors and arranging for the safeguarding of *Marne* before he left to fuel."[46]

Cunningham was a hard, but fair, taskmaster, not known to be over generous in his praise and this statement is a great compliment to the commanding officer of *Venomous*, but in the preceding paragraph Admiral Cunningham states that:

> "In my view there was a bad failure in A/S, quite apart from R.D.F. It was not until after the harm was done that A/S started to pick up echoes.

It appears that:

> (a) VINDICTIVE failed to ensure a proper co-ordination of R.D.F. arrangements, and, in consequence, R.D.F. results appear to have been completely negative.
> (b) An error in judgement caused VINDICTIVE to assume that what was, in fact, a U-boat, was VENOMOUS joining up. As a result no real attempt was made to identify the object sighted.
> (c) A/S was thoroughly unsatisfactory until the enemy had betrayed his presence by firing torpedoes. It is appreciated, however, that submarines were probably on the surface."[47]

Cunningham's assessment placed responsibility for the loss of *Hecla* on the shoulders of the senior officer present. After the loss of *Hecla*, Capt Acland never again commanded at sea, his future wartime service being in command of shore facilities.[48]

Falcon-Steward's report of success against the enemy during that very, very long night was considered over-optimistic by the U-boat Assessment Committee which downgraded the first attack to "insufficient evidence of damage" in March 1943. This turned out to be correct as *U-515*, still commanded by Korvetten Kapitän Werner Henke, fought on in the Battle of the Atlantic with considerable success until it was cornered and sunk by a US Navy Hunter-Killer Group, Task Group, TG 22.3, on 9 April 1944.[49]

Henke and forty of his men survived and were taken prisoners. Task Group 22.3 commander, Capt Daniel Gallery, USN, described his meeting with Henke when the German commander was brought aboard Gallery's ship the escort aircraft carrier, the USS *Guadalcanal*:

> "The man had a commanding personality and I knew in an instant he came in the cabin that he was the skipper. He looked like an All-American halfback whose team had just lost a close game and who was beaten but unashamed. I found out later that he was one of Dönitz' aces and though his crew respected his ability as a U-boat skipper, they hated his guts. They said he took unnecessary chances because he wanted an Oak Leaf for his Knight's Cross and they blamed the loss of their boat on his reckless confidence that he would sink the *Guadalcanal* before we got him. They were also bitter because for two years he had frozen promotions on his boat to prevent any of his hand-picked crew from being transferred to other boats when they were promoted."[50]

Shortly after his arrival in America as a prisoner of war, Henke was sent to Fort Hunt in Virginia. This coastal defence site, built during the Spanish-American War, was located on the Potomac River just south of Washington, D.C., and had been converted into a secret prison for interrogating high value German military personnel, saboteurs and spies. At this time there were very few captured U-boat commanders, and his value to US Naval Intelligence was critically important. His American interrogators apparently threatened to return Henke to Britain, and told him that he would be tried there as a war criminal for the sinking of the passenger ship SS *Ceramic*.[51] It seems that Henke would not talk and instead took his own life by committing suicide. On 15 June 1944 he walked out of his barracks, onto the fenced-in commons and across the commons towards the wire in full sight of the guards and climbed it, ignoring a warning by the guard to stop; he was shot and mortally wounded, dying shortly afterwards.[52]

Henke's fate and that of his crew would have remained unknown to those on *Venomous*. All they knew at the time was that *Venomous* was pitted against a determined and skilful enemy, and had saved hundreds of their fellow sailors and ensured that a crippled destroyer would not share the same fate as *Hecla*. Not a bad conclusion to a very, very long night.

• • • •

The survivors and their rescuers formed the HMS *Hecla*, HMS *Venomous* and HMS *Marne* Association in 1991 with Norman Johns as its Secretary. The following year more than two hundred members and their families attended a reunion in Stratford on the fiftieth anniversary of the sinking. Their numbers have declined with the passing years but there are still a few old sailors alive today who contributed their memories to this chapter and would be pleased to hear from former shipmates and their families.[53]

Notes

1   Dylan Thomas' poem, "Do Not Go Gentle Into That Good Night," was published in 1951.

2   Signal from Flag Officer Gibraltar to *Venomous* sent at 6/1200Z/11/42.

3   The record of Capt, later Capt Sir Herbert Guy Dyke Acland, RN DSC can be seen by visiting http://www.unithistories.com/officers/RN_officersA.html.

4   Charles Gibson, *The Ship with Five Names*, Abellard-Schman, London, 1965, p. 108. The damage to the ship's hull was massive. Her survival can be attributed to the very strict construction standards set by the Admiralty. Her construction would be a major factor contributing to the events of 11/12 November 1942. For more about *Hecla*, visit www.clydebuiltsshps.co.uk. Messrs Paul Strathdee, John Ward McQuaid, Bruce Biddulph and Stuart Cameron provided the information.

5   Admiral Andrew Browne Cunningham, The Naval Commander Expeditionary Force, Algiers cover letter to The Secretary of the Admiralty on 13 December 1942, No 82/00222/lp.

6   *Very Special Intelligence: The Story of the Admiralty's Operational Intelligence Centre 1939-1945*, Patrick Beesly, Naval Institute Press, Annapolis, 2000, p 150.

7   The top-secret intelligence information derived from deciphering the German Naval Enigma codes was passed to the Admiralty's operations centre. It would compose a brief, downgraded indications and warning signal (general enough as not to compromise the source) and then broadcast the signal directly to those ships needing the information. Admirals and senior captains would receive top-secret level signals directly from O.I.C. It is doubtful that Capt Acland would have received such a signal. Instead, he would have received a downgraded signal.

8   *Very Special Intelligence: The Story of the Admiralty's Operational Intelligence Centre 1939-1945*, Patrick Beesly, Naval Institute Press, Annapolis, 2000, p 150.

9   Paragraph No.2, Enclosure No.1 to N.C.X.F. No.82/00222/lp of 13th December 1942. Capt Arliss wrote the report on 16 November 1942. It was one of the enclosures cited in Admiral Cunningham's report to the Admiralty (National Archives, ADM 199/2068). One cable length equals 200 yards. The distance between *Hecla* and *Vindictive* was approximately 600 yards.

10 Anti-Submarine Division, Naval Staff, Admiralty, *Analysis of U-boat attacks on* (1) *HMS* Hecla, *11-12 November 1942*. Capt Arliss' report also notes the same information.

11 Despite the risk, Henke's U-boat followed the convoy on the surface. Henke was a bold and, in the eyes of his crew, a reckless commander. Robert Moore interviewed one of *U-515* crewmembers, Mr. Hans Hahn, who said that Henke was egotistical and highly aggressive, even reckless.

12 Admiral Cunningham's assessment is in the cover letter of the report on the loss of HMS *Hecla* to the Admiralty, 13 December 1942 No. 82/00222/lp. Other reasons which could explain why only *Venomous* detected the contact, include differences in the calibration of the radar equipment on *Venomous* and *Marne*, atmospheric conditions and differences in the expertise of the radar operators.

13 Ibid.

14 Acland's record of service can be seen at, www.unithistories.com/officers/RN_officersA.html.

15 *U-515* was a Type IXC Class submarine. This class was an improvement on the Type IX and IXB. The IXC was designed as a large long-range ocean-going submarine.

16 Paragraph No.4, Enclosure No. 1 to N.C.X.F. No.82/00222/lp of 13th December 1942.

17 Ibid

18 Ibid

19 Herbert McWilliams's letter was published fifty years later as *The loneliness of the long-distance swimmer* in *Sea Breezes*, January 1992, p11-9. His paintings of the sinking of *Hecla* are in the Imperial War Museum. He subsequently worked on the services magazine *Parade* as an artist and journalist.

20 Norman Johns, *My memory of the sinking of H.M.S. Hecla Nov. 11-12th 1942* (written in 2008 for the new edition of *A Hard Fought Ship*)

21 *Vindictive* was extremely fortunate to have executed the next zigzag to port at the time *Hecla* was hit, since the Anti-Submarine Division's report believed the two torpedoes that struck *Hecla* were part of a four-torpedo spread fired by Henke. Mr. Hans Hahn, a surviving crewman of *U-515*, confirms this.

22 Paragraph No.9, Enclosure No. 1 to N.C.X.F. No.82/00222/lp of 13th December 1942.

23 *Sea Breezes*, January 1992

24 Norman Johns.

25 Fred Lemberg was rescued the next morning from a Carley float. Only one of the New Zealand ratings died. Roland Fitzgerald was in the sick bay when the torpedo struck and was late in joining Fred at their action station on the bridge. He was covered with oil, and without his life jacket, he went down to get it and was not seen again. Fred is now 90 and e-mailed his memories of *Hecla* from his home in New Zealand.

26 *Sea Breezes*, January 1992.

27 Johnny Harbor not only survived the sinking of *Hecla* but also survived the war and he met up with George Male many years later on Plymouth Hoe. George Male's description of what happened can be seen on the Peoples War web site at:
http://www.bbc.co.uk/ww2peopleswar/stories/64/a5095064.shtml

28 Analysis of U-boat Attacks on (a) H.M.S. HECLA, 11-12 November 1942 (b) CONVOY M.K.F.1 (Y) – 15 November 1942, Anti-Submarine Warfare Division, Admiralty (NA ADM 199/2013).

29 Norman Johns.

30 Falcon-Steward's account can be cross-referenced through the report submitted by Admiral Cunningham. National Archives reference NA ADM 199/2068 NCXF, Algiers 13 Dec 1942: Loss of His Majesty's Ship Hecla.

31 The depth charges, which put *Venomous'* electric dynamos off-line, could also have affected the radar. The early radar sets were vulnerable to shock and many of their operators were not technically capable of fixing the sets. Specialists, often warrant officers, did onsite maintenance and repairs.

32 From an unpublished report written in 1972 by Lt Coleman.

33 From *The old V & W* (an account of the *Hecla* incident) first written in 1951 but reprinted unchanged in *Hard Lying*, the magazine of the V & W Association in 1996.

34 From the interview that Robert Moore conducted with Hans Hahn for the first edition of the book.

35 From Chapter 10 of *Navy Days* by Edward Coleman (Andrew Books, 1999), p76-91.

36 Ibid

37 Ibid.

38 Ibid.

39 Arthur J. ("Mervyn") Mansell MBE served on *Venomous* between September 1942 and January 1943 as a Commission Warrant (CW), and returned to Britain for training and commissioning. Lt Mansell served on the American lend-lease *Buckley* Class Destroyer Escort HMS *Riou* as her navigation officer. He received his M.B.E. for services to the game of cricket.

40 There are many possible explanations for the false echoes, which led to this 'non-sub' report. For example, marine mammals and schools of fish have been mistaken for submarines.

41 Greg Clarke was the "Schoolie" on Hecla whose job was the education of members of the ship's company preparing for a career when the war ended. Clark became the first Director of the Royal Navy Museum in Portsmouth and appointed Colin White, his successor, as his assistant.

42 Mr. Rowles account is from the first edition of *A Hard Fought Ship*.

43 From John Coleman's unpublished account written in 1972.

44 The aircraft carrier that helped the *Hecla* survivors and provided fuel to *Venomous* was not the USS *Boxer* since it was not commissioned until April 1945. It was the USS *Chenango* which is recorded by the US Navy's Historical Centre's records as being directed to enter Casablanca harbour on 13 November to provide fuel to 21 destroyers.

45 The *Official Admiralty Communiqué* (Serial No. 287) listed nine names who were known to have been killed since their bodies were recovered but included the names of twelve officers and 261 ratings as "missing presumed killed" out of the total complement of 39 officers and 799 ratings. This must be regarded as authoritative. No explanation has been found for the figure of 90 dead laid out on the deck of HMS *Venomous* at Casablanca that was given by Thomas in his account, first written in 1951 and reprinted in *Hard Lying*, the magazine of the V & W Association in 1996. Collister also gave a similar figure of 88 in an unpublished account written shortly before his death in August 2007.

46 Admiral Andrew Browne Cunningham's 13 December 1942 cover letter for the report on the loss of HMS *Hecla*, to the Secretary of the Admiralty, No. 82/00222/lp.

47 Ibid.

48 Acland's commands after *Hecla's* loss can be seen at: www.unithistories.com

49 By 1944, the USN had hunter-killer groups consisting of an escort aircraft carrier and several escorts.

50 Daniel V. Gallery, *Twenty Million Tons Under the Sea*, Naval Institute Press, Annapolis, 1956, p.262.

51 The SS *Ceramic* was steaming unescorted when torpedoed 400 miles west of the Canary Islands. Henke only realised that many of its passengers were women and children after he picked up the sole survivor, a British soldier. Rear Admiral Gallery describes the incident in his book. See *Lone Wolf: The Life and Death of U-Boat Ace Werner Henke*, by Timothy P. Mulligan (Praeger, 1993).

52 Henke is buried at Fort George G. Meade, Maryland. Fort Meade is the home of the National Security Agency (NSA). See website and, *Twenty Million Tons under the Sea*, p.269.

53 Write to: The HMS *Hecla*, *HMS Venomous* and HMS *Marne* Association, Secretary, Norman Johns, The Old Chandlery, New Road, Instow, Bideford, Devon EX39 4LN. Tel: 01271 860578 E-mail: norman.johns7@googlemail.com.

CHAPTER NINE

TO THE MED FOR THE LAST TIME
November 1942 – October 1943

"Death is sure
To those that stay and those that roam,
But I will never more endure
To sit with empty hands at home." [1]

Venomous had three days alongside in Gibraltar before getting underway on 17 November with the B Class destroyer, HMS *Boreas,* to rendezvous with the American built Long Island Class escort carrier HMS *Archer.* Just after midday on the 18th *Venomous* fell in with *Archer* and HMS *Velox,* a sister ship, escorting two tankers off Cape Spartel Morocco and they arrived back in Gibraltar without incident later that day, but *Venomous'* respite would be a short one. *Venomous* was to be very busy escorting convoys to ports on the coast of north Africa which had been under Vichy control. This was still a dangerous route, the Germans and Italians could attack the convoy with submarines and aircraft based in France, Sardinia, Sicily and Tunisia.

On the 21st *Venomous* slipped in company with her sister ships, *Wivern* and *Verity,* and with six other escorts steamed out into the Atlantic to meet Convoy KMS.3G from the Clyde.[2] This large convoy of 56 ships was one of the first to enter the Mediterranean with reinforcements and supplies for the newly established Allied First Army in North Africa. On entering the Mediterranean the convoy steamed eastward towards the recently liberated port cities of Oran, Algiers and Bone. After passing Oran it came within range of the German Luftwaffe and the Italian Regia Aeronautica and two of the merchant ships were lost to aerial torpedoes.

On the 26 November Falcon-Steward was ordered to escort several of its ships into the busy port of Algiers. CPO Herbert Button, the Bosun who had risked his own life rescuing survivors from HMS *Hecla,* had never fully recovered from his exertions. He was diagnosed by Surg. Lt Maxwell as having meningitis, taken ashore to hospital and died the following day. He was buried in the Dely Ibrahim War

Cemetery. His death was a great sadness to all in the ship.

Venomous remained in Algiers until the 29th, returning to Gibraltar on 4 December. With just enough time to replenish ammunition, fuel and food, Falcon-Steward took his destroyer back out on the 6th to escort another Mediterranean-bound convoy from the Clyde, Convoy KMS.4G of 62 ships. Again the convoy came under aerial attack, but lost only one ship. Falcon-Steward once more escorted several ships into Algiers, arriving safely just after midday on the 10th, but needing urgent repairs to a leaking condenser. The repairs were quickly made and *Venomous* returned to sea patrolling the coast off the port town of Bougie on the 13th.

Falcon-Steward with Max Horton (centre) and Capt G.C. Colville (right) examining evidence of a U-boat kill at Western Approaches HQ, 10 February 1945.
IWM Image Reference A 27253. *Courtesy of the Imperial War Museum*

Back at the Rock on 18 December it was time for Falcon-Steward to be relieved, and in a brief change of command ceremony he passed his responsibilities to Cdr D.H. Maitland-Makgill-Crichton DSO, DSC, RN. Thus went one of *Venomous'* most successful commanders. Cdr Hugh Falcon-Steward's next assignment was as Staff Officer for Tactics to C in C Western Approaches at HMS *Eaglet*, Liverpool. Admiral Max Horton had been appointed Commander-in-Chief, Western Approaches

Command, on the 19 November (a week after the "*Hecla* incident") and may have handpicked this highly experienced former anti-submarine officer. Horton adopted the ideas tried and tested by Captain "Johnnie" Walker RN.[3] He retained the existing convoy escorts but introduced support groups which operated independently of the convoys and were able to seek out and pursue submarines to the death. Horton's support groups proved to be decisive in the crucial spring of 1943, taking the battle to the U-boats and crushing the morale of the U-boat arm with persistent and successful counterattacks. Falcon-Steward returned to sea as a commander of a new frigate just before the war in Europe ended in 1945 and was promoted to Captain the following year.

Venomous' new commander, David Maitland-Makgill-Crichton, was a flamboyant personality. His previous command, the I Class destroyer HMS *Ithuriel*, was put into dockyard hands to repair damage sustained ramming and sinking the Italian submarine *Cobalto* during Operation *Pedestal*. Considered a dashing destroyer officer and notable "bon vivant," he was known to his contemporaries as "Champagne Charlie." His award of the DSC was in recognition of his conduct as Executive Officer of the E Class destroyer HMS *Express* during the Dunkirk evacuations, and he was to receive the DSO for his part in Operation *Harpoon* in June 1942. Three times mentioned in dispatches, Maitland-Makgill-Crichton was also a gifted linguist. He was known by the ship's company of *Venomous* as "four gun Crichton" after he read himself in with: "I observe this vessel has only three guns and my last ship, *Itherial,* had four guns so you will make up the shortage with enthusiasm and efficiency".[4]

His accomplished ship-handling abilities were immediately recognised by his junior officers. Midshipman Barney remembered:

> "I remember well on one occasion when we had to move berth from one part of Gibraltar harbour to another. He came up on the bridge with steam on main engines 'Let go – full astern both – atop both – full ahead both – starboard five – Midships – Port five – midships – stop both – full astern both – finish with main engines.' With that he went below leaving the First Lt to secure the ship."

Lt Cashman remembered another incident that testified to Maitland-Makgill-Crichton's ship handling skills:

> "Whilst we were doing a short refit at Gibraltar he and I had to go out to act as Pilots for some American Destroyers. As we came

slowly down the harbour the American turned to me and said 'say, where are the tugs', my reply was 'we don't use tugs to berth Destroyers' whereupon he stopped the ship and said 'say Lootenant I'm not putting this can alongside without tugs'. Eventually a couple of fussy little dockyard tugs came out and pushed her and her sister ship into the berth alongside each other.

The following day we went out on a trial and on return were told to berth astern of the two Americans. We came in the Northern Entrance, down the harbour at the maximum speed allowed and alongside in three engine movements. If I remember rightly the CO asked his two American opposite numbers over for a drink."

He was very popular with the men and according to Alex Campbell, who spent five months on *Venomous* as a Commissioned Warrant (CW) candidate "the crew would do anything for him". He organised keep fit classes and treasure hunts on deck, on one occasion with a "piece of bacon" as a prize, and made the officers join in. Harry Haddon recalled that he stopped the ship dead, out of sight of land, and announced "hands to bathe". Rope ladders and nets were dropped over the side and, without a boat being lowered, crew members not on duty jumped overboard for a swim; a non swimmer was lowered into the water on the end of a rope. William Collister described him approvingly as "very senior and an absolute toff".

It was at this time that *Venomous'* bows were reinforced with concrete. There had been a plan to use her to break her way into one of the disputed French ports by ramming the dock gates. Having rammed and sunk the Italian submarine *Cobalto,* Maitland-Makgill-Crichton certainly had the qualifications for the job but the need never arose. However, *Venomous* would retain her 'ram' until she went to the breaker's yard.

The new CO had four days to accustom himself to *Venomous* and her ship's company before he received orders on 23 December to take his elderly destroyer back out to sea to escort Convoy KMS.5G to Philipville on the Algerian coast.[5] Three other V & Ws - *HMS Velox, Vetch,* and *Wivern* – together with the *Starling* Class sloop, HMS *Woodcock,* joined *Venomous* in reinforcing the twenty escorts for the 48-ship convoy. *Venomous* and her charges spent Christmas 1942 at sea before reaching their destination on the 27th. The following day he was ordered by NOIC Bougie to escort the anti-aircraft ship HMS *Pozarica,* the stern of which had been blown off by an aerial torpedo, to Algiers.

Mediterranean operations, 1943.
Map graphic Kelly Erlinger. Map source Gordon Smith www.naval-history.net

Despite efforts to keep her afloat the converted merchant ship sank in Algiers Harbour.

Short haul convoys to ports on the North African coast were to become routine for *Venomous*, and Lt Cashman recounted a typical operation:

> "Our base was officially Gibraltar, but as the front moved further east, drawing the 1st and 8th Armies together, so we moved up. We escorted the Fleet to Mers el Kebir, the convoys to Algiers, and what became known as "club runs" to places further on such as Philipville and Bone. This was a night run as we were to a certain extent running the gauntlet."

They were "running the gauntlet" of aerial attacks from the Luftwaffe and Regia Aeronautica based on Sardinia and Sicily.

On 2 January 1943 Maitland-Makgill-Crichton received orders to place *Venomous* under the operational control of the Sixty-First Escort Group and in this capacity he took his ship from Algiers to Gibraltar as part of the escort for the damaged Dido Class anti-aircraft gun light cruiser, HMS *Argonaut*, reaching harbour on the 4th in company with *Velox* and *Wivern*.[6] At this point the six young CW candidates who had joined the ship at Londonderry in September left *Venomous* to return to Britain on a minesweeper for officer training at Lancing and King Alfred.

On 12 January Maitland-Makgill-Crichton's ship was one of thirteen destroyers protecting Force H (the battleships *Rodney*, *Nelson* and the

The six CW Candidates left *Venomous* at Gibraltar to return to Britain for officer training.
Rear row from left: Mike Fenn, Alex Campbell, John Dodd and John Carson.
Front from left: Mervyn Mansell and Dixie Dean. Only Mike Fenn failed to be commissioned.

fleet aircraft carrier *Formidable*) whilst en-route from Gibraltar to Mers el Kebir. *Venomous* returned to Gibraltar on the 17th but in less than 24 hours received orders to rendezvous in the Atlantic with a fast convoy of five American tankers from oil-rich Venezuela, Convoy TMF.2.[7] As the convoy approached Gibraltar, Maitland-Makgill-Crichton received orders to continue into the Mediterranean to protect a second damaged light cruiser, the Leander Class light cruiser, HMS *Ajax*. *Venomous* brought her back to Gibraltar late on the afternoon of 24 January. *Ajax* was so badly damaged by bombing that she had to be sent to America for repairs.

After four days in Gibraltar *Venomous* was ordered back into the Mediterranean, and together with her sister ship, HMS *Vanoc*, escorted the Adventure Class light cruiser minelayer HMS *Adventure* on a high-speed run to Oran. The small force arrived safely, but there was no time to linger, as Maitland-Makgill-Crichton received new orders to accompany the Hunt III Class escort destroyer HMS *Haydon* to reinforce the fast US bound Convoy GUF.4 from Oran to Gibraltar. On arrival in Gibraltar without incident the convoy was joined by several other merchant ships and escorts before continuing to Casablanca where they handed over to US naval escorts for the Atlantic crossing.

On arriving back in Gibraltar on 2 February, *Venomous* received a signal from the Admiralty that cheered all on board – "Your attack on 12/11/42 probably destroyed a U-boat." This was a small measure of recognition for her efforts to rescue the survivors from the *Hecla* and protect the damaged *Marne*.[8]

Here Midshipman Stephen Barney finally caught up with his ship. He described his first meeting with Cdr Maitland-Makgill-Crichton:

> "When I rejoined *Venomous* in the Mediterranean in February 1943, the CO called me to his cabin and asked me what my job had been in civilian life. On being told that I had been in an Advertising Agency, he said 'Right Mid – you're Correspondence Officer'. This meant that I had to handle all the paperwork for the Ship's Company of about 180 with no previous experience of how the Pusser works."

On that same day she was transferred to the Thirteenth Destroyer Flotilla and, in this capacity, she steamed out into the Atlantic to meet Convoy UGS.4 from the US to Gibraltar and escort it east to Oran.

On arrival off Oran *Venomous* and *Haydon* went to the naval base of Mers el Kebir (MEK) a few miles west where they arrived at 1445 on 3 February. That evening Cyril Hely wrote in his diary that the ship "had a good forenoon chasing a U-boat and shooting at a mine with Oerlikons and rifles. Play tombola with Taff [Harry Haddon] at night" and the following day "still in MEK. Cook of the mess in forenoon also whaler's crew". They spent the following day on anti-sub patrol off the harbour entrance.

On 7 February she was again at sea escorting Force H to Gibraltar where they arrived the following day at 1650. HMS *Nelson*, the flagship, entered harbour first followed by the other big ships. HMS *Formidable* only entered after it had flown off its aircraft and the destroyer escort entered harbour last, as was customary.

Midshipman Barney recalled how German submarines could easily slip through the straits of Gibraltar without detection:

> "At the time we were part of Force H in the Western end of the Med. Whilst waiting for the next operation, *Venomous* was frequently on

Floating dock at "MEK" naval base just outside Oran.

the overnight Anti-Submarine patrol in the Straits of Gibraltar trying to detect German submarines entering or leaving the Med. Different temperature layers, deep current flowing in, and less deep current flowing out, made it almost impossible to detect anything. In fact we never even made a firm A/S contact on anything resembling a submarine. Spanish fishing vessels galore with their diesel engines picked up at incredibly long distances in the comparatively still waters using a listening watch for hydrophone effect – hopefully from a submarine – and some quite remarkable long range identifications."

On 14 February *Venomous* renewed acquaintance with the young schoolboy she had rescued from Calais in the dark days of May 1940. True to his word, John Esslemont had joined the Royal Navy and was now serving in the Flower Class corvette, HMS *Balsam*:

"*Venomous* joined us in company with another Destroyer and believe me it did something to me to watch her plough her way

252

around our convoy of 60 ships KMS9 from Londonderry, bound for North Africa. We berthed at Gibraltar at 1900 on 16th. Our Escort Group comprised *Blackswan* (Sloop), *Carnation*, *La Malouine*, *Mallow*, *Myositis*, *Campion*, *Violet*, *Aubretia*, *Ubretia* and *Balsam*, all Corvettes of the Flower Class."

The return to Gibraltar on 16 February brought to an end Maitland-Makgill-Crichton's short period in command. Lt Henry Durell RN succeeded him on that day in another brief change of command ceremony that was all too typical of the war years. The appointment of Durell gave an indication of the old destroyer's reduced status as a warship. William Collister was sad to lose "our great skipper" and wrote, "it was quite a shock to go from senior escort captain to the other end of the scale."

Lt Durell was from Hampshire but his family originally came from the Channel Islands. He was a very senior lieutenant who looked older than his seniority indicated.[9] Despite this, Durell was a calm and charming man who became instantly popular with the Wardroom officers and the ship's company. Far from being aloof, he made himself very welcome in the Wardroom and did not live apart as much as his predecessors had appeared to do. Young Midshipman Barney recalled how on one occasion the Surgeon Lieutenant shaved off his beard, donned another officer's uniform and pretended to be a visiting officer from another ship. Durell courteously offered him a drink and talked to him politely for quite some time before realising his leg had been pulled. Stephen Barney also had fond memories of another young officer whom he thought of as an "Uncle":

> "Apart from Lt Durell, there is another man of whom I have very fond memories – Lt 'Slogger' Eaton RNVR. He was another kind Uncle to me. When I joined *Venomous* there were not enough cabins for all the Officers so I, being the most junior, had to sling a hammock in the cabin flat with nowhere to stow my clothes or belongings. This made it difficult to keep clean and smart so Slogger gave me the use of some of his cabin and desk space."

By the end of February, with Durell in command, *Venomous* had safely accompanied two further convoys to Oran and on 9 March she was detailed to escort the seriously damaged Hunt II Class escort destroyer, HMS *Avon Vale*, to Gibraltar. *Venomous* continued her local anti-submarine patrol operations in the Straits of Gibraltar until the end

Hot work in the Mediterranean under two Commanding Officers.
Cdr David Maitland-Macgill-Crichton RN and Lt Henry D. Durell RN.

Cdr David Maitland-Macgill-Crichton RN
in dress uniform.
Courtesy of Dr Alan Fleischman.

Lt H.D. Durell RN.
Courtesy of David Durell.

Lt Leslie "Slogger" Eaton RNVR
on left with Lt Colin Hunter,
wearing life jacket.
Note rails round radar dome above
left. *Courtesy of Chris Eaton.*

Midshipman Stephen
Barney RNVR.
Courtesy of Stephen Barney.

A striking double exposure
of Lt Tony Sangster RN.
Courtesy of Chris Eaton.

Warrant Officer Simms, "Guns"
with foot on torpedo tubes.

LS John C Robb.
Courtesy of Richard Bishop-Miller.

Lt F.L.W. Hunter RN on the bridge.
Stephen Barney commented "Officers
might be allowed to remove shirts in hot
weather but not their hats".
Courtesy of Chris Eaton.

A run ashore in Alexandria.
Able Seamen Hely, Hargrave,
Officers Steward George and
Harry Haddon.

of March. On the 30th *Venomous* was abruptly ordered to steam for the Clyde, while many of the crew were ashore in bars. They were rapidly recalled to the ship but Ordinary Seamen Harry Haddon and Cyril Hely, both teetotallers, had gone swimming off a local beach. On returning to the harbour they thought *Venomous* had shifted its berth but soon found it had left without them. They missed a trip home and were put on shore-based duties until its return. *Venomous* made the passage to the Clyde as a member and not an escort of Convoy MKF.11, and on arrival at Greenock on 6 April, spent six days having defects to her engineering plant repaired.

With not enough time to give the ship's company a longer run ashore, Durell received orders to take his destroyer back to Gibraltar. On 16 April she departed the Clyde, returning to Gibraltar on the 22nd with Convoy KMF.13, where Haddon and Hely rejoined their ship.[10]

Announcement of awards for HMS *Hecla*, signed by Lt H.D. Durell RN.
Posted on ship's notice board and kept as souvenir by Cyril Hely.

Whilst still in Greenock, the *London Gazette* of 13 April had announced that Cdr Falcon-Steward had been "Mentioned in Dispatches" (MID) for his part in the *Hecla* Incident. The news only reached *Venomous* on its return to Gibraltar and the ship's new CO posted a handwritten note on the ship's notice board, which Cyril Hely later retrieved from the bin and kept as a souvenir. Falcon-Steward's MID was scant recognition for the part that he and the ship's company had played during that night. The lack of recognition for the heroics of Bosun Button must also have been a disappointment, especially to those on the lower deck.

After five days in Gibraltar Durell received orders to take *Venomous* out into the Mediterranean. On the 28th she proceeded to Oran to link up again with Force H and escort the heavy ships back to Gibraltar where they arrived, without incident, on 7 May.

By now the Allies, advancing west from Egypt and east from Algeria, had squeezed the Axis Armies in North Africa into the Cape Bon Peninsula in Tunisia. Two hundred and fifty thousand men were encircled (an equal number to those who surrendered at Stalingrad). The C in C Mediterranean, Admiral Sir Andrew Cunningham, ordered

HMS *Venomous* crossing the stern of HMS *Formidable*, part of Force H, at high speed.
Photographed from the bridge of Formidable by Lt P.G. James between 20 – 30 May 1943.
IWM Image Reference A 17080. *Courtesy of the Imperial War Museum.*

all available destroyers and smaller craft for a close day and night patrol to prevent their evacuation. Named Operation *Retribution*, its objective was to ensure that none of the trapped German and Italian troops could be evacuated by sea. Cunningham must surely have had in mind the tragic evacuation of Crete by the British in 1941 when he ordered that Operation *Retribution* shall "Sink, burn and destroy. Let nothing pass."[11]

Venomous was present for this historic event, as Lt Cashman recalled: "When the two armies came together we were part of a tight ring around Bizerta, Tunis and the Gulf of Sirte to prevent any evacuation of enemy forces." Operation *Retribution* was concluded successfully, few if any of the beleaguered troops escaped, and on 13 May 1943 the Afrika Corps surrendered and the war in the desert was over.

As Roskill explained in his definitive work on the "War at Sea" two essential tasks remained:

> "The first was to sweep the Sicilian channel clear of the innumerable mines which had obstructed it for the last three years. Convoy escorts were reduced in order to release as many minesweepers as possible. The 12th, 13th and 14th Mine-sweeping Flotillas from Malta, two groups of mine-sweeping trawlers, motor launches and motor mine-sweepers all took a hand. By the 15 May a channel two miles wide and 200 miles long had been swept from the Galita Channel to Sousse, and thence on to Tripoli. Nearly 200 moored mines were cut. That day Cunningham signalled that 'the passage through the Mediterranean was clear' and that convoys from Gibraltar to Alexandria could be started at once. The Admiralty sent its congratulations. The Navy thereupon took up the second of the two duties mentioned – that of escorting these ships safely through the waters which had for so long been closed to our shipping.
>
> The first convoy consisted of four fast merchant ships. Escorted by the A.A. cruiser *Carlisle* and four destroyers, they reached Tripoli on the 22nd. Four more destroyers joined up there, and the Malta destroyers strengthened the escort for the second part of the journey. All ships arrived safely at Alexandria on the 26th. It was the first through-Mediterranean convoy to run since Operation *Tiger* in May 1941."[12]

The four destroyers chosen to escort KMS.14X, the first through convoy in two years to leave Gib for Alex, were two elderly V & Ws, *Venomous* and *Velox*, plus the Hunt Class destroyer, *Liddesdale*, and the Tempus Class *Troubridge*.[13]

Aboard HMS *Velox* was Lt Christopher R.V. Holt RNVR who kept a diary on which most of what follows is based.[14] On the 17 May the four destroyers assembled the convoy off Europa Point, with the Commodore of the Convoy in SS *Macharda,* and they left Gibraltar shortly after 2000. The crew on the escorts "did not know they were going any further east than Bone but rumours were rife". The next morning, after a quiet night, they were buzzed by a JU88 and late in the afternoon saw an Italian warship out of Spezia going south. On the 19th a convoy ahead, code named "Polecat", had two ships torpedoed and they were joined by the elderly anti-aircraft cruiser, HMS *Carlisle*, which Christopher Holt "found comforting."

They went to action stations that evening, "there were alarms and excursions, one or two softly purring aircraft passed over and we went to the alert during the first watch" – but nothing further. At 0800 the next day they followed the convoy through the swept channel into Bone which was "looking rather battered – two merchant ship wrecks and a mine-sweeper beached in the harbour and quite a lot of damage visible ashore." They were joined by two I Class destroyers, HMS *Isis* and HMS *Ilex*, and were off by 2130 forming single line through the swept channel. "The morning was marvellously still and it was difficult to believe that so calm and detached looking a place should have been a battlefield."

On the 21st they passed Bizerta, "five damaged ships and a Liberator aircraft, on the beach" and at about 1120 "*Carlisle* reported a 'bogey' (aircraft) but seemed unable to make the fighters play". After passing Cape Bon, the northern tip of Tunisia, they passed several floating mines but no aircraft as "it seems pretty obvious we have air supremacy around here."

At this point we must leave Lt Holt on *Velox* and rejoin *Venomous* which had gone to investigate a "large aircraft life-saving raft" off the Kerkennah banks, near the islands of the same name in the shallow Gulf of Gabes on Tunisia's east coast. They found it contained the body of a German, "his fingers full of rings". Christopher Holt went aboard *Venomous* on arrival in Tripoli and was told "a pretty grisly story":

> "The Hun had been dead for two days and had on him the personal effects of about seven other men, their rings, wallets, etc. French and Russian money and some pictures of naked females. He had also been keeping a diary."

One by one, his companions had died and he had removed their personal possessions before sliding their bodies over the side into the sea, only to die himself without an opportunity to return their possessions to the families. After removal of these (and a fine pair of leather boots) they gave him a Christian burial, sewn into a hammock in the traditional way, and added the life raft to the ship's sports equipment.

Venomous rejoined the convoy which headed south and with some difficulty found the swept channel into Tripoli, the chief port in the Italian colony of Libya and until recently the main supply point for the Axis forces. Lt Holt described their entrance to the harbour at 0800 on the 23 May:

> "Tripoli Harbour was a pretty amazing sight, at least half a dozen big wrecks and across the harbour entrance three blockships and a small gap which had been blasted by us. There was quite a big hospital ship and one or two good looking ITIs all wrecks.
>
> We eventually didn't get a pilot being furthest from the shore but followed the other two in. It looked as though we would touch either side going through the gap and were then confronted with a formidable array of wreck buoys. There was just room to scrape though there and sidle up alongside *Liddlesdale* who was berthed on an oiler astern to a big ITI.

Passing the blockships at the entrance to Tripoli harbour on the 23 May 1943.
Photographed from HMS *Velox* with Lt Barstow on the bridge (left).
Photographed by Lt Christopher R.V. Holt RNVR from HMS Velox.

HMS *Venomous* (left) and the Hunt Class destroyer HMS *Liddersdale* refuelling in Tripoli harbour.
Photographed by Lt Christopher R.V. Holt RNVR from HMS Velox.

They were given leave in the afternoon, went ashore and "found the whole town was filled with soldiers" and the shops, such as they were, selling souvenirs "pieces of silk with Tripoli and the date of the occupation". He met up with Lt Cashman, 'No 1' on *Venomous*, and was amused to find – "he wanted an umbrella!" Midshipman Barney recalled that he and "Slogger" Eaton were followed by some very persistent ladies and had problems shaking them off. Holt thought "the town itself was not at all badly damaged considering the amount it had been bombed; the Captain said that most of the damage to the harbour works had been done by the Germans' demolition." He observed that there was not much to drink: "There was one party of our libertymen who were drunk but I gathered that no one else had anything to drink at all. They were seen off by an equally intoxicated army sergeant."

Sadly, they were not to be with the convoy when it made its triumphant entry into Alexandria. Six new escorts took over and when they sailed at 2000 it was to head back to Bone to pick up a westbound convoy. They went "down the searched channel at 20 knots and thence N.W. cutting off the long crooked corner round the Gulf of Gabes. The next morning, the 24th, we were warned by a large party of mine-sweepers 'that there are definitely mines off Cape Bon' – we must have passed half a dozen. The Captain and Guns fired at the first two (with rifles) … and I got a biff at a third without much result." They went into

Bone at 1800 to refuel and on leaving at sunset two hours later the convoy and the town were attacked by bombers:

> "On arriving off Cape de Garda we got a signal that we would be required at 20.00 - an E.T. convoy it looked like. *Kelvin* and *Javelin* were also there and coming with us. We went in alongside the oiler and started oiling, however we were soon hoiked out again and at sunset were following the convoy down the (swept) channel. Several of the ships had German prisoners on board - we passed one quite close, big hulking fellows most of them looked, one of them had a squeezebox on his back. It was definitely a good sight.
>
> It was just about dark when we got to the end of the channel and suddenly the air was full of aircraft noises, two or three or more, and as we were speculating there appeared a stream of tracer to the NE up in the sky and a sheet of flame as the Hun went down. By the light of the burning plane we saw the night fighter bank steeply away, another grand sight. Almost at the same time a stick of bombs fell some distance away to the north (I gathered later that they were quite close to *Kelvin*). We started making smoke around the tail-end ships. There were one or two aircraft still around in our direction but most of them went for Bone; the flak was pretty terrific. The searchlights directed the fire. I believe that one and possibly two more were shot down."

Searchlights directing the fire on German aircraft attacking Bone.
Painted by Lt Christopher R.V. Holt RNVR from HMS Velox.

Lt Christopher R.V. Holt RNVR.
Courtesy of Nicholas Holt.

A caricature of HMS "Verminous" presented to its Commanding Officer, Lt H.D.Durell RN.
The 'artist' was Lt C.R.V. (Christopher Robert Vesey) Holt RNVR (1915-97).
Courtesy of David Durell.

Holt was "feeling rotten with tummy trouble" and his Diary ended when the convoy entered Algiers on the 26 May but he notes that "they were back in Gib by the 29th having, I suspect, escorted more ships from Algiers to Gib, but I have no record of this." The euphoria following the end of the North African campaign and the re-opening up of the sea route to Alexandria may explain the presentation of the light hearted sketch of HMS '*Verminous*' to its CO on the occasion of its

24th birthday. It is a surprisingly accurate depiction of a V & W and its weapons. It was painted on the back of an old chart, dated the 4 June and signed by Lt Holt with his initials, CRVH, following a family tradition that is maintained today by his artist daughter who lives in South Africa. The painting is still in the possession of Lt Durell's family.

Although *Venomous* was privileged to be one of the escorts for the first convoy to Alexandria after the clearing of the Sicilian Channel they had not gone all the way to Alex. Their chance came on the 21 June as Lt Cashman described:

> "Now that the Med was open and the whole of North Africa in our hands, we took the first convoy GTX.3 through from West to East all the way to Alexandria. We had heavy air attacks in the Narrows opposite Sicily. Only one ship was damaged but on the radio that evening Lord Haw-Haw claimed we had lost over 100,000 tons!"

Lt Sangster also described the attacks and a curious occurrence, which undoubtedly saved the convoy from further harm:

> "The convoy was negotiating the long swept channel off Cape Bon, which being shallow, was ideal for laying mines. As a result, the whole convoy was in single line ahead, because the swept channel was not wide. There had been no serious incidents, one FW190 having dived and attempted to bomb a Landing Ship Tank (LST) being the only action so far. The convoy must have stretched for 12 miles.
>
> I was on watch at about teatime, a *Hunt* class destroyer, *Ledbury* I think, signalled a submarine contact and dropped a pattern of depth charges about a mile ahead of us. She then must have lost contact because no more were dropped and she hauled down her signal.
>
> As Officer of the Watch [OOW] I was determined always to keep a good lookout. If I kept sweeping with my binoculars then the two sailors on 20-minute spells of lookout would also sweep diligently and the result would be at least four times better than the normal lookout kept on other watches. I also determined that if any sighting or contact was made, I would act immediately to change course and speed and then tell the Captain. About 20 minutes after the depth charging I sighted an object on the starboard bow. I recalled the depth charging and thought that a submarine might be surfacing.
>
> 'Starboard ten, full ahead both engines, prepare to ram, sound off action stations.' The words all carefully rehearsed poured out of me. 'Captain Sir' down the voice pipe, 'object on starboard bow am turning to ram' but he had already heard the ring of the telegraphs and was on his way.

'Midships, meet her, steady' to the quartermaster.

The whine of the engine noise increased and dear old *Venomous* leapt towards the object now only half a mile away. The Captain was now with me and was studying it.

'Revolutions 212, half speed ahead' ordered the Captain – he did not want to overshoot out of the swept channel.

At that moment, a wisp of smoke appeared just by the object and thickened rapidly, flames appeared.

'Hard a'starboard' shouted the Captain and the ship heeled over as her stern started to slide round to port. By the time it passed down the port side, flames 30 feet high were rising from the sea and we could feel the heat radiating from them.

The Captain reduced speed and we resumed our station in the convoy. This all happened about teatime and the fire caused an enormous plume of black smoke. Shortly afterwards the Italian air force started high level bombing. No bombing is fun, but if you cannot manoeuvre because of the minefield it is that much less fun.

But glory be! They concentrated on what they thought was a ship on fire for the next three hours until darkness fell. The smoke from the fire was 3000 feet tall.

I have never had a satisfactory explanation for this combustion taking place. *Ledbury* presumably must have attacked a wreck and not a submarine. The depth charges must have damaged fuel tanks in that wreck and must also have released air from a nearby compartment so that ignition could take place. But for all this to continue for three hours was really extraordinary. If science could provide a way of burning fuel on the sea it would surely have been used against oil slicks from tankers."

William Leslie Collister on "B" Gun vividly recalled this incident:

"Halfway across the shallow Gulf of Gabes … we, "B" Guns crew, noticed something unusual happening in the water ahead, like a giant dimpled saucer. We drew the Bridge's attention but before any action could be taken we were enveloped in a vast bowl of flames. I ordered all exposed ammunition to be flung over the side, meanwhile, our hair was singed and eyebrows likewise. We emerged the far side with paintwork very badly scorched. Of course, the flames attracted German planes, which had been paying us a lot of attention. They thought they had scored a hit on a troop ship … so now being the junior or scrap boat we were ordered to lay a smoke ring round the flames for twenty four hours and, of course, the convoy carried on peacefully."

Interestingly, even after so many years have passed, Stephen

Barney has not forgotten the watch-keeping philosophy of his old friend and shipmate, Lt Sangster:

> "Lt Tony Sangster and I used to keep a standing middle watch every night whenever we went out on the A/S Patrol in the Straits. He taught me a lot too – particularly about the necessity for keeping a constant lookout oneself in all directions even though we always had two bridge lookouts and a rather primitive radar set operating."

On arrival in Alexandria on 3 July they immediately began to prepare for yet another seaborne invasion as Lt Sangster related:

> "Once back in Alexandria we became aware of the great build up of shipping and guessed that another invasion was planned. When the printed orders were received on board I as Confidential Book Officer spent the first eight hours amending them. We were going to invade Sicily and our role would be to escort the second wave of troops to Augusta on the South Eastern corner."

The invasion was known as Operation *Husky* and like Operation *Torch*, the landings in North Africa, was a joint Anglo-American invasion with General Dwight D. Eisenhower as the Commander-in-Chief and Admiral Sir Andrew Cunningham as Allied Naval Commander of the Expeditionary Force. The British were to land their troops on the South East coast extending from the toe of Italy to the southern tip of Sicily. *Venomous* would be an escort for Support Force East, which included two monitors, each carrying two 15-inch guns to bombard German and Italian shore targets.

Venomous left Alexandria with HMS *Witherington* and HMS *Wishart* as an escort for Convoy MWF.37 on the 10 July 1943 and ERA Harry Wilmott described the problem which could so easily have brought their participation in Operation *Husky* to a premature end:

> "I joined the *Venomous* in early 1943 and stayed with her until she paid off at Falmouth in October of that year. A seaman and myself were the only Chatham ratings in the ship, her being a Devonport Destroyer.
>
> In 1943 the *Venomous* was all over the Med, North Africa and at the Invasion of Sicily, escorting the 8th Army from Alex to the landings. I remember that well, as we were told to do our own repairs on one of our extractor pumps at sea. So the ERAs worked day and night to repair, knowing too well that if the other one goes the ship stops. Our ERAs were first class but the old ship was breaking down completely – in our engine room we used to go on

watch with a bucket and an extra pair of underwear – at 143° you were drenched with sweat in ten minutes but somehow everyone did their job and survived.

In our branch were PO Johnston, PO Conybear and PO Evans who was a survivor of the *Prince of Wales*, we used to call him Roggy. In the Stokers Mess was Sharky Ward from Scotland and Paddy Boles from Ireland."

Recognition of the efforts of Warrant Engineer Lapthorne and his men was promulgated much later in a 7 December 1943 signal from Admiralty Bath:

"Sir,
With reference to Admiralty Letter dated 4 November 1943, D.026482/43, concerning engine room defects in *Venomous*, I am commanded by My Lords Commissioners of the Admiralty to acquaint you that they desire that an expression of their commendation may be conveyed to the Engineer Officer, and ratings named in the Commanding Officer's letter dated 27 July 1943, No. 23/2763, for the zeal and initiative displayed in connection with the improvised repairs to the steam stop valve of the port extraction pump.

I am Sir,
Your obedient servant,
The Commander in Chief
H.M. Ships and Vessels
Mediterranean."

Escorting convoy for landing in Sicily (taken from *Venomous*), 1943.
Courtesy of F.N.G. Thomas.

The convoy continued to its destination without incident, the big passenger ships having no difficulty in entering the port of Augusta and landing their troops on the 13 July, while the Warships patrolled to seaward. Lt Sangster described what happened that night:

> "The BBC news was perhaps our only source of reliable news and we gathered that the airfield just north of Augusta at Catania was still held by the Germans and needed capturing for use by our allied air forces. After a whole day of disembarkation, the big troopships formed up in convoy again at dusk outside Augusta. When it was dark a most dreadful thing happened. The convoy was overflown by a fleet of gliders and tugs and Dakotas carrying paratroopers. Their friendly identity could not be established and the convoy opened fire with every gun they had. It was a real firework display of tracer from all the Oerlikon 20mm guns. I gather from historians that this attack on Catania was a costly failure because of navigational errors as well.
>
> *Venomous* was dive bombed that night, which was a nasty noisy experience. A near miss but thankfully no casualties. Shortly after this we picked up a paratrooper in the dark whose plane had I think been hit by fire from the convoy. He was a Glaswegian and his vocabulary was limited but repetitive. He left those within earshot in no doubt of his opinion of the whole operation. I had every sympathy for him. Good staff Officers do not route the precious elite of paratroopers over convoys at night.
>
> His rescue was extraordinarily lucky. The depth charge crew on the quarter-deck reported to the bridge that they had heard a man shouting from the water. Lt Durell turned the ship on to the reverse course and slowing down searched the calm black sea with a 10 inch signalling lamp. His head, a tiny object in the sea was sighted and rescue followed."

The escorts did not open fire on the gliders and troop carrying planes flying towards the coast from offshore and Stephen Barney was in no doubt that the fault lay with the merchant ships in the convoy which ought to have known that they could only have been carrying British troops. He described the attacks on *Venomous* by Italian bombers in a letter written shortly afterwards to an old army friend:

> "… on the day the convoy arrived we went at 'Action Stations' eleven times. That night when the convoy had unloaded and we were leaving we had most excitement. We went to 'Action Stations' at dusk as usual and stayed there all night. One of our night fighters shot down an opposition bomber quite close to us and it jettisoned its bombs and then exploded in mid air. I saw three chaps bale out

and we went to pick them up. As we were doing so someone dropped a stick of bombs quite close. We picked one chap up but he was already drowned – he was an Italian. We were just going to pick up another when one of his chums dropped another stick of bombs even closer so we said "To Hell with this" and rejoined the convoy. Things seemed to happen all night and there were crowds of our own aircraft going over."

Harry Haddon described why they abandoned attempts to save the second airman:

"During the night we were under attack by Italian dive-bombers one of which we shot down (I think it was Cyril Hely on the starboard Oerlikon who got it). The pilot parachuted down and we tried to haul him aboard but a voice from the bridge called out "cut him loose, cut him loose!" which we did. As *Venomous* pulled away a bomb fell near the stern and probably did for him. I still have a piece of his parachute."

ERA Harry Wilmott thought the dead pilot was one of theirs:

"We hauled the airman on board and thought he was one of ours as the Italian navy wear a curl on their braid just like the Royal Navy. With all his flying gear on it took several minutes to hoist him on board but he died and we buried him early in the morning in the traditional hammock".

The following day *Venomous* poked its nose inside the harbour at Syracuse a few miles north of Augusta and Stephen Barney saw the shattered remains of gliders lying where they had crash landed in an olive grove on the south side of the harbour.

American lives were also lost and both the British and the Americans commanders reported on the cause of the disaster to General Eisenhower. Air Chief Marshal Arthur Tedder, head of allied air forces in North Africa and the Mediterranean, considered the airborne mission to have been operationally unsound because it had required aircraft to fly over thirty-five miles of active battle front:

"Even if it was physically possible for all the troops and ships to be duly warned, which is doubtful, any fire opened either by mistake or against any enemy aircraft would almost certainly be supported by all troops within range – AA firing at night is infectious and control almost impossible."[15]

Admiral A.B. Cunningham gave his explanation for the tragedy in the

Catania area on the night of the 13 July:

> "... the decision to carry out the operation was taken too late to enable routeing to be certainly promulgated to all ships. The airborne troops representative at my H.Q. was apprised of this danger at the time. This late decision in combination with the unexpectedly late sailing of a convoy from Augusta led to a number of aircraft being shot down by merchant vessel gunfire. In this instance too, enemy aircraft were present to complicate the issue."[16]

The report of Vice Admiral B.H. Ramsay, Naval Commander of the Eastern Task Force, contained a more detailed account:

> "It is greatly regretted that a number of our troop-carrying aircraft were shot down by our ships off the east coast on 13th July. The question of the rules for the engagement of aircraft off the beaches was always a vexed one during planning, and the orders were twice altered by agreement with the R.A.F. As finally framed, ships were free to open fire at night at aircraft whose approach indicated hostile intent, and it was stated that if friendly aircraft had to fly over our convoys they would do so above 6,000 feet. All troop carrying aircraft were routed in lanes to avoid our convoys on the night of D- 1/D, but for the second airborne attack on D + 3, they flew low over the Gulf of Noto. It is understood that Mediterranean Air Command had obtained the agreement of Commander-in-Chief, Mediterranean to this some hours earlier, and warning signals were at once sent by the latter to all ships and forces concerned. It is not certain that they did in fact reach all the merchantmen, and by unfortunate chance a small number of enemy aircraft was in the vicinity at the time our aircraft were approaching. As might be expected, firing which started spasmodically soon became general, and it is hard to blame ships for engaging low-flying aircraft which appeared to be menacing them during an air raid. It is considered that in only very exceptional circumstances should ships be deprived of their right to open fire at low-flying aircraft approaching them. The solution must be always to route transport aircraft clear of our shipping."[17]

Cyril Hely's relief at their safe return is clear from the entry in his diary on the 14 July: "arrived Malta after three near misses on us with heavy bombs. Luck was with us last night." *Venomous* escorted the convoy back to Alexandria but soon returned to Malta, where it was assigned to escort a convoy for Algiers before finally securing alongside at Gibraltar on 31 July.

It was here that Lt F.L.W. Hunter joined *Venomous* and almost immediately found himself with a ticklish problem:

> "I joined *Venomous* at Gibraltar as a young watch-keeping Lt in July 1943. That month being Duty Officer one hot afternoon, ship alongside, no other Officer on board, there was a knock on the cabin door, which was the Quartermaster with a top-secret message. The QM returned on deck above whilst I opened and read the message which ordered *Venomous* with other named Warships to sail 1800 next day with convoy for Malta.
>
> Whilst reading this I became aware through the open porthole that someone above deck was talking in almost exact detail about what I was reading. I rushed on deck and spoke to the QM, who confirmed that the Royal Marine messenger had been telling him the details. I tried to recall the Royal Marine, but he was cycling away along the jetty some 100 yards away. I rang the Duty Commander in the C in C's Staff in Naval Headquarters Officers under the rock, and said I had reason to believe the signal had been compromised. As a result the convoy was delayed 24 hours, sailing as usual into the Atlantic to fool the German agents in nearby Spain. We then doubled back, blacked out of course, into the Med during darkness.
>
> The QM and Bosun's Mate had to go to an identification parade to pick out the Royal Marine, which they did. Subsequently it transpired that the Admiral's secretary had gone into the Admiral's office next door, leaving the message open on his desk, which the Royal Marine had read."

After this convoy *Venomous* remained in Gibraltar until 18 August, spending part of the time in dry dock and afterwards painting ship as Cyril Hely grumbled in his diary on 10 August, "Painted ship all day. Chocca, chocca, chocca." Time ashore also gave the men a rare opportunity to participate in sporting activities, which in Midshipman Barney's case at least, were entered into with great enthusiasm:

> "Playing hockey in Gibraltar for *Venomous* against a vastly superior Indian Hockey Team, Henry Durell led us to defeat with great courage and calm. He gently reprimanded me for getting too excited and reminded me to play to the instructions of the Umpires."

Harry Haddon had volunteered to be goalkeeper despite never having played hockey and his rashness must have contributed to their defeat.

Her next mission took *Venomous* back into the Atlantic as recorded by Lt Hunter:

> "We left Gibraltar with other Warships and four British Merchantmen, for Lisbon. Off Portugal all Warships and Merchant ships hoisted

French flags instead of British. The Merchant ships went in and
fished off about 5000 French who had escaped through Spain to
Portugal. We conveyed them safely to Casablanca on 23rd August."

Venomous returned to Gibraltar on 24 August. Her remaining weeks in
the Mediterranean would be exacting, but repetitive. Cashman
remembered those last few weeks as a fleet destroyer:

> "From now on life became routine. We escorted convoys or the Fleet
> wherever their destination. I remember on one occasion we went into
> Malta low on victualling stores, ammunition, fuel etc. I cleared the
> Lower Deck and said, 'let's work until the job is finished then we will
> have Watch and part leave. Tomorrow we will clean ship in the
> morning and again have Watch and part leave from 1300.' Needless to
> say the lads worked their hearts out until the job was done."

Midshipman Barney expanded upon problems faced in the Engine Room:

> "Back in Gibraltar later in the year 1943, we were made very much
> aware that *Venomous* was nearly on her last legs. The Engineer
> Officer, Warrant Officer Laptborne, and the Chief ERA and the Chief
> Stoker fought a losing battle against old worn out equipment. Henry
> Durell was very understanding of the problems of the engine room,
> when strong feelings caused by constant breakdowns under trying
> 'hot' conditions, caused tempers to fray somewhat."

Barney's account was confirmed in a series of signals between C.S.
Gibraltar, C in C Mediterranean Fleet and the Admiralty in which
C.S. Gibraltar reported to Mediterranean Fleet that, "*Venomous* has
considerable hull and machinery defects which require at least eight
weeks to make good, etc."[18] This initial signal was followed-up later when
C.S. Gibraltar signalled to C in C Mediterranean that, "condition of hull
and machinery necessitates immediate return of 'V' to UK for thorough
refit. Bad hull leak must be made good before departure."[19] C.S. Gibraltar
conveyed its assessment in stronger terms in its signal to the Admiralty.
"'V' is at present unfit for sea. Necessary to dock make good bad hull
leak."[20] This signal led to *Venomous* being dry-docked at Gibraltar.

On 14 September, temporary repairs to *Venomous* completed, C.S.
Gibraltar signalled C in C Mediterranean, "*Venomous* undocked 14/9.
Hull leak made good. Ship now ready for passage UK for refit."[21] C.S.
Gibraltar placed limits on *Venomous*' return voyage, "Consider 'V'
should be limited to 22 knots except in emergency. Still consider
essential ship return UK for full refit at first opportunity."[22] Finally, on

11 October, C in C Mediterranean signalled its intentions to the Admiralty: "Intend to sail 'V' to UK in MK.27 for refit. Cannot receive this refit at Gibraltar unsatisfactory with other work."[23]

Concurring orders came the following day and *Venomous* sailed for the UK on 12 October. Cashman recalled the voyage home:

> "The war moved away up through Italy and the old lady began to feel her age. Finally in October we were ordered to take her home, to pay her off into the Dock at Falmouth. The voyage home was very rough but otherwise uneventful. We had to go well out into the Atlantic round the North coast of Ireland and down the Irish Sea."

Midshipman Barney also remembered his last voyage in the old ship:

> "Finally it became obvious that poor old *Venomous* was in so much need of a refit that her usefulness as an operational Destroyer in the Mediterranean had come to an end. We were sailed in company with one Merchant ship, with a short call for her in Lisbon in Portugal on the way back – but not us. We had to wait outside the harbour so no run ashore in another country. We were so expensive on fuel by this time that we had to sail a straight course, rather than zigzag as the Merchant ship we were escorting did! Fortunately we met no U-boats across the Bay of Biscay and we eventually made Falmouth in November 1943. The time came to pay off and leave dear old *Venomous*."

Gibraltar, October 1943, before *Venomous* limped home for a refit.
"The battleship, HMS *King George V,* turned round in Gibraltar Harbour. Submarines *Untiring* and *Unbroken* alongside HMS *Venomous*", Cyril Hely (the photographer).

The arrival at Falmouth on 20 October was not without its lighter moments as Lt Hunter related:

> "We arrived off Falmouth at about 0100. It was pitch black with no lights ashore, a gale blowing, raining like stink, and very rough. I was on the bridge but the CO had control with Digger (Lt Byrne) the Navigator, with his sopping wet chart under the flap of his dimly lit makeshift chart table:
>
>> CO: 'Where are we Digger?'
>> Navigator: 'Well, er – off Falmouth somewhere."
>> I suddenly (we were moving ahead slowly) saw white breakers ahead. I grabbed the voice pipe and shouted down to the QM below 'stop both engines, full speed astern.'
>> CO: 'What on earth are you doing?'
>> 'I can see water breaking ahead Sir.'
>> CO: 'By golly you're right.'
>> Digger: 'The chart shows a Naval Signal Station up on the cliffs to the East of Falmouth.'
>> CO: 'Signalman, use your Aldis Lamp to signal in the general direction of the signal station – just call him up on any pretext – if we can get him to reply we can get a bearing and find out roughly where we are.'
>> Signalman: 'Against regulations to use a light in wartime Sir.'
>> CO: 'Rubbish, get on with it.'
>> Signal Station replies 'Do not use lamp, out.'
>> CO: 'OK Digger, have you got a bearing?'
>> Digger: 'Yes sir, I think we're backing into a minefield.'
>> CO: 'Stop both engines.'
>
> At this time a violent thunderstorm broke over Falmouth and in the lightning flashes we could see we were off the cliffs to the East of Falmouth. Then lightning struck a barrage balloon at the entrance to the harbour, it caught fire and the whole area was lit up beautifully like daylight. We sailed in and met the pilot boat coming out to meet us."

So *Venomous* safely reached her destination. She was now scheduled for a protracted stay in the yard of Messrs. Silley, Cox Limited, Falmouth. On 22 October, two days after their arrival in Falmouth, the Admiralty signalled the Flag Officer in Charge Falmouth that *Venomous* was not to be converted into an L.R.E., "Pending decision of future of 'V' refit shall proceed...Is not to be converted to long range E.V. [Escort Vessel]."[24]

With *Venomous* taken in hand by Silley, Cox, most of the officers and ship's company soon departed for new appointments, leaving only a "care and maintenance" crew aboard. Few would meet again, but their memories of stirring moments remained.

Notes

1   Alfred Lord Tennyson, "The Sailor Boy", 1809-1892. To read the entire poem go to the following website: http://home.att.net/~TennysonPoetry/

2   Information on Convoy KMS.3G, and other convoys *Venomous* escorted, can be found on the following website: www.convoyweb.org.uk. It's a fascinating website, which honours the memory of one of Britain's noted experts on the history of the Royal Navy during WW2 – Mr. Arnold Hague. Mr. Hague died in 2005. *Venomous* is listed as one of the escorts for both convoys.

3   See http://www.mikekemble.com/ww2/walker.html for an account of Walker's contribution to the defeat of the U-boats in the Atlantic.

4   David Maitland-Makgill-Crichton (1910-87) could speak twelve languages fluently and translate forty languages into English. He was a translator during the visit of the Soviet leaders, Bulganin and Krushchev, and an expert witness at the Portland spy case. After resigning from Naval Intelligence in 1964 he made a living as a translator. An obituary was published in the *Daily Telegraph* and included in The *"Daily Telegraph" Book of Naval Obituaries*, edited by David Twiston-Davies (2006). See also: http://www.unithistories.com/units_index/default.asp?file=../officers/personsx.html

5   Philipville is the modern Algerian port city of Skikda, the third largest port in Algeria after Algiers and Oran. To see what the port of Algiers looks like today, use Google Earth.

6   HMS *Argonaut* Association Website: www.hmsargonaut.co.uk. *Argonaut* had been part of a cruiser destroyer group that attempted to intercept an Axis convoy. The group missed the convoy and the Italian submarine *Moncenigo* torpedoed *Argonaut* whilst the group was returning to Bone, Algeria. Two torpedoes struck the ship; one blew off part of the ship's bow, whilst the second blew off the stern. The ship made it to Gibraltar on two of its four propellers.

7   Refer to Convoy Web at www.convoyweb.org.uk for more information about Convoy TMF.2

8   Admiralty signal 7/1934/2/43 sent to *Venomous*. Further analysis by the Admiralty reversed the assessment.

9   Henry Dumaresq Durell (1912-44) joined the Royal Navy in 1937 and served on the battleship, HMS *Rodney*, and the destroyer HMS *Tartar* before being appointed as CO of HMS *Venomous*. His next appointment was as CO of HMS *Isis*. HMS *Isis* "dropped its pick [anchor]" (Stephen Barney) on a mine off the Normandy beaches on the 20 July 1944 leaving only twenty survivors out of the ship's company of 175. There is a memorial to those who died on HMS *Isis* in Portsmouth cathedral.
    See Unithistories http://www.unithistories.com/officers/RN_officersD6.html

10 Refer to Convoy Web at www.convoyweb.org.uk for more information about Convoy KMF.13 and the entire KMF series of convoys. These convoys were primarily troop convoys and many of the ships were large passenger liners bound for Algiers with American and British troops.

11 Correlli Barnett, p. 626.

12 Roskill, *War at Sea*, Vol. 2, p. 442.

13 Not to be confused with the far more famous HMS *Troutbridge*, the setting for the "Navy Lark", a popular BBC comedy radio series broadcast on the "Light Programme" from 1959-76. See: http://navylark.0catch.com/index.html

14 Lt Cdr C.R.V. Holt RNVR (1915-97) was the eldest son of Vice-Admiral Reginald Vesey Holt, and entered the Navy in 1939. He left the Navy as Lt Cdr and returned to his pre-war profession of stockbroker. He was also a talented amateur artist. His diary is in the RN Museum, Portsmouth (Ref. 1991.57/4). For his naval career see: http://www.unithistories.com/officers/RNVR_officersH.html#Holt_CRV

15 See: http://www.ibiblio.org/hyperwar/USA/USA-MTO-Sicily/USA-MTO-Sicily-9.html

16 Published as a Special Supplement to the *London Gazette,* 28 April 1950. See: http://www.ibiblio.org/hyperwar/UN/UK/LondonGazette/38895.pdf

17 Ibid

18 C.S. Gibraltar's signal 15/1422/8/43 sent to C in C Mediterranean Fleet.

19 C.S. Gibraltar's signal 10/1225/9/43 sent to C in C Mediterranean Fleet.

20 C.S. Gibraltar's signal 13/1114/9/43 sent to Admiralty.

21 C.S. Gibraltar's signal 14/1623/9/43 sent to C in C Mediterranean.

22 C.S. Gibraltar's signal 01/1134/10/43 sent to F.O.C. Gibraltar.

23 Signal from C in C Mediterranean Fleet to Admiralty sent 11/10/43.

24 Admiralty signal 220341/10/43 sent to F.O.C. Falmouth is proof *Venomous* was not converted to a Long Range Escort at Falmouth. Her weapons and sensors had been upgraded at Troon in 1942 but she would soon loose them.

CHAPTER TEN

ON OTHER DUTIES ASSIGNED
November 1943 – May 1945

'God save thee, ancient Mariner' [1]

Silley, Cox & Company Limited, Shipbuilders, Repairers and Engineers at Falmouth took *Venomous* in hand at their yards on 23 October 1943. It was estimated that it would take some three to four months just to repair her defects. This was confirmed in a signal from the Flag Officer in Charge Falmouth to the Admiralty on the 23rd: "T.I.H. 23/10 for defects only. Time required 3-4 months."[2]

As confirmed in an earlier Admiralty signal, there was no intention of completing the conversion of *Venomous* into an L.R.E. New anti-submarine warfare escort ships were being introduced into the fleet in large numbers. Although they lacked the high speed of the V & W conversions, their accommodations, sensors and weapons systems were superior to those of *Venomous* and her sisters. They were specifically built to fight U-boats and, most importantly, had superior endurance and better sea-keeping capabilities; they could range across most of the Atlantic without refuelling. There was no longer any need to convert an elderly V & W destroyer into an L.R.E.

The Admiralty had other duties for the *Venomous*. The signal to Flag Officer in Charge Falmouth on 28 October spelt out what her new role would be: "My 220341 affirmed has been given for 'V' to be refitted for Target Ship duties…Work for those duties should be undertaken."[3]

Ironically, the conversion work that was to be done included the removal of her forward boiler, as confirmed by the following exchange of signals. Admiralty signal to Flag Officer in Charge Falmouth, "…'V' is to operate as a two-boiler ship. Re-tubing of No. 1 boilers is not to be undertaken."[4] The Admiralty's signal seemed too vague for Falmouth, which responded on 19 November: "Your 162115/11/43 in view of decision to use as a 2 boiler ship. Immediate decision required removal of No. 1 boiler."[5] The Admiralty reply to Falmouth was to make it so.

By the end of November the decision to strip *Venomous* of her boiler and convert her into a target ship was no longer seen as a priority by the Admiralty. The Admiralty had several competing priorities and none of them involved *Venomous*. The main priority for Britain's shipyards was constructing and fitting-out the large numbers of vessels required for the amphibious assault against Hitler's Atlantic Wall; preparations for Operation *Overlord* were in full swing. There was also an urgent need to overhaul, repair and refit the scores of newer vessels involved in ongoing operations, especially with a view to their use in the Pacific. A further concern was manpower. By 1943 Britain was running out of men of fighting age. The invasion of France, and the ground war to follow, together with the war in the Pacific to liberate the colonies lost to the Japanese, required the fleet to consider all possible means of reducing its use of manpower. Stripping *Venomous* of her armament, boilers and sensors would reduce the size of the ship's company and help in a small way to free up men for the campaigns to come.

The yard was directed to pull *Venomous* out of dock to make way for the urgent refit of the modern O Class Destroyer, HMS *Oribi*. The Admiralty directed that, "*Oribi* to be T.I.H. Silley Cox Falmouth. Refit of 'V' will be suspended."[6] F.O.C. Falmouth responded on 4 December that, "V out of progress 'Oribi' T.I.H. 4/12."[7] *Venomous* was towed out of dock and placed on a mud berth to wait her turn. Ironically, *Oribi* had been John McBeath's command after he left *Venomous* in December 1941.

This had the immediate effect of freeing the ship's company to other duties. Lt Frank S.H. Greenaway RNVR (nicknamed "Raffles") had joined the ship as its Executive Officer and Officer in Charge (O.I.C) of *Venomous'* refit. With the ship turned-out of dock, Greenaway left to serve as a liaison officer (L.O.) to a squadron of US Navy PT Boats operating from the Helford River. The ship's chief engineer, Lt William R. Forster, RNR returned to HMS *Forte*, the shore base at Falmouth, and was given a pier head posting to an escort for a convoy to Archangel in northern Russia. Both officers would return once *Venomous* re-entered dry dock to affect her conversion.

Work on converting *Venomous* was delayed far beyond the original completion date of April, only resuming after the dramatic success of the Normandy Campaign and the rapid advance by the Anglo-American-Canadian Armies across France.

HMS *Venomous* stripped of its armament after its refit at Falmouth.
The hedgehog and RDF have been removed (left) and also the torpedo tubes, 3-inch HA gun and
the pompom gun platform (right).

When work finally restarted on *Venomous* her new look began to take shape. She lost her forward boiler and her characteristic thin forward funnel. She was stripped of all her anti-submarine armament: her Hedgehog, torpedo tubes and depth charge throwers and support equipment were removed and stowage space provided between the funnel and after superstructure for twelve practice torpedoes. Her depth charge and Hedgehog magazines were converted to other uses or left as voids. Her gun armament was further reduced by the removal of the 3-inch H.A. gun. *Venomous* retained her 2 4.7-inch guns in "B" and "X" position and her 20-mm guns positioned on either side of the bridge. She also lost both of her radars.

There were also significant changes in the officers and ship's company. Very few returned to *Venomous*. They were almost entirely reserves (RNR), volunteer reserves (RNVR) and Hostilities Only (H.O.) Ratings. Only Greenaway and Forster returned to the ship and resumed their respective duties. As the Executive Officer, Greenaway was responsible for ensuring that all of the work performed on *Venomous* was correct, whilst Forster worked tirelessly to ensure the old destroyer's modified engineering plant was in a condition that would allow her to operate effectively in her new role. Lt D. Caudle RNVR joined them as the ship's navigator. Caudle already had four years service at sea prior to joining *Venomous*. These three officers were the only ones with significant seagoing experience.

Lt Cdr Derek Lawson RNVR was appointed as *Venomous'* new commanding officer. In civilian life, Lawson was a distinguished lawyer, whose wife was Lady Hesketh Pearson. Besides Lawson, Greenaway, Caudle and Forster, the other officers were:

> Sub Lt Martin RNVR, the Watchkeeping Officer
> Sub Lt Thorp RNVR, the Gunnery Officer (Guns)
> Mid. Beckerman RNVR (promoted to Sub Lt whilst on board)
> Warrant Officer Cannell RNR, the Torpedo Officer (Gunner T)

Before the war Messrs. Martin and Caudle were both solicitors. Thorp was a bank manager, whilst Wilfred Beckerman had just left school and after the war attended Trinity College, Cambridge (Derek Lawson's old college), and became a Professor of Economics and Fellow of Balliol College, Oxford.

The officers for *Venomous'* last commission, August 1944.
From left: Lt(E) W.R. Forster RNR, Sub. Lt T.V. Thorp RNVR, Sub. Lt Martin RNVR, Sub. Lt D.W. Caudle RNVR,
Lt Cdr D. Lawson RNVR, Lt F.S.H. Greenaway RNR, Mid. W. Beckerman RNVR.

The Skipper, Lt Cdr Derek Lawson RNVR.
Courtesy of Professor Wilfred Beckerman.

Young Midshipman Wilfred Beckerman RNVR.
Courtesy of Professor Wilfred Beckerman.

As for the more seasoned officers, Forster had been commissioned as a Sub Lt in the Royal Air Force during the First World War, serving as an Observer Gunner in seaplanes on anti-submarine patrol at Houton Bay Air Station on Scapa Flow, Orkney, before going to sea in the Merchant Navy as a junior engineer and becoming a Chief Engineer on 'tramps' and tankers. Greenaway, who had considerable wartime service in HM Destroyers said this about the ship's engineering officer: "Lt (E) Forster RNR ... was a good one & could be relied upon to run his engine room without worry."[8] The ship's midshipman, Wilfred Beckerman remembered the ship's engineer from a perspective of a young snotty:

> "My main recollection of him is as a frequent opponent in darts games on board, and sometimes ashore in some pub or other in Douglas, Isle of Man. But he was a most congenial and experienced colleague and I liked him a lot, and he was certainly highly respected by everybody on board even if he did sometimes come back on board slightly the worse for wear after an evening ashore."[9]

Frank Greenaway joined Forster as one of the most experienced officers. In civilian life he was a graphic designer but had joined the RNVR in 1933. Greenaway rose through the ranks and after being commissioned served on Hunt class escort destroyers between 1940 and 1943. Greenaway had seen plenty of action during that time, and was disappointed when orders to his new posting came. Years later in a letter reminiscing about his wartime service on *Venomous* he admitted to feeling slighted over having someone with Lawson's lack of experience in command:

> "He [Lawson] privately confessed that he'd no wish to displace me as he was intended for the Admiralty Legal Department, who had insisted he obtain no less than four to six months command experience. I asked to be relieved of my appointment and felt fully justified by my previous record to do so. I was a pre-war regular RNVR Lt with three and a half years seniority of qualified officer status, a qualified Asdic officer. I'd previously been No. 1 of a *Hunt* Class destroyer, operating as a Brigade H.Q. ship for D-Day and I didn't want to miss being in at the invasion. Derek Lawson did his best for me and I was seen by Admiral Edwards who strongly advised me to stick it out as the plan was for me to succeed Lawson after about four months and subsequently to get a new frigate command here after."[10]

As her Executive Officer Frank Greenaway would serve *Venomous* well. He would also get his chance for command. Leaving *Venomous,* he was selected to command a new Captain Class frigate, HMS *Hoste*.[11]

Frank Greenaway offered some insight into the kind of men drafted from Devonport as the ship' company:

> "Eventually we asked Devonport for the rest of our ship's company prior to commissioning. We then learned from Drafting Commander we were to have only 80/85 percent of original complement and of them the bulk were what he described as 'Rehabilitation' rates. Not one had less than warrant punishment, cells etc for desertion – assaulting superior rates etc – four of the ABs (RN) were disrated POs! Thank God we had from the previous commission a small nucleus of fine CPOs who knew how to handle them."[12]

Tom Arthur Russell, known as "Yorkie" Russell, a former coalminer from Derbyshire, joined *Venomous* as a stoker much later in April 1945 but his first impressions of the old "rust bucket" are worth giving here:

> "When I finally arrived at the ship, she looked ancient. I didn't realise at the time but she was used mostly as a target ship for the Barracuda torpedo bombers to practice on. She was slightly turtle backed and seemed far narrower in the beam. You could tell she was aged by the thickness of the paint below decks, the rivets didn't stand out as sharply as on a ship of younger years. Down below, the stokers' mess deck was far narrower; we were more crowded together. Her paintwork and overhead corking was tinged a dirty yellow from the thousands of cigarettes that must have stained it over the years of service. It smelled of a certain amount of dampness and paint. I got to know my messmates over the days ahead and I found them a great crew."[13]

By August 1944 *Venomous* was ready for her new role. Flag Officer in Charge Falmouth signalled that *Venomous* was ready for sea on 8 August but Greenaway declined to sign for the ship until he had seen a survey report. He had particular reservations regarding the mast. This was noted.

Venomous departed Falmouth on 18 August and rounded Lands End, heading north into the Irish Sea, arriving at the Clyde on the 20th. The following day she conducted her sea trials – in the very same waters that she steamed during her first trials in 1919. These proceeded satisfactorily and on 1 September she got underway for her new base at Douglas, Isle of Man.

The Isle of Man's main wartime role was the internment of enemy aliens, Germans and Italians as well as political prisoners – members of the British Union of Fascists (BUF) and the IRA. The camps also held Jewish refugees; many were German nationals who had fled Germany and other parts of Europe under Nazi control. The camps were requisitioned guesthouses and small hotels, many on the promenade in Douglas. Camps in Peel, Port Erin, Port St. Mary and Ramsey held much smaller numbers of detainees, sometimes only for a few months, until they were assessed not be a threat to national security. Numbers peaked at 14,000 in late 1940, but by 1944 most had been discharged and the camps took on a new role housing captured prisoners of war.[14]

Once in Douglas Lawson reported to the Naval Officer in Charge (NOIC), and introduced himself to the Officer in Charge at the Royal Naval Air Station (RNAS), HMS *Urley* (Manx Gaelic for Eagle), at Ronaldsway. The main role of HMS *Urley* was training the aircrew of Barracuda torpedo bombers. *Venomous* was ordered to work with the Barracuda training squadrons 710, 713 and 747. They launched dummy torpedoes at target destroyers, which were also on hand to rescue the crew if the notoriously unreliable Barracuda had to ditch in the sea. The duties the ship was required to perform during the exercises had to be agreed with the Fleet Air Arm staff at HMS *Urley*. As navigation officer Lt Caudle would not only ensure that *Venomous* was present at the correct exercise area and on time, but would also be involved with radio communication between his ship, the exercising flight crews and the air station. As torpedo officer Lt Cannell was responsible for the recovery of the exercise torpedoes. This required training those members of the ship's company who would recover and then secure the expended practice torpedoes on *Venomous'* deck. This could be difficult if the seas began to pick up. It is ironic that in her last days of commissioned service, *Venomous* would once more be involved in the torpedo exercises she had undertaken twenty years earlier, but gone were the days when, with the dash and élan of a new, destroyer she unleashed her deadly fish against a practice target ship. Now she was the target.

At the time it was thought that the Barracuda would play a major role in the fight against the Imperial Japanese Navy. Despite the success of the aircraft and its crews in neutralising the battleship *Tirpitz* during the spring and summer of 1944, the Barracuda was shown to be inadequate in the Pacific. The aircraft was very difficult to fly; it was slow, its range was limited and it had a high accident rate. *Venomous'* new role as a target ship was invaluable in giving the Barracuda aircrews the opportunity to became proficient at dive-bombing and torpedo attack.

HMS *Venomous* working as a target ship in the Irish Sea, August 1944.
Courtesy of Professor Wilfred Beckerman.

Stoker Francis Notton, who had just joined the ship, described the routine of the following weeks:

> "As regards our time at sea our duties were to operate with the Fleet Air Arm as an aircraft tender – any pilots who crashed in the sea we were always around to fish them out. We also operated in the Irish Sea as escort for the Irish Ferry from Douglas to Bangor – that was a good number."

"Yorkie" Russell gave more details of the routine work of a target ship:

> "...Sometimes, the torpedoes fired would take some spotting and at times they must have given our captain a lot of anxiety, for to lose a 'fish' entailed the loss of around a £1,000, a large sum in those days. The sea boat's crew and the cutters would curse at the time taken to spot the nose of the torpedo as it bobbed in the troughs, especially if rain had set in."

From his perspective as the ship's 'snotty,' Beckerman described the at sea routine:

> "The routine was generally pretty boring since we were never in action. But we left harbour (Douglas, Isle of Man) most days, though I

am not sure why! We were involved with exercises with Barracudas sometimes, I remember we had to occasionally go out and search for pilots who had come down in the drink, sometimes at night. We never found any of them, I'm sorry to say. When it happened at night we would cruise up and down the allocated area with searchlights full on for a few hours until told to return to base. I hope ships in some other zone picked them up, and that the area we had been allocated was just not at the right place. Apart from that I really do not know what our function was. Perhaps just to keep some sort of presence in that part of the sea in order to frighten away potential German subs or something. If only they had known! At that time (i.e. when I was on it) there was absolutely nothing about our ship that ought to have frightened anybody. We did have a 4" gun for'wd but not much else. No radar! No Asdic or depth charges."[15]

This mundane work would be of short duration as on 1 October, while *Venomous* was entering the harbour at Douglas, she struck the Battery Pier. This mishap resulted in her spending the next month in dockyard hands. Lt Caudle recalled the sequence of events and the navigation difficulties of entering harbour:

"On entering harbour *Venomous'* stern was swept by an eddy on to the South Breakwater and she had to dock at Holyhead for repair. With the benefit of hindsight NOIC decreed that HM ships should not attempt to enter the inner harbour under the precise tidal conditions at the time in question."

Caudle remembered the humorous solution devised by NOIC Douglas to resolve the problem of ships returning to harbour at night and under difficult weather conditions:

The blackout was still in force of course and another slight navigational problem arose from the fact that returning in darkness from a night exercise to anchor in Douglas Bay, it was not easy to pick up a suitable leading mark on which to make one's run in to the position line formed by the appropriate cross bearing on Douglas Head, where one would let go anchor. Accordingly NOIC was asked to provide a suitable light in a prescribed position to be shown for the limited time when it was needed as a leading mark. NOIC obliged with three red lights vertical which it was discovered were shown from the Wrens' Quarters."

Repairs completed, *Venomous* sailed from Holyhead to Douglas on 2 November to resume her duties as target ship and sometime escort until early in 1945.

Venomous in home waters – but still with a job to do

Lt(E) W.R. Forster RNR.
*Photographed by Percy G Beer,
Southsea, 1943.*

The CO, Lt Cdr D. Lawson RNVR.
*Courtesy of Professor
Wilfred Beckerman.*

Lt F.S.H. ('Raffles') Greenaway RNVR.

Sub Lt Martin RNVR.
*Courtesy of Professor
Wilfred Beckerman.*

Lt D. Caudle RNVR.

Lt "Jimmy" Blair RNVR
replaced "Raffles" as "No 1" in
February 1945.

Chief ERA Arthur "Wiggy" Bennett.
Courtesy of Leon Bennett.

Thomas "Yorkie" Russell,
1st Class Stoker.
As a 'sprog' at HMS *Drake*, 1939.

CPO William L. Collister.
Served on *Venomous* from 1940-5.
Courtesy of John Collister.

On 10 January Lawson received orders to take *Venomous* to the east coast of Scotland where it would be assigned to Rosyth Command. *Venomous'* service was indeed coming full circle. She sailed for Rosyth on 8 January, a difficult voyage, as Lt Caudle described:

> "It was not the easiest of passages, especially without radar. Fog in the North Channel was followed by a blizzard in the Minch and a Force 8 gale. *Venomous* sought shelter in Loch Ewe whilst Chief sorted out some problem with his 'vacuum' or whatever and she then rolled her way round Cape Wrath. Thereabouts, St. Elmo's fire danced briefly along the yardarm and about the rigging – the only time I saw it during five years sea time (despite a fair bit of bad weather).
>
> Our entry into the Firth of Forth and passage up to our anchorage below the Forth Bridge also took place in a blizzard, and in darkness, which required, let us say, attention to our duties."

They had been sent to Rosyth to act as a torpedo target ship on the Firth of Forth for the Barracuda training squadrons at HMS *Jackdaw*, the RNAS station at Crail, but Collister grumbled that "as European hostilities drew to a close we spent more time anchored in the Tay estuary cleaning and painting ship".

At the end of January 1945 *Venomous* sustained considerable damage as the result of a very severe storm. Wilfred Beckerman, by now Sub Lt Beckerman, was OOW when the weather changed abruptly and the initial decisions made by him helped save the ship. He described what happened:

> "For some reason why I still cannot fathom, we had anchored in a small deserted and unsheltered bay, and the skipper was holding 'Captain's Defaulters' on the quarter deck. I was left in charge on the bridge to keep an eye on things. I realised – by means of taking constant bearings on landmarks ashore – that we were dragging anchor and could be driven onto the rocks nearer the shore. For some other mad reason the engine room had been allowed to shut down to half and hour (or an hour's) notice. As soon as I realised what was happening, I somehow managed to send a message down to the skipper on the quarterdeck (there was no intercom) and I also told the engine room that we needed to get steam up immediately. Whoever was on the other end of the phone from the bridge to the engine room told me that would take an half hour (or an hour, I don't remember which), so I told them that by that time we would all be in the drink and given the state of the sea with little chance of survival. So they did manage to get steam up in a few minutes, thanks, no doubt, to the energetic direction from Lt Forster.

When the skipper got to the bridge and took over he ordered dropping a second anchor. Unfortunately, at the time it was being released the ship was swung around by the waves and it 'fouled' the first anchor. It was then pretty chaotic, so neither of the anchors was holding and we were still gradually drifting back towards the shore, so that the only thing to do then was to weigh both anchors and get out to sea as fast as possible. But, with the anchor chains crossing, this was a very difficult operation, which the skipper handled very skilfully. But at one point, I remember we were going backwards away from the shore line and into the incoming big waves, and I clearly remember standing on the back of the bridge watching fascinated as big waves just came rolling over the stern and down the ship! However well we were battened down a lot of water must have gone down below decks. We then made our way out of the swept channel."

CPO William Collister, who had been with *Venomous* since 1940, was in charge of the tricky operation of buoying and slipping the crossed anchors:

"I was responsible for supervising all upper deck work so I let go with my only available AB, an old three stripe pensioner, but still the wind increased beyond gale force. Luckily, it was around midday the force of the wind pinned the ship over to an angle of around 40 degrees, so the CO decided to take the ship to sea for safety's sake. He ordered me to buoy and slip both anchors so my AB and I crawled on our bellies onto the lower guardrail for safety and eventually carried out what was a very dangerous operation. We then proceeded into the comparative safety of the North Sea. It was impossible to move around the upper deck even with lifelines rigged in ever worsening conditions so I ordered the cox'n and one AB to stay on duty in the wheelhouse or until I could spare an efficient relief. There was no question of watches. It was a case of 'stay where you were', seamen in the galley flat under my supervision, the engine room staff below in engine and boiler room and officers on the bridge."[16]

Beckerman's recollection of events before *Venomous* freed her fouled anchors and made a run to the open sea, concludes with the following observation:

"In retrospect, I think the skipper made a serious error of judgement in anchoring in such an unprotected bay in such conditions and then holding 'Captain's Defaulters' and partly shutting down the engine room. If we had gone ashore I am certain he would have been court-martialled (if still alive) and found guilty."

Greenaway's insight is that of a more senior officer who knew the operational reason for *Venomous* being at Lunan Bay when the storm broke, and the reason for the dismasting and subsequent events:

> "What contributed to dismasting had its root in being told 'anchor in Lunan Bay and await exercise signal the following day,' by Flag Officer Air, Arbroath. Any quick view of the Admiralty chart for the area proclaims Lunan Bay a bad, exposed anchorage, with bad holding ground. The Met. People [Meteorological Office] (upon whom F.O.A. relied on for weather forecasts in order to organise flying training programmes) had promulgated rapidly worsening conditions and we would have been ordered to sheltered waters nearby until the weather allowed flying operations.
>
> I'd sent Caudle down to supper, after he'd fixed us on the chart and instructed him to keep anchor watch when he returned. I surmised we were dragging rapidly at about 2000. Advised the C.O. and the E.R. that we'd not reduced notice to steam, had the ship stemming the cable, as the cable party and watch were closed up and the C.O. took over. I went down for my supper.
>
> I had already rigged lifeline from the break of the foc'sle to after screen on both port and starboard sides when we were on passage from Cape Wrath across to top of Scotland. But at this time the weather was no worse than that commonly met in these waters from the time of the year.
>
> It wasn't until we were on the southerly leg of our run down the swept channel that the blizzard and whiteout conditions arose. We'd been told to steam up and down between two points…until the first light and report our position as necessary.
>
> I'd found the old lady in her present form very manoeuvrable and responsive and in her present guise not as tender as she appears to have been in her fully operational fighting role."

Lt Caudle was also on the bridge during these perilous and turbulent few hours. His account described the difficulties and dangers faced:

> "Whilst we anchored in Lunan Bay waiting for a night 'Navex' [navigational exercise], there occurred an incident which resulted in *Venomous* dismasting. As dusk approached, a N.E. gale had sprung up. Notice for steam was reduced from one hour to immediate, which was as well, for the anchor watch showed her to be dragging her anchor onshore.
>
> Cdr Lawson decided to head out through the one-mile gap in the mine barrage, that being the only way to obtain sea room at all, and at the same time to keep *Venomous* head to the wind. *Venomous* proceeded at slow ahead and with meticulous attention to the

bearing given every minute by the Read Head beacon astern, in order to maintain the critical course through the gap. By now the wind must have been up to Force 11 (storm) or Force 12 (hurricane) or even more in the gusts.

In order to check the distance made good, the echo sounder was switched on with the intention of checking a series of soundings against the chartered depths. However, as is not unknown at critical moments – at least in those days – the machine refused to work, and whilst the Navigating Officer and the E/L Artificer were both together in the Chartroom trying to get it to function properly, a loud crash and grating were heard against the outside of the screen which faced aft. Both knew instinctively that the mast had gone, but when the Navigator asked the E/L Artificer if he knew what that meant, he replied with a knowing smile '10 days leave each watch'.

The mast had broken just above bridge level, the foretop having parted. Fortunately no-one was injured either on the bridge where Cdr Lawson had been so intent peering through the bridge's glass screen that he had not realised the mast had gone, until his attention was drawn to the fact by the OOW (Lt Thorp) or elsewhere. The Leading Telegraphist rigged a jury aerial and communication with the shore was restored."

After Beckerman was relieved he went straight to the Wardroom where he shared a few moments of relative peace with Lt Forster before returning to the bridge for his 2000 to midnight watch. Beckerman recounted what happened when he went on watch:

"I remember I had the 'first watch' (2000 to midnight), and shortly before having to go up on deck to go on watch I was sitting in the Wardroom in the company of Lt Forster, who had been sitting in an armchair, being thrown to the floor and sliding along it.

At 2000, I made my way, with great difficulty for'd (it was dark, of course, as well as snow flurries) and as I got near the for'd superstructure in order to go up the ladders that led to the bridge I felt a lot of clutter of wires and things around my feet, but I could not see what it was. Anyway, when I finally got to the bridge I immediately noticed that there was no masthead light and I pointed this out to the skipper, who had not noticed it before. We then both discovered that this was because there was no longer any mast!

So we just ploughed up and down keeping in sight some buoy in the swept channel, which, of course, meant that every now and again we had to do a U-turn in the course of which we had to be broadside on to the direction of the waves so that the ship rolled like mad."

Collister described the steps taken when the mast went:

> "During the middle watch there was a terrific crash. The wooden
> pole mast snapped off around fifteen feet from deck level and owing
> to the rolling wrecked both of the boats. After a terrific struggle we
> secured the wreckage. Then came the job of rigging an emergency
> oil lamp to the stump of the mast so Lt Greenaway and I tied
> ourselves together with a four foot [line, and with the] oil lamp
> scrambled as high as we could. It was the only time I have seen salt
> water slopping down the funnel."[17]

Even in times of war, the first enemy faced by a ship is the sea itself.
Down in the engine room conditions were also, to say the least,
uncomfortable. AB Frank Notton remembered:

> "One incident which I and all the rest of the crew will remember for
> the rest of our lives was one of the worst gales on the N.E. Coast for
> years. We were at anchor when a storm blew up so we slipped
> anchor and made for the open sea to ride out the storm. Then our
> mast snapped off, just like a matchstick, and fell across the
> motorboat, smashing it to pieces. The upper deck was a complete
> shambles. I had the afternoon watch in the engine room. All hands
> were forbidden on deck so my afternoon watch lasted about 30
> hours instead of four hours. Fortunately we had some pusser's kye
> in the engine room, which we boiled up in the steam drains – it was
> the best drop of cocoa I tasted. Through that incident we went to
> Grangemouth for repairs and were in dock about a month."

Caudle's recollection provides an additional insight into the perils
Venomous faced that night:

> "But *Venomous'* troubles were not over, for having passed right
> through the mine barrage, the point came where the ship had to be
> turned through 180° in order to return through the gap on a
> reciprocal course. Warning was passed through the ship of the
> impending measure so that all members of the ship's company
> would be prepared for the intense rolling motion, which would
> ensue. Slowly the ship was turned to starboard. As the turn
> progressed the rolling increased until the ship was beam on to the
> wind and sea, when it became quite violent and extreme. The 180°
> alternation of course was eventually completed – a fine piece of
> seamanship by Cdr Lawson. The violence of the rolling at its
> extreme can be gauged from the fact that the heavy Wardroom
> table, which was bolted to the deck, sheared its bolts and shot
> across the Wardroom to where Lt Forster was sitting. Fortunately,
> he was able to 'field it' without sustaining injury."

The ship's survival can be attributed to a combination of factors: a Clyde-built ship, the skill of her ship's company and – luck. *Venomous* returned safely to Rosyth in the early morning hours, looking very much the worse for wear. Another storm awaited Lawson and his officers as Frank Greenaway remembered: "F.O.A. was foaming at the mouth, having lost his previous target ship (a Yankee four stacker) in the minefield. We were all waiting to be court-martialled." However, because Greenaway had refused to accept the mast as re-rigged during the last refit, the F.O.A. came to an unexpected decision:

> "...the heavy gold at Rosyth who recognised Devonport's failings regarding the mast seemed pleased to have something to clobber them with, and I was congratulated on my presence in stopping the boys from casting the mast overboard (I was worried about getting the shrouds round the screws, rather than for saving the evidence of neglect)."[18]

It was during this time in late winter of 1945 while *Venomous* was being repaired at Grangemouth, that Lt Cdr A. Guyon Prideaux, RNVR succeeded Lt Cdr Lawson as the ship's CO. Prideaux recalled his appointment to *Venomous*:

> "At the end of an inevitable round of courses, I found myself appointed in command of the elderly Destroyer *Venomous* on routine duties in the North Sea, based on Rosyth. I passed several very happy months in *Venomous* and found myself greatly enjoying 'a quiet number' after five fairly eventful years."

Lt James "Jimmy" Blair relieved Lt Greenaway as Executive Officer, and remembered his arrival:

> "I found *Venomous* at Rosyth in February 1945 after 2 1/2 years in *Hunts* in the Med. and was surprised to learn that I was No. 1 when I boarded her. At that time she had actually been taken off active service as such and was serving as a torpedo target for the Fleet Air Arm from Crail, Donibristle etc. We left Rosyth on a Monday morning and returned to port most weekends."

A further new arrival was Sub. Lt Miroslav Stanley Lansky RNVR, a Russian émigré.

While the repair work was being undertaken at Grangemouth, the men of *Venomous* experienced the hospitality of the good people of that town, but sadly it was following one such gesture that *Venomous* was to lose one of her popular young ratings. Frank Notton remembered:

"The local laundry girls collected a few shillings each week and this they used to give a party to any small ship that was in for repairs. Our party was held one evening in the works canteen and although they were a little short of champagne, oysters and caviar, they really did us proud. Homemade cakes, sandwiches, no doubt from their own small rations. It was really a great night, only to end in tragedy for one of our messmates. His name was John Pelling, known to all of us as 'Cockney'. He must have gone back to the ship on his own, slipped and fallen in the docks.

We of course knew nothing of this and when he was absent for duty next morning he was reported AWOL. Anyway we sailed without him. He was found about three weeks later in the harbour and no one ever found out how it occurred.

His kit was sold to the crew by auction and I bid £2 for his lanyard, which I could normally have for 5d. The lads were able to send his parents a fair sum of money plus a contribution from the Officers and the ship's fund."

Throughout March and April, as the war in Europe came to an end, *Venomous* continued to fulfil her duties. It was during April 1945 that Lt John Coleman was able to take one last look at his old ship: "Just before VE Day, I was navigating an aircraft carrier in the Firth of Forth. I became interested in an old V & W towing a target. Close inspection revealed *Venomous* herself, reduced to a humble degree, but still working."

Then on 8 May 1945 it was all over, Germany had surrendered.

Notes

1   *The Rime of the Ancient Mariner*, by Samuel Taylor Coleridge, 1772-1834.

2   F.O.C. Falmouth signal sent to the Admiralty at 23/1104/10/43.

3   Admiralty signal sent to F.O.C. Falmouth at 28/1542/10/43.

4   Admiralty signal sent to F.O.C. Falmouth at 16/2115/11/43.

5   F.O.C. Falmouth signal sent to Admiralty at 19/1025/11/43.

6   Admiralty signal sent to F.O.C. Plymouth at 30/1831/11/43.

7   F.O.C. Falmouth signal sent to Admiralty at 04/1410/12/43.

8   Frank Greenaway's reminiscences were in a letter to Robert Moore on 8 February 1990.

9   Beckerman's account is from an e-mail to Bill Forster forwarded to Robert Moore in 2005.

10 Frank Greenaway's letter to Robert Moore dated 8 February 1990.

11 The *Captain* class was an American design classified as destroyer escorts.

12 Frank Greenaway letter to Robert Moore dated 8 February 1990.

13 Russell's account of his experience on *Venomous* can be found at the BBC's WW2 People's War website, www.bbc.co.uk/ww2peopleswar/stories/80/a7275080.shtml.

14 For a comprehensive bibliography of the internment camps, visit the Isle of Man Government's Manx National Heritage website at http://www.gov.im/mnh/heritage/library/bibliographies/internment.xml.

15 Professor Beckerman's account sent by e-mail to Bill Forster and forwarded to Robert Moore.

16 Collister's account was written for the new edition of this book in December 2006 and he died in August the following year.

17 Ibid

18 From a letter written by Fred Greenaway to Robert Moore, dated 8 February 1990.

CHAPTER ELEVEN

A LAST HURRAH
12 – 17 May 1945

The People of Norway Wish to Thank You. [1]

The war at sea in Europe was, for all practical purposes, over. The Royal Navy had shifted the bulk of its capital ships, the modern aircraft carriers and battleships, to the Pacific Theatre of Operations. The fast carriers of the British Pacific Fleet and many of the smaller escort carriers were now fully engaged with their American counterparts in the final campaigns of the Pacific war. [2]

Despite this there were still operations in Europe requiring the attention of Allied Forces, in which the Royal Navy would play a part. These included accepting the surrender of German forces and dismantling their instruments of war. *Venomous* was still needed and after years of arduous service, it would be her last hurrah.

Norway had not been liberated, and there was some uncertainty as to whether it would require armed force to effect the liberation. Hitler, fearing that the attack from the west on the German heartland would come through Norway, had made it an extension of the much-vaunted Atlantic Wall. Even with the Soviet Army fighting in the streets of Berlin the German High Command and the Allies both thought that "Festung Norwegen" could become a fortress of last resort when resistance in central Europe came to an end. [3] The Allies knew that the Germans had nearly 400,000 troops in "Festung Norwegen", and that the port cities, population centres and landing beaches were heavily defended by a network of coastal artillery batteries, anti-aircraft guns, coastal mine fields, and mobile artillery and infantry units.

The Germans were fighting the Red Army along the Norwegian border with Soviet Russia. It was recognised there would not be enough Allied soldiers to maintain order in Norway, dismantle the German defences, provide relief supplies to the Norwegian people and also act as a counterweight to the Russians. Plans for the liberation of Norway were drawn up during the first four months of 1945. There were to be two related operations. The first, Operation *Doomsday*, was launched on the 8 May (VE Day) when a small Allied staff led by a British Brigadier flew into Lillehammer and accepted the surrender of General Franz Böhme, the Commander in Chief of German forces in Norway, at midnight on the 9th. After the surrender approximately 3,500 British and 13,000 Norwegian troops entered the country and secured strategic points within Norway.[4]

The second was Operation Apostle in which *Venomous* and her ship's company would play a part. Allied forces (many Norwegian) took control of port towns up and down the Norwegian coast but the German Naval commander in Norway would only surrender to the Royal Navy. It was decided that British naval forces would be sent to four coastal towns to accept the surrender of German naval forces. One of these was the port city of Kristiansand and Prideaux took it upon himself to convince Capt Ruck-Keene, Captain (D) of the Rosyth Escort Force and commander of the naval component of the operation, to choose *Venomous* as one of the destroyers:

> "There was keen competition among COs to be in this party and I stressed to Captain (D) my considerable experience of carrying stores in Destroyers during the Tobruk and Leros affairs. I doubt if he was impressed, but *Venomous* was eventually among those selected and was detailed with *Valorous* to proceed to Kristiansand South. *Valorous* embarked Capt Lord Teynham, DSC, RN, who was NOIC designate of the port and we both had a number of British and Norwegian Army Officers, as well as stores."

Lt Cdr J.A.J. Dennis RNVR, the CO of HMS *Valorous*.
Courtesy of Alan Dennis.

One wonders if Lord Teynham intervened on *Venomous'* behalf. After all, he had been one of her commanders, though only briefly during its refit at Troon.

Lt Cdr John Alexander Jeffreys Dennis, DSC explained how HMS *Valorous* came to be selected: "Then word went around that the Rosyth Escort Force was to 'liberate' Norway, and there was much speculation about which ships would go. Being in Ruck-Keene's good books, I was lucky."[5]

Valorous, a sister ship of *Venomous*, had been converted to a WAIR (W-Class anti-AIRcraft) destroyer, and as an operational destroyer had the accommodations, communications and sensors (radars) to support the senior officer commanding the force. *Venomous* had lost that capability and it appears that her role was more that of a cargo ship that delivered most of the supplies carried by the force.

Caudle described the objectives and the formation adopted for the passage:

> "Soon after V.E. Day, *Venomous* was ordered to take part in the only Operation of this commission being part of a flotilla of eight destroyers (all the others being operational ships) which was to accept the surrender of the Germans at four coastal towns in Norway. Two ships were to be detached to each. *Venomous* and *Valorous* being allocated to Kristiansand. Passage across the North Sea was made in two columns of four ships in line astern."

On 12 May the mixed flotilla of destroyers and minesweepers departed Rosyth as described by Alex Dennis in his memoir:

> "On May 12th we embarked two or three tons of stores, some soldiers equipped with walkie-talkies and, eventually, Capt Lord Teynham, RN, who was to be the Senior Naval Officer, Kristiansand, South. Next morning, *Valorous* and *Venomous* (John Prideaux) embarked a German naval pilot with charts of the minefields off the Norwegian coast, and off we set at 20 knots for Kristiansand."[6]

On reaching the Norwegian coast several Kristiansand-based German minesweepers met Lord Teynham's force. Even with this sign of accommodation by the Germans, Dennis still felt uneasy as to what awaited his ship when it entered German controlled waters:

> "Early next morning, May 14th, we rendezvoused with some German minesweepers at the entrance to the swept channel and felt our way along the coast. We were, of course, at action stations,

prepared for a nasty reception in case the local command wanted to go out in a blaze of glory. On the approach we could see some very large coast defence guns, reputed to have been taken from the *Scharnhorst's* sister ship the *Gneisenau*, which had been written off after mine and bomb damage."

During the afternoon of the 14th *Venomous* and *Valorous*, together with six minesweepers, approached the entrance to Kristiansand Fjord. The Fjord is located near the southernmost point of Norway at the western entrance of the Skagerrak, the body of water separating Norway from Denmark's Jutland Peninsula. The port town of Kristiansand is located halfway up the Fjord. The Fjord's entrance is rather wide, and dotted with several small islands, among which is Oksøy, on the western side of the entrance, with its lighthouse Oksøy Fyr, and Grønningen on the east, with its lighthouse Grønningen Fyr.[7]

On *Venomous* Prideaux remembered his sense of wariness:

> "The squadron split up on arrival off the Norwegian coast and our party steamed up a narrow Fjord, passing close by several large German guns whose crews were gathered round their weapons. We hoped none of them would suddenly decide to repudiate the surrender. In Kristiansand's large natural harbour we found a number of German Merchant ships, each with the Swastika flag at the stern. These were sullenly dipped as we passed, but they were soon hauled down for good and confiscated."

Frank Notton's feelings were probably shared by all in the force: "I remember sailing up the Skagerrak to Kristiansand for the liberation – sailing through minefields, thinking to ourselves the war was over and hoping we didn't hit a mine." His fellow stoker, Stoker Thomas "Yorkie" Russell, remembered:

> "There was a crackle of small arm fire and an occasional Oerlikon burst. Mines had been swept and the sweepers were firing at them to sink or to explode them. I heard no heavy explosions …but I did see on one occasion, a mine coated in red lead bobbing up and down in the choppy sea. This did nothing for my peace of mind.
>
> Soon I saw another amazing sight; small craft that I can only describe as smaller than cobbles which used to take anglers out of the east coast ports. They were Norwegian fishing boats and I noticed that in them were kids looking about nine or ten years of age and they were fishing with hand lines."[8]

Inside the Fjord, as the British ships neared the town, apprehension changed to relief, and then to exhilaration. AB Bert Upton was on deck as *Venomous* neared Kristiansand and he never forgot the scenes that followed: "What a fantastic reception we had. The Norwegian men, women and children came out to us in small crafts, boats, rafts, anything, which would float. I can still see them climbing up the ship's side."

At a certain point in the Fjord a strange sight greeted them. Atop a very tall factory chimney flew a still recognisable British Flag. CPO William Collister remembered that "…on a tall factory chimney I saw a Union Jack tattered and filthy but still recognisable." He asked an elderly woman who came on board *Venomous* if she could explain how it came to be there:

> "…I got talking to a white haired old lady and asked her if there was a story attached to the flag…she told me there was, and told me the

HMS *Valorous*, known as "Lucky Loo", anchored in Kristiansand harbour.
Note the crowded deck and the fishing boat pulling up alongside with more guests.
Courtesy of Alan Dennis.

HMS *Venomous* anchored in Kristiansand harbour soon after arrival on the 14 May 1945.

factory in fact was the building which pre-war brewed British beer, and when the Germans arrived they took it over, but of course not as a brewery. One of the brewery's workers knocked all the metal rungs to the top of the chimney and all their attempts to remove the flag failed. But, after all the shooting, as I said you could still recognise the tattered flag."[9]

From *Venomous'* bridge Prideaux looked at the scene before him:

"The shores of the harbour, despite the cold wet weather, were crowded with cheering Norwegians, and as soon as we had anchored a tender came alongside us crammed with highly excited children, who rushed the ship and were soon swarming everywhere. The sailors, always in their element on such occasions, cleared the canteen of its stocks of sweets and chocolate for our young guests (many of whom had never seen chocolate before and at first regarded it with some doubt). The din was terrific."

Among the crowds on the waterfront was a young Norwegian, Christian Bogh-Tobiassen who captured the prevailing atmosphere amongst his fellow Norwegians:

"To anyone who was not there it is impossible to understand what the sight of these ships meant to the Norwegian people of the town, and to me it is impossible to describe the enthusiasm that greeted the ships and ships companies – it was all joy."[10]

However, *Venomous'* commander faced a dilemma, as Caudle recalled:

"Fraternising with the Norwegians was forbidden but to have complied with that order to the letter would have involved the truly repugnant task of repelling the friendliest of boarders who came out in their own boats and swarmed aboard, feelings pent up during five years of German occupation required release."

Not surprisingly Prideaux decided to turn a blind eye to events on deck. His own account shows the personal challenge he faced regarding the non-fraternisation orders:

"Later in the day the Wardroom entertained more mature visitors. They were all anxious to celebrate the occasion, largely by consuming alarming quantities of whisky in the gayest and most rapid possible manner. Most of our visitors spoke English and we had plenty to talk about.

As the evening wore on I found myself in conversation, on a wide range of subjects, with a most disarming Norwegian journalist. Next day this gentleman came alongside with a local paper carrying a

headline "The Captain of the Wanamoos (sic) speaks". As we had
strict orders to make no statements to the Press I was greatly
disturbed but luckily NOIC apparently did not see that particular
journal and I heard nothing about it officially. As I lost the article
before I could get it translated I shall now never know exactly what
I did say that evening."

It appears that Prideaux had nothing to worry about, despite the local
newspaper, *Christiansands Tidende,* reporting the arrival of
Venomous and *Valorous* in its headline: "HMS *Venomous* and HMS
Valorous together with six Minesweepers arrived Kristiansand harbour
at 6.20p.m, on the 14th May being the first Allied Warships to arrive in
the harbour since the break out of peace." The paper didn't even
mention his name, but it did refer to Dennis as "a very sympathetic
young gentleman," and Lord Teynham as "a typical English aristocrat."[11]

Lord Teynham and Brigadier "Mad" Mike Calvert of the SAS go ashore in Kristiansand.
Courtesy of Alan Dennis.

Dennis' *Valorous*, the force's flagship, faced the same challenge of
reconciling orders banning fraternisation with the successful execution
of the mission. Teynham had left his flagship to meet with British,
German and Norwegian officials to discuss the task for which his force
was originally dispatched, accepting the formal surrender of German
Naval forces stationed at Kristiansand. With Teynham ashore, a large

party had broken out in *Valorous'* Wardroom and mess decks with British sailors and Norwegian citizens becoming happier with each glass of spirits. Teynham returned unexpectedly with news that the Germans would soon be arriving on board *Valorous* for a formal surrender ceremony. One can imagine the hustle and bustle that followed but, according to Dennis, this had a humorous side to it:

> "Almost as an after thought he [Capt Lord Teynham] told me that he had arranged for a German surrender delegation to repair on board [*Valorous*] in half-an-hour's time. This didn't give us much time to set up a suitable venue for such high-priced visitors, ex-enemy or no. Teynham thought they'd never make it on time, anyhow. But, being German, they were on the dot and I had to keep them kicking their heels on the quarterdeck whilst we cleared away the Norwegians, the girls, the drinks and the tables."[12]

German naval officer is piped aboard HMS *Valorous* for the surrender.
Courtesy of Alan Dennis.

German naval officers waiting on the quarterdeck whilst preparations for surrender are made.
Courtesy of Alan Dennis.

Once the setting was arranged for the German delegation the proceedings began. Dennis remembered the atmosphere:

> "It was quite a moment. The Germans were, as always, punctilious, correct, straight-backed, and poker-faced though clearly crest-fallen (mixed though the metaphor may be). There was no question of resistance and they were going to co-operate… In general, as had already been arranged by Mike Calvert [the SAS commander], the Germans were to keep their arms, take care of their own discipline whilst they evacuated the town and started on the road trip to Oslo and thence back to prisoner of war status in Germany."[13]

With the formalities concluded both destroyers began to unload their supplies. These were urgently needed by the civil authorities and their timely arrival is a testament to Allied planning. The overall approach and subsequent effectiveness of the planning can be seen in the work of the British Army's 2/19 Civil Affairs Unit.[14]

Under the command of Major C.I. Lee, the unit had arrived in Kristiansand on 10 May. By the end of the second day Lee and his staff had met with local Norwegian town and county officials; conferred with the Kristiansand German Garrison Commander and his staff; begun the evacuation of German troops and civilians; obtained an estimate as to how many refugees and displaced persons there were in the area; determined the condition of the telephone and telegraph systems; assessed the condition of the town's fishing fleet, the need for oil stocks to power it and established that there was sufficient fuel to resume fishing. By the third day Lee reported that the town and its county urgently required coal, diesel oil, meat, flour, coffee and fats, including 300 tons of herring oil for margarine. The supplies the destroyers off-loaded (14 - 15 May) included oil, flour and coffee.

On 15th Capt Lord Teynham came aboard *Venomous* to accept the surrender of the German Admiral and the commanding officers of the German U-boats berthed further up Kristiansand Fjord at Marviken, as described by Prideaux:

> "On the 15th of May German Officers came on-board *Venomous* – they had to row their own boat – to sign over the necessary handover documents. Present on board on the occasion were the Allied Naval Area Commander, Capt Lord Teynham, and the Norwegian Navy District Commander, Commodore Landgraff, who actually followed *Venomous* from England".

Fred Mercer was sent in the whaler to collect the German admiral who congratulated Fred on his seamanship as he brought the boat alongside *Venomous*. Some of the officers personally surrendered by presenting their Lugar revolvers to Lt(E) Forster and Lt Caudle and when their 'guests' had left, one of them accidentally discharged his unfamiliar sidearm piercing a bulkhead and nearly hitting the CO. Fred Mercer remained in Kristiansand and returned later on one of the captured U-boats.

Dennis visited the Marvika submarine base and gives an idea as to the composition of the U-boat flotilla:

> "Next day we had a similar surrender meeting for the U-boat flotilla. There were 26 in all. I still remember some numbers: U281, 299, 369, 712, 1163 (Type VII C): U2312, 2325, 2334, 2335, 2337, 2350, 2353, 2354, 2361, 2363 (Type XXIII): and U2529 (Type XXI). The Type XXI and XXIII were the very latest, streamlined and very fast underwater. We were indeed lucky that they had hardly been in service long enough to affect the war at sea...I walked around some of them and was tremendously impressed with their equipment, their cleanliness and the high morale of the officers and men. This was indeed remarkable considering the appalling losses they had suffered..."

Later that day *Venomous* was able to turn her attention to more relaxing matters although, as Prideaux recalled, one needed to be on one's guard, especially as it concerned the standing orders on fraternisation!

> "On one occasion, as we were at luncheon, the Quartermaster came in and announced the arrival of a boatload of Norwegians. As visits from the shore had by now been forbidden he was told to send them away. He looked worried, and said he had already tried to do this, but that they refused to go without seeing the Captain personally. I decided to deal with them myself and went sternly up the ladder to do so. On the upper deck I was taken aback to find a bevy of lovely blondes waiting for me, carrying flowers, and surrounded by an appreciative crowd of sailors. As soon as I appeared the leading lady dashed forward, thrust a large bouquet into my arms, and embraced me warmly. The sailors were delighted."

The ladies turned out to be Kristiansand's hospitality committee.

In addition to the official guests that were entertained, the hospitality offered by *Venomous* created a deep impression on many

Norwegian youngsters who crowded the ship. None more so with the young Christian Bogh-Tobiassen:

> "The ship's company gave parties on board serving drinks and food of a kind that people in town had just dreamed of for years. All your Officers and sailors were very popular visitors indeed. Personally I remember practising my school English for the first time. To listen to your sailors, even to come on board your ships, to me 16 years old, was such a great experience that I joined our own Navy some three years later and stayed there ever after."

Prideaux did manage to get ashore and recalled how strange it seemed:

> "We did manage to get ashore one afternoon to the little wooden housed town, and it was most strange to walk round the streets rubbing shoulders with German soldiers, who still carried side arms whilst we were as usual quite unarmed. Their Officers too were driving round in staff cars whilst we had to walk. It occurred to us that things would have been different if our roles had been reversed."

Stoker "Yorkie" Russell was not very impressed with what he saw when he and some of his messmates had shore leave in Kristiansand:

> "The people seemed few and far between and not so talkative either. They seemed in a state of shock, as they couldn't believe that they had been liberated. What struck me was a squad of German sailors marching past, still armed and we not so much as a knife between us. We went back aboard early, an hour or two was long enough in that lifeless place."[15]

Upon his return to *Venomous* Russell and a messmate decided to take a bath in the very confined washroom space allocated to the ship's company. His description of the facilities gives an excellent insight into the bathing and washing conditions for members of the lower deck serving in the old V & W Class destroyers:

> "This compartment had only one hatch into it and you had to bath, in a large round bowl. There were only two of these bowls and you didn't always have enough hot water anyway to fill the two. This day we were in luck; we took our washing down and with it, the usual bar of pusser's soap and a knife to shave some onto the washing. I had got one of the metal tubs and as I was filling it, I decided to kill two birds with one stone and I would wash my clothes and bathe in the same water; my mate decided that it was a good idea. There we were both in the nude, perched with our buttocks on the edge of our respective tubs, rubbing our washing in the lather the soap shavings had created."

Unknown to both sailors *Venomous* had just welcomed on board another contingent of Norwegian citizens. What occurred next was an embarrassing moment for "Yorkie" and his friend, but very amusing for their Norwegian guests and his shipmates on the lower deck:

> "My back was towards the washroom entrance and I was concentrating on the job in hand. Suddenly, I heard a clattering of feet on the hatchway's steel ladder, nothing wrong with that but then I heard the unmistakable sound of female laughter. "Cor Yorkie," my mate said, "Look behind you." I turned and it must have been one of the few times that a sailor has blushed. There, laughing and pointing, were several Norwegian girls; what do you do in such a situation? We just carried on with our washing. I'd never felt so embarrassed. The b******s on the mess deck had actually directed the girls down to the bathroom and had had a good laugh at our expense. The girls had been invited aboard on a goodwill trip; they certainly had something to tell their folks. The boys on the mess deck, said, "Did you give them a flash, Yorkie?" But as luck had it, my back was towards them."

These were not the only unlikely visitors to be entertained by the lower deck. Russell remembered another unexpected guest:

> "One day as some of the boys were returning aboard, they came across a stranger in a uniform that they had never seen before. He wasn't German and he had only a very slight knowledge of English. He managed to get across that he was very hungry, doing this mostly by sign, pointing to his mouth and to his stomach. His uniform was a green shade, nearly the so-called Lincoln green of Robin Hood. He was escorted off the dockside, down to the mess deck and was seated whilst someone went off and brewed the mess deck tea up to the half way mark. A large tin of baked beans was opened and half a large loaf was cut up into thick slices and liberally coated with butter. This repast was placed in front of him as he literally drooled at the sight. I think he would have kissed us all if we had let him. His thanks were embarrassing; I'd never seen anyone starving like this man. He wolfed the food down and we just sat and watched him. His words were Russian sounding and he did claim that he was a Russian prisoner of the Germans and said that the Germans had shot some of his mates before we arrived. We made sure that he had his fill and then we packed him off before any officers arrived on the scene and kicked a stink up. We had after all, managed to get him aboard unbeknown to the officer of the day."

The Germans had approximately one hundred thousand prisoners of war in Norway, the great majority of which were Russian, and most were returned to Stalin's Russia where they were either shot or imprisoned in Stalin's Gulags.

SAS driving through Kristiansand in their jeeps are welcomed by children and adults alike.
From *A picture book of Kristiansand: Southern Norway in War and Peace, 1940-45*;
edited by Erik Lauritzen (Prolibro, 1988).

Children wave the national flag as they watch the parade on National Day, 17 May 1945.
From *A picture book of Kristiansand: Southern Norway in War and Peace, 1940-45*;
edited by Erik Lauritzen (Prolibro, 1988).

Sailors from HMS *Valorous* join with the army to parade through Kristiansand on Norway's National Day, 17 May 1945, whilst HMS *Venomous* returns to Rosyth.
Courtesy of Alan Dennis.

Venomous was ordered back to Rosyth after only two days and Prideaux, his officers and the ship's company, were unable to attend the parties arranged by the Norwegians to welcome their liberators. They left on the 17 May, Norway's National Day, which was celebrated by the people of Kristiansand with parades and parties. As the old destroyer weighed anchor, all on board could see the preparations being made ashore, and must have thought a more suitable time for departure could have been chosen. Their sister ship, HMS *Valorous*, would remain in Kristiansand for three weeks but this is the prerogative of a flagship. Caudle's disappointment must have been shared by all on board:

> "The time came to return to Rosyth. Ironically this was 17th May –
> Norway's National Day and at 0700 *Venomous* weighed and preceded
> just as the band was tuning up ashore ready for the celebrations later
> in the day. As might have been foreseen by those in *Venomous* she
> spent the three days after her arrival moored at a buoy."

Shortly after *Venomous* returned to the Firth of Forth she was spotted by Midshipman Beckerman when his ship, the modern destroyer HMS *Oribi* (John McBeath's command after he left *Venomous*), anchored nearby. *Oribi* had joined a much larger force of cruisers and destroyers dispatched to liberate Copenhagen where two of the Kriegsmarine's surviving major warships, the Hipper Class heavy cruiser, KMS *Prinze Eugen* and the Königsberg Class light cruiser, KMS *Nürnberg*, had at first "seemed a bit reluctant to surrender." Beckerman visited his old ship and one can imagine what his former Wardroom members thought when he told them that he "...spent two wonderful weeks in Copenhagen, eating like princes (there was no food shortage there at all), and having a lovely time with the ladies, who, we quickly discovered, were liberated already. Our ship was almost a floating night-club." This did not sit very well with *Venomous'* gunnery officer, Lt Thorp, who told Beckerman all he got from the ladies of Kristiansand "...was when one of them held his hand!" Beckerman left his old ship the following morning after a "terrific party and I got very drunk and sick".

After this "last hurrah" it was by now all too obvious that there was no future for *Venomous* other than the breaker's yard.

It would be much later that those who served on *Venomous* and everybody who had participated in the liberation of Norway received a certificate of appreciation from the people of Norway that proclaimed,

A commemorative scroll signed by King Olaf was presented to each member of the crew of HMS *Venomous*.

Courtesy of Thomas "Yorkie" Russell.

Notes

1   From a scroll presented by the Norwegian Government to all those British servicemen that participated in the liberation of Norway from German occupation.

2   The *Illustrious* Class carriers, *Illustrious, Victorious, Formidable* and *Indomitable,* together with the *Implacable* Class carriers, *Implacable* and *Indefatigable* formed the centrepiece of the British Pacific Fleet's (BPF) fast carrier force.

3   Festung Norwegen (Fortress Norway) was the German phrase used to describe the system of air defences, coastal fortifications, minefields and quick reaction armour and infantry units built by the Germans to defend Norway from invasion by the Allies as part of Hitler's vaunted "Atlantic Wall."

4   The Norwegian force came from Sweden.

5   As a junior officer, Cdr Dennis was awarded his DSC in the heroic action that resulted in Britain obtaining the key that broke the German's famous 'Enigma' encryption system. Cdr Dennis DSC, RN (Ret.) died in July 2008 at the age of ninety before we could discuss his role and that of *Venomous* in the liberation of Kristiansand but his unpublished memoir is in the Imperial War Museum, London (IWM Ref. 3129 95/5/1).

6   Ibid

7   Use Google Earth to obtain an excellent view of the Fjord and the town of Kristiansand. You will note that one of the icons superimposed on the satellite photograph identifies the approximate location of the sunken German *Königsberg* Class light cruiser KMS *Karlsruhe.* The submarine, HMS *Truant*, sank it after the cruiser departed Kristiansand on 9 April 1940. Prior to the sinking, *Karlsruhe* had successfully led a German Navy assault past the defences of the Fjord and the town to land the Wehrmacht during the Nazi invasion of Norway. In all likelihood, *Venomous* sailed over the wreck.

8   From Russell's account of his time on *Venomous* on the BBC's WW2 People's War website, www.bbc.co.uk/ww2peopleswar/stories/80/a7275080.shtml.

9   From Collister's account of his time on *Venomous* written for the new edition of this book in December 2006.

10 Christian Bogh-Tobiassen would later become a Captain in the Royal Norwegian Navy. His account of the liberation of his hometown was taken from his letters to Robert Moore.

11 *Christianstands Tidende* 1945 63(6) Tuesday 15 May

12 From the unpublished memoir of Cdr Dennis in the Imperial War Museum, London (IWM Ref. 3129 95/5/1).

13 Ibid.

14 War Diary of 2/19 Civil Affairs Unit (Christiansand Sub-Zone) from 10 May 45 to 30 May 45 with Appendices A to O (NA Ref. WO 171/8449)

15 From Russell's account of his time on *Venomous* on the BBC's WW2 People's War website, www.bbc.co.uk/ww2peopleswar/stories/80/a7275080.shtml.

CHAPTER TWELVE

THE END OF THE ROAD

"Keep right on to the end of the road, Keep right on until the end,
Tho' the way be long, let your heart be strong,
keep right on round the bend.
Tho' you're tired and weary still journey on,
till you come to your happy abode,
Where all you love you've been dreaming of will be there
at the end of the road." [1]

The end was near for *Venomous*. She had been living on borrowed time, and upon her return from Norway it was evident that her active life was over. AB Norton remembered that upon, "returning to base at Rosyth after six days we paid off."

Prideaux recalled what happened next: "On returning to Rosyth I found orders waiting to take *Venomous* up the river to Grangemouth to pay off and not long afterwards we said a sad farewell to the old ship, whose days of active service were obviously over for good."

Prideaux and most of his officers (with the exception of the engineering officer, Lt Forster) transferred to H Class destroyer, HMS *Havelock*, which carried on the duties of a torpedo target training ship.

Lt Jimmy Blair believed himself to be the last officer aboard *Venomous* when: "Shortly after [return from Norway], the Admiralty decided to scrap *Venomous* and I had the sad task of taking her up to Grangemouth, ignominiously by tug!"[2] Caudle also remembered the final voyage of *Venomous*:

> "Not very long after this episode *Venomous* made her last passage to Grangemouth further up the Forth to de-store and be finally paid off. That accomplished she was subsequently flooded and left to lie in the shallows, virtually no more than a hulk. A sad ending to a proud ship bearing a proud name."

AB Notton remembered mostly his fellow stokers: "After 40 years I still remember the other Stokers – Skuse, Ryan, Daly, Glennon, Wright from Oldham, Overthrow from Gloucester and Ken Payne from Southport – all of 'em good lads. I would like to think they are still around."

Venomous paid off into the Reserve Fleet on 11 July 1945, ending her long and distinguished career. Lt Forster remained aboard the ship for some months as the only officer but on 9 January 1946 she was paid off for disposal, being passed to the British Iron and Steel Corporation on 4 March 1947. Her demise, however, would not be immediate. The breakers yards were at full stretch demolishing the residue of six years of war, and it would be a further eighteen months (November 1948) before the name of *Venomous* became history.

Venomous and those other destroyers that inspired Rudyard Kipling performed duties beyond his poetic imagination. Kipling had eulogised the destroyers as "Maidens of the slain" whose "Flash, Dash and Boom" brought death and destruction but this ship did not confront the great battle fleets with her torpedoes. Indeed, she never once used her torpedoes to attack an enemy ship. Instead she was an escort for convoys of largely unarmed merchant vessels and used her anti-submarine armament to defeat the underwater menace of German U-boats. She fired at German tanks at point blank range, shot down aircraft during her heroic dashes between France and England and aggressively counter attacked a very determined and skilful U-boat commander.

Ironically, she saved many more lives than she took. From the Baltic in the early 1920s through operations such as *Pedestal* and *Torch*, *Venomous* saved approximately six thousand lives. Her operational life which began with contributing to the liberation of the Baltic States came full circle with her contribution to the Liberation of Norway. How would Kipling have penned this ship's exploits had he known the role it would play?

Thus passed a fine destroyer, also a lucky ship that successive crews remembered with affection. The last words are left to one of those who served in her often-crowded lower deck, a man typical of those described in Professor Christopher McKee's book, *Sober Men and True*, AB James Eaton: "She was a very happy ship and I am very proud to have served in her. I would do the same again if I could – good old *Venomous*."

Notes

1   This is the chorus from the song *Keep Right on to the End of the Road* written by Sir Harry Lauder.

2   Extract from *Landlubber in the Navy*, the privately published memoir of Lt Jimmy Blair RNVR.

POSTSCRIPT

There were sixty-nine V & W Class destroyers built at the end of World War I and all of those which survived went to the breakers' yards at the end of World War II. Within thirty years of the first V & W being launched not one remained afloat but during that time countless thousands of men served on them and in 1993 the V & W Destroyer Association was formed to keep former "shipmates" in touch with each other. The Association has HRH The Duke of Edinburgh as its Patron, publishes a magazine, *Hard Lying*, and meets at least once a year. Although many of its members have "crossed the bar" it is still active and relatives of those who served on V & W destroyers are eligible to join as Associate Members.

Further details are available on request from the Secretary:

John S. Appleby, F.R. Hist. S.
Honorary Secretary
V & W Destroyer Association
Little Pitchbury
Brick Kiln Lane
Great Horkesley
Colchester
Essex CO6 4EU

Telephone: 01206-271458

The members of the V & W Association are drawn from the officers and crew of the fifty six V & Ws which fought in World War II. A complete list of all the V & W Class destroyers and their fates is given as an appendix.

APPENDICES

Specification

Displacement:	1,120 tons
Length:	300' 0"
Beam:	29' 6"
Draught:	10' 8"
Machinery:	2 shaft geared turbines SHP 27,000 3 Yarrow boilers
Speed:	34 knots
Bunker capacity:	367 tons
Armament:	4 x 1 – 4.7-inch 1 x 1 – 12 pounder 1 x 3 – 21-inch torpedo tubes
	After conversion: 2 x 1 – 4.7-inch 4 x 1 – 20mm Hedgehog

Battle honours

Atlantic	1940-3
Arctic	1942
North Africa	1942-3
Dunkirk	1940
Malta Convoys	1942
Sicily	1943

APPENDIX TWO – COMMANDING OFFICERS

	From	To
Cdr S.P.B. Russell RN	28 Apr1918	14 Jul 1921
Lt Cdr L.G. Gardner RN	14 Jul 1921	1 Sep 1923
Lt Cdr D. McGrath RN	1 Sep 1923	13 Dec 1924
Lt Cdr L.F.N. Ommanney RN	13 Dec 1924	11 Dec 1926
Lt Cdr F.G.N. Rushbrooke DSC RN	11 Dec 1926	14 Jan 1929
Lt Cdr C.A.N. Chatwin RN	14 Jan 1929	3 Sep 1929

Whilst in reserve

	From	To
Cdr (E) R. Grieve RN	3 Sep 1929	20 Jun 1933
Lt (E) W.H. Hicks RN	20 Jun 1933	Nov 1933
Lt (E) F.A. Taylor RN	Nov 1933	26 Jul 1935
Cdr (E) G.N. Goodyear RN	26 Jul 1935	14 Sep 1936
Lt Cdr (E) T.H. Hunter RN	14 Sep 1936	30 Apr 1937
Lt Cdr (E) E.O. Stallybrass RN	30 Apr 1937	31 Jul 1939

	From	To
Lt Cdr D.G.F.W. MacIntyre RN	31 Jul 1939	8 Jan 1940
Lt Cdr J.E.H. McBeath DSO RN	8 Jan 1940	23 Dec 1940
Cdr H.P. Henderson DSO RN	23 Dec 940	3 Jul 1941
Cdr H.W. Falcon-Steward RN	3 Jul 1941	18 Dec 1942
Cdr The Lord Teynham RN	Feb 1942	Apr 1942
Cdr D.H. Maitland-Makgill-Crichton DSO DSC RN	18 Dec 1942	18 Feb 1943
Lt H.D. Durell RN	18 Feb 1943	23 Oct 1943
Lt Cdr D. Lawson RNVR	1 Aug 1944	6 Feb 1945
Lt Cdr A.G. Prideaux RNVR	6 Feb 1945	31 May 1945

APPENDIX THREE – LIST OF OFFICERS

Officers are listed under their ships in quarterly issues of the *Navy List*. Back runs of the *Navy List* are held at the National Archives in Kew and major naval libraries.

This may not be a complete list of all officers who served on HMS *Venomous* but it will be updated with links to information elsewhere on the web at:
http://www.holywellhousepublishing.co.uk/

Name	Rank	Speciality branch	Service dates
Adams, E.O.	Sub Lt, RN		1920-1
Allen	Commissioned Warrant, RN	Gunner Torpedo	1922
Allen, H.M.	Lt Cdr, RN	Engineer	1928-9
Alleyne, R.M.	Lt, RN		1921-2
Baker, H.L.S.	Sub Lt, RN		1919
Barlow, P.	Mid., RN		1924
Barney, S.J.	Sub Lt, RNR		1943
Beckerman, W.	Mid., RNVR		1944-5
Blair, J.	Lt, RNVR		1945
Botley, T.W.	Mid., RN		1919
Brice, L.W.	Mid., RN		1921
Browning, R.	Lt, RNVR	Surgeon	1941-2
Burges, R.Y.	Sub Lt, RN		1922
Buchanan, H.J.	Sub Lt, RAN		1922
Byrne, R.C.A.	Lt, RNVR		1943
Carray	Mid.		1924-
Cashman, M.	Lt, RN		1942-3
Caudle, D.W.	Lt, RNVR		1944-5
Chatwin, C.A.N.	Lt Cdr, RN		1929
Clark, I.T.	Lt, RN		1928-9
Coleman, J.F.	Lt, RNR		1942-3
Corby	Gunner Torpedo		1926-
Corries, J.D.	Mid., RNR		1922
Crossman, J.D.	Sub Lt, RN		1923-5
Cottam, G.M.	Lt, RNR		1940
Courcy-Ireland, S.B. de	Lt, RN		1920-1
Dawnay, P.	Mid., RN		1919?
Donald, C.G.W.	Lt, RN		1926-7
Douglas-Watson, F.	Lt, RN		1922
Duff, D.A.R.	Lt, RN		1939
Dunn, F.A.	Commissioned Warrant, RN		1920-2
Durrell, H.D.	Lt, RN		1943

Esson, A.F.	Mid., RNR		1939-1
Eaton, L.C.	Lt, RNVR		1942-3
Ellad		Schoolmaster	1926
Elliot, R.C.	Mid., RNVR		1942-3
Fretwell, V.E.W.	Mid., RNR		1922
Falcon-Steward, H.W.	Cdr, RN		1941-2
Forster, W.R.	Lt, RNR	Engineer	1944-6
Gotto, R.	Mid., RN		1919-20
Gannon, E.D.	Sub Lt, RN		1919-20
Gardner, L.G.	Lt Cdr RN		1921-3
Green, R.A.W.	Mid., RN		1925
Gregg, C.J.M.	Sub Lt, RN		1928
Gregory, S.C.	Commissioned Warrant, RN	Gunner Torpedo	1928-9
Greenaway, F.S.H	Lt, RNVRR		1944-5
Grieve, P.	Cdr, RN	Engineer	1929-33
Hare, M.	Mid., RN		1928
Harrison, C.E.P.	Lt, RN		1927-9
Harrow, C.C.	Mid., RN		1940
Helps, G.A.	Mid., RN		1927
Henderson, H.P.	Cdr, RN		1940-1
Hicks, W.H.	Lt, RN	Engineer	1933
Hollins, W.F.	Lt, RN		1924-5
Hunter, F.L.W.	Lt, RN		1943
Hunter, T.H.	Lt Cdr, RN	Engineer	1936-7
Hurry, E.	Sub Lt, RN		1919
Jackson, R.J.	Lt, RN		1929
Jocelyn, Viscount	Mid., RN		1929
Kershaw, P.	Lt, RNVR		1940-1
Knight, J.T.	Mid., RN		1941
Lansky, M.S.	Sub Lt, RNVR		1945
Lapthorn, C.G.	Commissioned Warrant, RN	Engineer	1943
Lawson, D.	Lt Cdr, RNVR		1944-5
Lewis, R.A.W.	Mid., RN		1925
Lewis, W.F.H.	Commissioned Warrant, RN	Gunner Torpedo	1939
Mackenzie, A.A.	Lt, RNR		1940-1
Maitland-Makgill-Crichton, D.H.	Cdr, RN		1942-3
Manton, R.	Lt, RN	Engineer	1924-5
Martin, J.N.	Lt, RNVR		1944-5
Maxwell, I.L.	Surg. Lt	Surgeon	1942-3
Maunsell, F.R.G.	Lt, RN		1925-7
McBeath, J.E.H.	Lt Cdr, RN		1939-40

McGrath, D.S.	Lt Cdr, RN		1923-4
McIntyre, D.C.F.W.	Lt Cdr, RN		1939
McPhee, A.D.	Lt, RN		1941
Prawle	Sub Lt		1925-
Milner, C.W.B.	Lt, RN		1939-40
Milner, G.C.	Surg. Lt, RNVR	Surgeon	1942
Moore, R.	Sub Lt, RN		1923-4
Mundy, H.M.S.	Sub Lt, RN		1919-20
Nicholl, R.A.F.	Sub Lt, RN		1919-20
Norman, P.	Mid., RN		1923
Ommanney, L.F.N.	Lt Cdr, RN		1925-6
Owen, A.L.	Mid., RN		1922
Pawle, E.	Mid., RN		1925
Pearson, Robert	Mid, RN		1921
Pemberton, R.H.S.	Mid., RN		1929
Perry, A.E.	Commissioned Warrant, RN	Gunner Torpedo	1919
Philip, J.H.	Commissioned Warrant, RN	Gunner	1919
Philpott, T.	Commissioned Warrant, RN	Gunner Torpedo	1922-3
Pinckney, E.P.H.	Lt, RN		1926-8
Portal, N.H.	Sub Lt, RN		1922
Prentice, J.D.	Sub Lt, RN		1919
Pudner, W.H.	Lt Cdr, RN	Engineer	1918
Redman, W.R.J.	Lt, RN		1928-9
Robertson, C.L.	Sub Lt, RN		1920
Robertson-MacDonald, A.D.J.	Lt, RN		1922-3
Rodger, R.H.S.	Mid., RN		1920
Rushbrooke, E.G.N.	Lt Cdr, RN		1927-8
Russell, S.P.B.	Cdr, RN		1919-20
Russell, S.Y.	Lt, RN	Engineer	1922-3
Sangster, A.D'E.T.	Lt, RN		1942-3
Scott, D.C.	Lt, RN	Engineer	1921-2
Simms, A.N.	Commissioned Warrant, RN	Gunner Torpedo	1941-3
Sims, L.	Lt, RN	Engineer	1926-7
Stokes	Mid., RN		1925-6
Taylor, E.A.	Lt, RN	Engineer	1935-6
Thomson, C.D.	Commissioned Warrant, RN	Gunner Torpedo	1940-1
Thompson, G.H.	Sub Lt, RN		1921-2
Thorp, T.B.	Lt, RNVR		1944-5
Tod, D.	Mid., RN		1921
Tomkinson, M.W.	Mid., RN		1927
Tonkyn, E.D.	Commissioned Warrant, RN	Wt. Engineer	1939
Tucker, J.C.	Sub Lt, RNR	Gunnery Officer	1941

Vaughan-Lewis, J.R.	Lt, RN		1939-40
Voil, L.C. de	Commissioned Warrant, RN	Gunner Torpedo	1920-2
Weatherall, A.T.H.	Mid., RN		1921
Welby-Everard, P.H.E.	Sub Lt, RN		1922
Wells, Walter R. DSC	Lt, RN		1939-41
Wheele, W.E.	Commissioned Warrant, RN	Gunner Torpedo	1923-4
Whitfield, J.F.	Mid., RN		1922
Willson, J.A.B.	Lt, RN		1919-20
Wood, G.E.C.	Lt, RN		1922-3
Wood, J.H.I.	Lt, RN		1922
Woodyatt, P.B.	Surg. Lt, RNVR	Surgeon	1940
Young, R.S.	Mid., RN		1921

Obtaining service records of commissioned officers

Commissioned officers who entered the service before or during 1924:

> The National Archives Office, Ruskin Avenue, Kew, Richmond, Surrey TW9 4DU
> Telephone: 0208-876 3444 Web: http://www.nationalarchives.gov.uk/
>
> You can also search and download service records online from the National
> Archives: http://www.nationalarchives.gov.uk/documentsonline/adm196.asp

Commissioned officers who entered the service between 1924 and 1939:

> Navy Records Office, TNT Archives Service, Tetron Point, William Nadin Way,
> Swaddlincote, South Derbyshire DE11 0BB
> Telephone: 01283 227913 E-mail: navysearchpgrc@tnt.co.uk

Service records from 1939 onwards:

> DNPers, Disclosure Cell, MP G-2, Room 48, West Battery, Whale Island,
> Portsmouth PO2 8DX
> Telephones: 023 92 628667/8666/8671/8670/8654

For further details see:
http://www.royalnavy.mod.uk/contact/obtaining-royal-navy-service-records-and/

APPENDIX FOUR – LIST OF RATINGS

Unlike the Merchant Marine there are no crew lists for Royal Navy ships. The ship's complement of 120-70 changed each time HMS *Venomous* was re-commissioned and this is inevitably a very incomplete list mainly based on information supplied by the seamen themselves or members of their families.

It will be updated on the web at:
http://www.holywellhousepublishing.co.uk/

Name	Rate	Service dates
The Ackerman twins	Able Seamen	1939-41
Addis, Michael "Mick"	Petty Officer (Quartermaster)	
Back, Robert T.	AB (Gunner)	1942-3
Ball, Charles	Petty Officer (Officers' Cook)	
Battersby, Arthur M		1942-3
Bennett, Arthur Malcolm "Wiggy"	Chief Engine Room Artificer (CERA)	1944-5
Billings, Fred	Petty Officer (Gunnery Instructor)	1939-40
Birkin, George Arnold "Arnie"	Gunlayer	1939-41
Boles, "Paddy"	Stoker	1942-3
Bordiss, J. P.	Petty Officer (Gunnery Instructor)	1940
Box, "Jan"	AB	1940
Brewster	AB	1925-6
Brown, T.I.	Petty Officer	
Butt, Wally		
Button, Herbert J. B. DSM	Chief Petty Officer (Bosun)	1942
Campbell	AB	1939-40
Campbell, Alexander M.	OD (CW Candidate)	1942-3
Carson, John	OD (CW Candidate)	1942-3
Carter, Nick	AB (Gunner)	1939-40
Charles, Sidney Thomas	AB (Bosun's Mate)	1939-42
Christian, "Bob"		1940
Collister, William Leslie	Chief Petty Officer (Gunlayer)	1940-5
Compston, Sydney	AB (Gunnery Dpt)	1940-1
Conybear	Petty Officer (Engine Room Artificer)	1942-3
Craddock, Robert	AB (the "tankie")	1942-3
Crowley, J. F.	Petty Officer	1941
Dagley, L.W. DSM	Petty Officer (Electrician)	1939-40
Dean, Dixie	OD (CW Candidate)	1942-3
Daily	Stoker	1945
Dalton, "Joe"	AB	1940
Dodd, John	OD (CW Candidate)	1942-3
Downing, Jan	Officers' Steward	1940
Duckworth	AB	
Dusty, Jack	Chief Storeman	

Eaton	AB	1940
Easton, W. S.	AB	1921
Edwards, J.	AB	1940
Eley	AB	
Emery, Charles J.	AB	1920
Evans, "Roggy"	Petty Officer (Engine Room Artificer)	1942-3
Fenn, Mike	OD (CW Candidate)	1942-3
Fisher, "Jacky"	AB	1940
Foxe, R.D.L. DSM	CPO	1942-3
Freeman, Harry	LS	1940
Fry, Albert	LS	1941
Glennon	Stoker	1945
Gorman	Petty Officer (Quartermaster)	
Grabham, Richard	AB	1939-43
Haddon, Harry "Taff"	AB ("B" Gun)	1942-3
Hargreaves	AB	1942-3
Hatton, Alfred	Chief Stoker	1926
Hayes	AB	1942-3
Hely, Cyril	AB (Starboard Oerlikon)	1942-3
Henderson, J. G.	AB	1940
Hicks, Geoffrey	Petty Officer (Torpedo Instructor)	1939-
Holgate, Tom	AB	1940
Holywood	Chief Petty Officer (Ship's Cox'n)	
Hopwood	AB	
Horner, "Jackie"	AB	1940
Hyde, Bernie	NAFFI Manager	
Irlam, James	Engine Room Artificer	1941
Jamieson, Jimmy	Electrical Artificer	
Johns	AB	
Johnson	Petty Officer (Engine Room Artificer)	1942-3
Knapton, W. DSM	AB	1940
Ledguard	Petty Officer	1940-
Liddicoat, Arthur		1939-42
Lockerman	AB	
Lodwick, William DSM	AB	1939-40
Lofthouse, Albert	Chief Petty Officer (Yeoman of Signals)	1942-3
Mann	Petty Officer (Seaman)	1939-
Mansell, A.J.M. "Mervyn"	OD (CW Candidate)	1942-3
Marshall	AB	
McGeeney, Hugh H. DSM	Chief Petty Officer (Ordnance Artificer)	1939-40
McCabe	AB	

Mayland, O. G.	Signalman	1940-1
Maxfield, "Maxi"	AB	1940
Mercer, Frederick	AB	1944-5
Metcalf, Percy	AB	1940
Mitchell	"Tankie"	1940
Moon	AB	
Munro	Yeoman of Signals	1940-1
Newby, "Willie"	AB	1940
Newton, J. A.	LS	1941
Nicholas, "Tubby"	Quartermaster	1939-41
Nickless, W. H.	Telegraphist	1940
Notton, Francis "Frank"	Stoker	1944-5
Orwell		
O'Sullivan, Michael J. DSM	Petty Officer (Seaman)	1939-
Overthrow	Stoker	1945
Passmore, Don DSM	Chief Engine Room Artificer (CERA)	1939-
Payne	Yeoman of Signals	1940
Payne, Kenneth	Stoker	1945
Pelling, John "Cockney"	Stoker	1944-5
Poole, Thomas Henry	Leading Seaman (Ship's Writer)	1939-5
Poultney, Eric Arnold	Signalman (Wireless)	
Prew	AB	
Price, Alfred J	Leading Stoker	1920
Rick, Percy	Ordnance Artificer	1942-3
Robb, John Cleland	LS	1942-5
Robinson, Thomas William	Stoker	1925
Robinson	AB	1940
Russell, Thomas "Yorkie"	Stoker	1944-5
Ryan	Stoker	1945
Scargill, "Jock"	AB	1939-41
Sefton, Len	AB	1940
Sheel, "Gordie"	Petty Officer (Telegraphist)	
Shepherd	AB	1942-3
Sinclair	AB	
Skuse	Stoker	1945
Smith, "Jock"	AB	1940
Speechley, George	Signals	1940
Sprosson, Henry Rolland	Engine Room Artificer	1927
Stafford, H. DSM	LS	1942-3
Stallard, E. Roy DSM	AB (Gunlayer)	1939-40
Squibb	Chief Petty Officer (Coxwain)	1939-
Thomas, F.N.G. "Freddo"	RDF Operator	1941-3
Tonner, James Andrew	Wireless Operator	1944-5

Upton, A.G. "Bert"	AB	1944-5
Vicary	AB	
Walton, William Taylor "Billie"	Petty Officer (ship's NAFFI)	1944-5
Ward, "Sharky"	Stoker	1942-3
Watts	Petty Officer (Cook)	1939-
Weeks, William E.R. ("Teddy")	AB (Bosun's Mate)	1939-41
Wharton, Fred ("Scouse")	AB	1942-3
Wilmott, Harry	Engine Room Artificer	1942-3
Wilson, Francis George	Asdic Operator	1942-3
Wright	Stoker	1945
Yelland, W. P.	AB	1942-3

Obtaining service records of ratings

Royal Navy ratings who entered service up to and including 1924:

The National Archives Office, Ruskin Avenue, Kew, Richmond, Surrey TW9 4DU Telephone: 0208-876 3444. Web: http://www.nationalarchives.gov.uk/

You can also search and download service records online from the National Archives: http://www.nationalarchives.gov.uk/documentsonline/royal-navy-service.asp?WT.hp=Registers%20of%20Seamen's%20Services

Royal Navy ratings who entered service from 1924 to 1972:

Director of Naval Personnel, Navy Search, TNT Archive Services, PO Box 7814, William Nadin Way, Swadlincote, Derbyshire DE11 1EG Tel: 01283 227912 Web: www.navysearchpgrc@tnt.co.uk

APPENDIX FIVE – SHIPBOARD ORGANISATION

The organisation of the ship's company aboard *Venomous* was the same as that for any destroyer during the first half of the twentieth century and remained virtually unaltered from the time of her first commissioning until she was scrapped after the Second World War. Apart from the lack of sails a sailor from Victoria's steam navy would have felt very much at home. The Victorian sailor would, however, have stood back in wonderment at the new technologies of asdic, radio and radar.

A typical warship of the period was organised by functions performed. Deck, communications, navigation, engineering, weapons and supply functions were common to all warships and naval auxiliaries. *Venomous* was no different.

Although the departments and their functions did not change, the manner in which they were organised falls into two distinct phases. The first extended from her first commissioning in 1919 to being placed into reserve in 1929 and the second from being brought back into service in 1939 to being scrapped after the war.

The table shows how the line departments and the divisions within each department are accountable to the commanding officer and the executive officer (an age-old delineation of authority at sea). These departments and subordinate divisions comprised the major functional organisations of a steam-powered warship.

The Second World War brought about a rapid advance and expansion in electronics and weapons technology. Ships such as *Venomous* saw the divisions within the signals and gunnery departments expand to support these new technologies. In the case of the signals department, for example, the introduction of improved radio equipment and radar required specialists to support them.

The removal of the forward bank of torpedoes, additional depth charge capacity and the introduction of the hedgehog brought change to the gunnery department. Despite the loss of two of her 4.7-inch guns there was a requirement for additional men with specialist skills to maintain and operate the new weaponry such as the 3-inch gun and the three 20-mm Oerlikons.

Authority and responsibility descended from the ship's commanding officer to the individual departments and divisions and their officers and chief petty officers through the ship's executive officer ('Jimmy-the-One' or 'Number One' in the RN and XO in the USN). The executive officer, who was responsible to the ship's commanding officer for everything onboard, was also directly responsible for the seaman or deck department. This differs from most modern navies where the seaman or deck department has its own officer as department head reporting to the commanding officer through the XO.

The ship's coxswain (the senior rating onboard), also known as the Bosun, was in the seaman department, and together with the XO, was the kingpin that ensured that the entire ship ran smoothly.

The table also shows that the ship's medical officer (MO) reported to the commanding officer through the XO. In a small ship such as *Venomous*, the MO, when not working medical issues, usually supported the commanding officer with miscellaneous correspondence and provided support to signals by decoding/encoding radio signals. Today's warships have a significantly larger medical staff, and they are treated as a separate division or department with the medical officer in charge and reporting to the commanding officer through the XO.

The following table illustrates the shipboard organisation aboard HMS *Venomous*:

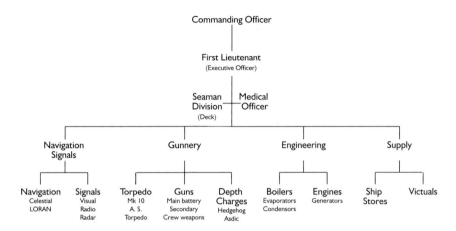

There were four line departments with two or more divisions. A junior line officer or a specialist officer such as an engineering officer was in charge of each department. A commissioned warrant officer, specialising in engineering or gunnery, might also be a department head as was the case for *Venomous*.

The number of men in each department varied with the Seaman and Engineering Departments being two of the largest departments.

Seaman Department

The Coxswain was the chief petty officer and under him were three petty officers, one of whom looked after the upper deck (the fo'c'sle) and another the quarterdeck. The third PO, the chief bosun's mate, was known as the "Chief buffer" and was responsible for routine maintenance of the external and much of the internal ship's structures – chipping and painting comes to the fore in this sailor's mind. The Coxswain had overall responsibility for the department and reported to the first lieutenant, the XO.

The Coxswain took the helm at action stations or when entering or leaving harbour but the Quarter Master, an able seaman, was at the helm on cruising stations (and was in charge of the gangway in harbour). There were two bosun's mates on each watch to act as bridge messengers (communicating when appropriate with their bosun's pipes) and engine telegraph operators. This department would be responsible for providing special sea duty men who would work the ship when departing and entering port – weighing anchor, casting off lines, etc. They would perform replenishment evolutions, such as taking on stores. The latter would usually involve the entire ship's company.

Signals Department

The ship's navigating officer was solely responsible for celestial navigation and for obtaining, maintaining and updating the Admiralty charts used onboard. Navigation had not changed much since the nineteenth century. Celestial fixes and dead reckoning were still the main basis for determining the ship's position. It was only late in the war that radar was used for inshore piloting. *Venomous* came dangerously close to running aground when she arrived in Falmouth during the early hours of 20 October 1943 due to a failure to use her radar for inshore piloting.

In addition to the obvious functions of sending and receiving or transcribing signals, the department was also responsible for the ship's gyrocompass as well as the use and maintenance of the ship's signal flags and signal books. The radio equipment, including the radio aerials, was also the responsibility of this department. The torpedo men were responsible for all electrical maintenance on the ship including the equipment in the signals department – they had the electrical expertise.

LORAN (LOng Range Aid to Navigation) was invented during the war. LORAN "is a terrestrial radio navigation system using low frequency radio transmitters that use multiple transmitters to determine location and/or speed of the receiver." There is no evidence that *Venomous* ever had the ability to receive LORAN signals. By late 1943 her days as an A.S. escort were over and only the frontline escorts and capital ships would have been given that capability.

Signals handled the visual as well as electronic communications for the ship. Visual signals involved operating signal flags and signal lamps. Encoding and decoding those signals was part of the job, and the yeoman of signals would have been responsible to the department head and directly to the commanding officer for the efficient operation of the division. Signals was also responsible for maintaining the equipment. Wireless was available but rarely used on convoy duty for reasons of security and visual signals continued to be important. Transmissions between Ships (TBS) was not introduced into the Royal Navy until 1942. *Venomous* may have been equipped with a TBS-like system during her 1942 refit but if she was why wasn't it used during the *Hecla* sinking? We know she had such a system when she was working as an aircraft target ship in 1944. The communication between *Venomous* and the airfield on the Isle of Man when a Barracuda aircraft crashed in the Irish Sea indicates a fairly robust radio capability.

As for electronic communications, High Frequency (HF) Continuous Wave (CW) radios using Morse code was the mainstay for the Fleet at the beginning of the war. The telegraphists were also responsible for the sending and receiving of signals. This required decoding and encoding encrypted signals. Signals was also responsible for ensuring the safekeeping of classified materials. In addition to the coding work, the ship's radio telegraphists were responsible for the radios' operation, maintenance and minor repair. Later in the war radio mechanics were trained to repair the equipment, freeing the telegraphists to concentrate on signal matters. This may not have been the case on *Venomous* since her usefulness as a frontline A.S. destroyer was over by mid 1943. More modern destroyers would have had the specialist onboard.

Gunnery Department

Maintenance of the torpedoes was the responsibility of a specialist officer, usually a warrant officer such as Mr. F.A. Dunn, the Gunner (T) who served onboard *Venomous* in 1921. He was also responsible for the maintenance of the ship's guns (main and secondary batteries) and the ship's small arms (revolvers, rifles, automatic weapons and ammunition, including illumination devices such as star shells). The Ordinance Artificers reported to him. The department had three divisions: torpedo, guns and depth charges. A chief or a senior petty officer specialising in each weapon system would probably lead each division – a chief torpedo man would have been the senior rating for the department. After all, *Venomous*' primary weapon was still the torpedo.

The torpedo division's ratings were responsible for the operation and the maintenance of the torpedo mounts and the three tubes on each mount. They were responsible for the loading, maintenance and firing of the torpedoes. They would also be responsible for the recovery of practice torpedoes used in exercises. The torpedo men were also responsible for all the low power electrical systems on board the ship (such as the Asdic). "There were half-hearted attempts to split the branch [rate] into torpedo men proper and electricians, but most men continued to learn both aspects of the job and the navy failed to set up a proper integrated electrical branch [rate] during the war."

During the war years, the emphasis on ship-killing torpedoes was reduced in favour of a more specific combat capability, which was dependent on the role the particular destroyer played. *Venomous* became a short-range anti-submarine escort (S.R.E.). Her after torpedo tube mount (three tubes) had been replaced in 1940 by a high-angle (H.A.) 3-inch quick firing gun to improve her A.A. defence and short-range surface-to-surface capability. Her forward torpedo mount and its upper torpedo tube accommodated the Mk. 10 Anti-Submarine Torpedo with a 2,000-pound warhead.

The gunnery division ratings were responsible for *Venomous*' main battery of four 4.7-inch guns and the two single barrel pom-pom guns as well as the personal weapons in the ship's armoury – rifles, pistols, grenades and ammunition. We saw that by Dunkirk, *Venomous* had acquired Lewis and Bren Guns for close in action and these would have been the responsibility of the gunnery division too.

A captain of the gun was in charge of each 4.7-gun and its crew of seven consisting of a gun layer (elevation), gun trainer (direction), sight setter (who set the range), a loader, breech worker, and two ratings to handle the cordite and the shell. A mop on the end of a pole dipped in a 'bucket' of water was used to clean and cool the barrel after firing. AB Sydney Compston recalled that Nick Carter (an old WW1 veteran) backed into and sat down in the 'bucket' whilst engaged in his continuous search of the skies for aircraft and was badly scalded and discharged as medically unfit shortly afterwards. The gunners were responsible for the maintenance and operations of the guns and the handling and storage of the ammunition, including the ship's magazines but not for firing.

The Gunnery Officer, a commissioned officer, was responsible for operational control of the main guns assisted by a CPO. Their action station was the Director, a rotating observation and control unit above and at the rear of the bridge, which was equipped with special binoculars, which automatically transmitted the direction of the target to the Transmission Station (TS) beneath the bridge. Data transmission was used to notify the guns of the type of shell to be used and to give the range to the TS. At the TS a PO assisted by several ratings entered the settings into a type of mechanical computer to determine the elevation and this was automatically transmitted to the gun layers and gun trainers at the four 4.7-inch main guns. When the guns were loaded and ready for firing, the interceptor closed and lights appeared on at the Director for each of the four guns. When all four lights showed the Gunnery Officer fired the guns as a broadside. The gun captain could only fire the guns when there was a breakdown in data transmission from the Director or the TS.

The depth charge division was responsible for the operation and maintenance of the ship's two depth charge throwers and the single depth charge rail that was originally fitted on *Venomous*. Under the direction of the Gunner (T) and his senior petty officer, the ratings of the division were also responsible for the handling and operation of the depth charge throwers in combat, including the depth charge magazine. As with the gunners, the torpedo men were augmented by the able and ordinary seamen from the seaman department.

The chart shows the expansion in the division as new weapons were introduced on *Venomous*. The division was responsible for the operation of the Hedgehog mortar and its projectiles and the maintenance of the system (including its electrical components) and its associated magazine (part of the forward magazine for the 4.7-inch guns). It was also responsible for the two 20-mm Oerlikon guns, which were added to complement the two 2-pounder pom-pom guns. Later, two additional 20-mm Oerlikons would replace both pom-pom guns.

Engineering Department

The engineering department was a large department consisting of two divisions. One division was responsible for the boilers and the other for the engines. In peacetime a warrant officer usually headed the engine room department but in wartime a chief engineer in the merchant marine such as Lt (E) William R. Forster RNR who led the department during the last year of *Venomous'* service might be in charge. The boiler division was the responsibility of a chief petty officer stoker and fourteen stokers and in charge of the engine division was a Chief ERA (Engine Room Artificer), a chief petty officer, with a team of six ERA under him. The ERAs were responsible for the operation of the ship's turbine engines (also the ship's boat engines) and electric generators. The stokers were responsible for the operation and maintenance of the ship's oil burners, boilers, condensers, evaporators and the spaces of the three boiler rooms. On average each boiler needed cleaning every 720 hours and as their condition deteriorated the hours between cleaning was markedly reduced, putting a great strain on the engine room department.

The stokers were also responsible for the fuel oil and fuel tanks, including refuelling in port and at sea, an essential task for an elderly ship with a high fuel consumption. *Venomous* would have not had the range to escort Arctic convoys had she not been able to refuel at sea. Seamen from the seaman department supported refuelling operations.

Before the war the engine department also had enginemen and shipwrights. Shipwrights repaired every part of the ship from the anchor windlass to the steam pipes and all wooden fittings. During the war years, those skills were in high demand, and ships such as *Venomous* did not have the skilled artificers, which could affect more complicated repairs.

Supply Department

The next department was supply. On a ship such as *Venomous*, this department consisted of two divisions, one responsible for the ordering, inventorying, storing and dispersing of the ship's stores, whilst the second was responsible for the personal needs of the ship's company, such as food, pay, beer, wine and spirits. The "tanky" dispensed fresh food, a position of some importance in the eyes of the ship's crew. This division included the ship's cook and officer steward. There would be one petty officer for the officers, and a petty officer and leading hand for the rest of the ship. Each mess had a daily duty cook, which was rotated among the members of the mess. A civilian employee ran the NAAFI canteen; a small cubicle, which stocked biscuits, chocolates, cigarettes, etc. came under this department.

Notes

1   In the US Navy, a ship is organised by department with divisions within each department. I have used the US Navy's terminology to explain how *Venomous* was functionally organised.

2   The breakdown of the Seaman Department comes from Mr. Peter Smith, who had obtained the listing of a former crewmember of one of the V&W Flotilla Leaders, HMS *Faulknor* with additional information provided by former AB Sydney Compston.

3   For more information on LORAN go to http://en.wikipedia.org/wiki/LORAN#History

4   Lavery Brian, *Churchill's Navy: The Ships, Men and Organisation 1939-1945*, Conway London, 2006, p. 143.

5   The last torpedo attack by Royal Navy destroyers occurred during the night of 15-16 May 1944, when HMS *Saumarez, Venus, Verulam, Vigilant,* and *Virago* executed a classic attack against the Japanese cruiser, IJN *Haguro. See Sink the* Haguro: *the last destroyer action of the Second World War;* by John Hinton. Seeley Service, London, 1979.

APPENDIX SIX – LIFE ABOARD HMS *VENOMOUS*

Officers and ratings lived quite separate lives, divided by rank and class as well as by the conditions under which they lived in the cramped conditions on a V & W.

Accommodation for the officers was in the cabin flat at the stern below the quarterdeck but above the waterline, with access through a round bolt-down hatch set in a larger square hatch which was only opened when in harbour. The sketch drawn by Stephen Barney, a midshipman and sub lieutenant on *Venomous* in 1943, shows the layout of the cabins and wardroom. A ladder descended to a short corridor which had the wardroom at the stern and the captain's day cabin for'ard with smaller cabins for the officers on either side. There was a shared washroom with hand basin and toilet. The wardroom pantry was connected to the wardroom by a serving hatch and across the corridor from the pantry was the office for the ship's writer. The wardroom had a bolted down table on the port side with bench seating on the starboard side. There was a small electric fire and a drinks cabinet, the cost of which was shared by the members of the wardroom. The officers had their own cook and an officers' steward to serve in the wardroom.

The officers had bunk beds with cupboards for stowage of personal possessions but no washing or bathing facilities. Officers were entitled to a personal servant, a seaman who volunteered for this additional duty and received a small supplementary payment. He would bring his officer hot water for shaving and, on rare occasions, fill a galvanised metal bath. The midshipman would have to sling his hammock in the corridor and if he was lucky be allowed to store his belongings in the cabin of a fellow officer. There was also a small cabin forward of the searchlight platform which ran athwartship and was shared by two officers

STERN

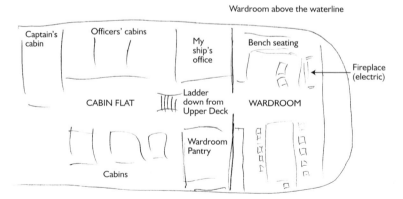

Sketch of officers' accommodation and wardroom at stern of HMS *Venomous*.
Drawn by former Midshipman Stephen Barney RNVR.

who had to learn to sleep whilst alternatively standing on their feet and their head as the ship rolled. The commanding officer's day cabin was larger and had its own wash basin and desk and could be used for private meetings with his officers. The CO also had a sea cabin beneath the bridge where he could be on call at a moment's notice when on active duty.

In the early years of the war the COs were always regular navy, usually a Lt Cdr or a Cdr, but the junior officers on the V & Ws were mostly RNVR and mainly drawn from the professional classes who had been to public school and university. Warrant officers, promoted from the ranks, often filled the more technically demanding positions. RNR officers with long service in the merchant marine were also recruited but eventually the Admiralty ceased to use this source as "more could not be taken without weakening the Merchant Navy unacceptably".[1] In the latter years of the war RNVR officers came from all walks of life and were eventually given the opportunity to command their own ships and served with distinction.

The conditions under which the officers lived at the stern of the ship were very different from those endured by the ratings in the fo'c'sle and on the deck below.

• • • •

The Royal Navy based its ships on one of the three manning ports: Chatham on the Medway near London which was known as "Chats", Portsmouth ("Pompey") and Devonport ("Guz"), a district of Plymouth. Each port had a naval base, a barracks and a dockyard. HMS *Venomous* was a Devonport ship during World War II and many of the ratings moved their families there only to find that after 1940 she rarely visited her "home port". The ratings despatched from Devonport to Rosyth when *Venomous* was brought out of reserve in July 1939 were nearly all regular RN but that soon changed.

Enlisted men were sent to HMS *Drake,* the barracks at Devonport, for training in the strange ways of the navy before being posted to their ship. They were allocated an official number and retained it until leaving the service. Its initial letter (D, C and P) indicated the home port and was followed by letters designating the branch (J for seaman, S for stoker, etc.) and finally a serial number. They were issued with the "square rigged" sailor's uniform of a woollen jumper (replaced in summer with a short-sleeved white tunic shirt) and a three striped square collar, the traditional slim-cut bellbottomed trousers without pocket, a belt with a pouch for carrying money and the distinctive round flat sailor's hat which in peacetime bore the name of the ship but for security reasons only "HMS" in wartime. The food was far better than at home where strict rationing was in place but they found it difficult to adjust to sleeping in a hammock, naval dress and petty regulations. Despite this period of adjustment conditions aboard *Venomous* whilst at sea must have come as a shock.

Each department had its own mess rooms but the petty officers messed together separate from the ratings for whom they were responsible. The main mess for the Seaman Department was beneath the raised foredeck and extended up to the chain locker in the bow with lockers lining both bulkheads and with four or more wooden tables bolted to the deck in front of each line of lockers. Portholes above the lockers provided light but were often covered whilst at sea. Each locker had a padded hinged lid which opened upwards and was large enough to take a kitbag. There was just room for a man to squeeze between the lockers and the tables and sit on the padded top of his locker to eat at the mess room table.

The ratings were divided into three messes with up to thirty to a mess with a leading seaman in charge of each mess. Ordinary Seamen (OD) and Able-bodied Seamen (AB) had no distinguishing marks but a Leading Seaman (LS) had an anchor on his sleeve. After three years' service a seaman received one stripe, a second stripe after seven years and a third after twelve. A seaman's department was indicated by an appropriate symbol, e.g. a gun for a gunner, a torpedo for a torpedo man. Each mess occupied a separate area of the fo'c'sle.

Hugh McGeeney described the catering arrangements aboard *Venomous:*

> Canteen messing operated in the ratings' messes i.e. each mess received a ration (by weight) of basic foods, meat, flour and vegetables according to the number victualled. The mess cook's duty was to present the food to the galley ready to be cooked (properly tallied of course in mess dishes and pots). Any other food was bought by each mess caterer from the victualling allowance [of 1/9d per day per man] supplemented from the pocket of mess members where necessary. The mess caterer planned the meals using basic rations and his own purchases together with the mess cook's skill in preparing a meal for the galley to cook."

Collister described:

> how the two mess cooks "were also responsible for dishing out the food and cleaning the mess." By 1939 the traditional square wooden plates (the origin of "a square meal") had been replaced by cheap white crockery and the mess tables had a raised lip to help prevent breakages.

The men slept in hammocks slung from hooks in the stanchions supporting the main deck, hanging from bow to stern, above the mess table where others might be eating. Each man had a mattress and one blanket. Nobody undressed and they used their lifebelts as pillows. The height of the mess was about seven foot and a tall seaman would have to duck to avoid the swaying hammocks above his head. John Garforth, an AB on HMS *Valorous*, a sister ship, described the conditions:

> "The mess deck was very small with tables down each side with lockers to sit it on with water draining all the time from the deck heads into the bilges. When the ship rolled a deluge of water rushed across the mess deck, sometimes taking the 'gash bucket' with it, the contents having spilled, slopping back and forth each time the ship rolled.
>
> The mess deck was just like a bathroom with condensation dripping from the 'deck head' all the time. We had to sleep with oilskins over our hammocks and with the hammocks being so close together (we were only allowed eighteen inches for each hammock) they were always touching each other

when they were slung, and when anybody stirred water on the oilskins just seeped into the hammock and they were constantly wet as there wasn't much chance of drying them in winter."

Hugh McGeeney described how:

"Lash up and stow' was the cry heard early in the morning from the Duty Petty Officer charged with the task of getting everybody up. The hammock was secured by seven lashings or turns of a rope to keep the mattress, blanket and pillow inside and the hole was then stored vertically in special hammock stowages."

Heavy watertight hatches sealed the mess from the open area at the break of the fo'c'sle. This open area was some twenty feet in length and had three toilets on the port side and four washbasins on the starboard side, all fed with seawater (hot fresh water might occasionally be obtained from a stoker in the engine room). AB "Freddo" Thomas described the procedure:

"There were no baths or showers available for lower-deck ratings and only four washbasins at the break of the forecastle on the upper deck, exposed to the cold wind. The usual practice was to fill a bucket with water and pour it over the head and body. Not too bad if the water was warm and fresh, but often it was not. If fresh water was in short supply and needed by the ship's boilers and machinery, the only solution was to tie a bucket to a rope and drop it over the side, then haul it up filled with cold sea water – a forbidden practice – which was very dangerous if the ship was moving at more than a few knots."

Some men slung their hammocks here, disregarding the green water slopping around below and the men washing or using the 'heads'. The PO Cook was ever present in his galley which was across the ship at the break of the fo'c'sle between the washbasins and the heads. Opposite the galley was a raised hatch (to minimise water ingress) with a ladder to the petty officers' mess on the deck below.

The petty officers (PO) and chief petty officers (CPO) were "fore and aft rigged" with jacket and peaked hat like an officer. The PO had crossed anchors on their sleeves and the CPO three brass buttons low down their sleeves instead of the crossed anchors. The Chief and PO's Mess with the Coxwain, the senior rating as its President, was on the port side and the Engine Room Mess, with the Chief ERA as its President, was on the starboard side. The ERA were also fore and aft rigged like the POs. Each had a separate hatch and ladder for access from the break of the fo'c'sle. As a result of being lower and more central there was less movement and they were more private. Two of the ratings were required to act as servants to the Petty Officer's Mess, preparing their food for the galley and keeping the mess tidy. Hugh McGeeney, who joined *Venomous* at Rosyth in July 1939, drew the layout of these two messes for the senior ratings.

Also on the lower deck but further forward was the mess of the communications ratings on the starboard side (WT operators, signalmen, Asdic and RDF operators – the "headache men" – and the coders) and that of the torpedo men and depth charge crew on the port. The Stokers mess was also on this deck. Access

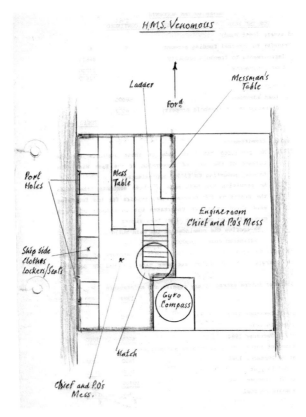

Plan of Petty Officers' Mess on lower deck of HMS *Venomous*.
Drawn by CPO Hugh MacGeeney RN. Courtesy of his daughter, Monica Budden.

to these three messes was from ladders in the fo'c'sle. New weapons requiring ratings with special skills meant there were not always enough lockers or hammocks to go round in these messes and men would sleep on the lockers.

"Freddo" Thomas, the RDF operator, described the cramped conditions in the communications ratings mess:

> "*Venomous* was an old ship and when the war began did not have anti-aircraft guns, R.D.F. and other modern weapons. Consequently, her crew, including officers, numbered about 120. During the first year of the war modernisation slowly progressed and her crew began to increase in numbers but there was no commensurate increase in the number of hammock spaces on the lower deck to accommodate the extra men. I, for one, had to wait six months before a hammock sling became available. Meanwhile, I had to sleep on the lockers on the seaward side of the mess-table, lashed to the bars of the boot-rack above, or I should have rolled off the lockers and under the mess-table! Somehow, I accustomed myself to this, but I could never good-humouredly tolerate being woken up by a mess-mate who needed to obtain a duffel coat or gloves from the locker directly beneath me."

The engine room was mid-ships and the ship's magazine, the store for the ship's munitions, was towards the stern extending as far as the tiller flat. The next deck down contained the drive shaft and other engine room spaces.

• • • •

The daily routine at sea was determined by the watch keeping system. Ratings were assigned to the port (red) or starboard (green) watch and the watches changed every four hours except for the two "dog watches" of two hours between 1600 and 2000:

> First Watch: 8pm to midnight (2000 to 0000)
> Middle Watch: Midnight to 4am (0000 to 0400)
> Morning Watch: 4am to 8am (0400 to 0800)
> Forenoon Watch: 8am to noon (0800 to 1200)
> Afternoon Watch: Noon to 4pm (1200 to 1600)
> First Dog Watch: 4pm to 6pm (1600 to 1800)
> Last Dog Watch: 6pm to 8pm (1800 to 2000)

The short two hour dog watches meant watches advanced every day making it impossible to develop a regular pattern of sleep. Ratings off duty during the first watch from 2000 to 0000 would try to sleep and when they next came off watch at 0400 the mess cooks would prepare a meal. This left little time for sleep before going on watch at 0800. Even this routine of advancing alternating four hour watches was disrupted by the call to action stations when every officer and man on the ship had to go to his action station. The call to action stations was traditionally done by the Bosun's mate with his "pipe" or call but Tannoy was also used. Sydney Compston recalled that in 1940 "they used to play 'Begin the Beguine' by the Joe Loss Orchestra every time they left harbour over the system."

Up spirits

All hands were entitled to a daily tot of rum and water known as "grog", a tradition going back to the time of Admiral Vernon. The Bosun's mate called "Up Spirits" on his pipe at 11 am. Collister described the time-honoured tradition:

> "After the age of 21 a rating (but not an officer) could if he so wished at noon each day request to 'draw his tot' [of Jamaica rum]. If he did not wish to draw his tot he could draw 3d a day in lieu. He was not allowed to draw it neat [Admiral Vernon, known as 'Grogram', decreed in 1740 that the 100% neat spirit was to be diluted 2:1 hence 'grog']. Senior ratings, Pos and above, were allowed 'neats', one gill of raw rum, but no one was allowed to 'bottle his tot'!"

"Freddo" Thomas was amused that

> "One or two of the older 'salts' having enjoyed their neat tots of rum before a meal seemed to spear a piece of meat, raise it to their cheeks first, before finding their mouths with difficulty. The tales they told about lurid shore-leave incidents, real or imagined, were extremely entertaining."

The members of a mess might pool part of their daily tot to give a seaman "sippers" on his birthday but sometimes the daily tot could have fatal consequences as Sydney Compston recalled: "poor Lodwick, a WW1 veteran who had his Christmas dinner and his tot, went to sleep and never woke up."

Leaf tobacco

Another tradition which "Freddo" Thomas found hard to bear was the smoking of leaf tobacco:

> "One thing that was hard for me to endure on the mess-deck was the smoking of leaf-tobacco. An old custom allowed seamen to buy leaf-tobacco on board. A method of converting it to a smokeable form was to roll it into 'pricks'. The leaves were rolled into sausage-like shapes, sprinkled with neat rum and bound up tightly with thick string. One end of the string was then tied to one of the hammock bars and the other end to another bar, so that it hung loosely two or three feet from the deck. The seaman then squeezed the 'sausage' by sitting on it with a leg either side and raising and lowering himself. The finished product, after drying, could then be flaked into a smoking pipe a number of times."

White Duster

When in harbour the "bunting tosser" (a signals rating) would raise the White Ensign (the white duster) at 0800 every morning and lower it at 1800 and any officer or rating on deck at the time would be required to stand at attention facing the flag.

Captain's Rounds

Captain's rounds was usually carried out on a Thursday or Friday morning and involved a cleanliness inspection of a part of the ship below decks and would be attended by the officers responsible for the department.

Divisions

Divisions was a routine muster of all ratings by department on the quarterdeck on Sunday mornings. The Captain would inspect the muster and there would then be a brief church service after which the Captain might address the ship's company.

Captain's Defaulters

Any offences against good order and discipline as laid down in King's Regulations (KR) and Admiralty Instructions (AI) were dealt with at "Captain's Defaulters" when the Bosun would present those enlisted men with discipline problems (defaulters) to the Executive Officer and the CO on the quarterdeck. A typical offence would be failure to report back aboard by the due time or overstaying leave. The culprit would be marched to the Captain's table, "Off Caps", the charge would be read, he would be asked if he had anything to say in his defence, the opinion of his divisional officer would be sought and he would then be sentenced, typically to loss of two days' liberty or the loss of a good conduct stripe.

Payday

This would only be held when required, possibly monthly or even less frequently, usually when going into harbour. The crew were assembled on the quarterdeck by divisions in front of the paymaster table. They would be called forward in order of rank, gave their rank and number, "Off Caps", the cap would be placed upside down on the table and the pay due placed in it which would then be picked up, the pay removed and the cap donned before retiring. A rating whose papers had been lost might be given a "North Easter" (not entitled). An AB was paid seven shillings a week, some of which he spent at sea on biscuits, soap and tinned food in the NAAFI.

Shore Leave

The usual watch system was discontinued when the ship was in harbour and the two watches would alternate between day duty and leave ashore. Dungarees were usually worn when working aboard ship but when given leave ashore they dressed up smartly in the traditional square rigged sailor's uniform.

When the ship was in dockyard hands for a refit the crew returned to barracks in their home port and were sent on longer leave before being posted to a new ship.

Service Certificates and "flimsies"

The officer responsible for the work and welfare of men in his division records their performance on their service certificates which are kept on the ship and are far more detailed than the service records for most officers which were held at the Admiralty. The only records kept on ship for officers were the "flimsies" (Form S 206) completed by the CO when an officer left or when there was a change of CO. The CO was required to provide the officer with a copy before forwarding to the Admiralty. Details of how to obtain service records are given in appendices three and four.

• • • •

This account is based on what I have been told by the officers and men who served on *Venomous* or one of its sister ships. I would like to acknowledge the invaluable contributions made by John Appleby, the Secretary of the V & W Association, and former AB Harry Haddon, over the course of several lengthy phone conversations and the account of life on the lower deck written by "Freddo" Thomas, the RDF operator.[2]

Notes

1 Roskill *War at Sea*, 1960.

2 For more about life on the lower deck of a destroyer during World War II see: *Very Ordinary Seaman;* by J P W Mallalieu (Victor Gollancz, 1944).

APPENDIX SEVEN – TS *VENOMOUS*

HMS *Venomous* was finally broken up for scrap at Charlestown on the Firth of Forth in 1948 but the name of *Venomous* has been kept alive by the Sea Cadet Unit in Loughborough, TS *Venomous*, which received its commissioning pennant that year.

Amongst the proudest possessions of the Unit is the ship's crest of HMS *Venomous* and the bronze plaque presented to HMS *Venomous* to commemorate her adoption by the town of Loughborough during Warship Week in February 1942.

For many years until 1980 the Unit enjoyed commodious accommodation by the side of the Grand Union Canal in Nottingham Road, Loughborough, establishing a sound reputation in many fields. Malcolm Whiteside and Robert Sibbald became Sea Cadets Corps National Boxing Champions and a cadet of that era is now Vice-Admiral Sir David Dobson (retired). The Commanding Officer was Lt Cdr (SCC) Maurice Hewitt RNR, a taciturn man, who had experienced the same hostile waters as *Venomous* during his service in the escort carrier *Trumpeter*.

From 1980 until 1984 the Cadets experienced the Spartan conditions of a converted cricket pavilion on their new site at Beeches Road, Loughborough, but the following year a new sectional concrete building was completed, with regular improvement undertaken thereafter.

In 1986, under their Commanding Officer Lt (SCC) Malcolm Turner RNR, the Unit distinguished itself with the award of a Burgee and fifth place in the National Pulling Competition. Lt (SCC) Iain Crighton RNR assumed command in early 1987, and both in that year and in 1988 a Pennant award was earned, together with further national representation in swimming and pulling (fourth place).

Bob Moore joined the Sea Cadet Unit in Loughborough in 1985 and in 1990 became Officer in Charge. After promotion to Lieutenant he was confirmed as Commanding Officer in 1992. The normal period of service for a CO of a Sea Cadet Unit is five years but by the time Lt Cdr (SCC) R.J. Moore RNR stood down in 2003 he had served for thirteen years. Bob became Assistant District Officer for Northants and Leicestershire Sea Cadets and remained in that post until his death at the tragically early age of 63 in 2007. He went to immense lengths to track down the surviving officers and crew of HMS *Venomous* and his interviews with them formed the basis of the first edition of this book when it was published in 1990.

In October 1987 the Unit was honoured to host a reunion of former officers and men of HMS *Venomous* during which their guests attended a reception given by the Mayor of Charnwood and a memorable Reunion Dinner. Those present were: Captain J.R. Coleman RD RNR, Cdr. D.A.R. Duff DSC RN, Lt. Cdr. A.G. Prideaux RNVR, Lt. Cdr. H.H. McGeeney DSM, RN, Lt. Cdr. M. Cashman RN, Lt. Cdr. S.J. Barney RD RNR, Lt. P. Kershaw RNVR, Lt. D.W. Caudle RNR, Lt. J.N. Martin RNVR, Mr. H. Knapton DSM, Mr. A.G. Upton, Mr. F.W.A. Notton, Mr. J. Irlam and Mr. H. Worsnip. A further honoured guest was Mr. John Esslemont, who travelled from his home in Bethune, Northern France, to meet for the first time the men who had rescued him from Calais in May 1940.

The HMS *Hecla*, HMS *Venomous* and HMS *Marne* Association held a reunion and service at Stratford in 1992 on the fiftieth anniversary of the sinking of

HMS *Hecla* which Bob Moore and twenty sea cadets from TS *Venomous* attended. The old sailors marched with the sea cadets to the war memorial. In 2004 the Association presented TS *Venomous* with the money to purchase a new standard.

In addition to perpetuating the memory of HMS *Venomous* the Unit has formed a strong affiliation with the Hunt Class minesweeper *Quorn,* the third ship in the Royal Navy to bear the name of the Quorn Hunt, which was launched in 1988.

For twenty years the annual Nelson Day Dinner hosted by the officers and cadets of TS *Venomous* has brought together former cadets, many of now serving in the Royal Navy, with distinguished guests to keep alive the spirit of Nelson's navy. Guests include Captain John Rodgaard USN, co-author of the new edition of this book, George Male, one of the survivors of HMS *Hecla,* and Captain John Kingwell Royal Navy, the CO of HMS *Albion*. Whilst reading history at Loughborough University in the 1980s John Kingwell served as seamanship officer, midshipman and sub lieutenant at TS *Venomous,* returning to his ship during the summer vacation. TS *Venomous* is one of very few SCC units to have had a regular Royal Navy officer on its books and it is particularly appropriate that Captain John Kingwell Royal Navy should have written the introduction to the new edition of this book.

In 1998 Loughborough achieved the Stephenson's Trophy for Best Unit in the Eastern Area, but just missed out on the Canada Trophy for Best Unit in the United Kingdom. On the 24th July 2001, His Royal Highness the Duke of York opened the new Boat shed.

Bob Moore's successor as CO of TS *Venomous* was Sub Lt (SCC) Kay Adey RNR who is still in post today. In 2009 the Loughborough Sea Cadet Unit has 34 fully enrolled cadets over twelve years of age, half of which are girls, plus a junior branch.

The prospects for future years are bright.

APPENDIX EIGHT – THE SIXTY-NINE V & Ws

ADMIRALTY 'V' CLASS, LEADER – 5 SHIPS

Name	Builder	Laid down	Launched	Completed
Valentine	Cammell Laird	7 Aug 1916	24 Mar 1917	27 Jun 1917
Valhalla (Ex *Montrose*)	Cammell Laird	8 Aug 1916	22 May 1917	31 Jul 1917
Valkyrie	William Denny	23 May 1916	13 Mar 1917	16 Jun 1917
Valorous (Ex *Malcolm*)	William Denny	25 May 1916	8 May 1917	21 Aug 1917
Vampire (Ex *Wallace*)	J. S. White	10 Oct 1916	21 May 1917	22 Sep 1917

ADMIRALTY 'V' CLASS - 24 SHIPS

Name	Builder	Laid down	Launched	Completed
Vimy (Ex *Vancouver*)	Beardmore	15 Mar 1917	28 Dec 1917	9 Mar 1918
Vanessa	Beardmore	16 May 1917	16 Mar 1918	27 Apr 1918
Vanity	Beardmore	28 Jul 1917	3 May 1918	30 Aug 1918
Vanoc	John Brown	20 Sep 1916	14 Jun 1917	15 Aug 1917
Vanquisher	John Brown	27 Sep 1916	18 Aug 1917	2 Oct 1917
Vectis	J.S. White	7 Dec 1916	4 Sep 1917	5 Dec 1917
Vega	Doxford	11 Dec 1916	1 Sep 1917	14 Dec 1917
Vehement	William Denny	25 Sep 1916	6 Jul 1917	16 Oct 1917
Velox	Doxford	Jan 1917	17 Nov 1917	1 Apr 1918
Vendetta	Fairfield	Nov 1916	3 Sep 1917	17 Oct 1917
Venetia	Fairfield	2 Feb 1917	29 Oct 1917	19 Dec 1917
Venturous	William Denny	9 Oct 1916	21 Sep 1917	29 Nov 1917
Verdun	Hawthorn Leslie	13 Jan 1917	21 Aug 1917	3 Nov 1917
Versatile	Hawthorn Leslie	31 Jan 1917	21 Aug 1917	3 Nov 1917
Verulam	Hawthorn Leslie	8 Feb 1917	3 Oct 1917	12 Dec 1917
Vesper	Alex. Stephen	7 Dec 1916	15 Dec 1917	20 Feb 1918
Vidette	Alex. Stephen	1 Feb 1917	18 Feb 1918	27 Apr 1918
Vimiera	Swan Hunter	Oct 1916	22 Jun 1917	19 Sep 1917
Violent	Swan Hunter	Nov 1916	1 Sep 1917	Nov 1917
Vittoria	Swan Hunter	Feb 1917	29 Oct 1917	May 1918
Vivacious	Yarrow	Jul 1916	13 Nov 1917	29 Dec 1917
Vivien	Yarrow	Jul 1916	16 Feb 1918	28 May 1918
Vortigern	J. S. White	17 Jan 1917	18 Oct 1918	25 Jan 1918
Verulam	Hawthorn Leslie	8 Feb 1917	3 Oct 1917	12 Dec 1917

Conversion	Fate
WAIR	Bombed and abandoned in the Scheldt Estuary on 15 May 1940. Salvaged and scrapped in 1953.
Not converted	Sold for disposal 17 Dec 1931 and scrapped in 1932.
Not converted	Handed over 24 Aug 1936 and scrapped.
WAIR	Scrapped 1947-8
Not converted	Transferred to the Royal Australian Navy in 1933. Bombed and sunk by Japanese aircraft Bay of Bengal 9 Apr 1942.

Conversion	Fate
	Originally named *Vancover*. The name then given to the Royal Canadian Navy in 1928. Sold for disposal in 1947.
Long Range Escort	Sold for disposal in 1947.
WAIR	Sold for disposal in 1947.
Long Range Escort	Sold for disposal 1945 and wrecked off Penryn en route to the breakers in 1946 – salvaged and scrapped.
Long Range Escort	Sold for disposal 1947.
Not converted	Sold for disposal 1936.
WAIR	Sold for disposal 1947.
Not converted	Mined in North Sea 1 Aug 1918 and sank the next day.
Long Range Escort	Sold for disposal 1947.
Not converted	Transferred to Royal Australian Navy – scuttled off Sydney 2 Jul 1948.
Not converted	Mined 19 Oct 1940 and sank in the Thames Estuary.
Not converted	Handed over for disposal in 1936.
WAIR	Sold for disposal 1946.
Long Range Escort	Sold for disposal 1946.
Not converted	Mined and sunk off Seiskari Island in Gulf of Finland 3/4 Sep 1919.
Long Range Escort	Sold for disposal 1947.
Long Range Escort	Sold for disposal 1947.
WAIR	Mined and sunk 9 January 1942 off the Nore, Thames Estuary.
Not converted	Handed over for disposal 8 Mar 1937.
Not converted	Torpedoed and sunk by the Bolshevik submarine *Pantera* in Gulf of Finland 1 Sep 1919.
Short Range Escort	Sold for disposal 1947.
WAIR	Sold for disposal 1947.
Not converted	Torpedoed by E-Boat 15 Mar 1942 off Cromer, Norfolk 1942.
Not converted	Mined and sunk off Seiskari Island in Gulf of Finland 3/4 Sep 1919

ADMIRALTY 'W' CLASS – 19 SHIPS

Name	Builder	Laid down	Launched	Completed
Voyager	Alex. Stephen	17 May 1917	8 May 1918	24 Jun 1918
Wakeful	Beardmore	17 Jan 1917	6 Oct 1917	30 Nov 1917
Walker	William Denny	26 Mar 1917	29 Nov 1917	2 Feb 1918
Walpole	Doxford	May 1917	12 Feb 1918	7 Aug 1918
Walrus	Fairfield	Feb 1917	27 Dec 1917	8 Mar 1918
Warwick	Hawthorn Leslie	10 Mar 1917	28 Dec 1917	8 Mar 1918
Watchman	Beardmore	17 Jan 1917	2 Nov 1917	26 Jan 1918
Waterhen	Palmers	Jul 1917	26 Mar 1918	17 Apr 1918
Wessex	Hawthorn Leslie	23 May 1917	12 Mar 1918	11 May 1918
Westcott	William Denny	30 Mar 1917	14 Feb 1918	12 Mar 1918
Westminster	Scotts	Apr 1917	25 Feb 1918	18 Apr 1918
Whirlwind	Swan Hunter	May 1917	15 Dec 1917	15 Mar 1918
Whitley	Doxford	Jun 1917	13 Apr 1918	14 Oct 1918
Winchelsea	J. S. White	25 May 1917	15 Dec 1918	15 Mar 1918
Winchester	J. S. White	12 Jun 1917	1 Feb 1918	29 Apr 1918
Windsor	Scotts	Apr 1917	21 Jun 1918	28 Aug 1918
Wolfhound	Fairfield	Apr 1917	14 Mar 1918	27 Apr 1918
Wrestler	Swan Hunter	Apr 1917	25 Feb 1918	15 May 1918
Wryneck	Palmer	Apr 1917	13 May 1918	11 Nov 1918

THORNYCROFT 'V & W' CLASS – 4 SHIPS

Name	Builder	Laid down	Launched	Completed
Viceroy	Thornycroft	15 Dec 1916	17 Nov 1917	5 Feb 1918
Viscount	Thornycroft	20 Dec 1916	29 Dec 1917	25 Mar 1918
Wolsey	Thornycroft	28 Mar 1917	16 Mar 1918	1 May 1918
Woolston	Thornycroft	25 Apr 1917	27 Apr 1918	28 Jun 1918

THORNYCROFT MODIFIED 'W' CLASS – 2 SHIPS

Name	Builder	Laid Down	Launched	Completed
Wishart	Thornycroft	18 May 1918	18 Jul 1919	Jun 1920
Witch	Thornycroft	13 Jun 1918	11 Nov 1919	Mar 1924

Conversion	Fate
Not converted	Transferred to Royal Australian Navy. Bombed by Japanese aircraft and beached 1942.
Not converted	Sold for disposal 1946.
Long Range Escort	Sold for disposal 1946.
Short Range Escort	Mined North Sea 6 Jan 1945 and written off as a constructive loss. Sold for disposal Feb 1945.
Not converted	Stranded in Filey Bay 12 Feb 1938 and written off as a loss. Sold for disposal 1938.
Long Range Escort	Torpedoed and sunk by U-413 off Trevose Head 20 Feb 1944.
Long Range Escort	Sold for disposal 1945.
Not converted	Transferred to the Royal Australian Navy in 1933 Bombed and sunk by the Luftwaffe & Regina Aeronautica off Libya 30 Jun 1941.
Not converted	Sunk by Luftwaffe off Calais 24 May 1940.
Short Range Escort	First use of Hedgehog to register a kill – *U-581* on 2 Feb 1942. Sold for disposal 1942.
WAIR	Sold for disposal 1947.
Not converted	Torpedoed and sunk by *U-34* SW of Ireland 5 Jul 1940.
WAIR	Bombed by Luftwaffe and beached off Oostend, Belgium 19 May 1940.
Long Range Escort	Sold for disposal 1945.
WAIR	Sold for disposal 1946.
Short Range Escort	Sold for disposal 1947.
WAIR	Sold for disposal 1948.
Long Range Escort	Mined off Juno Beach on 6 Jun 1944 and written off as a total loss. Sold for disposal Jul 1944.
WAIR	Bombed and sunk by Luftwaffe on 27 Apr 1941 during the evacuation of Crete.

Conversion	Fate
WAIR	Sold for disposal 1948.
Short Range Escort	Sold for disposal 1945.
Short Range Escort	Sold for disposal 1947.
Not converted	Sold for disposal 1947.

Conversion	Fate
	Sold for disposal 1945.
	Sold for disposal 1945.

ADMIRALTY MODIFIED 'W' CLASS, FIRST GROUP – 8 SHIPS

Name	Builder	Laid Down	Launched	Completed
Vansittart	Beardmore	1 Jul 1918	19 Apr 1919	5 Nov 1919
Vimy (Ex *Vantage*)	Beardmore	13 Jun 1918	11 Nov 1919	Mar 1924
Venomous (Ex *Venom*)	John Brown	31 May 1918	21 Dec 1918	Jun 1919
Verity	John Brown	17 May 1918	19 Mar 1919	17 Sep 1919
Volunteer	William Denny	16 Apr 1918	17 Apr 1919	7 Nov 1919
Wanderer	Fairfield	7 Aug 1918	1 May 1919	18 Sep 1919
Whitehall	Swan Hunter	Jun 1917	11 Sep 1919	9 Jul 1924
Wren	Yarrow	Jun 1918	11 Nov 1919	27 Jan 1923

ADMIRALTY MODIFIED 'W' CLASS, SECOND GROUP – 7 SHIPS

Name	Builder	Laid Down	Launched	Completed
Veteran	John Brown	30 Aug 1918	26 Apr 1919	13 Nov 1919
Whitshed	Swan Hunter	3 Jun 1918	31 Jan 1919	11 Jul 1919
Wild Swan	Swan Hunter	Jul 1918	17 May 1919	14 Nov 1919
Witherington	J. S. White	27 Sep 1918	16 Apr 1919	10 Oct 1919
Wivern	J. S. White	19 Aug 1918	16 Apr 1919	23 Dec 1919
Wolverine	J. S. White	8 Oct 1918	17 Jul 1919	27 Jul 1920
Worcester	J. S. White	20 Dec 1918	24 Oct 1919	20 Sep 1922

Sources:
V&W Class Destroyers 1917-1945, Antony Preston, Macdonald & Company 1971.
Conway's All the World's Fighting Ships, 1922- 1946, Ed. Robert Gardiner, Naval Institute Press
"V & W Class Destroyers" (Man O' War No.2), Alan Raven & John Roberts, A&P 1979.

Conversion	Fate
Long Range Escort	Sold for disposal 1946.
	Sold for disposal 1945.
Short Range Escort	Sold for disposal 1947.
Long Range Escort	Sold for disposal 1947.
Long Range Escort	Sold for disposal 1947.
Long Range Escort	Sold for disposal 1946.
Long Range Escort	Sold for disposal 1945.
Not converted	Sunk by Luftwaffe off Aldeburgh, North Sea 27 Jul 1940.

Conversion	Fate
Not converted	Torpedoed and sunk by U-404 southwest of Iceland 26 Sep 1942. Lost with all hands.
Short Range Escort	Sold for disposal 1947.
Not converted	Bombed and sunk by the Luftwaffe in the Bay of Biscay on 17 Jun 1942. Shot down 6 of the 12 attacking aircraft.
Short Range Escort	Sold for disposal 1947, but wrecked enroute to the breakers 29 Apr 1947.
Short Range Escort	Sold for disposal 1947
Short Range Escort	Sold for disposal 1947
Short Range Escort	Mined and damaged in North Sea 23 Dec 1943; written off but used as an accommodation hulk named *Yeoman*. Broken up 1946.

ÅPPENDIX NINE – LIST OF ABBREVIATIONS

AA	Anti-aircraft	HMNS	His (Her) Majesty's
AB	Able Seaman		Netherlands Ship
AI	Admiralty Instructions	HMSO	His (Her) Majesty's Stationary
AS	Anti-submarine		Office
A/S	Anti-submarine	HO	Hostilities Only
AWOL	Absent Without Leave	IRA	Irish Republican Army
BEF	British Expeditionary Force	KBE	Knight Commander of the
BPF	British Pacific Fleet		British Empire
BUF	British Union of Fascists	KCB	Knight Companion of the Bath
CAM	Catapult Aircraft Merchant [ship]	KCVO	Knight Commander of the Royal
CB	Companion of the Bath		Victorian Order
CBE	Commander of the British Empire	KMS	Kriegsmarine Ship
C in C	Commander in Chief	Kts	Knots
CPO	Chief Petty Officer	KR	King's Regulations
CO	Commanding Officer	LO	Liaison Officer
CS	Cruiser Squadron	LRE	Long Range Escort
CW	Commissioned Warrant Officer	LST	Landing Ship Tank
(D)	Destroyer	MBE	Member of the British Empire
DEMS	Defensively Equipped	MC	Military Cross
	Merchant Ships	Met.	Meteorological
DP	Dual Purpose	MID	Mentioned In Dispatches
DSC	Distinguished Service Cross	Mk	Version of a particular weapon or
DSM	Distinguished Service Medal		electronic system
DSO	Distinguished Service Order	MO	Medical Officer
(E)	Engineer	MTB	Motor Torpedo Boat
ERA	Engine Room Artificer	MV	Motor Vessel
EU	European Union	MVO	Member of the Royal
EV	Escort Vessel		Victorian Order
FAA	Fleet Air Arm	NAAFI	Navy, Army and Air Force
FL	Fully Loaded		Institutions
FOA	Flag Officer Arbroath	NATO	North Atlantic Treaty
FOC	Flag Officer in Charge		Organisation
FOIC	Flag Officer In Charge	NavEx	Naval Exercise
FX	Foc's'le	NCXF	Naval Commander Expeditionary
GCB	Knight Grand Cross of the Bath		Commander
GCO	Gunnery Control Officer	NM	Nautical Miles
GMT	Greenwich Mean Time	NOIC	Naval Officer In Charge
HA	High Angle	NSA	National Security Agency
HE	High Explosive	OBE	Order of the British Empire
HF	Home Fleet	OD	Ordinary Seaman (also used for
HM	His (Her) Majesty		Officer of the Deck)
HMCS	His (Her) Majesty's Canadian Ship	OIC	Officer In Charge
HMS	His (Her) Majesty's Ship	OOW	Officer of the Watch

Pdr	Pounder	WA	Western Approaches
PO	Petty Officer	WAIR	W-Class anti-AIRcraft
QM	Quarter Master	WRNS	Women's Royal Naval Service,
RAF	Royal Air Force		known as Wrens
RCN	Royal Canadian Navy	WT	Wireless Telegraphy
RDF	Radio Direction Finding [Radar]	WW2	World War Two
RAN	Royal Australian Navy	XO	Executive Officer
RCs	Roman Catholics		
Ret.	Retired	2d	Two Pennies (pre-decimal
RFA	Royal Fleet Auxiliary		currency, English)
RIC	Royal Irish Constabulary		
RMS	Royal Mail Ship		
RN	Royal Navy		
RNAS	Royal Naval Air Station		
RNB	Royal Naval Barracks		
RNLI	Royal National Lifeboat Institute		
RNR	Royal Navy Reserve		
RNVR	Royal Navy Volunteer Reserve		
RM	Royal Marine		
RPM	Revolutions Per Minute		
RV	Rendezvous		
SANF	South African Naval Force		
SAS	Special Air Service		
SBA	Sick Berth Attendant		
SCC	Sea Cadet Corps		
SMS	Seiner Majestät Schiff		
	(His Majesty's Ship)		
SP	Single Purpose		
SO	Senior Officer		
SRE	Short Range Escort		
SS	Steam Ship		
(T)	Torpedo		
TG	Task Group		
TF	Task Force		
TIH	Taken In Hand		
TS	Training Ship		
UK	United Kingdom		
US	United States		
USN	United States Navy		
V	HMS *Venomous*		
VC	Victoria Cross		
VE Day	Victory in Europe		
VJ Day	Victory over Japan		

BIBLIOGRAPHY

Primary sources

The following logs for HMS *Venomous* are held at the National Archives (NA), Kew:

> 4 June 1919 – 18 September 1929
> 29 September 1938 – December 1939 (NA Ref. ADM 53)

No logs for *Venomous* or any destroyers or small ships survive for the war years.

The main source for ship movements during World War II are the Naval War Diaries at the NA in Kew containing Admiralty signals. The index cards for ships at the Royal Navy Historical Branch in Portsmouth are the keys to unlocking this information. Further research at Kew can then lead to the detailed account of ship actions contained in the reports of proceedings written by a ship's commanding officer to his reporting officer. Online access to the National Archives via the Internet is no substitute for a personal visit as indexing is often superficial and the old card index which has not been digitised is still an essential tool.

The confidential edition of the quarterly *Navy List,* containing the complete information on officers and ships which was omitted from the published edition in wartime, is held at the NA in Kew at ADM 177. The *Pink* and *Red Lists* giving the location in port of HM Ships, but not at sea, are filed at ADM 187 and ADM 208.

A selective list of reports of proceedings relating to HMS *Venomous* held in the National Archives, Kew, arranged in date order:

Enemy air attacks – HMS *Venomous*. Report by Cdr John McBeath to Captain (D) 16th Destroyer Flotilla on four attacks on 19 May 1940. NA Ref. ADM 199/100 (Enemy Air Attacks on RN and Merchant Shipping, 1940-2).

Report on damage to HMS *Venomous* during attack by sixty Junker 87 bombers on 23 May 1940. With report on damage to HMS *Venetia* on 23 May 1940, photographs. NA Ref. ADM 267/101 (Shell and Bomb).

Action off Boulogne on 23 May 1940. From: The Commanding Officer HMS *Venomous*. To: Captain (D) sixteenth Destroyer Flotilla. Date: 26 May 1940. NA Ref: Not available.

Report on mine damage to HMS *Venomous* on the 30 December 1940 in Liverpool Bay. NA Ref. ADM 267/91 (Torpedo and Mine)

HMS *Venomous* – Convoy ON.28. Report of Proceedings, 21-5 October 1941. Includes report of Cdr H.W. Falcon-Steward, OIC for ON.28 in the absence of HMS *Keppel*. NA Ref. ADM 199/1147 (1941-2: ON, HX, SC Convoy Reports).

Findings of the Board of Enquiry into the collision between HMS *Keppel* and HMS *Venomous* on the 11-12 November 1941. NA Ref. ADM 1/12015(29)

Report by Capt H. Crombie RN of HMS *Bramble* on Convoy PQ.15 from 2 – 5 May 1942. NA Ref. ADM 199/721.
See also: http://www.halcyon-class.co.uk/Arctic/pq15.htm

Analysis of attacks by a U-boat on HMS *Hecla* at 2315, 11 November 1942. Anti-submarine Warfare Division, Naval Staff, 25 January 1943. NA Ref. ADM 199/2013.

Report on torpedoing of HMS *Marne*. From: The CO of HMS *Marne*, Lt Cdr H.N.A. Richardson RN. To: The Naval Commander Expeditionary Force. Date: 17 November 1942. NA Ref. ADM 1/14272.

Loss of HMS *Hecla*. From: Admiral Cunningham, Naval Commander Expeditionary Force, Algiers. To: Secretary of the Admiralty. Date: 13 December 1942. Enclosures include the report of Capt S. Arliss RN, CO HMS *Hecla*. NA Ref. ADM 199/2068.

Précis of attack by *Venomous*. Director of Torpedo, Anti-submarine and Mine Warfare Division (DTASW), Proceedings of U-boat Assessment Committee. NA Ref. ADM 199/184

Report from CO of HMS *Wishart* to Commander in Chief Levant on Convoy GTX.3 from leaving Gibraltar on 22 June to arrival at Alexandria on the 3 July 1943. NA Ref. ADM 199/1035.

Secondary sources

Select list of books on destroyers

Brooks, E. *Destroyers*, Jarrold, 1942

Chapman, T. *Water, Water Everywhere*, Aedificamas Press, 1986

Cocker, Maurice *Destroyers of the Royal Navy, 1893-1981*, Littlehampton, 1981

Fairweather, Cliff *Hard lying: the story of the V&W class destroyers and the men who sailed in them*, Avalon Associates, 2005

Friedman, Norman and Baker, A.D. *British Destroyers: From Earliest Days to the Second World War*, Seaforth, 2009

Friedman, Norman *British destroyers and frigates: the Second World War and after,* Seaforth, 2008

Gretton, Peter *Convoy Escort Commander*, Cassell, London, 1964

Hawkins, Ian *Destroyer: An Anthology of first hand accounts of the war at Sea, 1939-1945*, Conway Maritime, 2005

Jackson, D. C. *One Ship, One Company: the Story of HMS Worcester*, National Library of Australia.

Mallalieu, J.P.W. *Very Ordinary Seaman,* Victor Gollancz, 1944

Marriot, Lee *Royal Navy Destroyers since 1945*, Ian Allan, 1990

March, Edgar J. *British Destroyers: a History of Development 1892-1953:*

drawn by Admiralty Permission from Official Records and Returns, Ships Covers and Building Plans, Seeley Service, 1966.

Lenton, H. T. *British and Empire Warships of the Second World War,* Greenhill, 1998

Lenton, H. T. *British Fleet and Escort Destroyers* (2 volumes), Doubleday, 1972

Lenton, H. T. and Colledge, J. J. *Warships of World War II Part Two: Destroyers and Submarines,* Ian Allen, 1974.

Lewis, L.J. and Payne, M.A. *Scrap Iron Destroyers,* Garden Island, Australia, 1976.

Preston, Anthony, *V and W Class Destroyers 1917-1945,* MacDonald & Co. Ltd., London, 1971.

Raven, Alan and Roberts, John *V & W Class Destroyers* (Man o' War No. 2), Arms and Armour Press, 1979

Smith, Peter C., *HMS Wild Swan,* William Kimber & Co, London, 1985.

Whitley, M.J. *Destroyers of World War Two: An International Encyclopedia,* Arms and Armour Press, 1999

General reference works

The War In France And Flanders 1939-1940, by Major L.F. Ellis CVO, CBE, DSO, MC (London: HMSO, 1954). In: *History Of The Second World War: United Kingdom Military Series,* edited by J.R.M. Butler.

Conway's All the World's Fighting Ships 1906-1921, Conway, 1997, reprinted by the US Naval Institute Press, 2006.

The Royal Navy Officer's Pocket-Book, 1944, compiled by Brian Lavery, Conway, 2006.

A Seaman's Pocket-Book, June 1943, by Authority of the Lords Commissioners of the Admiralty, Introduced by Brian Lavery, Conway, 2006.

Books and periodical articles

Beesly, Patrick, *Very Special Intelligence: The Story of the Admiralty's Operational Intelligence Centre 1939-1945,* US Naval Institute Press, Annapolis, 2000.

Barnett, Correlli, *Engage the Enemy More Closely: The Royal Navy in the Second World War,* W.W. Norton & Company, New York, 1991

Bell, Christopher, M., *The Royal Navy, Seapower and Strategy between the Wars,* Stanford University Press, Stanford, 2000.

Bennett, Geoffrey, *Freeing the Baltic,* Birlinn, Edinburgh, 2002.

Blair, Clay, *Hitler's U-Boat War: The Hunted 1942-1945,* Random House, Inc., New York, 1998.

Brown, David K., *Atlantic Escorts: Ships, Weapons & Tactics in World War II,* US Naval Institute Press, Annapolis, 2007

Clayton, Tim and Craig, Phil, *Finest Hour,* Hodder & Stoughton, London, 1999.

Coleman, Edward *Navy Days,* Andrew Books, 1999

Colledge, J.J., and Ben Warlow, *Ships of the Royal Navy,* Chatham Publishing, London, 2006.

Courcy-Ireland, S.Brian de, *A Naval Life,* 2nd Edn, Englang Publishing, Poulton, Glou., 2002

Delve, Kevin, *The Story of the Spitfire: An Operational and Combat History,* Greenhill Books, London, 2007.

Gallery, Daniel V., *Twenty Million Tons Under the Sea,* US Naval Institute Press, Annapolis, 1956.

Gibson, Charles, *The Ship with Five Names*, Abellard-Schman, London, 1965

Greene, Jack and Massignani, Alessandro, *Naval War in the Mediterranean 1940-1943*, Chatham Publishing, 1998.

Howarth, Patrick, *Undercover: The Men and Women of the Special Operations Executive*, Routledge & Kegan Paul Ltd, 1980

Hughes, Wayne, P., *Fleet Tactics: Theory and Practice*, US Naval Institute Press, Annapolis, 1986.

James, Lawrence, *The Rise and Fall of the British Empire*, St. Martin's Press, New York, 1994.

Kemp, Paul, *The Russian Convoys 1941-1945*, Arms and Armour Press Ltd., 1987.

Lavery, Brian, *Churchill's Navy: The Ships, Men and Organisation 1939-1945*, Conway, 2006.

Macintyre, Donald, *The Battle of the Atlantic,* Pen & Sword Military Classics, Barnsley, 2006.

H.H. McWilliams, Herbert H., The Loneliness of the Long-distance Swimmer, *Sea Breeze*. January 1992, p11-19

Miers, Suzanne, *Slavery in the Twentieth Century: The Evolution of a Global Problem*, Alta Mira Press, 2003.

Owen, David, *Anti-Submarine Warfare: An Illustrated History,* US Naval Institute Press, Annapolis, 2007

Rohwer, Jürgen, *The Critical Convoy Battles of March 1943,* US Naval Institute Press, Annapolis, 1977.

Roskill, Steven W., *Naval Policy Between the Wars*, Vol. II, *The Period of Reluctant Rearmament*, US Naval Institute, Annapolis, Maryland, 1968.

Roskill, Steven W., *White Ensign: The British Navy at War 1939-1945*, US Naval Institute, Annapolis, 1960.

Smith, Peter C., *Hold the Narrow Sea*, US Naval Institute Press, Annapolis, 1984.

Smith, Peter C., *Pedestal: The Convoy That Saved Malta*, 5th Edition, Crécy Publishing Ltd, 2002.

Miscellaneous

Rudyard Kipling's poem, *The Destroyers,* was published in 1898, and it can be found at: http://www.poetryloverspage.com/poets/kipling/kipling_ind.html

Alfred Lord Tennyson, *The Sailor Boy, 1861*. The poem can be found at the following website dedicated to Tennyson:
http://home.att.net/%7ETennysonPoetry/index.htm

Websites

Links to these sites will be provided from: www.holywellhousepublishing.co.uk/

BBC – WW2 People's War	http://www.bbc.co.uk/ww2peopleswar
Convoy Web	http://www.convoyweb.org.uk
Fleet Air Arm Website	http://www.fleetairarm.com/
HMCS Sackville Website	http://steelnavy.com/Sackville.htm
HyperWar: World War II on the World Wide Web	http://www.ibiblio.org/hyperwar
Indicator Loops	http://indicatorloops.com/loops.htm
International Naval Research Organization	http://www.warship.org
Naval Historical Foundation	http://www.navyhistory.org
Naval History.Net	http://www.naval-history.net
NavSource Naval Photographic History of the USN	http://www.navsource.org
Official Royal Navy Website	http://www.royalnavy.mod.uk
Old Ships	http://www.oldships.org.uk
Royal Navy Flag Officers 1904-1945	http://www.admirals.org.uk
The Clyde Bank Story	http://www.theclydebankstory.com
Uboat.net – The U-boat War 1939-1945	http://uboat.net
V and W class destroyer – Wikipedia	http://en.wikipedia.org/wiki/ V_and_W_class_destroyer
World War II unit histories & officers	http://www.unithistories.com

A

Achates, HMS, 122-123

Acland, Capt Herbert G.P. RN (Ret), 211-213, 215, 240

Admiral Hipper, KMS, 182

Admiral Scheer, KMS, 181

Admiralty: Naval Intelligence Division's Operational Intelligence Centre, 193, 212

Admiralty, The, 120, 168, 172, 197

Adriatic Sea, 43, 49

Adventure, HMS, 250

Aegean, 58

Agar, Lt Augustus RN, 19, 127

Ailsa Shipbuilding Co, 168, 172

Ajax, HMS, 250

Akureyri Fjord, 180, 182, 206

Albatross, HMAS, 211

Aldenham, HMS, 206

Alexander-Sinclair, RAdm Edwyn, 19, 27, 36-37

Alexandria, 50, 58, 128, 196, 248, 257, 260, 262-263, 265, 269

Algeria, 197

Algiers, 59, 211, 245-246, 249, 262, 269

Alleyne, Mid Reynold H. RN, 31

Allit, Mr. W.J. RN, 82

Amazon, HMS, 170, 198-199

Ambuscade, HMS, 122

Andrei Pervozvanni, Soviet Battleship, 19

Antelope, HMS, 205

Anti-Submarine Warfare (ASW), 152

Anti-Submarine Warfare Division, 172, 213-215

Archangel, 141, 179, 190, 277

Archer, HMS, 245

Arctic, 137, 184

Argonaut, HMS, 249

Argostoli Bay, 55, 57, 59

Argus, HMS, 129-130, 198-199, 205-206

Arliss, Capt Stephen RN, 212-219, 226

Armed Merchant Cruiser (AMC), 150-151

Arrow, HMS, 124

Asdic, 73, 152, 208, 213, 216, 223, 229

Asia Minor, 43-44

Atherstone, HMS, 207

Atlantic, Battle of, 114, 144, 212

Atlantic Escort, Brown, David K., 142

Atlantic Fleet, 37, 41

Aubretia, HMS, 253

Augusta, Port of 267-269

Augusta, USS, 234-236

Aultbea, 149

Ausma, HMS, 141

Autroil, Russian Minelayer, 36

Avon Vale, HMS, 253

B

Back, AB Robert, 185, 208

Bacon, Capt C.H.C. RN, 57

Badsworth, HMS, 180, 184, 188-189, 195

Baker, S/Lt Henry RN, 28

Baltic, 18, 20, 25, 35, 37, 42, 108, 156, 211, 312

Balsam, HMS, 252-253

Barham, HMS, 55

Barlow, Mid Peter RN, 49

Barnett, Correlli, 64, 74, 194

Barney, Mid Stephen RNVR, 197-207, 247, 251, 253-254, 260, 265, 267-268, 270-272

Barracuda Torpedo Bomber, 283-284, 287

Basilisk, HMS, 103, 106

Baynham, Mid B.H.G.M RNVR, 161

Beatty, Adm of the Fleet David, 49

Beckerman, Mid (later S/Lt) Wilfred RNVR, 279-280, 284, 287-288, 290, 308-309

Belgium, 77, 102

Belfast, 131-132, 207

Bennett, Chief ERA Arthur RN, 286

Biarritz, SS, 85

Bicester, HMS, 205

Bingham, Capt B.S. RN, 54

Biorko Sound, 19, 22-25

Birkenhead, 132, 137, 172

Birkin, AB George, 68, 157

Bismarck, KMS, 150

Bizerta, Port of 195, 257

Black Ranger, RFA, 189

Black Swan, HMS, 253

Blair, Lt James RNVR, 286, 292, 311

Blyskowica, Polish Destroyer, 71

Bodicia, HMS, 63, 180, 188

Bogh-Tobiassen, Christian, 300

Bolsheviks, 18-19, 23

Bone, Algeria, 245, 249, 260-261

Boreas, HMS, 245

Botavon, SS, 185

Boulogne, 80, 84-89, 99-100, 107, 126, 169

Boxol, RFA, 44

Bramble, HMS, 182

Brambleleaf, RFA, 54-55

Brand, Adm Sir Hubert, 59

Bray Dunes, 102-104, 109

Britain, Battle of, 118, 126

British & Commonwealth Army Units:

  First Canadian Div, 119

    20th Guards Bde, 84, 90

    2nd Bn Irish Guards, 84, 95, 99

    1st Bn Welsh Guards, 84, 93, 95

  51st Highland Div, 119

British Expeditionary Force (B.E.F.), 69, 71, 75, 80, 84, 109, 119

Broke, HMS, 54-55, 208

Broome, Cdr J.E. RN, 141, 155, 160-161, 165

Browning, Surg Lt Robert RNVR, 155, 157, 159

Bryony, HMS, 49, 58

Buckel, Lt K.W.S. RN, 63-64

Burham, SS, 132

Burrough, VAdm, 184, 198

Bush, Col W.E., Green Howards, 109

Bussum, SS, 77

Button, CPO Bosun Henry, 227, 229-230, 238-239, 245, 255-256

C

Calais, 80-84, 107, 252

Calais Base Hospital, 82

Calcium, SS, 136

Caledon, HMS, 19, 48

Calvert, Brig Michael, 301, 303

Calypso, HMS, 50

Cammell Laird, 136-138

Campbell, HMS, 16

Campbeltown, HMS, 177

Campion, HMS, 253

Cape Bon, 44, 256, 260, 263

Cape Corso, SS, 184

Cape Wrath, 37, 163, 287, 289

Cardiff, HMS, 123-125

Carlisle, HMS, 257-258

Carnation, HMS, 253

Caroline, HMS, 57

Carysfort, HMS, 16

Casablanca, 212, 231-232, 234-236, 251

Cashman, Lt Michael RN 176-177, 182, 188, 193, 198-200, 209, 225, 227, 232, 247, 249, 257, 260, 263, 272

Cassandra, HMS, 19

Catapult Armed Merchant (CAM) ship, 180-182

Caudle, Lt David W. RNVR, 278, 283, 285-287, 289, 297, 300, 304, 308, 311

Ceramic, SS, 241

Chamberlain, PM Neville, 62, 68

Charles, AB T. Sydney, 158

Charybdis, HMS, 205

Chatham, 26, 28-29, 31, 33, 35, 47, 54, 60, 125, 265

Chatwin, Lt. Cdr (later Cdr) Cecil A.N. RN, 59, 71

Chenango, USS, 235

Cherbourg, 69-70, 75

Chiltern, HMS, 185

Churchill, PM Winston, 125, 156

City of Christchurch, SS, 85

Clarke, S/Lt Greg RNVR, 230

Clarke, Lt I.T. RN, 59

Clyde, The, 15, 129-131, 149, 189, 193, 197, 199, 206-209, 245-246, 255, 292

Cobalto, Italian Submarine, 247-248

Coleman, Electrical Artificer (EA) Edward, 226, 231, 233

Coleman, Lt John RNR, 206-207, 223, 235, 293

Collister, CPO William Leslie, 171-172, 184, 186, 230, 248, 253, 264, 286-288, 291, 299

Commander in Chief
    Atlantic Fleet, 34
    Home Fleet, 170, 177, 207
    Mediterranean Fleet, 48, 58-59, 240, 256, 266, 269, 271-272
    Middle East, 129
    Nore, 127-128
    Western Approaches, 29, 130, 163, 170, 176, 207-208

Commission Warrant (CW) 206

Compston, AB Sydney, 72-73, 76-77, 82, 101, 111-113, 115, 118, 123, 134-135, 142

Conder, Cdr E.R. RN, 90

Conquest, HMS, 57

Convoy to Scatter, Broome, Capt J. RN, 153

Convoys:
    CF.7, 211
    CF.7A, 211-212, 214
    FN.223, 124
    FN.224, 124
    FN.225, 124
    GTX.3, 201, 263
    GUF.4, 251
    HX.96, 135
    HX.113, 141
    HX.115, 142-143
    HX.126, 148
    HX.129, 150
    HX.133, 153
    HX.146, 156
    JGF.2, 231
    KMF.13, 255
    KMS.3G, 245
    KMS.4G, 246
    KMS.5G, 248
    KMS.9, 253
    KMS.14X, 257
    KX.4A, 208-209
    MKF.11, 255
    MWF.37, 265
    OB.297, 141
    OB.302, 141-142, 145
    OB.307, 144
    OB.323, 149

    OB.330, 150
    OB.336, 151
    OB.343, 154
    OB.349, 155
    OG.54, 141
    ON.10, 156
    ON.15, 157
    ON.28, 160
    OS.35, 161
    PQ.13, 186
    PQ.15, 170, 179-182, 184, 186
    PQ.16, 187
    PQ.17, 197, 206
    PQ.18, 207
    QP.11, 182, 184, 187
    QP. 12, 187, 189
    SC.14, 132
    SC.27, 144
    SC.34, 150
    SC.43, 157
    SC.48, 160
    SC.50, 161
    SL.56, 131
    TMF.2, 250
    UGS.4, 251
    WA.4A, 207
    WS.21S

Copenhagen, 20-22, 25, 27, 309

Cornflower, HMS, 51

Cottam, Lt G.M. RNVR, 75

Courcy-Ireland, Lt (later Capt) S. Brian de RN, 16-17, 30-33, 35

Courtauld's Calais, 81-82

Coventry, HMS, 54

Cowan, Adm Sir Walter, 19-20, 23, 27, 37

Craddock, AB Robert J., 187, 239

Cricket, HMS, 46

Crombie, Capt, Harvey RN, 182, 185-186

Crowley, PO J.F., 162

Cunningham, Adm Andrew Browne, (See also Commander in Chief Mediterranean Fleet) 128, 212, 215, 240, 256-257, 265, 268

Curacoa, HMS, 193

D

Dagabur, Italian Submarine, 205

Dagley, PO Lesley W., 103, 108, 126

Danzig (Gdansk), 36

Darlan, Adm, 68

Dawnay, Mid (later VAdm Sir) Peter, 49

D.E.M.S., 185

Dennis, Lt Cdr, John Alexander Jeffrey RNVR, 296-297, 302-303

Defender, HMS, 66

Delhi, HMS, 36, 193

Derry, see Londonderry

Derwent, HMS, 170, 198, 205

Despatch, HMS, 130

Destroyer Flotillas (RN):
  First, 20, 55, 211
  Second, 55
  Third, 16, 29, 33, 55
  Fourth, 25, 37, 41, 44, 47 49, 54-57
  Sixth, 35
  Thirteenth, 18, 251
  Sixteenth, 69, 123, 126
  Eighteenth, 121, 123
  Nineteenth, 153
  Twenty-First, 123

Destroyers, The (Kipling), 1-2

Devonport (Dockyard), 63, 97, 115, 118, 120, 265, 282, 292

Dianella, HMS, 141

Director of Naval Construction, 10

Domala, MV, 72

Donald, S/Lt (later Cdr) C.G.W. RN, 54, 90

Dönitz, Gross (Grand) Adm Karl, 138, 143, 152, 212-213

Dorcasia, SS, 136

Douglas-Watson, Lt Francis RN, 37

Dover (Harbour), 71, 75, 78, 80, 83, 86-87, 100, 105-106, 110, 120

Dow, S/Lt J.A. RNVR, 105

Dragomesti Bay, 55, 59

Dragon, HMS, 22, 36

Dreyer, Adm Sir Frederick, 59

Duff, Lt D.R. RN 66-69, 71

Dunedin, HMS, 25

Dunkirk, 84, 100, 102-103, 107-108, 111-113, 118

Dunn, Mr. F.A. RN, 34-35

Durell, Lt Henry D. RN, 253-255, 262, 263, 267, 270-271

E

E-Boats (Schellboote), 71, 121-122

Eagle, HMS, 53, 57, 195, 199-202

Eaglet, HMS, 246

Easton, AB W.S., 35

Eaton, AB James, 68, 77, 80, 94, 144, 312

Eaton, Lt Leslie C RNVR, 170, 176-178, 183, 197, 233, 235, 237, 253-254, 260

Edinburgh, 16, 33, 190

Edinburgh, HMS, 187

Edsall, USS, 46

Edwards, AB J., 99

Eglington, HMS, 128

Egypt, 49, 129, 194, 256

Eisenhower, Gen Dwight D., USA, 265, 268

Elliot, Mid R.C. RNR, 177

Emden, SMS, Light Cruiser, 28

Empire Morn, SS (CAM), 180, 188

Endrass, Lt Engelbert, KM, 142

English Channel, 54, 77, 84, 120-121, 123

Erebus, HMS, 23

Escapade, HMS, 188

Escort, HMS, 139

Escort Groups:
  First, 132, 134, 135, 138, 141-142, 144, 160
  Twenty-First Escort Group, 170, 194
  Sixty-First Escort Group, 249

Eskimo, HMS, 205

Esslemont, John, 81, 83, 252

Esson, Mid Alan F. RNR, 80, 92-93, 98, 101, 126, 148, 169

Estonia, 18, 21, 27, 36

Evacuation of Dunkirk, The, Gardner, W.J.R., 114

Excellent, HMS, 71

Exmoor, HMS, 132

Express, HMS, 247

F

Falcon-Steward, Cdr (later Capt) Hugh W. RN, 153, 160-162, 165, 168-169, 172, 175-177, 183, 194, 204-207, 209, 211, 213, 215-217, 222-223, 228, 231-232, 235, 239-241, 245-247, 255-256

Falke, KMS, 128

Falmouth, 265, 272-273, 277-278

Famagusta, 49, 55, 58

Festung Norwegen, 295

Fifth Torpedo Boat Flotilla, Kriegsmarine, 128

Finland, 18, 156

First Sea Lord of the Admiralty, 49, 128

Firth of Forth, 16, 67, 287, 293

Flag Officer in Charge
  Falmouth, 273, 276-277, 282
  Greenock, 163-164
  Liverpool, 137

Fleet Air Arm, 150

Fleur de Lys, HMS, 134-135

Folkestone, 83, 86, 97

Force F, 196, 205

Force H, 249, 251, 256

Force Q, 182, 189

Force R, 196

Force X, 195-196, 198

Force Y, 195-196

Force Z, 195-196

Foreign Office, 51-52

Formidable, HMS, 131-132, 170, 250-251, 256

Forster, Lt (E) William R. RNR, 277-279, 281, 286, 290-291, 304, 311

Forte, HMS, 277

Forty, Stoker George, 219, 222, 233

Fourth Battle Squadron, RN, 48, 55-56

Freetown, 195, 211, 213, 217

Fremantle, Adm Sir Sydney, 19, 27

Frobisher, HMS, 54, 195

Furious, HMS, 130-131, 198-200, 203-205

Fury, HMS, 205

G

Gala, Yacht, 105

Gallipoli Campaign, 46, 58

Ganges, HMS, 119

Gannon, S/Lt Eric RN, 28

Gardenia, HMS, 134-135

Gardner, Lt Cdr Lewes G. RN, 33-35, 44, 46-48

Garland, HMS, 71

German High Sea Fleet, 1, 16, 18, 28

Germanic, SS, 145

Gibraltar, 31, 44, 47, 54-56, 59-60, 130-131, 141, 196, 204-206, 209, 211-213, 216-217, 225, 230-231, 235, 237-239, 245-247, 249-251, 253, 255-258, 262, 269-272

Glaisdale, HMS, 231

Glorious, HMS, 67

Goltz, Graf von der, Gen Gustav Joachim Rüdiger, 18, 20, 22-23

Goodenough, Cdr RN, 78

Gotto, Mid (later Capt) Renfrow RN, 20-22, 25-26, 108

Grangemouth, 292, 311

Greco-Turkish War, 45

Greece (Greek), 44-46, 53, 55

Greenaway, Lt Frank S.H. RNVR, 277-279, 281-282, 286, 289, 291-292

Greenock, 129-130, 194, 255-256

Greif, KMS, 128

Gretton, Lt Cdr Peter RN, 204

Grey Rover, RFA, 182

Grieve, Cdr (E) P. RN, 60

Grom, Polish Destroyer, 71

Guadalcanal, USS, 241

Gulf of Finland, 19, 23, 25

H

H-31, HMS, 149

Haddon, AB Harry, 186, 188, 193, 227, 229, 248, 250-251, 255, 268, 270

Hahn, Hans, (U-515 Crewmember) 224, 229

Haifa, 49, 58, 196

Halifax, 135, 141-142, 153

Harrier, HMS, 77

Harwich, 29, 68, 71, 120, 122-123, 125-127, 129, 161

Harwich Flotilla, 55, 120

Hatton, Chief Stoker Alfred, 54

Havant, HMS, 107

Havelock, HMS, 130, 311

Havock, HMS, 3-4

Haydon, HMS, 251

Hebrides, 139

Hecla, HMS, 149, 154-155, 160, 211-213, 215-220, 222-223, 225-226, 230, 232-237, 240, 242, 245, 247, 255-256

Hedgehog anti-submarine mortar, 170-171, 278

Heinkel He-111, 72, 76, 185

Hely, AB Cyril, 183, 197, 200-201, 203, 230, 238-239, 251, 255, 268-270, 272

Henderson, Cdr H. Pitcairn RN, 135, 137-138, 142, 147-149, 152-153

Henke, Korvettenkapitän Werner KM, 216-218, 220, 241-242

Hesperus, HMS, 71, 131

Hetherington, Surg Lt S.L., 232

Hewitt, RADM H. Kent USN, 235-236

Heworth, SS, 124

Hill, Alderman George, 174-175

Hindenburg, 62

Hitler, Adolf, 62, 73, 138

HMS Wild Swan, Smith, Peter, 90

Holt, Lt Christopher R.V. RNVR, 258-263

Holy Land, 49, 58

Home Fleet, 141, 194-195

Hood, HMS, 13, 52, 150

Hook of Holland, 75, 77

Hopwood, AB, RN, 183

Hornet, HMS, 3-4

Horton, Admiral Sir Max, 64, 67, 246-247

Hostilities Only (HO), 67, 278

Howard-Johnson, Cdr RN, 134

Howe, HMS, 194, 206

Hughes, Capt Wayne P. USN (Ret), 1, 41-42

Hunter, Lt Colin RN, 254, 269-270, 273

Hurricane, HMS, 130

Hurry, S/Lt Edward RN, 14-15, 28

Hvalfjord, 144, 149, 155, 206-207

Hylton, SS, 142, 145

Hyperion, HMS, 76

I

I/KG26 (Coastal Group), 185

Iceland, 143-144, 149, 154, 156, 179, 189, 211

Ilex, HMS, 258

Indomitable, HMS, 195, 199

Inglefield, HMS, 180, 188

Ireland, 29, 37-38

Irlim, ERA James, 82, 162

Isis, HMS, 258

Isle of Man, 282-284

Isle of Man Steam Packet Co, 100

Ithuriel, HMS, 247

Ivanhoe, HMS, 107

J

Jackal, HMS, 122

Jaguar, HMS, 122

Jastrzab, PS, 184

Javelin, HMS, 261

John Brown & Company Ltd, 13

Johns, 2nd Class Stoker Norman, 217, 219, 221-222, 227-228, 231, 233, 242

Jones, S/Lt D.H. RNR, 91

Jones, Telegraphist Air Gunner Arthur Eric, RN, 204

Jonquil, HMS, 232

Junkers, JU-88 Bomber, 182-188, 258

Jutland, Battle of, 1, 17, 41

Jutland, SS, 185

K

Kaiserhafen, 36

Kalkara Naval Cemetery, 53

Kearney, USS, 160, 168

Keith, HMS, 88-92, 106

Kelvin, HMS, 261

Kemper, Paul, 182

Kendall, Pilot Officer J.B. RAF, 188-189

Kenya, HMS, 170, 194-195, 198, 205

Keppel, HMS, 141, 160-163, 165, 170, 173, 197, 201, 203, 205-206

Kershaw, S/Lt Peter RNVR, 72-73, 76, 79, 83, 85-86, 92, 96, 101-103, 105, 107, 110-111, 113, 124-125, 128, 132, 135-136, 138, 142-143, 145, 147-148, 151, 153, 156, 169

Kilkis, Greek Battleship (see Mississippi Class), 56

King Alfred, HMS, 72

King, Cpl Douglas,109

King George V, HMS, 181-182, 272

Kingcup, HMS, 141, 163

Kipling, Rudyard, 1-2, 15, 312

Knapton, AB Harold, 65-66, 72, 77-78, 98, 126

Knight, Mid J.T. RNR, 137, 152, 176

Kola Inlet, 182, 185-186, 188

Kondor, KMS, 128

Kouts, VAdm Tarmo, 36

Kriegsmarine, 74, 77, 122, 181, 309

Kristiansand, 35, 296-297, 301, 303-304, 307-309

Kronstadt Naval Base, 23-25, 36-37, 127

L

L'Orage, FS, 89

La Malouine, HMS, 253

Lady Elsa, HMS, 141

Lady of Mann, SS, 75

Laforey, HMS, 202-203, 205

Lancastria, RMS, 119

Lansky, S/Lt Miroslav Stanley RNVR, 292

Lapthorne, WO (E) RNVR, 266, 271

Lassos Bay, 55

Latvia, 18, 22, 36

Lawson, Lt Cdr Derek RNVR, 279-281, 283, 286-287, 289-292

Ledbury, HMS, 182, 263-264

Lemberg, Fred, RN (New Zealand), 218-219

Lemnos Island, 46, 53

Lend Lease Programme, 5, 184

Lewis, Commissioned Gunner W.F.H. RN, 65, 75

Libau, 20-22

Libya, 129, 194, 259

Liddlesdale, HMS, 259-260

Lightning, HMS, 205

Liguria, SS, 141

Lithuania, 18

Liverpool, 130, 135, 139, 141, 144, 154, 161, 212, 246

Liverpool, HMS, 36

Liverpool Light Vessel, 138

Llanstephen Castle, RMS, 194

Loades, AB Bill, 200

Loch Ewe, 139, 141, 149, 153, 155-156, 160-161, 164, 177, 180, 190, 287

Lockerby, Capt R., 108

Lodwick, PO, RN, 66

Lohmeyer, Korvettenkapitän Peter, KM, 153

London, 32, 62

London, HMS, 181-182, 184

London, HMS (Frigate) 190

London Gazette, 125-126, 256

Londonderry (Derry), 130-132, 138-139, 141, 149, 153, 157, 161, 169, 173, 177, 189, 206, 208, 249

Long Range Escort: See L.R.E.

Lookout, HMS, 205

Lough (Loch) Foyle, 153, 157, 160

Loughborough, 173-176

Loughborough & Shepshed Echo, 173-175

Louisville, HMCS, 232

L.R.E. (Long Range Escort) 168-170, 173, 216, 273, 276

Luftwaffe, 73, 80, 119, 157, 185, 196, 205, 245, 249

Lützow, KMS, 182

M

MacDonald, PM Ramsay, 41

Mackenzie, Lt Angus A. RNR, 75, 98, 101-102, 111, 134

Mackintosh, Capt L.D. RN, 203

Maitland-Makgill-Crichton, Cdr David H. RN, 246-251, 253-254

Majorca, 49, 52, 75

Malay, HMS, 56

Malcolm, HMS, 69-70, 75, 80, 102, 123, 126, 170, 197-199, 201 203, 205, 208-209

Male, AB George, 149, 219, 221, 230, 236

Mallard, HMS, 127

Mallow, HMS, 253

Malta, 44, 47, 52, 54-59, 129-130, 194-196, 199, 201, 204, 257, 269

Man O'War, HMS, 141

Manchester, HMS, 122, 195

Mannerheim, Gen Baron Carl Gustav, 18

Marlborough, HMS, 25-26

Marne, HMS, 211-214, 216, 219-223, 225-229, 231-232, 236, 239, 242, 251

Marr, Private D.J.W., 103

Martin, S/Lt RNVR, 279, 286

Matchless, HMS, 180, 195

Maunsell, Lt F.R.G., RN, 54

Maxwell, Surg Lt RNVR, 206, 245

May, AB Leslie, 188

Mayland, Signalman O.G., 94, 98

McBeath, Lt Cdr (later RAdm Sir) John E.H., RN, 71-72, 75-80, 82, 84 87, 90-91, 93, 95-97, 102, 104-109, 111-112, 115, 123, 126, 130-132, 134-135, 149, 277

McGrath, Lt Cdr Donal S., RN, 48-50

McGeeney, Ordinance Artificer 3rd Class (CPO) Hugh H., 65-66, 70-71, 78, 89, 94, 97-98, 101, 105, 111-112, 118, 121-123, 126

McIntyre, Lt Cdr (later Capt) Donald G.F.W., RN, 66-70

McPhee, Lt Arthur D. RN, 137, 163, 169

McWilliams, Lt Herbert Hastings, SANF, 217-221, 227, 236

Mediterranean, 43, 47-49, 52, 54, 129, 170, 194-195, 206, 245-246, 249-250, 256-257, 268, 271

Mediterranean Fleet, 41, 43, 47-49, 52, 54, 57, 128-129, 195-196, 208

Medway, 33, 54

Mellor, Lt Cdr B.H. de C. RN, 91

Mers el Kebir, 249-252

Mid Ocean Meeting Point (MOMP), 138, 144, 152

Miers, Suzanne, 52 (see Slavery in the Twentieth Century)

Milner, Lt C.W.R. RN, 71, 75

Milner, Surg Lt RNVR, 206

Minches, 139, 144, 161, 164, 205, 287

Mona's Queen, SS, 85-86, 100

Montrose, HMS, 121

Moore, S/Lt Richard RN, 37

Morocco, 165, 197, 209

Mosquito, HMS, 107

Moville, 155, 157

Mudros, 46, 49, 57

Munich Agreement, 63

Murmansk, 141, 179-180, 186-187, 190

Myositis, HMS, 253

N

Nab Tower, 69-70

Nalon, SS, 130

Napoleonic Wars, 47, 119

Navarin, 56-57, 59

Neale, Lt Cdr J.K. RNVR, 122

Nelson, HMS, 59, 195, 198, 205, 249, 251

Nelson, Horatio, 33, 50, 52, 54-55

Nethercott, AB Ian, 92

Neutrality Patrols, 144, 160

Newcastle, HMS, 122

Newton, Leading Seaman J.A., 162

Nicholls, S/Lt Rob, RN, 28

Nickless, AB W.H., 99

Nicosia, 58

Nigeria, HMS, 170, 180-181, 184, 198

NOIC Douglas, 283, 285

NOIC Greenock, 194

Nore, 130-132

North Africa, 129, 217, 236, 245, 249, 256, 262-263, 265, 268

North Cape, 156, 185

North Goodwin Patrol, 77-79

North Sea, 1, 120-123

Northern Dawn, HMS, 141

Norway, 35, 74, 179, 182, 185, 295-297, 307, 309, 311-312

Notton, Stoker Francis, 284, 291-292, 298, 311

Nova Scotia, 135, 141

O

Operation:

Aerial, 119

Apostle, 296

Ascendant, 196

Baritone, 201, 205

Bellows, 195, 201, 204-205

Berserk, 199

Cycle, 119

Doomsday, 296

Dynamo, 100, 106, 112, 114, 120

Harpoon, 247

Hurry, 129

Husky, 201, 265

Lucid, 127

Middle August, 195

Neptune, 177

Overlord, 177, 277

Pedestal, 170, 194, 196-197, 201, 247, 312

Retribution, 201, 257

Tiger, 257

Torch, 197, 209, 211-213, 312

Weserübung, 73-74

Oran, 212, 245, 250-251, 253, 256

Oribi, HMS, 135, 149, 277, 308

Orkney Islands, 16

Orwell, AB, 183

O'Sullivan, PO Michael J., 65, 98, 126

Oslo, 74

Osprey, HMS, 68, 72, 153

Ottoman Empire, 43

Oxfordshire, 157

P

Palestine, 129

Palma, 49, 52, 59

Palmas Bay, 54

Panzers, 80, 84, 88

Pantera, Soviet submarine, 19

Parkes, Warrant Engineer, A.E., RN, 74, 101, 112, 128, 137-138, 147-148, 154-155, 162, 169

Parsons, Lt S.J., RN, 169

Passmore, Chief ERA Don, 137

Pead, Warrant Engineer H.R., RN, 176-177

Pembroke, HMS, 60

Percival, Gen Arthur, BA, 111

Petrograd (formerly St. Petersburg, later Leningrad), 23

Petropavlovsk, Soviet battleship, 19

Phaeton, HMS, 22

Pinckney, Lt E.P.H., RN, 54, 59

Plymouth, 63, 102, 115, 118, 120, 122, 171

Polyarnyy (Polyarnoe), 186-189

Pontevedra, 31

Port Edgar, 16, 20, 31-33, 35, 37

Port Said, 49-50, 52, 58, 196

Portland, 68, 153

Portsmouth, 68, 70, 72, 74-75, 120

Pound, First Sea Lord, Adm of the Fleet, Sir Dudley, 128

Pozarica, HMS, 248

Prague, 64

Prescott, HMCS, 231

Preston, Anthony, 10, 42, 108, 112, 169-172

Prideaux, Lt Cdr A Gunyon RNVR, 292, 296-298, 300-301, 303-305, 308, 311

Prien, Korvettenkapitän Günther, 66

Prince of Wales, HMS, 150, 266

Prinze Eugen, KMS, 150, 309

Proes, S/Lt RNVR, 177

Puffin, HMS, 125

Punjabi, HMS, 182, 184

Pytchley, HMS, 132

Q

Queen Elizabeth, RMS, 193

Queen Elizabeth II, 36

Queen Mary, RMS 193

Queen of the Channel, SS, 85, 100

Queen Wilhelmina, 77

Queenstown (Cobh), 29

R

Radio Direction Finder (RDF or RADAR), 118-119, 137-138, 165, 213-216, 223-224, 229, 240, 278

RDF Types:

ASV Mark II, 156,

Type 271, 138,

Type 271M, 172, 177, 214, Type 286M, 138, 140, 165, 172, 214-215

Ramsay, VAdm (later Adm Sir) Bertram, 80, 99-100, 106-107, 269

Reading, HMS (former US Navy), 141

Regia Aeronautica, 245, 249

Repulse, HMS, 150

Reserve Fleet, 60, 63-64, 67, 311
Resolution, HMS, 55
Restigouche, HMCS, 157
Reval, 20-21, 25
Revenge, HMS, 56, 151
Reykjavik, 144, 154, 160, 206
Riga, 36-37
Richardson, Lt Cdr H.N.A. RN, 213-216, 220
Robb, LS John C., RN, 254
Robertson, S/Lt Charles RN, 29
Rockingham (former Belmont Class Destroyer, USS *Swasey*), HMS, 134-135
Rodger, Mid Robert H.S. RN, 28
Rodney, HMS, 195, 198, 249
Roosevelt, President F.D.R., 144
Rosenbaum, Lt Helmut, KM CO of *U-73*, 200
Roskill, Capt Stephen RN, 144, 257
Ross, acting S/Lt C.P. RN, 63
Rosyth, 18-20, 28-29, 60, 62-63, 67, 130, 194, 287, 292, 308
Rosyth Escort Force, 296-297
Rowles, Les, 230, 236
Royal Air Force (RAF), 27, 138, 269, 281
 Coastal Command, 143-144, 156
Royal Australian Navy, 35, 41, 211
Royal Canadian Navy, 138, 157
Royal Marines, 75, 77, 144, 270
Royal Oak, HMS, 55, 59, 66, 141-142
Royal Sovereign, HMS, 56
Royalist, HMS, 19
Ruck-Keene, Capt Philip RN, 132-133, 296-297
Rushbrooke, Lt Cdr Edmund G.N. RN, 55, 58
Russell, Cdr Somerville P.B. RN, 14-15, 20, 22-23, 25, 28, 31, 33
Russell, 1st Class Stoker Thomas Arthur, 282, 284, 286, 298, 305-306, 309

S

S Class Destroyers:
 Sabre, HMS, 154-155, 169, 193
 Saladin, HMS, 193
Sampson, USS, 47
Sardonyx, HMS, 194
Scimitar, HMS, 193
Shikari, HMS, 157, 194
Sportive, HMS, 48
Stuart, HMS, 48

Salamander, HMS, 107
Sambuks, 51
Sandhurst, HMS, 20, 178
Sangatte Loop Station, 80-81
Sangster, Lt Anthony de E.T. RN, 177, 180, 184-185, 189, 203, 205, 209, 213, 216-217, 223, 232, 236, 254, 263, 265, 267,
Sardinia, 49, 198, 245, 249
Scapa Flow, 16, 18, 27-28, 66, 141-142, 205-206, 281
Scott, RFA, 16
Scotland, 31, 141
Seagull, HMS, 184
Sebenico, 55
Seeadler, KMS, 128
Seidisfjord (Seydisfjordur), 177, 179
Shearwater, HMS, 125
Sheerness, 33, 37, 59-60, 122
Sheffield, HMS, 122
Sheldrake, HMS, 125, 127
Shepherd, HMS, 183
Short Range Escort (S.R.E.) 170, 173
Sicily, 245, 249, 265-266
Silly, Cox, Ltd, 273, 276-277
Simms, Mid Arthur RN, 155, 169, 176
Simpson, Capt D.J.R. RN, 90
Sims, Engineer Lt L. RN, 54
Sirius, HMS, 195
Skiathos, 57, 59
Skipjack, HMS, 107
Slavery in the Twentieth Century, Miers, Suzanne 52
Sliema Creek, 53-54
Smith, CPO Mervyn, 147
Smith, Peter, 170
Smyrna (Izmir), 43, 45
Sober Men and True, McKee, Christopher, 312
Solent, 69, 72
Somali, HMS, 180, 205

Spartak, Russian Minelayer, 36
Speedwell, HMS, 122
Spezia, Naval Base, 52
Spikenard, HMCS, 157
Springbank, HMS, 150-151
St. Albans, HMNS, 180, 184, 188
St. Croix, HMCS (former USS *McCook*), 157
St. Laurent, HMCS, 157
St. Olive, HMS, 124
Stallard, AB Ernst Roy, 93-94, 99, 101, 126
Stanier, Lt Col Sir Alexander, 1st Bn Welsh Guards, 95
Stella Leonis, HMS, Trawler, 124
Stork, HMS, 124
Straits of Gibraltar, 251-253
Straits of Messina, 58, 196
Straits of Sicily, 44, 130, 195
Stuka, Junkers 87, 77, 80, 89, 106-107, 124
Sturgeon, HMS, 180
Suez Canal, 51-52
Suffolk, HMS, 150
Sweden, 20

T

Tallinn, 21, 26-27, 36-37
Tangiers, 54
Tartar, HMS, 205
Task Group (TG) 22.3, 241
Task Force (TF) 34, 230
Teynham, Lt Cdr Lord Christopher John Roper-Curzon RN, 176-177, 199, 296-297, 301-303
Thames estuary, 122, 127
Thesiger, Adm Sir Bertram, 27
Thomas, RDF Operator F.N.G.,118, 146, 158, 172, 175,187, 190, 198, 224, 229, 266
Thompson, Sub Lt RN, 34,
Thompson, Commissioned Gunner (T), RN, 75, 90, 101, 148, 152, 155
Thorpe, S/Lt T.V. RNVR, 279, 290, 309
Tiger, HMS, 31
Tirpitz, KMS, 182, 206, 283
Tonkyn, Warrant Engineer, E.D. RN, 64, 74

Torbay, 31, 33

Torpedo Boat Destroyers, 3,

Torpilleur, FS, 90

Treaties:

Brest-Litovsk, 18

Lausanne, 45

Versailles, 5, 42-43, 62

Trinidad, HMS, 186

Tripoli, 257, 259-260

Troon, 168-169, 177, 296

Tucker, Sub Lt John C. RNR, 139, 147, 150-152, 156, 163, 169

Tugs:

Atjeh, 78-79

Jaunty, 195, 201, 231

Marauder, 163

Mastadonte, 163

Respond, 28

Savly, 28

St. Abbs, 107

St. Cyrus, 28

Swarthey, 72

Tunisia, 245, 256, 258

Tuscaloosa, USS, 181

Twiss, Lt (later Admiral Sir) Frank RN, 70, 123

U

U-boats:

U-46, 141

U-47, 142

U-48, 142

U-73, 200-201

U-110, 151

U-201, 151

U-515, 216, 221, 241

U-652, 160

Ulster Queen, HMS, 180, 188

V

V82, SMS, 18

V100, SMS, 28

Vaughn-Lewis, Sub Lt (later Lt) RN, 66, 93, 169

Vetch, HMS, 248

Victoria and Albert, Royal Yacht, 50

Victorious, HMS, 181, 195, 198-199

Vindictive, HMS, 211-218, 240

Violet, HMS, 253

Voil, Gunner (T) L.C. de RN, 54

V and W Class Destroyers:

Valkyrie, HMS, 16

Valorous, HMS, 18, 22, 296-297, 299, 301-302, 308

Vampire, HMS, 36

Vancouver, HMS, 142

Vanessa, HMS, 24

Vanity, HMS, 23

Vanoc, HMS, 250

Vanquisher, HMS, 104

Vansittart, HMS, 49, 54, 63

Velox, HMS, 130, 245, 248-249, 258-259, 262

Venetia, HMS, 86, 89-91, 96

Venomous, TS, 173-176

Verdun, HMS, 29-30

Verity, HMS, 13, 18, 24, 30, 75-77, 121, 123, 125, 245

Verulam, HMS, 19

Vesper, HMS, 129-131

Veteran, HMS, 13, 48, 121, 126

Viceroy, HMS, 24, 48

Vidette, HMS, 198

Vimiera, HMS, 48, 85, 88, 90, 96

Vimy, HMS, 85, 88-90, 168

Viscount, HMS, 168

Vittoria, HMS, 19

Vivacious, HMS, 105, 107

Volunteer, HMS, 54-55, 63

Voyager, HMS, 56

Wallace, HMS, 23

Walrus, HMS, 52

Wanderer, HMS, 18, 22, 25, 30, 43, 49

Watchman, HMS, 18, 132

Westcott, HMS, 16, 160, 171

Whitehall, HMS, 53-54, 102

Whitley, HMS, 18, 20, 22

Whitshed, HMS, 33, 35, 45, 54-55, 80, 84, 88, 90, 121

Wild Swan, HMS, 31, 76, 88-91, 96, 121, 125-127, 134-135

Winchester, HMS, 18, 22

Windsor, HMS, 96, 129-130

Wishart, HMS, 170, 198, 205, 265

Witch, HMS, 54

Wivern, HMS, 53, 69, 121, 124-125, 127, 245, 248-249

Wolsey, HMS, 33, 85

Wolverine, HMS, 52, 170, 198-199, 201, 204-205

Woolston, HMS, 43, 53

Worcester, HMS, 44, 54, 121, 139

Wren, HMS, 54, 69

Wrestler, HMS, 201, 208-209

Wryneck, HMS, 22, 52

Wyvern, HMS, 75

Vulcan, USS, 160

W

Warn, Sergeant L.F., 109-110

Warspite, HMS, 55, 58

Washington, USS, 181

Washington Naval Treaty, 42

Watts, PO Cook, 66

Weeks, AB Teddy, 157

Welby-Everard, S/Lt Philip RN, 35

Wellington, HMS (former US Navy), 141

Wells, S/Lt (later Lt) Walter R. RN, 66, 95, 98, 105, 125-126, 147-148, 162

Western, Lt James G.T. RN, 63

Weymouth, 67-68

Wichita, USS, 181

Wilmott, ERA Harry, 265, 268

Wilson, Lt John A.B. RN, 14, 31

Witherington, HMS, 265

Woodcock, HMS, 248

Woods, AB Fred, 229

Woodyatt, Surgeon Lt Peter RNVR, 120, 147, 152, 154-155

Y

Young, Mid Reginald S. RN, 31, 33

Z

Zagloba, SS, 124

Zetland, HMS, 170, 198

FORTY YEARS AT SEA
A voyage with my father

"My younger brother and I were brought up by an elderly housekeeper and sent to boarding school at the age of seven and eight. My mother was a determined hard working career woman. My Father was a stranger, frightening but romantic, whose return home changed the domestic routine until his departure by taxi to join a new ship."

The author changed his mind about going to sea when his father told him that "I shall throw you out of the house if you do" but on leaving school he worked his passage to the West Indies on his father's ship and in his early twenties, whilst travelling the world, worked as a deck boy and a junior officer on merchant ships in the East Indies and Pacific and was shipwrecked crewing a schooner.

In retirement he set out to discover who his father really was by "following the paper trail which even the most ordinary person who has been in the services or the Merchant Navy leaves behind." His search uncovered a life which began with an apprenticeship as a fitter at a shipyard on the Tyne interrupted by service in the RAF as an eighteen year old Observer Gunner on anti-submarine patrol in Orkney. In 1921 he went to sea as a marine engineer on oil tankers, an Antarctic whaler, tramp steamers, cargo liners and a Royal Fleet Auxilliary tanker.

Wartime service in the Royal Navy on a destroyer was followed by a regular run across the Atlantic to the Caribbean sugar estates of Tate and Lyle until retirement to the seaside resort of Exmouth in Devon after forty years at sea.

This book is both a personal journey of discovery and the story of ships and shipping in the last century, revealed through the life of a typical marine engineer.

William Redvers Forster (1900-75)

FORTY YEARS AT SEA: A VOYAGE WITH MY FATHER; by William A. Forster.
Holywell House Publishing, Autumn 2011.
ISBN 9-780-9559382-1-4

Holywell House Publishing
88 Holywell Hill, St Albans, Hertfordshire AL1 1DH, Britain.
http://www.holywellhousepublishing.co.uk/